THINKING WITH BALIBAR

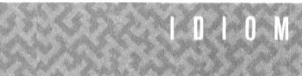 INVENTING WRITING THEORY

Jacques Lezra and Paul North, series editors

THINKING WITH BALIBAR

A LEXICON OF CONCEPTUAL PRACTICE

ANN LAURA STOLER, STATHIS GOURGOURIS,
AND JACQUES LEZRA, EDITORS

Fordham University Press *New York*   2020

Copyright © 2020 Fordham University Press

All rights reserved. No part of this publication may be reproduced, stored in a retrieval system, or transmitted in any form or by any means—electronic, mechanical, photocopy, recording, or any other—except for brief quotations in printed reviews, without the prior permission of the publisher.

Fordham University Press has no responsibility for the persistence or accuracy of URLs for external or third-party Internet websites referred to in this publication and does not guarantee that any content on such websites is, or will remain, accurate or appropriate.

Fordham University Press also publishes its books in a variety of electronic formats. Some content that appears in print may not be available in electronic books.

Visit us online at www.fordhampress.com.

Library of Congress Control Number: 2020904889

Printed in the United States of America

22 21 20   5 4 3 2 1

First edition

CONTENTS

Preface   vii

Introduction: Balibar and the Philosophy of the Concept
Warren Montag   1

Anthropological
Bruce Robbins   15

Border-Concept (of the Political)
Stathis Gourgouris   28

Civil Religion: Secularism as Religion?
Judith Butler   45

Concept
Étienne Balibar   54

Contre-/Counter-
Bernard E. Harcourt   71

Conversion
Monique David-Ménard   85

Cosmopolitics
Emily Apter   94

Interior Frontiers
Ann Laura Stoler   117

Materialism
Patrice Maniglier   140

The Political
Adi Ophir   158

Punishment
Didier Fassin   183

Race
Hanan Elsayed 193

Relation
Jacques Lezra 211

Rights
J. M. Bernstein 230

Solidarity
Gary Wilder 253

Bibliography 275

List of Contributors 311

Index 315

PREFACE

Étienne Balibar is among the most important political thinkers of our times. This is not only because of his long and influential trajectory, with numerous philosophical innovations over the years in an array of subjects, but also because of his consistently active participation in current political problems, in the realm of politics as it happens and the situations in which it happens. The fact that a theorist and creator of political concepts engages consistently with the elusive dimension of real social-historical contingencies makes Balibar a rare figure in contemporary thought. More than almost any other in the formidable group of European intellectuals of his generation—who write and teach in France, Italy, and Germany in particular—Balibar has extended himself beyond the limited reference points of European metropolitan circles, and has built an oeuvre out of extensive conversations not only with the requisite classical thinkers of antiquity and modernity but with contemporary interlocutors worldwide.

Thinking with Balibar is the first publication of collective reflections on Balibar's work. Adhering to the lexical method of the Political Concepts project (seven years of annual workshops, an ongoing online journal, and a first collection in print—*Political Concepts: A Critical Lexicon*, 2018), it engages Balibar's intellectual creativity at its most elemental: the microlevel of conceptual invention at which he has consistently excelled.

The texts collected here are expressions of real-time conversation—debate, dialogical inquiry, collaborative critical reflection. By virtue of Adi Ophir's initiative, a number of thinkers who have been Balibar's interlocutors for many years and in a variety of ways were gathered together with Balibar at Brown University in December 2016 to engage with his thinking and with his participation. The *Political Concepts* impetus and format remained as always: reflection and contextualization of a concept in a specific framework and disciplinary language—in this case, of course, within or in relation to Balibar's oeuvre—and elaboration according to one's own manner and decision, aspiring ultimately to elucidate the open-ended questions of the political across geographical and societal contexts currently and in historical terms.

The intent of *Thinking with Balibar* is thus to *think* and *work with* some of Balibar's major concepts while defining and in some cases putting pressure on them. Each of the essays/lexemes/scholars tries, in its/his/her way, to think with Balibar. This means more than "thinking with" the concepts that Balibar furnishes, as if his work offered a tool kit for digging into various problems and circumstances. The "with" that we find in "thinking with" is not only the "with" that we use when we say that one digs ditches *with* a shovel or a backhoe, as one thinks not just *with* concepts or in concepts but also in the companionable and conversational and challenging mode that silently and clamorously goes *with* every technique when it's *thought* that we're thinking and talking about. "Thinking with" is thinking alongside, across the table, over a glass of wine, *with* Balibar. As proper acknowledgment of Balibar's restless handling of concepts, disciplines, methods, and political or theoretical problems, this collection of voices privileges a contrapuntal—and indeed, a dialectical (in its utmost sense)—arrangement of critical reflections fully commensurable and responsible to Balibar's multiplicity of disciplinary languages and political concerns.

Thus, whatever epistemological framework each author brings to the table—philosophy, political theory, psychoanalysis, feminism, anthropology—enters the space of Balibarian conceptual invention self-consciously open to the dialogue of methodologies that this work makes trenchant in the current social and political sphere. Respecting Balibar's own care never to lose sight of the difficult political problems of our time even when immersed in the most theoretical of meditations, the ultimate target of these collected reflections is how to conceptualize not merely political ideas and notions but the world's real situations, in which actual men and women struggle to create conditions of life that resist or elude mechanisms of exploitation and oppression.

"Thinking with" thus means "with" in the most challenging-companionable, even agonistic senses—which was the project pressed on the editors by Balibar himself when we proposed the volume to him. Each lexeme/entry/essay thinks *with* Balibar *about* one of Balibar's concepts but also from *outside* of Balibar's lexicon, in a different language (sociology, psychoanalysis, literary criticism; via Spinoza, via contemporary analytic philosophy; and so on). One could call it a project of translation, but this grants privilege to one term that is both not universal in the essays collected here and, however powerful and compelling, inadequate to some of the more meaty thought-encounters in the volume. The contributors are thinking with Balibar about one of Balibar's concepts, but they're doing it from a position that generally falls outside of Balibar's own way of reflecting upon his own concepts. (The most fascinating example of this inside-outside performative topology is perhaps Balibar's own essay on "Concept," a reflection, *by* Balibar but from outside of Balibar's customary way of reflecting on his own work, on the concept that holds the volume together.)

In some cases, thinking with Balibar means thinking with the conversations he has had over time while writing, publishing, and debating. In other cases, the matter is approached differently—as a matter of structure, as the result of an encounter with a text reread under different circumstances than those of its production or first reception, or on account of a shift in orientation brought about by historical events (1989, 2001, the 2008–9 crisis). It is *en passant* but not as their central focus that most of the lexical essays that the volume collects describe the intellectual, social, and political milieux in which Balibar's work has developed.

This volume shows how to do things with Balibar's thought—in some cases, real-world and extramural things; in every case, how to do things with the work of thought about real-world and extramural things. The essays in *Thinking with Balibar* show that one of the things one does with Balibar is explain some of Balibar's concepts, but from rather different positions and disciplinary formations. This multiplication of possible approaches, by no means exhaustive in intent or in practice, is tribute to the fecundity of Balibar's thinking—but this isn't a celebration volume. It is at best a chronicle of discovery with an eye toward collective and collaborative learning, and the performative aspect of these essays is central to the book's pedagogical vocation.

The texts in this volume are then distillations of collaborative contestation and elaboration both in the actual time and space of the event and in subsequent reflection and exchange of views. The editors have sought to provide some stylistic uniformity to these interventions, but we retain many of the traces they bear of the circumstances that brought the authors together, hoping thereby to capture some of the conversational, social, and societal drive of Balibar's thought, and to guard to a degree the signature of the contingency of the encounter.

Why a *lexicon in formation*, and in what sense? *Thinking with Balibar* provides a second iteration of the lexical project proposed in the collective's first publication, *Political Concepts*, but with a more focused and tightly shared framework. The rather unstable combination of the project of definition ("What is an 'Internal Border' in Balibar's work? How is it a *political* concept?"), a self-interrogative take on a sort of Socratic mode of political inquiry, and acknowledgment of the unfinished quality of both ("in formation") is channeled here through a conceptual universe created over a significant number of years and complexities of conjuncture (social, historical, cultural, political) always with an impetus to pierce through the cracks of often enigmatic ideological situations that, moreover, tend to change with alarming speed and scale. A collective practice of reading is on offer: the reading of a long and complex oeuvre simultaneously with a reading of the often opaque world situation that brought this oeuvre to life in the first place.

Given that Balibar has been an exceptional pedagogue of reading in such double fashion since the earliest phase of *Reading Capital* (1965)—a collaborative project radically exemplary in itself—this is only just and could not be conducted otherwise. The most uncompromisingly *sub specie aeternitatis* standpoint of critical reflection will falter if the most brutally temporal standpoint—the unstable realm where forms shape-shift, decay, or disappear—is not simultaneously engaged. Training this unusual mode of collaborative inquiry upon the work of a specific thinker, albeit a thinker of great disciplinary range, enables, both methodologically and philosophically, a concentration on the specific political underpinnings of the world that elicits this thinking in the first place. *Thinking with Balibar* does not so much demarcate the horizon of Balibar's interpretation of that world, as open it further to the vicissitudes of its own time and the time to come.

THINKING WITH BALIBAR

INTRODUCTION: BALIBAR AND THE PHILOSOPHY OF THE CONCEPT

Warren Montag

Étienne Balibar's work may be understood as an uninterrupted process of the production of concepts. And even when the concepts he produces are not precisely political concepts, formulated with the aim of conferring intelligibility on some part of what is, perhaps only by convention, determined to be the political, we inevitably discover that they both are imbued with and exude what he calls "politicality." To read Balibar is to be reminded that if it is not the case that everything is political, we can nevertheless acknowledge the politicality that saturates the medium of language (or, more precisely, discourse) in which every concept must be formulated. I refer here not simply to the concepts he has designated with a neologism, such as equaliberty, but also those, such as civility, citizen, stranger, or perhaps politicality itself, on which, through his labor, he has conferred a new meaning. To say that he is the producer and not the creator of concepts is not to minimize his part in shaping their meaning but to recognize the work of differentiation and specification, as well as linkage and conjunction, necessary to transform what already exists into something new, something endowed with the capacity to allow us to think differently or *penser autrement*. There can be no immaculate conception in philosophy.

Central to his philosophical enterprise is the postulate of the singularity of "concept" in relation to apparently similar terms: idea, notion, doctrine, even argument. Balibar reminds us of the history that is congealed in the word: the verb *concipio* means both to grasp or seize something whether in one's hands or by seeing it, and also to conceive, to be impregnated; it is thus both active and passive, designating both a taking from and a receiving (although a receiving that will lead to the birth of something new). To a greater extent than the other terms invoked above, "concept" contains within itself the trace of the activity required to grasp that part of reality that is the object of the concept and make of it something new, something born of the object but distinct from it. Thus, the activity of conceiving distinguishes the concept from the contemplative reflection or "passive mimesis" that characterizes the notion of truth as *adaequatio rei et intellectus*, an adequation or correspondence between an object or thing, and an idea.[1] But the historical process of differentiation that Balibar invokes has perhaps become visible only retroactively, by means of a series of attempts to isolate "concept" from the semantically proximate nouns that have been used in its place. Of these, two are particularly important for any understanding of Balibar's thought: Jean Cavaillès's *Sur la logique et théorie de la sciences* (1947)[2] and a number of works by Georges Canguilhem, above all, the essay "Le concept et la vie" (1966).[3]

The penultimate sentence of Cavaillès's *Sur la logique*, well known to students of Althusser and Foucault, continues today to be enveloped in a politicality otherwise foreign to the formidably dense discussion of logical positivist and phenomenological approaches to a theory of the sciences that precedes it. The work was completed (or abandoned) shortly before Cavaillès was executed by a German firing squad in 1943 for his activity in the resistance, a fact that gave the sentence the force of a political slogan for the young philosophers at the École Normale in the period just prior to 1968: "It is not a philosophy of consciousness, but a philosophy of the concept that can provide a doctrine of the sciences."[4] To understand what is summarized in and by this sentence, it is not sufficient simply to note the critique of the subject it implies. The specificity of "consciousness" and the strangeness of its being set in opposition to the concept require our attention. Furthermore, to speak of a philosophy of the concept as if a concept could exist independently of the object or phenomenon of which it was precisely the concept, understood as something like the condition of possibility of the intelligibility of an object or phenomenon, can only appear to be a kind of provocation. Why would Cavaillès propose something like a philosophy of the means of the production of knowledge rather than of the knowledge it produces? Moreover, the fact that the sentence begins by rejecting any philosophy of consciousness, which should be understood here in the broadest sense, not limited to that given the term by Husserl and his followers that is the specific object of Cavaillès's critique, must in some sense call into question the meaning of "concept."

It is not mere coincidence that it is Balibar himself, notably in his *Identity and Difference: Locke and the Invention of Consciousness*, who without referring directly to Cavaillès allows us to understand what is at stake in his evocation of consciousness in opposition to the concept. The Latin *conscientia* originally designated a knowing with (*con-scientia*) others that was transformed over time into a knowing with or of oneself, a reflection or perception of one's own perceptions and ideas (that, for Locke, cannot be understood as an activity insofar as it is impossible not to perceive what passes in one's own mind). According to Cavaillès, Husserl's phenomenology as expressed in the different accounts offered in *Cartesian Meditations* (1931), *The Crisis of the European Sciences* (1936), and *Experience and Judgment* (1939), above all, although in certain, highly mediated, ways, his notions of intentionality and consciousness remain tied to a model of knowledge derived from the notion of the correspondence between an object or thing and the way that it is perceived, comprehended, or understood, and thus a correspondence between two levels of reality, one primary and the other secondary, one independent and the other dependent: the thing and the (activity of) mind by which a thing is perceived, discerned, or reflected upon. Against phenomenology, Cavaillès cites Spinoza, for whom consciousness, was best defined not as a reflection on or perception of that which would exist prior to and outside of it, but as the outside itself in an act of self-reflection that is coincident with the act of existing. If consciousness can be said to exist at all, it "exists in the immediacy of the idea, lost in it and losing itself in it."[5] This is Cavaillès's materialism: the concept is irreducible; it not only possesses a material existence, as Althusser said, but it is also a "thing" (*res*) with its own reality (a word derived from *res*). A philosophy of the concept takes as its starting point Spinoza's proposition that thought and extension, knowledge and reality are "one and the same thing."[6]

Canguilhem, too, at the very moment Balibar was occupied in a collective project to develop a theory of discourse and of discursive materialism, turned his attention to the relation of the concept of life to life itself. Beginning with an examination of Aristotle's reflections on both concepts and life, he makes the following observation:

> A primary, fundamental difficulty appears in Aristotelian philosophy concerning the relations between knowing and being, between intellect and life in particular. When the intellect is understood as a function of contemplation and reproduction, if it is given a place among the forms, even a prominent place, the thought of order is situated, that is, confined to a place in the universal order. But how can knowledge be at the same

time mirror and object, the reflection and the reflected? The definition of man as *zoon logistikon* or rational animal, if it is a naturalistic definition (similar to Linnaeus's definition of the wolf as *canis lupus* or of the maritime pine as *pinus maritima*), makes science, and the science of life as much as any other science, an activity of life itself.[7]

Although, according to Canguilhem, philosophy from Aristotle to Hume seeks precisely to avoid such a conclusion as the imminent danger that it would almost certainly encounter if left to wander freely, he argues that "the project of the naturalization of the knowledge of nature" as an answer to "the question of the conception of concepts" (conception here understood as both the genesis or production of concepts and as the question of their conceptual status), emerges regularly or "naturally" within its history.[8] The naturalization or materialization of knowledge (and not simply the knowledge of nature) places knowledge in history and poses the question of the materiality specific to it. In this sense, understanding the naturality of knowledge is the necessary condition of any understanding of its politicality.

Balibar has extended the positions of both Cavaillès and Canguilhem and, in doing so, increased their power of provocation by demonstrating that a philosophy of the concept must begin with a recognition that it has already begun—that is, to capture the full force of the paradox, that it necessarily precedes itself in the form of a "concept of the concept" and, therefore, a philosophy of the concept of the concept. If knowledge exists in the infinite concatenation of ideas—in that the knowledge of an idea always takes the form of another idea, an idea of the idea—then the knowledge of the concept must take place through another concept, a concept of the concept. I deliberately pose the problem this way so that we may confront the obvious objection: does not the very project of determining the concept of the concept involve us in a kind of hermeneutic circle? Without a concept of the concept, we cannot identify a concept as such or differentiate between concepts and nonconcepts. At the same time, we are confronted with the problem of how to identify the concept of the concept without first understanding (that is, having a concept of) the concept? And the problem with this particular aporia or "paralogism," as Balibar calls it, is that if we grant to the philosophy of the concept a central place in the production of knowledge, his project appears unnecessary, superfluous, or, even worse, the kind of intervention that leads not only to doubt but to infinite regression: if we must grasp the concept of the concept, are we not by the same logic required to determine the concept of the concept of the concept, and so on to infinity?

We may now see very clearly the extent to which Balibar, like Cavaillès before him, draws on Spinoza, in particular Spinoza's critique of Descartes' theory of method:

> To find the best method of seeking the truth, there is no need of another method for seeking the method of seeking the truth, and there is no need of a third method to seek the second method, and so on to infinity. For in that way we should never arrive at knowledge of the truth, or indeed at any knowledge. The case is analogous to that of material tools, where the same kind of argument could be employed. To work iron, a hammer is needed, and to have a hammer, it must be made. For this purpose there is need of another hammer and other tools, and again to get these there is need of other tools, and so on to infinity. In this way one might try to prove, in vain, that men have no power to work iron.[9]

How does one work iron without a hammer made from iron? How does one arrive at a true idea without an idea (or a true idea) of the true? Spinoza in this way allows us to answer the following question: if objects are known through concepts, must not the concept itself be known through its concept, and what would allow us to recognize the concept of the concept without presupposing the very thing of which it is the concept that allows it to be known? Before we begin to answer this question, however, we might first situate the paradoxical or circular nature of the question of the concept of the concept in the developments that followed Cavaillès's call for a philosophy of the concept. Of particular relevance to Balibar is Althusser's very Spinozist discussion of what he called "the necessary circle" of philosophy in *Philosophy and the Spontaneous Philosophy of the Scientists* (the text of a lecture to a seminar that took place in 1967 and in which Balibar was a participant): "When, with my first words, I said: 'Philosophical propositions are *Theses*,' and quickly added: '*This* proposition is itself a philosophical Thesis' by which I put Thesis 1 into play, you obviously noticed that my argument was circular: because I declared that the proposition by which I defined philosophical propositions as *Theses* was itself a *philosophical* Thesis."[10] The necessity of the circle derives from the fact that it is not possible "to provide a definition—that is, a knowledge—of philosophy that would be able *radically* to escape from philosophy: there is no possibility of achieving a science of philosophy or a 'meta-philosophy'; one cannot radically escape the *circle* of philosophy. All *objective* knowledge of philosophy is in effect at the same time a *position within* philosophy, and therefore a Thesis in and on philosophy; that is why you felt, on the contrary, that *I could speak of philosophy in general only from a certain position in philosophy*: demarcating myself, by distancing myself from *other* existing positions."[11]

In proposing to develop the concept of the concept, Balibar, too, has voluntarily and "consciously" entered the inescapable circle formed by the paradoxical act of having to determine the concept of the concept from the starting point of that of which it is the concept; the concept suddenly seems to lack the very foundation (the concept of the concept) that it necessarily precedes in the order of inquiry. The necessary circle of philosophy, however, Althusser insists, is not like a logical circle, that is, a trap from which there is no escape or an empty paradox that bars the way to thought. On the contrary, it is productive insofar as it reminds us that concepts cannot escape or transcend the reality that they allow us both to grasp or capture and to understand. We might recall Spinoza's famous response to Descartes's demand for apodictic certainty:

> A true ideal (for we do have a true idea) is something different from its object (*ideatum*). A circle is one thing, the idea of a circle another. For the idea of a circle is not something having a circumference and a centre, as is a circle, nor is the idea of a body itself a body. And since it is something different from its object, it will also be something intelligible through itself. That is, in respect of its formal essence the idea can be the object of another objective essence, which in turn, regarded in itself, will also be something real and intelligible, and so on indefinitely.[12]

This is the point at which the notion of a philosophy of the concept takes on its meaning. Cavaillès insists that both the logical positivist model of a syntax, an order that produces or generates every conceptual proposition, and the phenomenological notion of the intentionality that unites subject and object in a correlation represent a separation of knowledge and its object that renders the objectivity of knowledge a permanent and insoluble problem. The concept understood as the act of consciousness or subjectivity (whether transcendental or nor not) provides a foundation or origin outside of and prior to knowledge that serves as the guarantee of its adequation to an external object, as if this adequation were in turn the guarantee of its validity as a concept. Neither approach acknowledges the irreducibility of the concept to its object and thus its materiality.

In the text of a lecture delivered in 1966, "The Object of the History of the Sciences," Canguilhem returns to the themes of Cavaillès's critique. Taking the history of the science of crystals as his example, he argues that while crystals certainly have an independent existence as a natural object (although he insists that the natural object is "not naturally natural" but an object perceived in the context of a culture), "this natural object, outside of any discourse devoted to it, is not of course the scientific object. Nature itself is not cut up and divided into scientific objects and phenomena. It is science that constitutes its own object from the moment it invents a method to form, by means of propositions that are capable of being *composée intégralement*, a theory concerned with its own falsification."[13] In the same way, and here we see that Canguilhem is as profoundly Spinozist as Cavaillès, "the object in the history of the sciences has nothing in common with the object of a science.... The object of historical discourse is in effect the historicity of scientific discourse insofar as this historicity represents the effectuation of a project that is internally normalized but traversed with accidents, held back or diverted by obstacles, interrupted by crises, that is, by moments of judgment and truth.... The object of the history of the sciences is an object not given to it, an object to which incompleteness is essential."[14] The concept of the history of the sciences refuses to "identify science with its results," and instead takes as its object science in its "errancy," to use a term familiar to readers of Canguilhem, that is, the history of its errors and detours, a history inseparable from that of its truths.

Moreover, the history of the sciences has of a number of objects situated on different levels. There are "documents to be cataloged, instruments and technologies to be described, methods and questions to be interpreted, concepts to be analyzed and criticized."[15] Concepts inseparable from the discursive reality of documents or what Gaston Bachelard called the "technical materialism" or materiality of the instruments, machines, and spaces or institutions necessary to experimentation, as well as of the gestures and acts performed by bodies that are themselves part of the technical materiality essential to the sciences, can render sciences intelligible only insofar as they possess a discursive and historical materiality. Balibar suggests that what I have called, following Bachelard and Althusser, the materiality of concepts exists in three modes: discursivity, historicity, and politicality. Although he cautions that, if only in the last instance, it is impossible to separate these modes, each of which depends on the others for its existence, Balibar is led to isolate politicality from the other modes of conceptuality in order to capture the conflictuality proper to concepts as such. He does so by carrying out a kind of symptomatic reading of a classic of analytic philosophy, W. B. Gallie's "Essentially Contested Concepts" (1956).[16] Gallie's notion of contested concepts differs from Balibar's postulate of the essential conflictuality of concepts in fundamental ways: For Gallie, conflict is external to the object and resides in the inexplicably permanent (and therefore essential) multiplicity of perspectives concerning the meaning or use of a concept rather than in the concept. The task of philosophy in such cases is not to adjudicate the competing claims concerning their proper use and meaning, but precisely to determine them to be indeterminable, the contest of meanings undecidable. The question of why these cases and not others came to be essentially contested is excluded from the outset, as if to explain why "democracy," to use one of Gallie's examples, is the site of such conflict would be to participate in the very contestation that philosophy should refrain from attempting to resolve. It would not be inaccurate to refer to this phenomenon as the depoliticalization of concepts.

Balibar, in contrast, holds that concepts as such are essentially contradictory, not by virtue of what Gallie calls the "variety" of the interpretations applied to a concept, a variety for which the concept itself bears no responsibility, but in themselves, their discursive composition, and the histories present in and around them. His analysis converges with that of Canguilhem, above all in *La formation du concept de réflexe aux XVII et XVIII siècles* (1955).[17] For the latter, the question to be answered is not whether the variety of interpretations of a concept reaches the threshold that marks it as essentially contested but how a concept such as "reflex" can play an essential role in different sciences, that is, how concepts migrate or stray into new domains where they become naturalized in a new conceptual system and, like all immigrants, are neither completely the same nor completely different as before: "If a concept logically emerging from or formed in a given context later finds itself taken up by a theory that uses it in a context and sense different from the first, this does not mean that the concept in question is condemned to be a mere word emptied of meaning in the first context. For there are certain theoretically polyvalent concepts, such as the refraction and reflection of light relative to corpuscular and wave theory."[18] The use of the term "polyvalent" suggests the capacity of the concept to function in a number of different theoretical systems, as well as the capacity to bind or combine with other concepts and theories to form a new conceptual regime. Polyvalence derives from the heterogeneity of the concept's powers or capacities, a heterogeneity that in turn arises from the concept's historical and discursive existence. It is directly related to the errancy or drift of the concept, not in the current sense of its increasing inadequacy in the face of the unpredictable results of a data stream, but in a sense closer to the idea of semantic drift, to which the concept's drift is linked. Even the heterogeneity of the concept's meanings and powers is itself unstable, its instability a spillover from the constitutive disorder of the discursive world. For Canguilhem, the concept of the polyvalence of the concept makes intelligible its essential and necessary incompleteness.

It was none other than Foucault who would demonstrate the theoretical polyvalence not only of the concept but of the concept of the concept. In the *History of Sexuality* (*La volonté de savoir*), Foucault appropriates Canguilhem's formula but replaces "concept" with "discourses": the tactical polyvalence of discourses.[19] In fact, the term "concept" appears only twice in the *History of Sexuality* (1976) in contrast to the *Archaeology of Knowledge* (1969), in which the term appears nearly two hundred times and in which Foucault devotes an entire chapter to "the formation of concepts."[20] It is here that he provides a rationale for the substitution of discourse for concept in the later work. The objective of archaeology is "to describe—not the laws of the internal construction of concepts, not their progressive and individual genesis in the mind of man—but their anonymous dispersion through texts, books, and oeuvres. A dispersion that characterizes a type of discourse, and which defines, between concepts, forms of deduction, derivation, and coherence, but also of incompatibility, intersection, substitution, exclusion, mutual alteration, displacement, etc."[21]

In contrast to an ordering of discourse, an attempt to "subject the multiplicity of statements to the coherence of concepts," Foucault proposes "the inverse series: one replaces the pure aims of non-contradiction in a complex network of conceptual compatibility and incompatibility; and one relates this complexity to the rules that characterize a particular discursive practice."[22] In the later work, the near absence of the term "concept" can be linked to Foucault's increasing suspicion of the language of scientific inquiry, even as it is possible to argue that the concept of the concept is nevertheless present even where the word is missing, concealed perhaps behind phrases such as "discursive elements," "statements," and "formulas." Not only is Foucault interested in polyvalence in the sense Canguilhem gives it, namely, the capacity of concepts (or statements) to function in different conceptual systems for different uses, but he specifies one of the outcomes of polyvalence: "the shifts and reutilizations of identical formulas for contrary objectives."[23] This is the condition of what Balibar calls the politicality of concepts.

Foucault's notion of power-knowledge, that is, of the essential consubstantiality of the exercise of power and the production of knowledge, precisely because it rules out any clear and consistent division between science and ideology, compels us to see the ways in which the polyvalence of concepts in their discursive existence not only allows concepts to function in distinct conceptual systems, but it also makes them available for accomplishment of different and even opposing strategic ends in social and political struggles: "There is no question that the appearance in nineteenth-century psychiatry, jurisprudence, and literature of a whole series of discourses on the species and subspecies of homosexuality, inversion, pederasty, and 'psychic hermaphrodism' made possible a strong advance of social controls into this area of 'perversity.'"[24] But the same polyvalence that allows initially "innocent" concepts or discourses that originally emerged in fields such as biology and physics to be mobilized in support of social controls permits these concepts to be reutilized "for contrary objectives." The very concepts and discourses deployed in the attempts to confine and subject those to whom the category of homosexual was applied also made possible the formation of a "'reverse' discourse: homosexuality began to speak in its own behalf, to demand that its legitimacy or 'naturality' be acknowledged, often in the same vocabulary, using the same categories by which it was medically disqualified."[25]

Balibar's oeuvre offers another equally striking example of the theoretical polyvalence of a concept, this time a directly political concept: citizen. The publication of the essay "Citizen Subject" in 1988 marked a turn in his investigations of the relations between subject, subjection, and subjectivation. To the antinomy of subject (subject to/subject of), Balibar applied the notion of citizen as it emerged in the French Revolution as a way of breaking open the circle formed by the necessary primacy of subjection over subjectivation in the formation of the subject. In postulating the hyperbolic character of the citizen who must struggle to prevent the rights accorded to him (and, later, her) from contracting into a merely formal or symbolic existence, Balibar endowed the citizen and perhaps the citizen masses, with an essential role in preserving and extending democratic rights beyond the limits of the politics in the strict sense. The citizen as the bearer of equaliberty was thus an incarnation of a kind of universalism.

Within a very short time, however, the ideas of citizen and citizenship were invested, to a degree previously unknown, with meanings contrary to those that Balibar had attached to them. Citizenship, far from representing an overcoming of the exclusionary effects of social and economic hierarchies, became a legitimating principle of exclusion, its emancipatory tendency relativized to the nation-state, the community of equals that it (in theory) enabled limited to territorial borders. The concept of citizenship is today imbued with a very material existence of control and confinement, of state and nonstate violence, of abandonment, of the mass production of noncitizens increasingly without rights of any kind: its discursive existence is inseparable from institutions and apparatuses. As Balibar himself has noted, the opposite of the citizen is now less the subject than the stranger, the foreigner, the other who remains and must remain other (to use Levinas's expression).

The notion of the polyvalence of concepts, which is in some sense a theory of their uncontrolled and uncontrollable migration to foreign or antagonistic theoretical realms, however, in no way guarantees their successful assimilation or even their ability to fulfill the function they were invited to fulfill. Canguilhem's notion, as well as that of Foucault, appears to apply only to the cases in which the migration, importation, or borrowing of concepts has been successful, success being defined by the production of effects in the realm of knowledge or power-knowledge. It is not too much to say that it was left to another of Canguilhem's interlocutors—namely, Althusser—to investigate the possibility, which he soon recognized to be a necessity, of a theory of conceptual failure, of concepts transplanted or translated only to wither and die, of concepts whose only function in a new domain is to conceal the absence of the concept required by the theoretical problems that have emerged in it, of uninhabitable, because theoretically empty, domains in which concepts can be said to survive only in the sense that they have been preserved in a petrified state.

But the theory of conceptual failure depended on the existence of another theory that for Althusser existed but only "in the practical state," neither recognized nor recognizing itself as theory, "a theory which makes it possible to distinguish a word from a concept, to distinguish the existence or non-existence of a concept behind a word, to discern the existence of a concept by a word's function in the theoretical discourse, to define the nature of a concept by its function in the problematic, and thus by the location it occupies in the system of the 'theory'; this theory which alone makes possible an authentic reading of Marx's writings, a reading which is both epistemological and historical, this theory is in fact simply Marxist philosophy itself."[26] Althusser thus takes Foucault's notion further than did Foucault himself: it is not simply that concepts or discourses immanent in a field of conflicting and unequal forces can be "weaponized" by opposing blocs, but that these discourses and concepts are themselves sites of struggle. If we look carefully, we find that what we thought was a hill is in fact a ruined fortress, a ridge, a battlement—the declivity we thought was a dry creek, a series of trenches. In the face of what Althusser calls "the enemy's brutal assault," anything capable of serving as a weapon, will. This is what explains Marx's use of the Hegelian concepts "appearance and essence, outside and inside, inner essence of things, real and apparent movement, etc., that we find it at work in many passages of Engels and Lenin, who found a motive for its use in the ideological battles in which the most urgent parrying was required beneath the enemy's brutal assault and on his chosen 'terrain,' first of all by turning against him his own weapons and blows, i.e., his ideological arguments and concepts."[27] But Althusser also shows that in addition to the absence of concepts and the necessary dissimulation of this absence through the use of concepts imported from other conceptual and theoretical systems, the attentive reader of Marx's *Capital* is apt to discover the presence of concepts that have arrived prematurely, belonging to a theoretical system that does not yet exist because its historical conditions of possibility have yet to emerge, with the result being that concepts may precede the theoretical foundations that confer meaning upon them, if only retroactively. Such concepts may appear as answers to questions that have not been posed, questions that paradoxically arise only on the basis of the answers that historically precede them. In a striking passage, Althusser argues that the question "'What is the value of labour?' is a sentence identical to a concept, it is a concept-sentence which is content to utter the concept 'value of labour,' an utterance-sentence which does not designate any omission in itself, unless it is itself as a whole, as a concept, a question manqué, a concept manqué, the omission (*manque*) of a concept. It is the answer that answers us about the question, since the question's only space is this very concept of 'labour' which is designated by the answer as the site of the omission. It is the answer that tells us that the question is its own omission, and nothing else."[28]

The exploration of the forms of the realization and nonrealization of concepts in their historicity, discursivity, and politicality led Balibar to a kind of ultimate formulation of conceptuality, the limit-concept of the concept. Borrowing a phrase (or a concept) from Foucault, he provides not an absent concept but a concept of absence, a concept that makes intelligible the unfillable gap that prevents contradictory postulates from being reconciled or made consistent even in the most urgent historical and political circumstances: God is one and God consists of three persons; the economy is determinate in the last instance and the last instance never comes. This is the point of heresy, the point of an unresolvable paradox, between whose terms it is impossible in a given historical conjuncture to choose. It does not represent a lapse into an irrationalism of mysteries; on the contrary, it is an assessment of what it is possible and not possible to think, not a priori, but in the present. It offers a warning of the dangers of theoretical voluntarism, of filling absences with words or of denying their existence at all. Above all, it is a recognition of the limits that the conjuncture imposes on the production of concepts and, therefore, knowledge itself: it is what Hegel called the patience of the concept.

NOTES

1. Étienne Balibar, "Concept," *Political Concepts: A Critical Lexicon*, no. 4 (2012), https://www.politicalconcepts.org/concept-etienne-balibar.
2. Jean Cavaillès, *Sur la logique et la théorie de la science* (1947; Paris: Vrin, 1976).
3. Georges Canguilhem, "Le concept et la vie" [1966], in *Études d'histoire et de philosophie de la science* (Paris: Vrin, 1976), 335–64.

4. Cavaillès, *Sur la logique*, 78.
5. Cavaillès, *Sur la logique*, 78.
6. Spinoza, *Ethics* II, P7, sch.
7. Canguilhem, "Concept," 337.
8. Canguilhem, "Concept," 342.
9. *Spinoza: Complete Works*, ed. Michael L. Morgan, trans. Samuel Shirley (Indianapolis: Hackett, 2002), 9.
10. Louis Althusser, *Philosophy and the Spontaneous Philosophy of the Scientists and Other Essays* (London: Verso, 1990), 101.
11. Althusser, *Philosophy*, 102.
12. Spinoza, *Complete Works*, 10.
13. Georges Canguilhem, *Études d'histoire et de philosophie de la science* (Paris: Vrin, 1976), 16–17.
14. Canguilhem, *Études*, 17–18.
15. Canguilhem, *Études*, 19.
16. W. B. Gallie, "Essentially Contested Concepts," *Proceedings of the Aristotelian Society* 56 (1956): 167–98.
17. Georges Canguilhem, *La formation du concept de réflexe aux XVII et XVIII siècles* (1955; Paris: Vrin, 1977).
18. Canguilhem, *Formation*, 6.
19. Michel Foucault, *The History of Sexuality Vol. I: An Introduction*, trans. Robert Hurley (New York: Pantheon, 1978), 100.
20. Michel Foucault, *The Archaeology of Knowledge* (New York: Vintage, 1972), 56–63.
21. Foucault, *Archaeology*, 60.
22. Foucault, *Archaeology*, 62.
23. Foucault, *History*, 100.
24. Foucault, *History*, 99.
25. Foucault, *History*, 99.
26. Louis Althusser and Étienne Balibar, *Reading Capital*, trans. Ben Brewster (London: New Left Books, 1970), 33.
27. Althusser and Balibar, *Reading Capital*, 38.
28. Althusser and Balibar, *Reading Capital*, 23.

ANTHROPOLOGICAL

Bruce Robbins

The use of the term "anthropological" in common parlance can be illustrated by a postelection op-ed in the *New York Times* by Mark Lilla. Lilla writes: "The media's newfound, almost anthropological, interest in the angry white male reveals as much about the state of our liberalism as it does about this much maligned, and previously ignored, figure." To describe the media's newfound interest in the angry white male as "almost anthropological" is to imply that the media has suddenly begun looking at a newly discovered or at least somewhat exotic tribe or natural kind, gazing across a certain distance at a social collectivity with which it should already have been familiar, and perhaps also fixing that collectivity with a naturalizing stare that imposes on it a set of differences that it pretends to discover. For Lilla, observing this object from an "almost anthropological" angle is clearly a mistake. The angry white male ought not to have been ignored by the media or by the Democratic Party. Its likes and dislikes ought to have been better known—and perhaps there is an extra implication: better known than those of, say, women and minorities. Lilla does not quite say that the presidential election of November 8, 2016, would have had a different result if the situation had been reversed and it were women and minorities who were looked at anthropologically.[1] He does not reflect on one opposite but equally pertinent understanding of "anthropological" in common parlance—namely, showing excessive deference to the subjectivity of its subjects—or on how he would feel about an identity politics that would include the now-militant identity of the angry white Trump voter.

How the word "anthropological" might sound *to* an angry white Trump voter can perhaps be divined from the following passage, which I take from the first scene of George Saunders's short story "Sea Oak": "'There are times,' Mr. Frendt says, 'when one must move gracefully to the next station in life, like for example certain women in Africa or Brazil, I forget which, who either color their faces or don some kind of distinctive headdress upon achieving menopause. Are you with me? One of our ranks must now leave us.'"[2] The passage describes how a character gets fired. The reference to "certain women in Africa or Brazil, I forget which, who" do something distinctive upon reaching menopause, it doesn't really matter what, is intended to make the sacking of an employee seem as natural and inevitable as menopause. If, as anthropology informs us, women in some distant culture mark this life stage, then . . . well, the logic is not meant to be flawless, but it seems to follow that the resistance to firing that might be expected to arise in our culture is based on something provincial, trivial, illegitimate. The anthropological is offered as a bumbling stand-in for what is universal, hence as would-be authoritative support for the act of moving an employee or two with minimum fuss to the next station in life. It's a euphemism for a performative "You're fired!," a phrase that has accrued deeper and weirder resonance since so many working-class voters chose, in November 2016, to vote for the television personality known for performing it. Neither Saunders's protagonist nor Saunders himself could ever be mistaken for an angry white Trump voter—indeed, all of the story's legitimate class anger is displaced to a ghostly elsewhere. Still, "Sea Oak" offers a glimpse of what such a voter might feel when the home culture is overruled by the exotic, knowledge of which is obtainable only by those with higher education, time off for travel to distant places, travel grants to go with the credentials, and so on. We are only a step from the successfully resentful slogan of "liberal elites."

Though both of these examples of the anthropological in common usage are pertinent to the Trump presidency and both are critical of the concept, they are far from identical. In objecting to an anthropological view of white males as an exotic species, Lilla seems to be suggesting not only that white males ought to be familiar rather than exotic, but also that instead of being seen as a particular identity, they ought to be seen as representing the uninflected, identity-less norm. Saunders, however, seems to be objecting to the use of the anthropologically exotic to *create* a norm—a false, arbitrary, self-interested norm. I begin with these examples of the anthropological as it appears in popular discourse not because Étienne Balibar uses the word "anthropological" in either of these senses, though there is some overlap with each. Nor is it because Balibar is obliged to use the term to help directly with the rhetorical situation in which we Americans find ourselves under Donald Trump. He is not. I start here nonetheless for three reasons. First, because it would be irresponsible for Americans right now *not* to think of that rhetorical situation. Second, because attention to the history of common parlance, as opposed to a more strictly conceptual history, engages in an interesting way a founding premise of *Political Concepts* as a project—namely, the premise that although popular discourse is likely to be wildly abundant, random, and chaotic, more valuable political knowledge can be achieved by departing from it and shifting upward to the more rarified level of concepts, a level at which greater rigor and clarity are possible. This premise might have remained invisible, at least to me, were it not for Balibar's choice of addressing, at the Political Concepts conference that gathered the authors of this collection together, the metatopic of "the concept of concept." But it has also been brought to light by recent discussions of whether the rhetoric that helped elect Donald Trump is genuinely reflective of the reigning neoliberalism that preceded Trump or, on the contrary, is mere noise, as Philip Mirowski has suggested, intended only to entertain a deluded populace while distracting them from what is being done to them and in their name.[3]

My third reason for highlighting the anthropological in common parlance is its intimate relation to the "political," the word to which Balibar ultimately has recourse in working through the challenge of the anthropological and again, of course, one of the two words that define the Political Concepts project. It is obviously a related reason. It leads to some of the same questions: Does the commitment to politics send us ineluctably back from philosophical concepts to ordinary language as spoken by, to, and for "the people"?[4] Does the political allow us to settle the issue of whether Balibar's anthropological turn is or is not a return to the humanism that the Althusserians so strongly repudiated in the 1960s? Is it merely another way of saying, with Ellen Rooney, that theory in order to be effective cannot satisfy itself with a critique of ideology but must make itself into ideology?

The 1960s background for Balibar's engagement with the term "anthropological" is presumably to be found in Sartre's proposal for a "concrete anthropology" in *The Critique of Dialectical Reason* and the assault on that position by Levi-Strauss, who declared that the goal of the human sciences was not to constitute man as an object of knowledge but, on the contrary, to "dissolve" man. Gregory Elliott offers this context for Althusser, and Althusser's turn against the humanism of Sartre, Kojève, and Hegel, however complex and ambivalent, is the most obvious context for Balibar.[5] In *Saeculum: Culture, religion, idéologie* (2012), the phrase "anthropological differences" serves, accordingly, to point to a contrast with humanism's "ontological differences."[6] "Anthropological differences" are differences that cannot be denied or escaped yet are not (as ontological differences would be) fixed, univocal, or incontestable. The term is a bit misleading, but the intention is clear: anthropological differences do not presuppose a given human nature, the erstwhile object of anthropology.[7] In an interview conducted after the French publication of *Citizen Subject*, recently issued in English translation by Fordham University Press,[8] Balibar says that his personal interest in the term "anthropology" began with the early Foucault.[9] This accords with the selection he and John Rajchman made in 2011 in their anthology of post-1945 French philosophy; the second item on the table of contents is Foucault's "Introduction to Kant's Anthropology."[10] Foucault's point in that text, briefly summarized, is that the term "anthropology" promises a knowledge it can't deliver. It can't deliver because the supposed object of that knowledge, "man," does not exist. In the interview, Balibar says that he differs from Foucault, first of all, in that he is not as interested as Foucault was in the scholarly disciplines or the epistemological conditions necessary for the emergence of disciplines. (This is certainly true as far as the discipline of anthropology is concerned. Fascinated as he may be by particular anthropologists, such as Mauss or Levi-Strauss, and by how they can go wrong, as in the work of Talal Asad, he rarely uses the word "anthropological" to refer to the disciplinary perspective of anthropology.) The other sense in which he differs from Foucault on anthropology, he says, is that he is not interested in debating the ontology of the human, that is, in arguing either for or against a human nature or human essence. What he *is* interested in, and what he wants to distinguish from the human essence, can be described, he says, in two overlapping ways. First, as the human *condition*, where condition refers to being conditioned, or determined, or dependent. And second, as *politics*—politics, one might go on to surmise, conceived of here as a necessary response to being conditioned, determined, dependent.

I think it is fair to say that Foucault's rejection of the anthropological object "man," at that early stage of his career, was not intended as political in the usual sense of that term and indeed might be understood as discouraging politics in the usual sense of the term. (How we feel or ought to feel, at this moment in history, about politics in the usual sense of the term is of course a relevant question, and under present circumstances, I would not be sorry to see it raised.) At any rate, Balibar's disagreement with Foucault about Foucault's critique of the anthropology of Kant and about the anthropological in general does not mark a disagreement about human essence, as he sees it, but a desire on Balibar's part, but not on Foucault's, to make a case that those who share the human condition also and necessarily share a *political* condition—that the subject cannot be conceived without the citizen, to cite the argument of that book, or (to put this another way) that the proper object of the term "anthropological" is not "man" but politics.

To say this is to register the particular and characteristic ambition that goes into Balibar's use of the term. Political conflicts often pivot on the meaning of the past, but they do so by drawing the past into a concern with choices and directions that must be decided on in the present. The maxim that "all politics is local" is arguably still more true about the now than it is about the here; it has special force in the dimension of time. The word "anthropological" suggests not only differences existing in the present, differences that put at risk the project of a united or universal left politics, but also differences in time, which challenge politics from another angle. The anthropological marks a timescale measured in tens of thousands of years, including both recorded history and what we sometimes call "prehistory." It marks a timescale, therefore, on which the present-tense urgencies of politics cannot make the same claim to interpretive decisiveness. And I would argue that Balibar knows this very well, even as (like the rest of us) he flings "politics" against the solid wall of "anthropological differences," hoping to make a dent.[11]

The word "anthropological" does not appear in the index of *Violence and Civility* (2015), but as a noun it gets into a chapter title, and I think it was the background hum of that extraordinary book that made me reach instinctively for the word "anthropological" at the moment of concept-choosing, a moment that always comes too soon. Much of *Violence and Civility* is devoted to arguing, against the present-day liberal impulse to make violence the self-evident and decisive target of political energies, that "there is no nonviolence." In making this argument, the book takes on a very up-to-the-minute task. It speaks a good deal about capitalism and Marx's *Capital*—again, objects that are very much of our moment. At the same time, however, *Violence and Civility* also chooses to work within a *longue durée*, on a scale that goes back well before the advent of capitalism. "Violence" and "civility" might be described as civilizational concepts, concepts without which civilization could not be defined and which have therefore been involved in debate about its definition since the beginning of philosophy. No one who has ever read Balibar will have missed his extraordinary, one might almost say helpless love for the full length and breadth of the philosophical canon. My point here, maybe something too obvious to need to be said, is that the commitment to reflect on Hobbes and Hegel and Aristotle, in a book on violence and civility, is also a commitment to think *outside the frame* of Marx's critique of capitalism. It's a commitment to think about these subjects on a larger scale—a scale that it is helpful to think of as anthropological.

It is *Citizen Subject*, subtitled *Foundations for Philosophical Anthropology*, that announces what some readers have seen as an anthropological turn. Balibar says in that book that he is interested in the word "anthropological" because the word marks the limits of Marxism. This is of course an area that, whatever its known perils, he has been exploring for a long time. The problem is differences. Marxism, he suggests, may or may not agree that differences are "undefinable or impossible to localize," but it has definitely missed the other half of the double bind: the fact that they are unavoidable (it is impossible to imagine the human being deprived of them without being the victim of unbearable violence). Thus, it suffers from a "disastrous political blindness," an inability to recognize the "exclusions" and "disqualifications" that are both intrinsic to "civic-bourgeois universality" and irreducible to "any single model or procedure"—irreducible, that is, to Marxism's procedural model, which I assume to be a critique of capitalism, or an attribution of primary causal efficacy to capitalism. The implication is that Marxism, although critical of civic-bourgeois universality, by focusing on capitalism has also taken over some of liberalism's blindnesses. It's only fair to add, however, that from its beginnings Marxism has also been interested in the precapitalist past, if only so as to figure out where capitalism fits in a larger materialist history. In that sense, Marxism has always already been anthropological, and in taking on terms such as "violence" and "civility" since ancient Greece, Balibar is continuing that anthropological tradition.

It would be convenient for me if I could immediately point to a useful linkage between, on the one hand, the anthropological timescale (whether the narrower one inhabited by the philosophical canon or the vaster one inhabited by the history and prehistory of humankind) and, on the other hand, what Balibar calls (almost always within scare quotes) "anthropological differences": race, gender, sexuality, and so on. As of now, that's not a claim I can make. What his reflections on violence and civility suggest to me is the possibility of continuing to think ethically and politically in a newly expanded temporal landscape that most often seems to *disable* ethical and political categories, that sometimes even seems *intended* to disable those categories.

To me, at least, inhabiting that expanded temporal landscape does not seem optional. In the era that has finally acknowledged climate change, who does not feel the need for some materialist attention to the longer *durée*, a *durée* in which the effect of humans on the planet can be recontextualized—if not by another Copernican Revolution, then at least by a decentering and relativizing of, say, industrial capitalism that makes room for other, earlier causes of the extinction of species? (Characteristically, it was Balibar who first told me I had to read Dipesh Chakrabarty on the environmental decentering of capitalism.[12]) And speaking of the subalterns, who does not applaud the deprovincializing of Europe? But what happens when the deprovincializing of Europe, which has been mainly discussed in spatial terms—as an inclusion of perspectives coming from territories and peoples that had been colonized or otherwise abused—is carried out as a temporal enterprise, a widening of the time frame so that the roughly five hundred years of Europe's rise to preeminence and global hegemony no longer occupy the center of the story? One answer is that the ethical critique of empire is disabled. Again and again, it is suggested that an ethical vocabulary would be an alien, modern, European imposition on non-European and premodern empires. A more general answer, in literary criticism but also across other disciplines, sometimes under the influence of Bruno Latour, is that critique is disabled, or held, again, to be a mere fashion that has had its day. I have already referred to Talal Asad and the suggestion that now we are all "postsecular" if not frankly antisecular. At this scale, secular concepts such as democracy and equality can be redescribed as provincial. It's a familiar move: reactionary Anglo-Europeans using the supposed demographic weight of non-European opinion to back up a commitment to hierarchy, submission, and so on that actual non-Europeans today, if consulted, would most often be quite unenthusiastic about. Ethics is disqualified where ethics is necessary: with regard to premodern and/or non-European empires, which are discussed as if the anti-imperial judgments brought to bear on modern European empires would be hopelessly anachronistic, the effect being to disable judgment of the European empires, as well. And ethics is then applied, unconsciously, where it is totally inappropriate—for example, in the assertion that no world history can be valid unless, in any given case, causal agency is attributed equally to every actor and every geographical region. This is history as politeness. It's bad history, and it's also bad politics.

As I see it, it is this intellectual landscape that Balibar is trying to learn to maneuver around in when he uses "anthropological" to mean "not capitalism" or "not *merely* capitalism" and when, accordingly, he calls for a redefinition of terms such as "exploitation" and "surplus value" so as to admit the productive power of nature and the productive power of domestic labor, the latter dictated by the sexual division of labor, and both of them working on timelines distinct from the timeline of exploitation. Exploitation supposedly works by itself, a modern kind of machine that distinguishes capitalist society from all others, which have relied instead on violent coercion and therefore must be described as depending on domination, not exploitation. The anthropological turn, which allows exploitation to be absorbed back into the now-more-universal category of domination, forces us to confront the possibility that history, overflowing with empirical differences, may be much more random than Marxism has traditionally been comfortable with—a possibility that Perry Anderson raised decades ago in his book on E. P. Thompson, but that he himself arguably did not quite know what to do with, either.[13] As I read him, Balibar is unique among contemporary Marxists in refusing to stay out of this dangerous zone, a zone where Marxism threatens to dissolve *into* difference, historical as well as sociological or identitarian.

Violence, the anthropological-scale object to which Balibar has paid the most sustained attention, has much the same unsettling effect. The more history is determined by violence, the more random, capricious, and arbitrary history becomes—in other words, the less that history presents itself as structured, or even structurable. I mean structurable *by politics*. What the term "differences" really means, down and dirty, is that politics in the sense of the struggle for justice—or, if you prefer, as the struggle for more meaningful life for more people—becomes harder to conceive. This is one reason why the place of violence in human history remains one of the more interesting aporias for Marxism, as for example in Gopal Balakrishnan's book *Antagonistics*. I note in passing that, as Balibar already observed in *Citizen Subject*, here anthropological differences seem *opposed to* politics rather than being *constituted by* politics.[14]

But to return to the idea that anthropological differences are indeed constituted by politics: The word "politics" (Adi Ophir's word, more or less, at the Political Concepts conference) is, among other things, a way of insisting on what anthropological differences are *not*. It means that such differences are not pre-existing characteristics, which can be assigned to categories of persons. And it means they are not particulars, as opposed to the universal. So what are they? Balibar offers various answers, all of which seem to be versions of "politics," but in a slightly mysterious or work-in-progress sort of way. He says that differences are better considered as "relations"—the subject of Jacques Lezra's talk at the conference.[15] And reversing the idea of differences as particulars opposed to the universal, he says that differences are better considered on the contrary as *claims to universality*. The phrase "claims to universality" seems extremely promising. The question it raises, vis-à-vis the definition of anthropological difference as politics, is whether or not these are two ways of saying the same thing. If they are not, then one would be tempted to reframe their relationship by saying that, after all, "claims to universality" *function like* particulars in the sense that, when they conflict, as they must, they demand some sort of adjudication or settlement or negotiation. What happens when one claim to universality walks up to or runs into another claim to universality? Where are they when they meet? What do they say to each other, and in what language do they say it? These are not frivolous or subphilosophical questions. The problem of anthropological differences can't really be solved by kicking it upstairs. If difference is a claim to universality, it seems to follow that there must be a site or zone or field where conflicting claims to universality can meet and something can happen leading, if not to a resolution, then at least to some new settlement, arrangement, or equilibrium. The word "universality" may not be anyone's preference for designating that site or zone or field where claims to universality are mysteriously adjudicated—that is, another, higher order of universality or authority—but that's how it seems called upon to function. Balibar speaks against the liberal model whereby the state is the supposedly universal site where differences-as-particulars are measured and managed. We know he vehemently rejects the idea that the state has a monopoly on the universal. But (perhaps because I am too accustomed to the liberal model) I have trouble seeing what could happen to various "claims to universality," what the next step could be if it's *not* some version of that model: In other words, politics, located wherever, as the process by which various claims to universality are brought together with each other and some new fusion or balance or coalition between them is achieved. The state has no monopoly on this process, but surely the state will get a piece of the action. And one day, one hopes, a larger piece of that same action will devolve onto the institutions of an emergent but increasingly effective transnational democracy and, within those institutions, politics, somewhat retooled, will learn to operate at a transnational scale.

If Balibar is indeed saying that anthropological differences *are* politics while hesitating to imply that politics is (also) the process by which anthropological differences are induced to confront other anthropological differences and to *work out* their differences, so to speak, then the intention would presumably be not to think of politics as *exterior* to those differences, as manager of or mediator between them, but rather as *constitutive* of them. The differences, so I imagine the argument would go, are *nothing but* the encounter, the confrontation in which, Herr and Knecht-like, they are fashioned and refashioned—that is, constituted.[16] The interesting word here is "constituted." We make this term do a lot of work for us. I speculate that one key difference between Balibar and Foucault on the state—the presumptive place where differences-as-claims to universality would confront each other—is that Balibar won't allow the word "constitute" to do more work than it is capable of doing. They agree that the state, or governance, *produces* differences and discriminates on the basis of the differences it produces. But Balibar has more time for politics conducted at the level of the state because, unlike Foucault, he recognizes effective or successful impact on the state coming from below—presumably from particular collective agents who were not already fully formed by the state. That is, these agents possess something—call it characteristics or situation or whatever—in advance of their encounter with the state, something that is therefore not fully constituted by or in relation to the state. Balibar forbears from specifying them or how and where they *are* constituted. He does not want to give them any preexisting characteristics. But even more than that, he does not want to allot to the state or to governance or to "power" the theological omni-competence to constitute differences all by itself, without input from elsewhere.

In the interview I cited above, Balibar mentions being told by one of his examiners, "You are always looking for contradictions!"[17] This is of course true. To this, it must be added, however, that if he is always looking for contradictions, he often refuses to find those contradictions in the same old places—for example, as the necessary products of claims to universality.[18] Going out on a limb, I would speculate that he backs away from the assumption or premise, otherwise almost universally accepted, that the universal necessarily generates its exceptions and/or exclusions. For him, universality does not automatically generate paradoxes or contradictions. It may, and it may not. At any rate, exclusions can also come from somewhere other than from claims to universality.

Let me try to make this sound a bit less vague. At two places in the conclusion of *Citizen Subject*, the phrase "anthropological differences" is preceded by the adjective "great." The phrase is "great anthropological differences."[19] "Great" is a small word, but here it opens the door to a very large point. It implies, of course, that some differences are not great. It implies that the forms of discrimination and the sufferings that follow from "anthropological differences" can be compared. It implies, one might say, that (to abuse Orwell) if all suffering is equal, some suffering is more equal than other suffering. Differences are commensurable; there is a field or ground on which they can be compared or otherwise related to each other. Needless to say, this view is not universally held. It is awkward to say, but I think it's correct, and it is an exemplary act of courage on Balibar's part that he does say it. For example, nothing is more fundamental to Balibar's commitments than refugees. Technically speaking, refugees are merely citizens of *another* state; the state as such is not obliged to see them as other, to exclude or marginalize or discriminate against them. Their difference from natives may well be invisible. In other words, refugees, though they are arguably the exemplary sufferers of our time, may nevertheless not be bearers of "great" anthropological differences.[20]

In the context of contemporary American politics, it is worth adding that in this respect Balibar is not offering a variant of what has come to be called "intersectionality." Intersectionality, at least in its early iterations, meant adding on forms of suffering and discrimination, making sure that no form of suffering or discrimination went uncounted. For Balibar, there is the possibility of such calculations and indeed a need for them, but the arithmetical operations involved cannot be restricted to addition. At the very least, they include subtraction and division. A woman who is also black may also be wealthy and well educated. A white man who is poor and gay may also be a racist and xenophobe. And so on. Balibar's thinking suggests that adding angry white men as a category of difference, whether or not they themselves are respecters of difference, cannot be the end of our political calculations.

What the adjective "anthropological" adds to the plural noun "differences" is, of course, the question of the human. If I had to specify what kind of question the question of the human is, I would say, and I think I would be channeling Balibar here, that it is not an ontological or an epistemological question, but a political question. What I mean by this is that it can be settled, and settled again—never finally, never "resolved"—only by different claims to universality pushing up against each other, both struggling against and joining with each other, finding common ground both on which to join and on which to do battle. This happens in the loud and messy domain of popular usage, and not exclusively or perhaps even primarily at the level of concepts. But that does not mean it is entirely without civility. When we imagine many voices jostling to be heard, we should not imagine George Eliot's roar that lies on the other side of silence, a roar that Eliot declares to be unbearable, unlivable, in fact fatal to those who hear it. We have no reason to think that these voices do not listen to and even, sometimes, hear each other.[21] Civility is not a utopian placeholder. It is as much a political fact as differences are. Like violence, it is anthropological.

NOTES

1. Mark Lilla, "The End of Identity Liberalism," *New York Times*, November 18, 2016. I think Lilla misrepresents this disrespectful view of the angry white Trump voter in calling it "almost anthropological." It is true, as Balibar stops to note in *Citizen Subject*, that "ethnology" has sometimes naturalized differences. But nothing is more characteristic of recent anthropology than an excessive and sometimes

apparently perverse respect for the subjectivity of its subject. If I want our politics to include the angry white men Lilla mentions, as I do, it's not because I necessarily respect their subjectivity, for example in the groups they blame (women, minorities, liberal elites) or do not blame (bankers) for the situation in which they find themselves. (On occasions such as this, I tend to find anthropology at fault because it has too much respect for the subjectivity of its subjects, not too little.) It's because I believe history is objectively structured so as to create inequalities so vast that they cannot be contemplated without pain and confusion, even from the advantaged end.

2. George Saunders, *Pastoralia* (London: Bloomsbury, 2001), 92. Mr. Frendt seems equally open to ignoring "anthropological" references, as when he offers the employee he has fired the following advice: "I'd like to encourage you not to behave like one of those Comanche ladies who bite off their index fingers when a loved one dies. Grief is good, grief is fine, but too much grief, as we all know, is excessive" (111).

3. Philip Mirowski, *Never Let a Serious Crisis Go to Waste: How Neoliberalism Survived the Financial Meltdown* (London: Verso, 2014). Michel Feher's talk at the Political Concepts conference offers one instance among several others in which neoliberalism is credited with bringing into existence a new form of human nature. Feher's term "the investee" is in this sense a contribution to anthropology.

4. In his talk at the conference, Balibar declared that he was inviting politics to contaminate the domain of intelligibility that philosophy as a discipline is at pains to protect.

5. Gregory Elliott, *Althusser: The Detour of Theory* (London: Verso, 1987). See especially Elliott, *Althusser*, 60.

6. Étienne Balibar, *Saeculum: Culture, religion, idéologie* (Paris: Galilée, 2012), 80.

7. Balibar, *Saeculum*.

8. Étienne Balibar, *Citizen Subject: Foundations for Philosophical Anthropology*, trans. Steven Miller (New York: Fordham University Press, 2017).

9. Étienne Balibar, "Citizen Balibar," interview by Nicolas Duvoux and Pascal Séverac, trans. Michael C. Behrent, Collège de France, *Books & Ideas*, November 26, 2012, https://booksandideas.net/Citizen-Balibar.html.

10. Étienne Balibar and John Rajchman with Anne Boyman, eds., *French Philosophy since 1945: Problems, Concepts, Inventions*, trans. Arthur Goldhammer (New York: New Press, 2011).

11. A useful and characteristic instance of this temporally expansive intellectual move at the Political Concepts conference was Didier Fassin's reminder that punishment has not always involved inflicting physical pain—that in the past *poinè* often denoted compensation, the payment of a debt, with no assumption that physical pain would be involved. This is of course also evidence of how much of an intellectual debt we collectively owe to Foucault.

12. Dipesh Chakrabarty, "The Climate of History: Four Theses," *Critical Inquiry* 35 (2009): 197–222.

13. Perry Anderson, *Arguments within English Marxism* (London: Verso, 1980), 51.

14. Gopal Balakrishnan, *Antagonistics: Capitalism and Power in an Age of War* (London: Verso, 2009).

15. The seemingly counterintuitive idea that relations can be or simply are ontologically prior to the objects they relate has of course been a piece of poststructuralist common sense for decades. It is perhaps worth asking how expensive it would be, conceptually speaking, to surrender this premise, if only partially. Yes, it makes as much sense to say that society produces individuals as to say that individuals produce society. But society does not produce individuals out of nothing. *Citizen Subject* also defines anthropological differences as "less a matter of *differences between individuals or subjects*, the unequally recognized 'place' that they occupy within the framework or at the edges of the human species or society, than of the originary dissymmetry of 'bonds' or 'relations' themselves: the relations by means of which *individuals socially and politically constitute the human*" (Balibar, *Citizen Subject*, 65).

16. When we use the term "constitutive," we are holding off the potential randomness of differences. That randomness is what is most threatening about them. It is much more threatening than the risk of offending someone's sensibilities or counting one form of suffering as more significant than another. What is scariest about thinking of differences as *not* constitutive is the prospect that, like historical differences, they might lead away from the premise that history is meaningful, even potentially meaningful.

17. Balibar, "Citizen Balibar."

18. It will be obvious to Balibar's readers that everything he says about the concept of the anthropological is directly or indirectly relevant to his well-known arguments on the subjects of universality, secularism, and human rights.

19. At one point, the phrase "great 'anthropological differences'" (again with "great" not in quotation marks) is followed by a parenthesis and a list: "(whether it be sex, intelligence, 'race,' or—as we will see—abnormality)" (Balibar, *Citizen Subject*, 280, 282).

20. Balibar: "The anthropological dimension of this distribution only emerges when the division among nations is thought as the differentiation of humanity itself and thus appears as a quasi-transcendental trait" (*Citizen Subject*, 287). Ethnology, he goes on, undertakes to describe and interpret this trait in order to present it as "natural," "a 'natural' dimension of political multiplicity" (*Citizen Subject*, 287). This is of course what makes the foreigner seem unassimilable. The standard objection to anthropology is that, through its exaggerated respect for cultural differences, it exacerbates the logic that makes foreigners seem unassimilable and/or that makes assimilation seem like a violation.

21. This is to say that in order for the joining together to happen, there must first be recognition of those differences.

BORDER-CONCEPT (OF THE POLITICAL)

Stathis Gourgouris

My initial consideration was to examine the concept "border," bearing in mind Étienne Balibar's extensive work, going back to the 1980s, on the matter of geopolitical borders. Much of this work is animated by his incisive analysis of the problem of "Europe," which poses a twofold demand: first, a historical account of the trajectory of European thought and its political implications and, second, a philosophical account of the present as it unfolds, often unpredictably, in the real time of thinking and acting. To the first belongs a huge corpus addressing almost the entirety of modern European thought, from Balibar's early work on Marx and Spinoza onward, and to the latter, the work that encounters key landmarks of European reality (from those texts on capital, class, nation, and race to their eventual implication with questions of universality, secularity, citizenship, anthropology, and subjectivity). In a more pointed sense, this meditation on the concept of border in this European trajectory spans the range from the early analysis of the "interior frontier" in Fichte to multiple interventions regarding the institutional project of the European Union in its various manifestations in the last thirty-five years.

In this respect, the border—as a historically actual formation and not merely as a figure—is ever present in Balibar's writing, which is what leads me to risk the claim that Balibar's work relies largely on the "border-concept": on the capacity of ambiguous and self-contesting concepts to work their way through the barriers of established narratives and categorizations and pierce the cracks in those formidable walls of both conceptuality and periodization—that is, both the philosophical and the historical parameters of established logics that often, without our understanding, encumber our thinking even when we think against them.

Elemental in Balibar's mode is a double methodological path in the sense that it involves two different modalities that are, however, codeterminant and intersecting or intertwined, rather than just dialectical, parallel, or simply antithetical. Both these modalities have to do with what was signaled as necessary from the earliest years: the practice of reading, and indeed reading in a twofold way: (1) rigorously textual (even if the text is not literary, strictly speaking—I cannot emphasize enough how eye-opening it was to see one of the greatest idea-books of all time, Marx's *Capital*, be subjected to textual interrogation in the manner that literary critics devote to a difficult poem); and (2) rigorously historical, at times even genealogical—but this, too, is achieved by being strenuously attentive to language, to words themselves or to names, whether these may be "subject" or "Europe," "universality" or "monotheism."[1] These words can in fact be bona fide philosophical concepts as well, but even though their conceptual genealogy is always examined within the internal history of philosophy, they are never allowed to remain strictly abstract, but are always plunged right back into the mess that is human action, historical action.

Incidentally, let us underline that from the outset, Balibar's work is often collaborative: sometimes literally (as in the case of *Reading Capital* or the work with Immanuel Wallerstein) but also even when the work bears the single signature "Balibar," it is consistently engaged with the work of others, and I don't mean the canonical archaic others but a whole range of contemporaneous others, whose ideas are allowed to enter the trajectory and often even to alter it. So, for Balibar, reading is surely not the manifestation of the experience of one "ideal" reader but the work of readership (and I emphasize *work*), which can only be done through the antagonistic conversation of a multiplicity of experiences of reading focused on a shared object.

So let me put on the table some of those key notions in Balibar's thinking that I am calling border-concepts. The most obvious one would have to be "equaliberty," as the very name—and, indeed, the very act of radical naming that we call "neologism"—signifies the entwinement of two powerful established concepts whose common historical trajectory has always been marked by mutual contestation. But I can say this equally about "citizen subject," which has become, under Balibar's signature, a name: a composite name that, very much like "equaliberty," to which it bears direct connection, deconstructs both its components while emancipating each component from the hegemonic logic that safeguards its power through time. To these two names, I could quickly add a couple of others—say, "ambiguous universality" or "antiviolence"—although no doubt more can be found.

Whether single words or not, these names exemplify a border-conceptuality as method. It's possible, one can argue, that this border-conceptuality is a particular expression of the dialectical method. If we assume this to be the case, however, I would suggest that we speak of dialectics in the way that Walter Benjamin understood the dialectical image. For what takes place is not a process of sublation—especially not in the direction of a concept's ascent to a more enhanced, even if altered, state—but rather of the simultaneous deformation and transformation of a concept by its constitutive nature, whereby a concept is undone by its very properties while enabling the reconstitution of these properties in altered form by this very undoing. Sometimes this is denoted in a verbal manner, as, for example, the oft-used phrase "secularizing the secular" (borrowed initially from Bruce Robbins) or "democratizing the democratic," etc. It is important to underline here the simultaneity of a process by which a substantive or a concept is traversed by its property that at the same time enables an action of de- or trans-formation, which is why this is a peculiar dialectics. But we must remember that in Benjamin's terms, "dialectics at a standstill" does not mean a disempowered or static dialectics. Rather, the dialectical image is a pulsing entity; it's dynamic, even if it does not need the linearity of (progressive) time to enable dialectics to happen.

Moreover, I would add the reminder that the use of the word "border" itself entails more than simply matters of location. A border is always a historical institution, bearing a certain geo-temporality, even when it is made to do the philosophical work of "limit." Limits or thresholds, we all know, are constitutively ambiguous, serving at the very least as portals, alternately open or barred depending on a whole array of factors and conjunctures that can never be reduced to purely philosophical categories or historical conditions. From a strict standpoint, a border-concept defies precise definition, even if in a paradoxical sense, because every definition establishes a border of sorts—in Greek, *horismos* (definition) is of the same root as *horion* (limit, boundary, border)—in essence because a border occupies an ambiguous terrain and can never achieve pure permanence: finality, de-finition.

Useful here is also Jacques Derrida's inordinately enabling configuration of interdiction. Reading Kafka's parable "Before the Law," Derrida reminds us that what is forbidding (*l'interdit*) is also the interstitial (*l'inter-dit*): what lies between the lines, often unsaid and unperceived but always enabling the process of meaning even while serving as obstacle to meaning.[2] What brings together and what tears apart—a notion, a category, a meaning, a definition—happens simultaneously, as it were, and this very ambiguity becomes the working method. Thus, in engaging with Balibar's border-conceptuality in this fashion, I imagine an entwinement of Sandro Mezzadra's figure of "border as method" with Aamir Mufti's figure of "partition as method"—both being drawn, of course, from kindred political universes equally pertinent here, for in both cases what is European cannot be articulated apart from what is colonial and vice versa.[3]

To illustrate what I mean—and before I go on to address the implications of this sort of political methodology in my own thinking—I will engage in a little concept surfing, as it were: that is, to consider each of three border-concepts in turn, not by elaborating on its specific content, but with an eye to its borderline form.

EQUALIBERTY

From the outset, Balibar reveals that, in conjuring this word, he is displacing the use of the word "democracy," and I would like to suggest that, in this respect, he is restaging an original archaic displacement—though it would not have been consciously considered as a displacement per se in the language of the ancients—which we see, for example, in Herodotus, namely, that in place of democracy, as a specific form of politics (to be distinguished from monarchy or oligarchy), the word used is *isonomia*, a name that does not designate a political regime, strictly speaking, but rather a societal condition. Equaliberty may be thought of as the modern name of *isonomia*, if we understand the work that *nomos* conducts in that ancient figure as the closest we can come to configuring the work that "liberty" conducts in the post-Enlightenment conceptual sphere. For any notion of liberty or freedom in the ancient Greek political universe cannot be restricted to an existential condition (although this is where it begins) but achieves meaning in terms of how society is divided or apportioned (*nemein*), which is to say simply, how society is organized. In other words, I'm suggesting that, although a political name, equaliberty bears directly upon the question of social organization and, to be more precise, self-organization—*autogéstion*.

Equaliberty then derives from, but also accentuates further, the encounter of two paramount conditions of the modern democratic imaginary (equality and liberty), which are characterized by an irreducible and outmaneuverable struggle. This struggle emerges from and returns to the core of each condition so that, from the isolated standpoint of each one versus the other, it might seem to be debilitating. At their absolute point, both these notions work at cross-purposes for the simple reason that absolute equality presupposes a fundamental constraint that liberty cannot contain while, conversely, absolute liberty shatters any regulatory regime that thus makes equality impossible to achieve. Yet both are necessary conditions for radical democratic politics, which is why, given their constitutive antinomy, democracy enacts the aporia that makes it such precarious or high-risk politics.

This aporia permeates the project of the French Revolution, at least insofar as this project is announced in the *Declaration of the Rights of Man and the Citizen*, where a basic contradiction, to which the writers of the *Declaration* would have been impermeable, is presumed to be eradicated by the peculiar conjunction that couples the indefinite with the definite, the universal with the particular. Balibar takes this impossible equation as the departure point for a radical democratic politics that surely exceeds the historical parameters of its revolutionary emergence by literally merging the two terms (here, we can say "political concepts" without hesitation) and annihilating their declared sacredness that served—this is perfectly clear—as the transcendental guarantee of a new metaphysics of power. It makes sense to me, in this respect, that Balibar identifies equaliberty as "an absolute 'fiction,' or an institution with no foundation that is necessarily and irremediably contingent,"[4] a figure (or "truth effect," in Adi Ophir's language) that brings to mind Georges Sorel's description of the general strike as the quintessential myth of socialism.

The result of this wordplay is a fluid conceptuality whose limits are internal. As is the way of the portmanteau, the concept opens at both ends and renders permeable the hard and external conceptual boundaries of each component, so that, on the one hand, the whole equation is plunged into indeterminacy—another way of foregrounding its impossibility—and, on the other hand, the evident merger is fissured, so that conditions that are presumed to have been overcome, resolved, or sublated by the simultaneous pursuit of the two individual projects (equality and liberty) in their totalizing revolutionary pact, now take their place as inevitable mediations. I am thinking here of sexual difference, incommensurable sociality, ambiguous universality, or subjectivity as such mediating conditions for equaliberty.

CITIZEN-SUBJECT

One can argue that the concept "citizen-subject" is a sort of deconstruction of "equaliberty"—especially if we can envisage equaliberty to have an interior frontier. From another standpoint, however, one could also argue that "citizen subject" is another face of "equaliberty" or perhaps even a phase, so long as we don't understand either face or phase as a matter of sequence or consequence. I am not making a silly pun; face and phase are related at the root as epitomes of the tropic power of image. Both equaliberty and citizen-subject belong to the same imaginary, and not only because of their shared historical content but also, in Balibar's hands, because of their form, their borderline conceptuality.

Like "equaliberty," "citizen-subject," too, involves an inveterate wordplay, as the word "subject" in a number of Latin-derived or Latin-affected languages is caught in the interplay between the metaphysics of grammar (the subject of a verb or a sentence, *subjectum*, which becomes the subject of an action) and the metaphysics of sovereignty (the subject *to* power, *subjectus*, that is to say, the object whose action is authorized by some regime of subjection, which would include a self-making dimension, where subjection and subjectivation meet, as Foucault, Butler, and a range of other thinkers have elaborated). This constitutive perplexity of the subject is not alleviated by the coupling with the word "citizen"; on the contrary, Balibar uses it to complicate the presumed cognitive sovereignty of the term "citizen" precisely in the way that history itself, surely in its revolutionary moments, also does.

But the border-concept figure performs an action that exceeds the historical mark, even the revolutionary one. It brings the problem of citizenship within the contentious realm that characterizes the question of political anthropology since the time of Aristotle's equally problematizing figure of the political animal. It's difficult to imagine how Aristotle could have come to the term *zōon politikon* without the historical actualization of democracy. The great American political theorist Sheldon Wolin puts it succinctly: "There is an extraordinary element in this characterization" because there had to have existed (as always-already) "a powerful, undeniable experience of politicalness, an actual practice sufficiently widespread to justify claiming it not simply as a human possibility but as the teleological principle of human nature itself. What was captured, *a posteriori*, by Aristotle's formula was the revolution in the political accomplished by Athenian citizen democracy of the fifth century."[5] The revolution of the political may be otherwise configured to be a revolution of the natural. This tangible and fully actualized political mode of living being (*zōon*) leans on the very processes of subjectification, configuring the sort of subjectivity whose nature is interrogative and transgressive while being collaborative and collective against previous structures of communal hierarchy. The analogy in contemporary terms would be what Balibar configures to be the "becoming-citizen of the subject" (*le devenir citoyen du sujet*), which is always codetermined, in palindromic fashion as it were, by the "becoming-subject of the citizen" (*le devenir-sujet du citoyen*).[6]

I am risking the suggestion that, within the question of political anthropology, Balibar's reconfiguration of the historical trajectory of the *subjectum/subjectus* relation might be a symptomatic reading of Aristotle's notion as well, even if Aristotle is not the object of reading—rightfully so, for the trajectory that Balibar wants to elucidate is the history of European sovereignty, which is a Latin and indeed Christian trajectory. But insofar as the word "citizen" finds a semantic antecedent in the Greek conception of *politēs*—the "person of the *polis*" but just as well simply "political person"—then the connection is there. What is less obvious in the connection is the relation between the "animal" and the "subject," for the subject is already largely a political term as *subjectus*: the person who is subjected to the authority to the sovereign and, in that respect, may not even be quite a person but nonetheless represses the political animality that cannot be abolished by the action of "becoming citizen" except in the manuals of liberal humanism and its civilizing command of taming the beast.

Incidentally, insofar as in the Christian reference frame *subjectus* is also subjected to the grace of God, it entails a creeping notion of person, but discussing this would take us far afield. I note here how Balibar underlines the *coincidence* of the two in the double play of the trajectory between *fidèle sujet* (loyal subject—to the King) and *sujet fidèle* (faithful subject—to God). Having said that, insofar as the citizen enables a subjectification beyond the condition of subjection—this is how the "becoming-citizen of the subject" reconfigures the "becoming-subject of the citizen," that is, creates another mode of subjectivity—then we can say that the animus, the "natural" substance in the phrase *zōon politikon*—the *animal*, yes!—is qualified by the political, by becoming citizen. The verb "qualify" is used here in the strongest possible sense—that is, coming to bear specific qualities but not "civilized" or "humanized" or anything of the sort.

The other side, however, remains to haunt the process: "the becoming-subject of the citizen." Here, the detour would have to go through Spinoza, which would link Aristotle to the modern history of democracy by continuing a *de-Christianized* notion of politics and sovereignty. In reading backward through Balibar's admirable encounter with Spinoza, I was struck by various elements that are useful here and even tend to echo and elucidate Aristotle, even though they come from an entirely different historical context. I quote Balibar in a couple instances, which I will not have the chance to analyze, but I think are insightfully resonant in themselves: "Even before sovereignty can be defined as the 'sovereignty of the people,' a 'people' already exists, irreducible to a multitude of plebeians or a passive mob. . . . We cannot claim that men are sociable 'in their origins' but they *are* always already socialized."[7] This condition of *always-already* in the politics of society, which is surely not reducible to a simple a priori, remains the deconstructive element in the otherwise dialectical dynamic of how the "becoming-citizen of the subject" engages with the "becoming-subject of the citizen." Here, let us recall Peter Osborne's observation as to the transformative capacity of this engagement. The specific signification of "subject" in this equation is not quite equivalent, for what is transformed into citizen was initially *subjectus*, whereas what the citizen is transformed into is *subjectum*, a new subjectivity. So even the *subjectum/subjectus* relation is no longer the same once this "becoming" is animated by the engagement of the citizen-subject semantic field. What is the subject in citizen-subject and what is the citizen in citizen-subject are no longer questions that can be answered substantively and in equivalence. There is no "what" and no "is"—the border-conceptuality in this political ontology creates and sustains a dynamic condition of becoming.

ANTI-VIOLENCE

Of all the border-concepts I mention here, "anti-violence" is the most curious—or the least evident. This is because words bearing the prefix "anti-" are conventionally made to bear a position of some solidity that is rarely considered to be emancipated from its binding mirror condition. And yet this is precisely the point of this brilliant formulation. Balibar tells us from the outset that "anti-violence" is not at all "non-violence" or even "counter-violence"—these two being the quintessential negations that seal the conceptual sovereignty of violence. "There is no non-violence" he says characteristically at one point.[8]

Strangely, unlike non-violence, which means literally a negation of violence, anti-violence signifies an antithesis that is fully implicated in the thesis that nominally gives it meaning, which is to say that it recognizes the dangerous delusion of seeing violence as an existential appendage that politics allegedly can overcome—which is the cornerstone of the Western metaphysics of sovereignty. Instead, Balibar sets as a task the impetus to think not of how politics can eradicate violence, as if a social imaginary can ultimately be reduced to the rule of its institutions, but of how violence is permeated by politics, making thus the question of politics immanent and crucial in any consideration of violence. Incidentally, "the question of politics" always and unambiguously involves whatever is required in the decision of answering the question "Which politics?"—which to me signifies nothing less than the point where the political (*le politique*) intersects with politics (*la politique*). Using Balibar's language, I would risk saying that the political is the citizen-subject figure of politics. In simple terms, this means that anti-violence is a concept pertaining foremost to politics, not to ethics or metaphysics, and surely it does not signify (or even aspire to) an overcoming of violence, but it does signify—polemically, one might say—a way of imagining an emancipatory politics in which violence is neither the subject nor the object that authorizes politics but the "irreducible remainder over the institutional, legal, or strategic forms for reducing and eliminating it."[9]

This politics, which Balibar names "the emancipatory insurgency that simultaneously perpetuates and eclipses the constitution"[10]—notice here the parallel structure of excess between violence as remainder and the politics of insurgency—may be characterized by a sort of know-thyself recognition that enables the self-constitution of a collective political subject "in a world in which the political community no longer has natural or traditional bases but can arise only from a collective decision and practice."[11] Such politics cannot possibly be restricted to the politics of autochthonous citizenship (whether ancient or modern) and, in this respect, cannot be reduced to any sort of transcendental rights that somehow precede its institution in the name of the citizen-subject—nationalism being here the most indomitable culprit. Such politics is profoundly historical—in the sense of geo-temporal—and therefore as precarious as any radical democratic politics is by definition: a politics of citizenship in which anti-violence would be endemic, as a condition of internal otherness at the core of its constitution, but even more (or precisely, as a consequence of), a politics of "citizenship permanently in the making."[12]

It makes perfect sense to me, then, that Balibar will go on to recognize this politics as a tragic politics, and this resonates with various arguments I have made to this effect. In a brilliant moment, he sees the politics of "anti-violence" as a borderline condition that he names "Luxemburg's aporia," elaborating it further as the question "How can the balance between the ethics of conviction and the ethics of responsibility be democratically shared?"[13] In this aporetic encounter, neither of these contrary ethical realms—we can call the pairs alternately faith and knowledge, theory and practice, etc.—have any significance outside their *political* immersion in this paradoxical condition of democratic sharing, the proposition of equaliberty par excellence. Because no constitutional order of rights can possibly safeguard what always takes place in the precarious arena of contested collective practice, this sharing cannot possibly be restricted to a priori authorization. All ethical positions are tragic: they are groundless, without guarantees, and *meaningless* (in a literal, not pejorative, sense) in themselves outside the field of contention. Note that this tragic politics, Balibar, says, is not heroic—and I have argued the same as well. It is a matter of tragic life—in other words, of the limit point of a political anthropology, as he also says.

Left Governmentality

Keeping to Balibar's express request not to speak merely about his work but rather to use his work as a springboard for our own thinking on this occasion, I will now briefly consider a concept I have been recently exploring precisely in Balibar's mode of border-conceptuality in the political arena. What I have named "left governmentality" is a paradoxical concept par excellence, if we keep in mind the problematic relation of the Left—at least in both the Marxist and the anarchist tradition—to the politics of government as opposed to the politics of resistance, which is always instantaneously privileged. The problem emerges from the historical record of the Left's incapacity to govern without being absorbed by the institutions against which it stands, even when it has assumed power by force and by the violent dismantling of whatever is the *ancien régime* of the day. However, this particular historical legacy of violence does not concern me here. I am proposing that we consider the notion of left governmentality not in the frame of the Leninist revolutionary Left but within the limits of a liberal parliamentary system or, more precisely, within the democratic process whereby the Left coming to the position of government does not abolish the democratic process—any such action, regardless of where it comes from, is fascist. This means, right away, that any sort of left governmentality will have to account for the possibility that it might be overthrown in the same way that it came to be. Hence, it is a regime of struggle, a tragic regime.

The paradox is aggravated further if we consider how Foucault's notion of governmentality tends to be interpreted as a mechanism of population control, although there is great evidence in Foucault's thinking that would make governmentality a notion essential to a kind of autonomous, self-empowering politics. I am thinking especially of Foucault's extensive work on the disciplines involved in what he named "the government of the self," for there is no doubt that any sort of left governmentality worthy of its name cannot possibly be excised from the self-governance of the subject, however we might agree or disagree about what this might involve and how feasible it might actually be. Indeed, self-government, an old autonomist adage that is pertinent to the politics of society, has a "mirror" in the government of the self, with its extensive self-disciplinary practices that Foucault sought out in the Stoic period, as we know.

So if governmentality, in Foucault's writing, is the figure that moves out of the disciplinary or punitive society model and into, say, the biopolitical or micropower model, by analogy left governmentality is a figure that moves out of the counterpower model and turns the notion on its head, so that "societies of control" (to use a Deleuzian phrase) become societies of self-governance.[14] Left governmentality is as much a condition of governing the self (or governance by the self) as it is a condition of governing the other (or governance by the other)—departing in both cases from both liberal/individualist and Marxist/collectivist modes in which there remains a sharp division between self and other.

I invented the term "left governmentality"—initially without much thinking, I admit—in response to the 2011–12 political conjuncture that brought forth what we now summarily call the politics-of-assembly movements (the Arab Spring, the Spanish and Greek occupations of public squares, the Occupy movement in the United States, and subsequent assembly occupations of public spaces in various parts of the world—Istanbul, Hong Kong, Brazil, etc.), even though "movement" might be an inaccurate term of description because the operative politics involved in all these cases of assembly is in fact a kind of Benjaminian politics of arrest, of interruption.[15] Subsequently, this idea found more concrete and higher stakes historical content in the rise of Syriza to power in Greek politics, especially since this signaled the veritably rare event of the Left coming to power not by revolution but by the procedures of a liberal parliamentary system.

The key question in the actual politics of left governmentality is obviously how to move from resistance/opposition to government decision. I don't see this as a mere positional shift in the spectrum of power but rather something that requires the operations of a different political imaginary and a different framework of social organization. Left governmentality is a border-concept because it acknowledges—it *names*—the paradox of a political constituency that traditionally derives its authority from negation (resistance to established authority and, at the outer limit, revolution) having achieved a position of affirmation, the imperative to rule, especially if we understand rule, in a radical democratic sense, not to be reducible to an ideological partisanship that divides society between rulers and ruled, whatever may be the specific turns of representation. For this latter reason alone, left governmentality entails the sort of rule that pertains to all and is shared by all of society, not just the extension of the specific class interests presumed to authorize leftist propositions of rule—traditionally, the dictatorship of the proletariat on the way to communism or, more recently, the politics of left populism, to which I turn briefly below.

From my perspective, left governmentality has no meaning outside the problematic of democracy and, indeed, outside the paradoxical politics of equaliberty, ambiguous universality, and the citizen-subject. In this particular sense, the class politics that the Marxist legacy of the Left has indelibly established—and in fact the class struggle itself as a kind of epistemological framework that permeates all levels of political thought and action—cannot be presumed to work against the radical democratic imperative that, *anarchist* as it is in literal terms (where *archon* and *archomenos*, ruler and ruled, are one), aspires to an autonomous politics at all levels of life and for all involved, regardless of the social differences that are still in play. Rather, in this encounter of left governmentality with democracy, the epistemology of class struggle becomes a productive obstacle to the tendency to sublate social difference in the name of an emancipatory universality; it underlines the ambiguous universality that the proposition of equaliberty necessitates.

At a basic level, whatever governmental (state) politics that left governmentality enacts cannot obviously be restricted to typical institutional politics. The Left in power, when it comes to govern the society as a whole with the inheritance of the capitalist state, cannot sever itself from the social movements that bring it to power in the first place. By "social movements," I am not referring simply to politics of negation/resistance but more to radical affirmation politics: solidarity networks (which must always be international in the last instance), alternative modes of social organization and economy at the local level, collective self-instituted public services (neighborhood health care, schooling for immigrants, welfare for impoverished strata), extraparliamentary politics, and all kinds of performativities of difference.

The movement, in this respect, cannot be instrumentalized, whether as a potential pool for political party organization or even as a symbolic recipient and/or carrier of institutional alterity at the state level. Pierre Clastres's old argument of "society against the state" (unburdened, however, by his utopian politics of "society without the state") can be very useful here as an epistemological framework. A certain relative autonomy of society, as a field of self-organization, must remain in place in order to keep the movement from being instrumentalized and for the performativities of difference to flourish or, even more, to sustain a real political effectiveness and not to remain locked in ideological self-satisfaction. For this reason, the politics of the state in which the Left may have acceded cannot presume to dictate the terms of action to the movement that may have created the horizon of possibility for this accession, nor can it presume to harness a certain raw political power inherent in the movement that, no matter its specific form of social organization, must remain formless in some last instance.

So, in light of the notorious case of the Syriza government calling for a referendum in July 2015, I argued at the time that the referendum was decided by the government and was won, for the government, by the movement in order for the government to act on its basis. Nothing in this equation should be assumed to be linear or self-evident, or even simply causal. The components are irreducibly linked but cannot be collapsed into each other. Neither the government nor the movement is subservient to each other, and yet both the government and the movement are responsible for each other. They can exist just as easily in coincidence as in contestation, and indeed they must, if the radical democratic impetus of left governmentality is to be sustained.[16]

It is in this sense that left governmentality, in its full capacity as a border-concept, cannot be equated with any conceptual framework identified as left populism, either in the able hands of Chantal Mouffe or in the historical-political field in Venezuela, Spain, or Greece.[17] The sense of Syriza's failure, for example, which unleashed extraordinary waves of debilitating affect ranging from depression to rage among large constituencies of supporters, including activists in the movement as such, would have been more productively put to work if the symbolic structure of the whole affair did not have left-populist characteristics—whether these were a matter of psychical investment by the population (a sort of metaphysics of faith) or were instrumentally cultivated and engineered by central aspects of the Syriza organization itself. In reference to the latter, I do not examine whether this cultivation was intentional or unwitting, for the symbolic structures of left populism are machinelike in their ways and sweep political affect toward a monovalent direction, regardless of what might be the material conditions of social difference on the ground.

This machine-logic is what produced the disastrous way in which the Syriza referendum was constructed, conducted, and interpreted. The left-populist imaginary that engendered and prevailed over the referendum, at nearly all levels of society and state, prevented the differences of the social body (on both sides of the vote) from remaining active factors in the arena of political discourse, producing thus a debilitating homogenization of all political signifiers—the enraged polarization of affect being one of the most acute markers of homogenization. The complexities addressed symptomatically and brought forth causally by the referendum were thus nullified; the government's subsequent decision appeared to be total deception—for some, it spelled treason, for others, cynical confirmation of political realism. The roused population (on all sides) was simply deflated and any radical possibility in the next phase of political action was disarmed.

The us-against-them division, which Laclau and Mouffe always held on to in order to retain intact a certain register of the epistemology of the class struggle, is precisely what renders left populism a political machine-logic. (What this does to the epistemology of the class struggle as such cannot be discussed here in a substantial way.) Despite, of course, the consistent acknowledgment that the people is a heterogeneous entity, this elemental division inevitably homogenizes the framework of society. The machine reproduces simple 0/1 divisional pairs: people/elite, society/state, disenfranchisement/power, us/them. What happens then when, let us say, the people come to power? What happens to the state? To the people who now occupy the state? We presume that "we" do not become "them," but on what basis do we turn their house (the state) into ours, if by sheer constitutive division we have undersigned and sealed its alterity? What does it mean for us to have *come to power*? Had we no power before? If disenfranchisement means no power, then how do the powerless achieve power? Likewise, if we presume that there are two different modes of power, how do we account for a qualitative shift of power in real political and social-historical terms? Either the division "disenfranchisement/power" collapses, or the power that "we" now have in the place of "them"—say, the state—is really still "their" power, since, after all, we had no power of our own.

Notice that I have left out the inheritance of capitalism from this admittedly reductive set of queries in order to keep the matter focused on the governmental sphere, even though this inheritance can never be left out. In fact, it is impossible to field the problem of left governmentality without including as a key element the inheritance of capitalism, at least at this present planetary phase. Because the symbolic structure of left populism is so formalist, the actual politics that it mobilizes will be channeled, at some point in the process, toward inherited modes of oligarchic power: not only in the basic sense in which the movement will be subsumed by the political party form and its metaphysics of representation but, even more, in a kind of historically antecedent way, in the sense that the people's power will be subsumed by the power of national sovereignty at the apex of which remains the heroic sovereign, whether as the President of the Republic or the Popular Leader. For the same reason that I have always argued that popular sovereignty is, strictly speaking, a nonsensical notion, I also think that left populism is a nonsensical notion, if we want to retain within the content of the Left an undeconstructibly internationalist and radical-democratic (or, in my language, anarchist) ground.

The usual argument, which Mouffe reiterates, that the difference between Right populism and Left populism is that the first restricts democracy whereas the second doesn't, has proven insubstantial, since so many strains of left-populist politics have ended up in centralized sovereign power—literally, oligarchic power. Left populism is still a sovereign state politics, with all the ensuing horrific dimensions of nationalist thinking kept intact. Thus, no matter what might be the left-populist rhetoric, national borders must be preserved as sacred markers of difference as division—that is to say, safeguards of identity—that then serve either as pillars of self-enclosure or platforms for expansion and conquest of the other. This pertains to the internal space, as well: the paramount gesture of creating internal borders of division and self-enclosure, instrumental power and control over the performativities of difference. This is why left populism cannot possibly be a border-concept in the way that left governmentality is.

And it is also why left populism may pride itself on mobilizing a movement but ultimately has no respect for the autonomy of the movement past its point of instrumentalized power. Left populism claims to begin with the movement but is instead always-already grounded in the telos of governmental power as state power in the name of the people. In this respect, it remains entirely with the liberal framework and plays very well into the hands of neoliberal power. Instead, left governmentality is inevitably grounded in the problem of government—in how to move from resistance to government—but this can never be its telos, because it would mean de facto the conquest of the movement and the voiding of resistance by the formal power of rule. Without the movement—that is, civic action whose institutionality exists outside the state and sometimes against the state—there can be no left governmentality. In other words, although left governmentality begins with and has sufficient cause in the fact that the Left is in government, it cannot be solely conducted at the level of government. It cannot be exhausted within the purview of political institutions of government but must involve general social practices of *governance*, indeed self-governance.

For this reason, obviously, left governmentality cannot revert to simple party politics in the liberal system. In fact, its perpetually contentious relation between governance and insurgency, government and movement, is precisely why left governmentality is a border-concept that bears a tragic politics. The nonrevolutionary Left's notorious aversion to taking on the responsibility of government in its name might be the result of its fear of losing its authenticity as resistance or counterpower, which is curiously never the fear of revolutionaries despite the fact that historically this loss of authenticity seems to have happened every time, for how could it not? Yet, as Balibar incisively reminds us—and he lays out this reminder specifically as a mark of the tragic dimension of politics—"the risk that the revolt might be perverted is never sufficient reason not to revolt."[18] Permit me to add, especially in the conjuncture of present critical times, that the bloody tragedy of Left politics today is certainly never sufficient reason to think that Left politics now lies dead on the stage.

NOTES

1. Regarding the latter, I draw attention to one of Balibar's exemplary even if less-known texts: "Note sur l'origine et les usages du terme 'monothéisme,'" *Critique* 704–5 (2006): 19–45.

2. Jacques Derrida, "Devant la loi," in *Acts of Literature*, ed. Derek Attridge (London: Routledge, 1992), 181–220.

3. Sandro Mezzadra and Britt Nielsen, *Border as Method, or, the Multiplication of Labor* (Durham, N.C.: Duke University Press, 2013); Aamir Mufti, *Forget English!: Orientalisms and World Literature* (Cambridge, Mass.: Harvard University Press, 2016).

4. Étienne Balibar, *Violence and Civility: On the Limits of Political Philosophy*, trans. G. M. Goshgarian (New York: Columbia University Press, 2016), 146.

5. Sheldon Wolin, "Transgression, Equality, and Voice," in *Dēmokratia: A Conversation on Democracies, Ancient and Modern*, ed. Josiah Ober and Charles Hedrick (Princeton: Princeton University Press, 1996), 65–66.

6. See Étienne Balibar, "Bourgeois Universality and Anthropological Differences," in *Citizen Subject: Foundations for Philosophical Anthropology*, trans. Steven Miller (New York: Fordham University Press, 2017), 275–302.

7. Étienne Balibar, *Spinoza and Politics*, trans. Peter Snowdon (London: Verso, 2008), 34, 88.

8. Balibar, *Violence*, 149.

9. Balibar, *Violence*, 11.

10. Balibar, *Violence*, 144–45.

11. Balibar, *Violence*, 146.

12. Balibar, *Violence*, 147.

13. Balibar, *Violence*, 148.

14. Here, it would help to remember the resonance in the word of the French notion of *mentalité*. Namely, governmentality is not so much the substantive noun from the administrative qualifier "governmental" as it is the designation of a certain imaginary (a mentality) of governance.

15. This is brilliantly argued by Mehmet Dosemeci, "The Kinetics of Our Discontent: Toward a History of Social Arrest," in *Past and Present* (forthcoming).

16. For the full argument, which proved to be quite controversial at the time, see Stathis Gourgouris, "The Syriza Problem: Radical Democracy and Left Governmentality in Greece," *Open Democracy* (August 6, 2015), http://www.opendemocracy.net/can-europe-make-it/stathis-gourgouris/syriza-problem-radical-democracy-and-left-governmentality-in-g/.

17. It's useful to consult Chantal Mouffe's recent, succinct interview on the matter of left populism today and overall. Chantal Mouffe, "We Urgently Need to Promote a Left-Populism," interview with Gildas Le Dem (August 4, 2017), https://www.versobooks.com/blogs/3341-chantal-mouffe-we-urgently-need-to-promote-a-left-populism/.

18. Balibar, *Violence*, 150.

CIVIL RELIGION: SECULARISM AS RELIGION?

Judith Butler

In Balibar's 1985 *Spinoza and Politics*, he follows a complex and compelling trajectory through Spinoza's *Tractatus theologico-politicus*, and the *Ethics*, to show how a political structure of democracy is articulated through the reflections on religion, specifically on God, law, nature, and love.[1] Spinoza is said to lament the degeneration of religion into superstition on the one hand and dogmatism on the other. Furthermore, he seeks to distinguish both theology and theocracy from what he calls "true Religion"—the latter would ally the dictates of revealed religion with those of reason.[2] Balibar begins this text by claiming that one can find the contours of a theory of democracy in Spinoza's *Tractatus*, one for which actions or deeds prove to be central both to faith and to freedom. Balibar follows Spinoza closely as he seeks to understand how "true religion" differs from theocratic notions of institutional authority and its command structures. What does true religion mean when it not only is separated from theocracy but functions as a critical perspective on its operations? And how is true religion related to freedom understood as *potentia*, the immanent power of the individual that is irreducible to egotism or individualism?

By clearly opposing the mandates of religious institutions that seek to curb the operation of free thought, Spinoza seeks to know and to elaborate the very power of free thought, an inquiry that involves rethinking power not merely as *potestas* (external power) but as *potentia* (immanent power), and rethinking freedom not as individual prerogative but as an exercise of power crafted and intensified in relation to others. Theology is faulted politically for its deep ties to hierarchy and caste, which is why defeating one ruling theology by installing another is no solution, as it simply shifts the site of *potestas* while failing to reverse the priority of *potestas* over *potentia*. The radical critique of theology would have to take aim at the social hierarchy between the so-called elect and the masses, those it governs or subordinates. All this happens through recourse to a critical method that, in Balibar's language, "frees faith itself from theology."[3]

And though I cannot in these few pages reproduce the subtlety of Balibar's exposition, I do hope to underscore that this faith liberated from theology is not a merely subjective experience but, alas, "true religion." True religion restores and intensifies the immanent powers of freedom, ones that are exercised and actualized in the context of interaction or communication with others. If we move too quickly to the conclusion that that freedom has been successfully transposed into a form of social exchange, we forget that Spinoza identifies the will of God, associated with "true religion," "with nature itself, [nature] in its totality and its necessity."[4] For Balibar, this apparently speculative problem of understanding how the will of God can be so identified with nature is to be approached less as a metaphysical problem than as a practical one. In what sense, or where, is something called "God" operative in nature and true religion, and how are they then related to one another?

As Balibar points out, the philosophical problem that Spinoza confronts is how to relate human freedom to the order of the world. If both freedom and nature are "ordered" in some way, and related to one another, then that can only be understood by understanding how they both act. If faith shows itself in *works*, then any theocratic authority that intervenes in acts seeks to negate the freedom or potential expressed or actualized in those acts. If freedom is figured apart from acts and works, and if faith, too, is said to exist apart from deeds, then both are wrenched out of the structure of action that gives them meaning. Even as it is the task of the sovereign to determine the public good, according to Spinoza, the sovereign oversteps its mandate if it interferes at the level of deeds and works, thwarts their emergence, or curbs their expression. Deeds and works are expressions of what Spinoza calls the "freedom of religious conscience"[5]—and it is that practical determination of faith that constitutes "true religion."[6] There are checks on the sovereign and checks on the individual, and those limits articulate a sustainable bond. The individual checks her own freedom in transferring her own sovereignty to the external sovereign authority, which means that both sovereign and citizen are bound by practices of self-limitation, even though overstepping and interference happens, or threatens to happen, all the time.

As Balibar elaborates the nascent structure of a democratic theory found in Spinoza's theological writings, working always between the *Tractatus* and the *Ethics*, it becomes clear that consensus, for instance, is derived from faith, and that faith, or *potentia*, is the practical and social determination of freedom, close, we might speculate, to Marx's idea of "living labor." Something is alive in this *potentia*, enacting and exposing its relation to what is living in nature, to the animate order of nature, an order that is manifest less as principle than as *conatus*; that actualization of what is living in nature is what links human freedom to the order of the world. It also explains why theocracies that deny or destroy true religion are "essentially sad."[7] If and when true religion is suppressed, the living basis of the polity is destroyed. This is why the effective absorption of religion into theocracy is the death of religion, and precisely *not* its actualization. The success of theocratic rule, the triumph of *potestas* over *potentia*, destroys the very possibility of the determination of an action at once free and social, defining one version of tyranny. Conversely, there is something in religion that subverts theocratic rule. This may or may not be a fully deliberate or conscious strategy. As Balibar, following Spinoza, puts it, "There is a tendency already present within religion itself to pervert its own aims."[8] In other words, there is something in religion that resists its realization as the structure of a state. Its aim is less teleological than practical, and its institutionalization is in some sense its death.

Although I cannot lay out all the links of this argument, an argument that Balibar continues in a piece published in 2012 titled "Spinoza's Three Gods and the Modes of Communication," it is worth noting that Balibar finds that God takes several forms for Spinoza, some of them quite surprising.[9] There seems to be recourse to God as anthropomorphic sovereign, but God is also rendered distinctly as Law detached from all anthropomorphism; this happens when God, or the divine, is said to be love but also nature. These latter renditions lead Balibar to emphasize the ethical and political implications of a practical form of freedom that is always codetermined within and by a social and political world. The point is not only that the *conatus*, that desire to persist in one's own being, is enhanced or diminished depending on the dynamic interactions with other living beings, but that a desire to live together, a pulsation that belongs to cohabitation, emerges that forms the basis of consensus, and that this political principle and practice follows from the very exercise or actualization of the desire to persist in one's own being. One desires to persist in one's own being, but that can only happen if one is affected by the other, and so *without that fundamental susceptibility there can be no persistence*.

This is the point that Deleuze partially clarified about Spinoza.[10] But the political implications exceed his view. If one's one being is implicated in the being of others, then persisting in one's own life implicates one in a transitive situation of supporting and being supported by the persistence of another's life. My life is never exclusively mine, since life itself is a transitive relation. This persistence in one's being, which turns out to be constitutively linked with the entire order of social and natural life, is, moreover, not a substrate of action but action itself, since the desire, understood as a power, a potential, is acted upon and acting. In "Spinoza's Three Gods and the Modes of Communication," Balibar redefines Spinoza's God this way: the absolute meaning of God is "the idea of *agire*, acting (and agency), and more precisely of acting necessarily."[11] As I understand it, no God stands behind this kind of acting as a metaphysical phantasm; whatever God is, God is operative in that acting. We are not led to ask, then, what grounds the metaphysical justification of God. We ask whether and where and how this notion of God becomes operative. If what is called "God" proves to be an immanent feature of socially determined and free action, and that action is enabled and intensified as part of an exchange, then action emerges within a field in which the living body is acted upon and acting upon others, sometimes sequentially, sometimes simultaneously, sometimes in ways that do not allow us clearly to distinguish between active and passive modalities. This transitive field of acting and acting upon is one way of describing the operative domain of true religion, transitive in the sense that it passes over and incites. It is in fact this potential that is socially generated on the basis of the transitivity of the *conatus* that constantly contests the idea of God as sovereign lawgiver. I think it is fair to say that, for Spinoza, God may give the law in the form of command, but no sovereign may fully intervene upon the *conatus* and its actualization in action without losing its legitimacy as a sovereign. The command is issued, but whether or not action complies with the demand is not predictable. Such a formulation not only foregrounds the possibility of an embodied and social freedom, but it also exposes the sovereign as less than all-powerful. This last point becomes all the more clear when we learn from Balibar that Spinoza tends to identify God with Law, and specifically with the site of enunciation whereby law is communicated. At that point, the anthropomorphism of God falls away, and in its place emerges the performativity of lawgiving. The law is given in a situation in which obedience is not precisely secured. Indeed, if God is the law, God is also, it seems, love, which names the social, dynamic, and generative character potential of the *conatus*. One might say that in relation to law and to love, the operative moment of God is the performative. We find both features in Spinoza's work, which means that in his work we also find the textual theater for the mutual contestation of law and love.

Now that dimension of God called "love," the *Deus sive Amor sive Homo*, once again leaves the anthropomorphic conception of the divine in elaborating those affective relations among individuals freed from all ambivalence. This pre-Freudian account of love that is freed of hate centers on the mutuality of acting and loving or, perhaps better, the transitive generation of love at the expense of hate. At one point in the text, the idea of God is understood as precisely this middle region, if not that middle voice, where the actor's love is not altogether distinct from the lover acted upon: the augmentation and intensification of both passions depend upon a way of acting and being acted upon that is not easy to distinguish. On the one hand, it sounds like Merleau-Ponty's "The Intertwining," that unedited piece at the end of *The Visible and the Invisible*, but given that this scene of love is now called "true religion," it might all be closer to Martin Buber's "Between Man and Man"—the divinity in and as the relation. What is most timely, however, is the idea that "true religion" is to be found in that affective and loving relation among humans that, in Balibar's terms, "saves" them from their unhappiness.

In Balibar's Spinoza, we find as much on the topic of sadness as we do on happiness. Love acts, acts upon others, but love also is realized or actualized through works, which intensifies the *potentia* among humans, linking their lives to the living and natural process of the *conatus* in ways that cannot be fully determined by any commanding or exterior law. Indeed, what Balibar calls the "practical rule" to love thy neighbor—the one that, of course, struck Freud as so improbable (why would we not be prone to have hostility as our first relation to the neighbor?)—has a saving power. The argument follows neither from utility nor from any other measure of instrumentality. As Balibar puts it, to love one's neighbor performs its own result, generates its own intensity and enhancement, more fully actualizing true religion and even happiness. It also builds the rudiments of civil society that is not yet, or not ever, subject to external law.

There are of course many complex problems here, including the psychoanalytic argument that there is a constitutive ambivalence in all relations of love, and the various political insights into multiplicity and antagonism within political life that we find in democratic theory throughout many centuries. Since I cannot take all that on in this essay, I wish only to return to the critical relation between true religion and theocracy in Spinoza's text, guided by Balibar's reading. If theocracy is an attempt to destroy true religion, and true religion moves beyond various anthropomorphic and anthropocentric conceptions of God, this puts Spinoza not surprisingly closer to the Jewish tradition than the orthodoxy of his synagogue would have understood; at the same time, he takes up the Christian doctrine of love. Love may not be the basis of civil society, but it may articulate some of its basic structures. The multiplicity of desires ideally enhances one another within the context in which no repressive law, no command structure, intervenes upon their realization. One can see how Spinoza became the inspiration for antistatist politics on the Left.

My final question is whether this important framework that is elaborated by Balibar in his early and recent work functions in some way in his discussion of secularism and his proposals about how best to adjudicate religious claims within a state that defines itself as secular—or *laïc*, in the French sense. I will not here go into the various secularism debates—though it is important to note, as Aamir Mufti has shown, that the "secular" in Edward Said is not the same as "secularism" in Asad.[12] I take that point. But perhaps we would do well to think about the process of secularization as it is variously formulated by Talal Asad and Saba Mahmood but also by Carl Schmitt. In the study of religion, there is a debate about whether religion is, or should be treated as, a concept, or whether it needs to be understood as an embodied way of life, a set of practices or rituals, even a matrix of subject formation and its manner of reproduction. The idea of religion as a concept inserts the problem of religion into philosophical debate, transforms and readies the phenomenon for its place within a philosophical vocabulary. Whatever quarrel there might be between philosophy and religion is swiftly resolved when religion is treated as a concept. The history of its usage and meaning is at once presupposed and obliterated in that moment when it becomes consolidated as a concept. It does not matter which religion, or which practices, at the moment in which we arrive at the generalization that subsumes them all. The point is one that Reinhart Koselleck made about conceptual history, and one that Marx himself made about abstraction, namely, that the sedimented meanings of a term are covered over when it is transformed into a conceptual reality. Nietzsche's point was somewhat different, arguing in *Beyond Good and Evil* that concepts are the cumulative effects of dead metaphors. Similarly, secularization names the process by which religious practices are transformed over time into secular concepts—perhaps even deadened and sanitized for secular consumption. And though secularism is mainly figured as the stage or mark of a progressive history that ultimately leaves religion behind, it is itself defined and formed by the religious traditions that produced its basic terminology and structure its operations. One of the great features of Spinoza's *Tractatus* is that it shows us those moments of that conversion precisely without covering it over.

So if we turn to Balibar's consideration of those operations of arbitration and mediation used to negotiate among conflicting religious claims, we have to ask where this power of arbitration and mediation comes from. Is it a secular operation, the distinctive secular operation of mediating among religions claims, and is itself clearly outside, or beyond, the domain of religion? Spinoza refers explicitly to the secularization of many of the religious concepts that he analyzes in the *Tractatus*; in fact, that process of secularization articulates the possible structure of a democratic theory in that text. The enigmatic hyphen that joins the theological to the political in the title never did quite tell us how to read that relation.

In Balibar's recent work, including an article titled "La France aux laïques?," he explicitly criticizes those French cultural positions that take *laïcité* to be an identity.[13] The mandate of *laïcité* for the state, Balibar reminds us, was to maintain institutional neutrality in relation to its citizens, establishing a rigorous separation between church and state. *Laïcité* has at least two meanings, one that insists that religion should not represent public power, but another, derived from Locke, and the focus of much of Balibar's own reflections, that endeavors to preserve the autonomy of civil society and, in particular, the liberties of conscience and freedom of expression. In this light, the emergence of a *laïcité identitaire* appears as a contradiction in terms. Of course, one can maintain secularism as a set of personal beliefs or even as a self-proclaimed identity, even rally behind secularism as a personal cause, but those beliefs or that identity position belong to an indefinite number of beliefs that are, or should be, protected by *laïcité*. In other words, how can *laïcité* name that neutral operation of power that protects one's personal beliefs and also be a personal belief protected by that very power? On the one hand, if secularism names institutional neutrality, then it provides the possibility of mediating the conflicting views, including conflicting religious views. Secularism would not be one of the various liberties of conscience, including religious liberties, that it mediates. It stands apart as the neutral mediator. Secularism would not be distinguished as one of the cultural formations or identities in relation to which it is charged with maintaining neutrality. When secularism becomes a civil religion or what we might call now an identity position—a form of publicly avowed identity ready to fight with religious identities or, in the case of France, pitted against Islam—then it forfeits the very neutrality for which it stands and becomes one of the warring positions in need of mediation.

Of course, all this becomes more complex if *laïcité* preserves the religious foundation of the state in Catholicism precisely by enshrining the Catholic/republican distinction as the defining one for the understanding of *laïcité* itself. If the state is secular by virtue of not being Catholic, then Catholicism is negatively preserved as the defining religion for the state. Much has been written, especially about the Dreyfus affair, but the general point is that established forms of *laïcité* distinguish among religions worthy of protection and others figured as the force against which protection is needed.

Spinoza himself avowed the secularization of the religious concepts he considered, by which he did not mean that the religious meanings were negated by the secular ones but that the tension between true religion and theocracy formulated basic tensions between individual and state powers. For Spinoza, it was clear that the religious meanings continued to inform and shape secular concepts, even as secularism sought to separate itself from religious concepts and practices. Whether secularism reanimates certain religious traditions even as it insists upon its separation is, of course, of the utmost importance to people who hold strong views on all sides of the question. So one question I am left with is whether "true religion" in Spinoza limits theocratic power in the way that secularism is supposed to safeguard the religious neutrality of the state. Is the effort to separate religion from state already happening in the formulation of true religion, and if so, is true religion truly one precursor of what we now call *laïcité*? Is love not related to mediation, as it surely was for Hegel in his *Early Theological Writings*? Furthermore, the question of where and how to mediate among conflicting religious claims in civil society appeals precisely to a neutral party or to a neutral site for that mediation. What and who is vested with the task of conflict resolution, and for what reason? What is this model of love without any remainder of hate? Is true religion then, precisely as a way of articulating civil society in its multiplicity, precisely the framework for mediating not only between religious claims but the very conflict between secularists, conceived as identitarian and sectarian, and nonsecularists, understood as adhering to any number of religious views, or even as accommodating that multiplicity? If we thought that secularism were the name for institutional neutrality and neutral mediation, we might ask whether it is not the animated result of something like "true religion," in Spinoza's sense. Is secularism the true religion of civic life, or is the contemporary oscillation between religion and secular positions the new form of conflict within *civil religion*?

NOTES

1. See Étienne Balibar, *Spinoza and Politics*, trans. Peter Snowdon (London: Verso, 1998); Étienne Balibar, *Spinoza et la politique* (Paris: Presses Universitaires de France, 1985).

2. Spinoza writes, "I assert that in a state of nature everyone is bound to live by the revealed law from the same motive as he is bound to live according to the dictates of

his sound reason, namely, that to do so is to his greater advantage and necessary for his salvation" (Baruch Spinoza, *Theological-Political Treatise*, trans. Samuel Shirley [New York: Hackett, 2001], 182). See also Balibar, *Spinoza and Politics*, 6.

3. Balibar, *Spinoza and Politics*, 7.

4. Balibar, *Spinoza and Politics*, 12.

5. See Spinoza, *Theological-Political Treatise*, chap. 20.

6. Balibar, *Spinoza and Politics*, 49; Spinoza, *Theological-Political Treatise*, chap. 14.

7. Balibar, *Spinoza and Politics*, 47.

8. Balibar, *Spinoza and Politics*, 9.

9. Étienne Balibar, "Spinoza's Three Gods and the Modes of Communication," *European Journal of Philosophy* 20, no. 1 (2012), 26–49. "Spinoza's Three Gods" was first presented as "Thinking with Spinoza: Politics, Philosophy, and Religion" at Birkbeck, University of London, May 7–8, 2009.

10. See Gilles Deleuze, *Expressionism in Philosophy*, trans. Martin Joughan (Cambridge, Mass.: MIT Press, 1990).

11. Balibar, "Spinoza's Three Gods," 30.

12. Aamir R. Mufti, "The Missing Homeland of Edward Said," in *Conflicting Humanities*, ed. Rosi Braidotti and Paul Gilroy (London: Bloomsbury, 2016), 165–84.

13. Étienne Balibar, "La France aux laïques?," in *Lettre ouverte contre l'instrumentalisation politique de la laïcité*, ed. Christine Delroy-Momberger, François Durpaire, and Béatrice Mabilon-Bonils (Avignion, Fr.: L'Aube, 2017). An English version is available as Étienne Balibar, "Laïcité or Identity?," Verso, August 31, 2016, https://www.versobooks.com/blogs/2823-etienne-balibar-laicite-or-identity.

CONCEPT

Étienne Balibar

It is an extremely perilous task to offer a paper among a collection such as this, and especially to have to do it with a tentative definition of the concept of "concept." But it is also a challenge that I take gladly, because it provides me with a unique occasion to return to some philosophical questions that have occupied me throughout my life for various reasons, many of which were directly or indirectly evoked during the Political Concepts conference in late 2016. However, as I started to gather and organize the questions that I imagined should be addressed under this heading, I soon realized that I should select *only one* of the dimensions that intersect in any inquiry into this problem—which in a sense is the "final" one, in which philosophy reflects on its own method and its specificity as a discourse (called *noesis noeseôs* by Aristotle). And it was also clear that, even with greater space, I could only sketch a map of analyses and arguments in a programmatic way. However, I can try to indicate right away how, in my view, these questions relate to some issues that most of us struggle with whenever the term "philosophy" (or one of its partial equivalents, such as "theory" or "critique") was invoked as a necessary framework.

It seems to me that a theory of the concept, or a theory of "working with concepts," should be investigated in *four directions* at least: into the problem of the *scientificity of concepts*, or their relationship to the idea and practice of scientific knowledge; into the problem of their *discursivity*, or their dependency on the properties of language and its uses (including the problems of translation and translatability); into the problem of the *historicity of concepts*, whether intrinsic or extrinsic (or, more probably, both); and finally into the problem of *the politicality of concepts*, which as I will show may become identified to some extent with the question of the status of *conflict* within conceptual thinking. I don't believe that any of these four dimensions are really separable from the others, but their investigation does not proceed along the same lines, with the same references. I will focus here on the *politicality of concepts*, which is the aspect with which traditional epistemology (whether more positivist or more Kantian-leaning) is less comfortable—but also one that connects most directly with our objects in this group, despite the obvious paralogism that would be involved in the idea that the politicality of concepts reflects the fact that they are, one way or another, *concepts of the political*.

FROM METALANGUAGE TO POLEMIC ASCENT

We may begin with this remark: in contemporary philosophy, the term "concept" is immediately stamped with *divisions* that trace back to ancient divides.[1] The term "concept" in Latin (*conceptus*) seems to refer to an etymology *cum-capire* that is well rendered in the German word *Begriff*, denoting an appropriation or even a catching or a seizing of the "object" (or the "thought-object"). But this is not the only connotation. When Descartes, for instance, writes that a certain sentence is true "quoties a me profertur, vel mente concipitur, necessario esse verum" (each time I say it or I conceive it in my mind), he alludes to another etymology of *concipere*, which means "to create or generate life within a womb."[2] And when Kant attributes to "concepts" (*Begriffe*) as opposed to "intuitions" (*Anschauungen*) the active capacity to synthesize or impose unity upon a given diversity of representations, he directs our attention toward another great divide: that of intellectual activity and passive *mimesis*, be it in the proper form of images or models, or through the effect of naming. Deleuze is not very far from there when—in his book written with Guattari—he distinguishes immediately a *concept*, an *affect*, and a *percept* in order to delineate the fields of philosophy, art, and science—even if other significations are introduced afterward in the book, which make these standard divisions less mechanical.[3]

For my part, I remain very stubbornly attached to the idea that inside and outside official philosophy (if there is an "outside" of philosophy, or, rather, if philosophy is not entirely a "thought of the outside"), "concept" and "conceptualization" are names for an *intellectual* activity, in the sense of an activity that produces *intelligibility* or makes "things" *intelligible*, to create an "intelligible order" (*ordinare ad intellectum*, as Spinoza defined his "third kind of knowledge," while immediately associating it with an ethical injunction: *sed intelligere!*).[4] In other terms, we need concepts because we seek intelligibility, whether it is about nature, passions, or politics. I believe that the reference to concepts contains something like an injunction *not to give up on the necessity of understanding*, in the very middle of our affections and actions. And I interpret in this sense both the bizarre suggestion once made by Althusser to create a "party of the concept" (an expression he claimed to have found in Marx, although I can't say where that would be), and the famous line of demarcation once proposed by Foucault between "philosophies of the concept" and "philosophies of consciousness"—which is not very different from picturing philosophy as a battlefield for antithetic "parties."[5] All this clearly inscribes the question of the concept in a conflictual horizon, but it is a far cry from identifying *conceptuality* and *conflictuality*, and a fortiori *politicality*. It could even mean the opposite, namely, that the concept is in (external) conflict with the logic of conflict and therefore is not itself internally conflictual.[6]

There are reasons for the resistance of the concept to its own conflictuality that an ordinary positivism simply would identify with consistency or realism but that are better understood if we trace them back to the great Platonic divide between *rhetoric* (or "sophistic discourse") and *philosophy* (soon to become identified with ontology), a divide that is supposed to be foundational for *rationality*. As we know, this divide is not intent on separating the philosophical thinking from the political questions; far from it. But it is certainly intent on extracting philosophy from the "common" place where a multiplicity of political interests and discourses collide, considered a space for "opinions" and not for "truth": it thus installs philosophy in a transcendent position, with respect to conflicts, that seems to be the condition of its critical power or its capacity to bring about an "intelligible order." As we know, this extraction or separation entails an opposition between *logos* and *episteme* on one side, *agôn* and *stasis* on the other side, or in general what Lyotard (in an explicit return to the Sophists) called "the differend."[7] Hence the idea that there can be a "science" (or "concept" or "intelligibility") of the political *only* if science, concept, and intelligibility are not themselves political. The strength of this position comes from the fact that one can hardly reconcile the search for *objectivity* (be it an objectivity of ideal objects or essences, or an objectivity of empirical objects, *realia*) with a generalization of the differend. It also comes from the fact that knowledge and intelligibility are strongly and institutionally associated with the idea of *learning*—a practice that requires *teaching* (even "self-teaching"), as indicated by the quasi equivalence, in philosophical Greek, of the two concepts of *episteme* and *mathesis*. But learning and teaching obey rules that can be normative, even imperative, but not conflictual, unless the institution becomes destabilized, undermining its own authority.

At this point, before I undertake an examination of ideas and arguments that can undermine the separation—not in the sense of a retreat from intelligibility but in the sense of granting the concept a greater power of knowing things and "ordering" them in an intelligible manner, that is, increasing the capacity to know (and make known) of the concept through a recognition of its politicality—I want to indicate in a highly schematic manner two epistemological consequences of the "Platonic divide."

The first consequence has to do with the institution of "neutrality" in science, or the identification of objectivity and neutrality. Although Plato himself is much more dialectical than that (witness his treatment of the various "hypotheses" in the *Parmenides* and their relationship to the "method of division" in the *Statesman*), the great instrument used by epistemology to prevent conflict and politics from entering the field of intelligibility and from "contaminating" the concept is the creation of *a metalanguage of science*. Whether in its logical or its transcendental form (or, in a weaker manner, in the form of "scientific methodology"), a metalanguage is always a system of *rules* that are imposed *ex ante* on conceptualization (for the sake of truth): in fact, it is a *quasi-juridical* superstructure, whose function is analogous to that of a *Grundnorm* in legal theory, that imposes nonconflictuality in order to secure noncontradiction, or that—borrowing an expression from W. V. O. Quine—regulates *semantic ascent* toward generalities in order to prevent what, conversely, we could call *polemic ascent* toward irreducibly conflicting ideas or hypotheses.[8] It is therefore inseparable from an ideal of *normal science*, in which the conflicts are relegated to the "subjective" realm of conjectures, refutations, and moments of paradigm change. Normal science avoids conflict, or renames it a "contradiction" to be logically eliminated, because it fears that conflict destroys objectivity.

A second consequence follows from there that concerns the paradoxical effects of *metalanguage* and the isolation of the concept from conflict in the field (or the case) of "anthropological disciplines." Conventionally, I include in this field everything that ranges from history and philology to political and social theory—or, rather, that combines these disciplinary forms in various proportions, depending on the *problems* they investigate. The norm of neutral or neutralizing metalanguage is what condemns anthropology to the eternal return of the dilemma of antiscientific "critique" or "hermeneutics" (even when simply presented in terms of a critique of positivism, reification, etc.), and pseudoscientific "objectivism" (or naturalization). This dilemma is impossible to overcome if we do not attempt a revision of the regime of knowledge, based on a different understanding of the construction and the use of concepts. Of course, we know of several ways under which the attempt to rethink conceptualization was made in the anthropological realm: *dialectics* was (or could be) one of them, and *structuralism* was another one—respectively oriented toward the thinking of *processes* and the thinking of *relations*, which means that, in both cases, the "object" was perceived as an epistemological obstacle, or the attempt was made to conceive something like an "objectivity without objects," or to link concepts to an activity of *problematization* rather than *objectification*. It is this orientation that, in a sense, I want to try to radicalize, albeit through a different method that will directly discuss several attempts at bringing conflictuality into conceptuality, because I believe that dialectics and structuralism in their symmetry or opposition are still *metalanguages*—or, perhaps, "methodologies," which do not focus on the concept as *the unit of intelligibility* within knowledge but tend to impose abstract patterns on the construction of concepts.

I will examine (very schematically) the possibility of this *unity of opposites* (from the point of view of traditional epistemology) under three successive headings: first, *concept and ideology*; second, *concept and the "subject-object" antithesis*; and third, *concept and sensibility*. As will be seen, I will invent very little myself, except perhaps the order in which I assemble these discussions, relying on texts and philosophies that I found inspiring at various moments.

CONCEPT AND IDEOLOGY

My first approach to the conflictuality of concepts is through their relation to "ideology." I am not thinking of "ideological concepts" but of the relation of *all* concepts to ideology. At the same time, I assume that "ideology" always has an intrinsic relationship to the *political* and the conflictuality of the political, which is manifested in both typical uses of the term, referring to "dominant ideology" and "rival ideologies," respectively. But it is also clear that epistemology has a tendency to relegate ideology, as a factor of conflict, either on the side of the *prehistory* of concepts or on the side of their *uses* and *applications*, or both—therefore in their *outside*.[9] Althusser's early exposition of the idea of the "epistemological break" that was achieved by the invention of certain specific scientific concepts in the field of history is a perfect illustration of that tendency, with the interesting exception of his later rectification as to the unfinished (perhaps even infinite) character of the break, and to his references to "practical concepts" that would be located "in the middle" of the break, using contradictory languages at the same time (which bear a strange similarity to the idea of a "vanishing mediator," *à la* Jameson).[10]

But let me explore some alternative possibilities. I want to invoke, in the first place, my recent discovery (owing to the remarkable study by Nestor Capdevila on the concept of ideology[11]) of the paper that was presented in 1956 before the Aristotelian Society by Oxford philosopher W. B. Gallie, with the title "Essentially Contested Concepts."[12] One could say that the title here is the most important thing, but the content is interesting, as well. It is coined in a relatively light mixture of analytical argument and social psychology, but it raises a question that is in fact independent of this language. The important word is of course "essentially," as opposed to "contingently."[13] The idea is that the *external impossibility* to reach "universal agreement" on the use and meaning of certain concepts, in fact reveals an *intrinsic characteristic* of that meaning, which precisely generates the infinite or interminable process of their contestation. This is *also* the deepest reason for their use: they are not used *despite* their conflictual nature but precisely *because* of the *dissensus* they provoke and crystallize. To put it a little more strongly, such concepts are not made to reconcile viewpoints but to divide them, and to foster controversies, if not antagonism. This is linked to the fact that their internal complexity, or the composition of their parts, has no univocal form of synthesis. Playing with Deleuze's reversal of the Kantian definition of the unifying function of concepts, we may say that their internal composition relies on *disjunctive syntheses*, which resonates or communicates with conflicts of interests and commitments. Three examples are announced by Gallie in the original article: the concepts of "art," "democracy," and "religion." But in the course of the argument, they are substituted with "art," "democracy," and "social justice," with a special emphasis on the last two. "Religion" is dropped—perhaps because its way of being "contested" appears problematic to Gallie, since it could raise a symmetric question about "secularism" (not deprived of importance these days). Interestingly, the internal tension he identifies in definitions and uses of "democracy," as elaborated in the Western constitutional tradition, is the tension between equality, or equal participation, and liberty, or rather liberties in the plural, which appear to be much more concrete than the former.[14] And the internal tension, leading to opposite ethical choices, which he identifies in the case of social justice, is between meritocracy and cooperation (he doesn't say "solidarity"), which he labels respectively "liberal" and "socialist" understandings of justice, while tracing them back conceptually to the Aristotelian disjunction of "commutative" and "distributive" justice in the *Nicomachean Ethics*. A weak or minimal interpretation would thus locate these antitheses on the side of "practical" reason or understanding, as opposed to speculative or cognitive reason: this is supported by his terminology of the "appraisive concepts," that is, concepts that incorporate value judgments or require agreement, and his idea that one passes from one interpretation to the other for the "same" concept, through a process of "conversion," which he describes as rational or argumentative. But then there is the idea that such concepts exhibit dilemmas where it is impossible intellectually *not to choose a side*, thus suggesting a more radical, maximal interpretation (borrowing on a Kantian dialectical model): such concepts illustrate an antithetic of pure reason, or a logic of conflicting universalities that confer an ideological tenor to the constitution of the concept itself.

Equally interesting is the second reference that I want now to invoke. In 1975, Reinhart Koselleck composed an essay on the "historical-political semantic of asymmetrical antithetic concepts," which was later incorporated in the collection *Vergangene Zukunft* (*Futures Past*).[15] Koselleck's aim, in this essay, is to discuss modalities of the collective representations of Self and Other, through the examination of concepts that function as oppositional couples that draw a line of demarcation within the totality of humankind, while also "discriminating" one part on behalf of the other or structurally instituting a *denial of recognition* of some humans from the point of view of others (i.e., *universalizing discrimination* in language itself). There are three main examples, which are presented and discussed in chronological order, thereby delineating a kind of philosophical history of otherness: the ancient Greek opposition of Hellenic and Barbaric peoples, the medieval opposition of Christians and Pagans, and finally the modern opposition of the Superhuman and the Infrahuman (*Übermensch* versus *Untermensch*). These asymmetric oppositions are presented as specifically *political*, and it is with respect to the last one that Koselleck also uses the category "ideology" or "ideological weapon" (*Kampfmittel*) in order to describe a historical effectivity (or performativity) of concepts (*Wirkungsgeschichte von Begriffen*) that not only is not superimposed onto their structure but is made possible by the structure, coinciding with its construction. The very name *Gegenbegriff* is meaningful here because it can be glossed in two directions: as designating an internal opposition, which means that the concept here is *the coupling* itself, not each single "term," and as indicating that the coupling identifies an adversary (*Gegner*) from the point of view of its "dominant" term.

Two circumstances are important to recall here. One is the notorious fact that Koselleck has taken much of his inspiration from Carl Schmitt, whose "scientific achievement" in formalizing the concept of the political through the antagonism of "friend and foe" is evoked in the last page of the essay as an inspiration for the study of semantic oppositions in general, in a somewhat euphemistic juxtaposition with the "linguistic manipulation" that made it possible for the Nazis to define a "potential nonexistence" (*Nichtexistenz*, almost synonymous but not identical with *Vernichtung*) of "non-Aryan" people through the racial categorization of "Aryans" as *Übermenschen* and "non-Aryans" as *Untermenschen*.[16] The second circumstance is the fact that Koselleck is a founder and the main organizer of the huge encyclopedic project of *Geschichtliche Grundbegriffe* ("Fundamental Concepts of History"), whose affinities and differences with our own project of *Political Concepts: A Philosophical Lexicon* well deserve a discussion.[17] In Koselleck's encyclopedia, as in our own, concepts are essentially considered as unities bearing a single name—such as *Staat* or *Revolution*—that serves as the guiding thread for a more or less complex genealogy. From this point of view, the dialectical *Gegenbegriffe* appears as a limit-case, which crucially combines an insight into the conceptual structure itself and connects it with ideological and political performativity. I regret not having the space to enter the proper analysis of the three oppositions, which, as always in Koselleck, combines erudition with acute theoretical reflexivity, but I will indicate what seems to me certainly not to disqualify the whole construction but to affect it with a dangerous internal vacillation, which we cannot ignore if we want to investigate this mode of conceptual conflictuality further.

For reasons that anticipate my next point, I will call this *a subjective-objective vacillation*. In the first place, in order to isolate the typical oppositional asymmetry, Koselleck needs to discard conceptual pairings that either are not oppositional but simply distributive, or are oppositional but not dissymmetric (i.e., discriminating). As examples of (allegedly) nonoppositional couples, he gives such anthropological differences as "man and woman," "parents and children," "sick and healthy." As examples of oppositional but not dissymmetric, there are "the national and the foreigner," "the friend and the foe." In such cases, the conflictuality that may arise would be extrinsic, a matter of uses, not inherent in the concept. Then there is the fact that the three great asymmetric *Gegenbegriffe* discussed by Koselleck ("Greeks"-"Barbarians," "Christians"-"pagans," and "human"-"inhuman"), which have their distinct logics and in fact express *different formations of the political* forming a chronological succession, inherit certain representations of *Otherness* from their predecessors but also embody a continuous process of *interiorization* of the conflict to the Self. Barbarians are supposed to be external to the Greek in a way in which "pagans"—or rather "paganism" or "idolatry"—are not, with respect to the "Christians," or to the Christian redemption and messianic mission. But in the case of the "inhuman" with respect to the "human"—variously identified as criminal, as oppressor (particularly princes and kings, in the discourse of the Radical Enlightenment), or conversely as the oppressed and underdeveloped—there is no longer any exteriority but an inclusion or an incorporation that is perceived as the threat of a foreign body—I am tempted to say, *à la* Lacan, "a Thing." The fact that, paradoxically, the "human" or "humankind" (*die Menschheit*, which can also mean "humanness") is a universal category and must include (or perhaps annihilate, in auto-immunitarian fashion) its own negation produces a displacement and makes room for a "supplement," equally paradoxical, namely, the idea of the "human" that is *more* than "human" (*der Übermensch*). Reading Koselleck symptomatically, it seems to me that this vacillation must be granted not only an ideological function in the pejorative sense but a conceptual function, since it is what precisely permits to dispose all the previous divergences along the same line of evolution.

For want of room and time, I will skip here a third reference, which I hope to develop on another occasion, which would return to the Althusserian aporia of the "epistemological break," more precisely, to the solution proposed by Canguilhem for that aporia in his 1970 essay "Qu'est-ce qu'une idéologie scientifique?" ("What Is Scientific Ideology?"), in which he used an oxymoronic formula to liberate epistemology from the nondialectical disjunction of "science" and "ideology"—sketching a description of the alternative moves of ideologization and deideologization of such concepts as "mechanism," "evolution," or "regulation," which includes a transgression of disciplinary limits.[18] This is, I believe, a radical dismantling of the picture of "normal science" that involves another type of intrinsic conflictuality.

THE SUBJECT-OBJECT DISTINCTION

I will now pass to a *second* approach, which is centered on the discussion and critique of the subject-object distinction, on which both the empiricist and the transcendental representations of objective knowledge are founded, in such a manner that concepts are seen either as *instruments* for the preservation of the divide, or *a priori conditions* of its production. The second case is of course philosophically more demanding, but they are in fact two sides of the same coin.

Indeed, the idea of overcoming, neutralizing, or canceling the subject-object divide as a metaphysical heritage that can be also articulated with certain juridical and economic structures, such as private property and the commodity form, is nothing new in contemporary philosophy. It has produced particularly exciting developments in the postphenomenological tradition—in the wake of Merleau-Ponty's attempt (in his unfinished posthumous book, *Le visible et l'invisible*) to describe a preontological experience of the world (called *la chair*, the flesh), in terms of a "chiasmatic" exchange of the internal and the external places, also called an *entrelacs* or intertwining of body and world.[19] This approach was later complicated by Derrida and is now applied by Judith Revel in France to the reading of Foucault himself.[20]

However, I want to try a different approach here. I will return to the Foucauldian critique of the empirical-transcendental doublet (in *The Order of Things*) that was chronologically preceded by his close reading of the two sides of Kant's philosophy of knowledge: on the one side, there is the *Critique of Pure Reason*, with the famous Copernican Revolution, which describes the "subject" as a system of the conditions of possibility for the perception and knowledge of all "objects," more precisely a coincidence of the conditions of possibility of our experience of objects, and the conditions of existence of objects in general; on the other side, there is an empirical description, inspired by the method of "natural history," of those quasi-objective characteristics of the human individuals that can be considered either obstacles or instruments for their moral education and culture.[21] As Foucault perfectly demonstrates, there is a correlation between, on one side, the fact that the *knowing subject* is subtracted (or, as one may also say, *foreclosed*) from the world of objects (hence from reality and materiality) and, on the other side, the fact that processes of subjection and subjectivation are reified and objectified, that is, they are projected and constructed as calculable phenomena, or classified in typologies of the human that also have a disciplinary function, through a range of quasi-scientific patterns of explanation (which include game theory, behaviorist psychology, and psychiatric medicine). I suggest that we push this critique one step further and state that what is in fact foreclosed from the field of science is not only the *capacity* or "faculty" to know (i.e., to investigate and conceptualize) but also the *interests that generate the quest for the intelligibility* or the "desire for knowledge" itself. By stating that the neutralization of radical conflictuality, or the type of contradiction whose development and revolution is not calculable (or even definable in advance), becomes rejected into the unknowable, for which there is no experience and no concept, that which Kant famously called the *Ding an sich* or the "thing in itself." This in turn suggests that a restoration of the desire of knowledge *as such* within the field of objects and, more generally, *problems* that an anthropology must address, and a restoration of conflicts, antagonisms, and contradictions (admittedly not completely identical categories) as intrinsic characteristics of objectivity—perhaps an objectivity without "objects"—are two sides of the same question, for which the oxymoronic combination "subject-object" is as good a name as any other.

Again, here, several paths are open. One is the post-Kantian, in particular the Hegelian dialectical way, which I leave aside because it restores the antagonism only to eliminate it more perfectly in the final form of the "absolute knowledge." I prefer to indicate how the double restoration is at work in some limit-formulations of contemporary philosophers. I apologize for the very *French* character of this list—a limitation of my culture.[22] One such formulation is Althusser's late attempt at comparing the intrinsically conflictual development of Marxism and psychoanalysis, which, in an essay from 1976, "On Marx and Freud," he described as "schismatic theories" or theories whose scientific (knowing) capacities, are paradoxically linked to their progressing only through "deviations" or "*heresies*" without a stable "orthodoxy" (incidentally, a complete reversal of his earlier exposition of the "epistemological break"), by virtue of the fact that neither a psychoanalyst nor a Marxist political theorist are *external to the situation* they analyze.[23] Therefore their "subjective" position or interest forms a direct "objective" component of this situation, of which they must give a conceptual account—whether it is called "transference" (and "countertransference") or "party/class position." This is what led Althusser increasingly toward a *Pascalian* understanding of the risk, or the wager that is involved in knowledge, perhaps drawing on the identical meaning of *pari* (wager) and *parti* (choice, decision) in Pascal's text.[24] But isn't there something similar in the way in which Foucault elaborated the very strange idea or project of an "ontology of ourselves"—a veritable subversion of the philosophical grammar (even more so than an "ontology of relation"), which I also believe is a displacement and a recasting of his critique of the *will to knowledge*? It is through the definition of an *actualité* or an *untimely present* that Foucault sketches this "ontology." Its object is not so much *who we are* or have already become but rather *who we are becoming*, without predictable end: therefore it involves an essential element of uncertainty—which in turn intensifies the quest for intelligibility. But as we also know, this quest does not take the form of an individual or collective self-consciousness: it is entirely oriented toward the "outside"; it consists in interpreting the signs of time and the mutations of our culture that are taking place "now." For sure, a Foucauldian *becoming* oneself as another and an Althusserian subject who is divided by his/her *partisanship* are not exactly the same thing. But they seem to me to converge in the direction of overcoming the mirror image of subject-object in a conceptual rather than mystical or phenomenological manner, thus generating a greater rather than lesser intelligibility.[25] There remains an important difference, however, between the ways in which Althusser and Foucault represent conflictuality as inevitable effect of the "chiasmatic" relationship between subject and object—making each of the two poles an "enclave" in the other: for Althusser, the conflict is a political (or ideological) oscillation affecting individual and collective agency; for Foucault, it is more like an anthropological uneasiness affecting the self. Although one could say in Heideggerian jargon that in both cases, "being-in-the-world" is at stake.

DIVISION OF THE SENSIBLE

To conclude this discussion in a very provisional manner, I would like to propose a third approach to the conflictuality of concepts, which I attach to what is traditionally considered the *opposite* or *antithesis* of conceptual knowledge (therefore located by Kant in his first *Critique* in the "elementary" position as what must become "subsumed" under the law or power of the concept), namely, *the sensible*. I call it the *division of the sensible*, stealing an expression from Jacques Rancière or trying to push its meaning in the direction of my own question. In the original French, Rancière's title, which has also become a key category of his philosophy, is *Le partage du sensible*, and each of the two terms is hard to simply translate into English, because *sensible* means both "sense" and "sensibility," and *partage* evokes both "cutting" into parts—a division (or even, in Afrikaans, an "apartheid")—and distributing or "sharing" the parts.[26] As we know, the idea of the division/distribution of the sensible in Rancière's view tightly articulates aesthetics and politics, or it introduces an aesthetics of politics, which is neither a political aesthetics nor a critique of the aestheticization of the political *à la* Benjamin. It rejects the Deleuzian distinction of "concept," "affect," and "percept," and, although it may in part have been inspired by the idea of a "logic of sensation" (Deleuze) or "logic of the sensible" (Lévi-Strauss), this is rather an antithetic relation because Rancière's postulate is not that sensation or perception generates its own savage structures of intelligibility that are then expressed in the arts but that there is a poetic or literary *power* of the human (called *littérarité*) that is historically organized in different *regimes* of the arts: the modern or aesthetic regime would be only one of them, which "democratizes" the genres by calling into question their hierarchic distribution. It would make it possible therefore to develop an aesthetic production based on any technique or material activity that is socially recognized. It is precisely by means of this capacity of dividing, distributing, and redistributing the sensible, which includes the *vis-*

ible and the sayable (*dicible*), that the arts acquire their political function and intersect with the political in the true sense: that of confrontation between the radical declaration of equality, which is uttered by the *sans-part* (the "no-part," or radically unrecognized people), and the social classifications and exclusions that Rancière calls "police." As Rancière writes in *Politics of Aesthetics*, "political or literary utterances are effective in the real. They define models of speech and action but also regimes of sensible intensity."

So what is a redistribution of the sensible? It combines apparently two levels of conflictuality. At the most apparent level, it is a mapping or discursive representation of the social and symbolic roles of collectivities—particularly those that are public or domestic, valorized or devalorized: therefore, it coincides with a construction of the sociological conditions of the political order. And—if I am allowed to insert my own terminology—it involves the drawing and redrawing of *internal borders* that distribute and situate social differences and statuses or ranks. But at a more fundamental and also more decisive level, it is a pattern of the *visibility or invisibility* of actions, languages, and subjectivities whereby the absence of the invisible "no-part"—or, conversely, its intrusion into the realm of the visible (and the sayable)—obliquely determines the ways in which the possibilities of representation of all the other parts are configured. This is an idea that, like it or not, owes as much to Althusser as to Foucault—both of them secretly responding to Merleau-Ponty. It is beautifully illustrated in the final chapter of Rancière's more recent *magnum opus*, *Aisthesis*, through the interpretation of James Agee's (and, by implication, Walker Evans's) *Let Us Now Praise Famous Men*, the picture book invented and written on the roads of America's southern states in the middle of the Great Depression.[27] This is of course another way of conceptualizing the becoming present of "the absent cause" that strips it as much as possible from its persistent theological resonances—nothing to do, in Rancière's description, with a miracle or a *Parousia* of the Redeemer of politics (even if called "the proletariat"), but an operation that at the same time is *common*, creating common notions or common sense, and *exceptional*, or intensely disturbing. I submit that we have to do here—through the mediation of a singular alliance of the poetic or the literary in the broad sense and the political—with a reduction of the antithesis between concept and intuition, or a conceptual effect where there is no formal concept.[28]

Indeed, this takes us to a limit of any "epistemological" discussion of *concept production* in terms of its conflictual character, which I have chosen as my guiding thread. I am uncertain about how to pursue such a discussion or inquiry—for which fortunately I no longer have room. And in any case, that should not take the form of a synthesis or systematic assemblage of these different modalities of conceptual conflictuality or conceptual conceptualization, to which we can attribute a *political* meaning. But instead of a conclusion or in guise of an opening toward other reflections, something comes to my mind that I want to share. I realize that everything I have said or hinted at here is a kind of deferred discussion of the issue of *dialectics*, and especially the dialectics of Hegel, for whom *the concept as such* is an exposition and a resolution of conflict. And of course, that entails the vexed question of whether Marx reproduced that conceptual logic, even if under a different name or in a different field, or opened the way to its irreversible deconstruction. Intentionally, I did not embark on that discussion before: not only because I had no time or wanted to take a detour but because in fact I think that what Hegel calls *the concept* is not what we need to discuss as "concept" in the field of anthropology and philology. And in fact my implicit guiding thread, if there is any single one, is *not Hegelian*: it is really *Kantian*, or post-Kantian, or neo-neo-Kantian. It has to do with an attempt at modifying, inverting the function of "schematism," as it were, so that the concept—*der Begriff, das Begreifen*, which means "the formation of concepts"—does not work as an instrument to distinguish, to *isolate* the faculties or elements of intellectual activity that could generate conflicts from one another, be they ideologies, subjectivations, or sensibilities, but, on the contrary, to bring them together and transport them into a single *topos* in order to problematize the uncertain effects of their encounter.

NOTES

1. See Barbara Cassin and Emily S. Apter, eds. and comps., *Dictionary of Untranslatables: A Philosophical Lexicon*, trans. Steven Rendall (Princeton: Princeton University Press 2014), s.v. "concept."

2. *Œuvres de Descartes*, ed. Charles Adam and Paul Tannery, vol. 7, *Meditationes de prima philosophia* (Paris: Vrin, 1904), 25.

3. Gilles Deleuze and Felix Guattari, *What Is Philosophy?*, trans. Hugh Tomlinson and Graham Burchell (New York: Columbia University Press, 1995), chap. 7.

4. This injunction is to be found in Spinoza's *Tractatus Politicus* (I.4): "Actiones humanas non lugere, non ridere, neque indignari, sed intelligere." A similar formula features in Letter 30 to Oldenburg. *Ordinare ad intellectum* is the motto that permeates Part 5 of the *Ethics* (after Proposition V.10 and the scholium).

5. See Michel Foucault's Preface to Georges Canguilhem, *The Normal and the Pathological*, trans. Carolyn R. Fawcett and Robert S. Cohen (New York: Zone Books,

1989). The idea of philosophy as a battlefield (*Kampfplatz*), a formula often repeated by Althusser (especially in the "Soutenance d'Amiens," from 1975), comes from Kant's *Conflict of the Faculties*.

6. Hegel will *not* be my main reference in this discussion, although I need to characterize his position later. His dialectical "method" means that the logic of *contradiction* (of which conflict, or certain modalities of conflict, can be presented as specific cases—or to which they can be reduced) is inherent in the concept. This is, I believe, a very different orientation.

7. Jean-François Lyotard, *The Differend: Phrases in Dispute*, trans. George van den Abbeele (Minneapolis: University of Minnesota Press, 1988).

8. See Willard Van Orman Quine, *Word and Object* (1960; Cambridge, Mass.: MIT Press, 2015), 56. I proposed this symmetry of "semantic ascent" and "polemic ascent" for scientific arguments in a paper that was presented to the anniversary conference of the foundation of Paris Nanterre University, 2013, and published as "Que devient la théorie?: Sciences humaines, politique, philosophie (1970–2010); Réflexions et propositions," in *1970–2010: Les sciences de l'homme en débat*, ed. Yan Brailowsky and Hervé Inglebert (Paris: Presses Universitaires de Paris Ouest, 2013), 21–38.

9. "Prehistory" became a common term in epistemology in the wake of the discussions about the "epistemological break" and the "scientific revolution" in the mid-twentieth century. But the idea is there already in Kant's "history of pure reason," which separates the "safe way" (i.e., linear progress) of science from the conflictual and uncertain vicissitudes preceding the "Copernican revolution" (see the Preface to the second edition of the *Critique of Pure Reason*).

10. On "real humanism," see Louis Althusser, *For Marx*, trans. Ben Brewster (New York: New Left Books, 1969), 219–46. Jameson's celebrated article "The Vanishing Mediator: Or, Max Weber as Storyteller" is reproduced in Frederic Jameson, *The Ideologies of Theory* (New York: Verso, 2008).

11. Nestor Capdevila, *Le concept d'idéologie* (Paris: Presses Universitaires de France, 2004).

12. See W. B. Gallie, "Essentially Contested Concepts," *Proceedings of the Aristotelian Society* 56 (1956): 167–98; repr., in *Philosophy and the Historical Understanding* (London: Chatto & Windus, 1964).

13. I am aware of a subsequent discussion of the difference between "concept" and "conception," to which such luminaries as H. L. A. Hart, John Rawls, Ronald Dworkin, and Steven Lukes have contributed, each of them quoted in "Essentially Contested Concept," Wikipedia, last modified October 10, 2019, https://en.wikipedia.org/wiki/Essentially_contested_concept. It seems to me that, emphasizing a distinction between the semantic and the pragmatic (or the objective and the subjective) sides of the question, this discussion essentially serves to deflect the fact that Gallie pointed at conflicts originating in the concept itself, as indicated by Jeremy Waldron in his later

commentary "Is the Rule of Law an Essentially Contested Concept (in Florida)?," *Law and Philosophy* 21, no. 2 (March 2002): 137–64.

14. In a more recent book, Nestor Capdevila has pursued his critical use of Gallie's methodology, returning to the twin issues of democracy and revolution in a discussion of Tocqueville and Marx in *Tocqueville ou Marx: Démocratie, capitalisme, révolution* (Paris: Presses Universitaires de France, 2012).

15. Reinhart Koselleck, *Zur historisch-politischen Semantik asymmetrischer Gegenbegriffe*, in *Vergangene Zukunft: Zur Semantik geschichtlicher Zeiten* (Frankfurt: Suhrkamp Taschenbuch Wissenschaft, 1979); *Futures Past: On the Semantics of Historical Time*, trans. Keith Tribe (New York: Columbia University Press, 2005).

16. I speak of "euphemism," but it is difficult not to read it as a concealment of the "place of enunciation" where, *within* historical discourse itself, a reference to the subject *for whom* (*qua* historian trained inside the conflict that he describes) the "antithetic concepts" *appear dissymmetric*: perhaps a subject who "changed sides" during his lifetime.

17. Otto Brunner, Werner Conze, and Reinhart Koselleck (eds.), *Geschichtliche Grundbegriffe: Historisches Lexikon zur politisch-sozialen Sprache in Deutschland*, 8 vols. (Stuttgart: Klett-Cotta, 1972–97). See Elias José Palti, "Reinhard Koselleck, His Concept of the *Concept* and Neo-Kantianism," *Contributions to the History of Concepts* 6, no. 2 (Winter 2011): 1–20. Koselleck's introduction to the *Geschichtliche Grundbegriffe* is translated and commented upon in *Contributions to the History of Concepts* 6, no. 1.

18. Georges Canguilhem, "What Is Scientific Ideology?," *Radical Philosophy* 29 (Autumn 1981); see Étienne Balibar, "Science et vérité dans la philosophie de Georges Canguilhem," in *Georges Canguilhem, philosophe, historien des sciences*, ed. Bibliothèque du Collège International de Philosophie (Paris: Albin Michel, 1993), 58–76.

19. Maurice Merleau-Ponty, *The Visible and the Invisible*, trans. Alphonso Lingis (Evanston, Il.: Northwestern University Press, 1968).

20. See Judith Revel, *Foucault avec Merleau-Ponty: Ontologie politique, présentisme et histoire* (Paris: Vrin, 2015).

21. See Foucault's commentary of Kant's *Anthropology* in Michel Foucault, *Introduction to Kant's Anthropology*, ed. and trans. Daniel Defert, François Ewald, and Frédéric Gros (Los Angeles: Semiotext(e), 2008).

22. Adorno's *Negative Dialectics* certainly should be discussed here, but this is a whole world of thought in itself. For most of us, the combined concept "subject-object" owes its definition and prestige to contemporary post-Marxian thinkers such as Lukács and Ernst Bloch (who applies it to his reading of Hegel). The genealogy traces back to Hegel, but above all to Schelling.

23. My main reference here is an essay written by Althusser in 1976 for the Tbilisi Conference, the first conference on psychoanalysis to be held in the USSR, which he

did not attend in person. See Louis Althusser, "On Marx and Freud," trans. Warren Montag, *Rethinking Marxism* 4, no. 1 (Spring 1991): 17–30. In the French original, Althusser did not exactly use the quasi-theological category "schismatic" but the more politically oriented "scissionist." This term was introduced in the German translation. Althusser's reformulations involve an often dramatic confrontation with the Great Schism of the international Communist movement, in which he found himself caught, and also a complex confrontation with Lacan, which I cannot discuss here.

24. "Or quel mal vous arrivera-t-il en prenant ce parti? . . . Je vous dis que vous y gagnerez en cette vie, et que à chaque pas que vous ferez dans ce chemin, vous verrez tant de certitude de gain, et tant de néant de ce que vous hasardez, que vous connaîtrez à la fin que vous avez parié pour une chose certaine, infinie, pour laquelle vous n'avez rien donné" (Blaise Pascal, *Pensées*, ed. Louis Lafuma [Paris: Points, 2018], § 418).

25. I developed this comparison at greater length in my essay "La philosophie et l'actualité: Au-delà de l'événement?," in *Le moment philosophique des années 1960 en France*, ed. Patrice Maniglier (Paris: Presses Universitaires de France, 2011).

26. Jacques Rancière, *Le partage du sensible: Esthétique et politique* (Paris: La Fabrique-Editions, 2000); Jacques Rancière, *The Politics of Aesthetics: The Distribution of the Sensible*, ed. and trans. Gabriel Rockhill (London: Bloomsbury, 2004).

27. Jacques Rancière, "The Cruel Radiance of What Is (Hale County 1936—New York 1941)," in *Aisthesis: Scenes from the Aesthetic Regime of Art*, trans. Zakir Paul (New York: Verso, 2013).

28. That would of course include Rancière, although in an indirect way, in the great discussion about the theses of Kant's third *Critique*, that of Aesthetic Judgment, that has so deeply determined recent philosophy.

> The terrorist and the policeman both come from the same basket. Revolution, legality—counter moves in the same game; forms of idleness at bottom identical. He plays his little game—so do you propagandists. But I don't play.
>
> —The Professor in Joseph Conrad's *The Secret Agent* (1907)

CONTRE- / COUNTER-

Bernard E. Harcourt

Is it possible to imagine a concept that is so productive that it leads us beyond the ordinary play of "countermoves in the same game"? Is it conceivable that the prefix *contre-* or, in English, "counter-" could overcome the opposition from which it is born and generate a fully autonomous conceptual form? Not in the Kantian or Hegelian sense of a synthesis that resolves an antinomic opposition (not the least of which because the prefix *contre-* functions differently than the prefix "anti-" does) but rather as an original counterpoint that itself becomes so powerful as to liberate itself from the oppositional relationship and transform itself into a freestanding concept, intervention, or even mode of governmentality?

I suspect this is what Étienne Balibar aspired to in his essay in *Equaliberty* when he urged us to institute "a counterpower" to the force of conventional government and administration.[1] Such a counterpower would have to become greater than simply resistance to governmental power. In order for it to achieve its full potential, it would need to liberate itself from its originary opposition and transform itself into an autonomous, self-referential, fully articulated form of governance. This alone could guarantee that the *contre-* move develop into its own independent mode of governing. It is an ambitious ideal but a realizable goal. At least, it is one that we have witnessed in our own lifetimes—though in an inverted way. But then again, we do not always have total control over our concepts. Often, they escape us. Sometimes they come back to haunt us.

A model for this concept-making—for this conceptual fabrication—can be found in Joseph Conrad's novel *The Secret Agent*, which serves as the epigraph to this essay. The character of the Professor in that novel had strapped on him, at all times, a flask of explosives and carried a small detonator in his hand—ready to blow himself and everyone around him to bits. By means of these devices, he claimed to have gotten past the conventional opposition between revolutionaries and the police. He claimed to have overcome the mere "game" of moves and countermoves and reached a higher—and more threatening—stage. He claimed to have transformed his reactivity into a pure force. Into perfection.

Readers will recall that it was the figure of the Professor, more so than Conrad's other characters, who inspired later anarchists and some terrorists, prominently among them the Unabomber, Ted Kaczynski. Conrad, who always labeled his characters for us, referred to the Professor as "the perfect anarchist."[2] And what exactly, one may ask, was the ambition of this "perfect anarchist"? "What is it you are after yourself?," his comrade Ossipon would ask him with indignation. "A perfect detonator," Conrad writes, in a response he describes as "the peremptory answer."[3]

One can infer from Conrad's novel that the Professor himself had begun as an anarchist caught in the counter-moves that he himself disparaged—caught in the play, in the game, in the parry. One can assume that the Professor was originally part of that dance or that judo of counter-moves. But the implication is clear: the Professor had gone beyond the mere tit for tat and had achieved instead a more *perfect* form of anarchism. What made this the most perfect or peremptory anarchist state was precisely getting beyond the *contre-* move to another level—a level that was autonomous of the opposition itself and, in that way, absolute. It was a pure state, independent from the back and forth between the revolutionaries and the police.

Because of the explosives that he strapped on himself at all times, the Professor remarked, "they know . . . I shall never be arrested. The game isn't good enough for any policeman of them all. To deal with a man like me you require sheer, naked, inglorious heroism."[4] The Professor may have sounded almost delirious, and self-aggrandizing for sure, but the Professor had achieved something unique: he had gotten beyond the ordinary relation of opposition.

The Professor ultimately has the last scene of the *Secret Agent*. After the counter-intelligence and counter-espionage is over—after Winnie Verloc's story has reached, in Conrad's words, "its anarchistic end of utter desolation, madness, and despair,"[5] after her brother's accidental explosion at Greenwich Station, her own murder of her husband, and her suicide—it is the Professor who closes the book—"the incorruptible Professor," as Conrad adds. Conrad closes:

> He was a force. His thoughts caressed the images of ruin and destruction. He walked frail, insignificant, shabby, miserable—and terrible in the simplicity of his idea calling madness and despair to the regeneration of the world. Nobody looked at him. He passed on unsuspected and deadly, like a pest in the street of full men.[6]

The Professor had become sheer force, ruin, and destruction. He had overcome his opposition to the system to become something as deadly as the pest. He had achieved the full effect of the *contre-* move. Not a very attractive overcoming—but as I mentioned, we do not always have total control over our conceptual moves—but a remarkable one.

A similar conceptual movement runs through the writings of Balibar and through much of Michel Foucault's thought, as well. A good illustration in Foucault's work is from an early passage in his inaugural lesson, on April 2, 1981, of the Louvain lectures titled *Wrong-Doing, Truth-Telling: The Function of Avowal in Justice*. At the close of that inaugural lecture, Foucault evokes, as the very framework or core of his interventions to come, the notion of a "*counter-positivism*" that, he explains, "is not the contrary of positivism, but rather its counterpoint." The full passage reads as follows:

> We often speak of the recent domination of science or of the technical uniformity of the modern world. Let's say that this is the question of "positivism" in the Comtian sense, or perhaps it would be better to associate the name of Saint-Simon to this theme. In order to situate my analysis, *I would like to evoke here a counter-positivism that is not the opposite of positivism but rather its counterpoint.* It would be characterized by astonishment before the very ancient multiplication and proliferation of truth-telling, and the dispersal of regimes of veridiction in societies such as ours.[7]

The notion of counter-positivism conveys something different than "antipositivism" does because Foucault actually embraces a positivistic sensibility toward the proliferation of truth-telling forms. There is a history here, a truthful one. Foucault is tracing a history of truth telling regimes—more specifically, of regimes of veridiction and of speaking truth and, in the larger arc of his years at the Collège de France, of the different bases (legal, historical, political, economic) that ground claims of truth over time.

Foucault's method, then, is not antipositivist. It is instead a "counterpoint": it deploys positivistic sensibilities against narrow positivism. Most importantly, his method culminates in a philosophical intervention that is autonomous of positivism and of antipositivism, that does not depend on either, and that no longer responds or relates merely to the opposition—it becomes its own autonomous method: a pure philosophical method, a way of seeing the world. It overcomes positivism while always indexing it.

Foucault's counter-positivism, in the end, is a full-fledged method, fully detached from any dispute with positivism. In fact, it is perhaps the most important compass for deciphering the Louvain lectures—which is why, incidentally, the passage ended up on the *quatrième de couverture*, where it remains in the French edition as the most significant words of those lectures. It is the point of perfection.

The *contre-* move—by which I mean, to be clear, the movement of thought and practice, the action that is captured by adding the prefix *contre-* or "counter-" to another concept—is a conceptual factory. Its generative power is remarkable. It is not so much a concept itself but instead the creator, the producer of concepts. The *contre-* move produces rich, constructed mental representations. It practically defines the distinction between concept and notion: nothing here is intuitive and immediate, as are notions; on the contrary, the *contre-* move is complex, constructed, and stabilized over time. It is the intellectual work product. It is the infrastructure to myriad new concepts. In fact, if one looks in the *Oxford English Dictionary*, for instance, the entry for "counter" becomes a litany, a catalog, an enumeration of counter-concepts: "Counter-address; counter-advise; counter-affirm; counter-ambush; counter-avouch; counter-beat; counter-bid; counter-bore,"[8] and I am still only at the beginning of the *B*'s. Each term with its own early etymological use and history.

Foucault made use of the *contre-* move extensively—in fact, one could argue that it was one of his most productive devices, a veritable conceptual-production technique. Nietzsche did, too, referring for instance to "art" as the "counter-movement" against nihilism.[9]

In conversation with Balibar, during his seminar on Foucault at Columbia University in fall 2015, we began to identify and catalog the occurrences of the *contre-* move in Foucault's work, including the concept of *contre-pouvoir* in his debate with Maoists;[10] the concept of "counter-history" in *"Society Must Be Defended"*[11]; the concept of "counter-conduct" in *Security, Territory, Population* or, in the same lectures, the concepts of "counter-society" ("In some of these communities there was a counter-society aspect, a carnival aspect, overturning social relations and hierarchy"[12]); or the concept of "counter-justice" again in his debate with Maoists,[13] of the "counter-weight" to governmentality in the *Birth of Biopolitics*,[14] of the idea of psychoanalysis as a "counter-science" in *The Order of Things*.[15] Throughout his writings, his lectures, his interviews, Foucault constantly returned to the prefix *contre-* to create concepts, to fashion new and autonomous ideas.

And it is of central importance in reading Balibar. There are, in his *Equaliberty* essays and many other brilliant writings, multiple deployments of the *contre-* move: Balibar speaks of "counter-racism"[16] and counter-populism—as Michel Feher has discussed, there is the "counter-city" and the "counterpower."[17] Then, there is also this important *contre-* move, which may fall on the darker side of the ledger:

> The crisis of the national-social state correlative to globalization and the reproletarianization that constitutes both its result and one of its objects from the side of the dominant classes (of financial capitalism) gives rise to a whole series of national or international political initiatives that relate to what could be called a *preventative counterrevolution*, even more than neoimperialism.[18]

There is also the *contre-* move that counters the counter-revolution with a "counter-counterrevolution," setting things somewhat more straight for the resisters and the disobedients:

> The whole question is whether a policy of this kind, more or less deliberate but perfectly observable in its effects, which combines financial, military, and humanitarian aspects and which I believe can be characterized as preventive counterrevolution, elicits a revolutionary response, or, if you like, a counter-counterrevolution, according to the schema of "going to extremes" that was largely shared among Marxist and Leninist representations of the socialist transition after the experience of the insurrections of the nineteenth century.[19]

In his culminating seminar in fall 2015, Balibar proposed that Foucault had developed a "counter-politics"—in contrast to *le politique*, the apolitical, or even the unpolitical. Following that, at a conference at the University Paris–Est Créteil on "Assujettissement et subjectivation" on June 1, 2016, Balibar developed his *contre-* move further, suggesting that the central element of truth-telling in Foucault's work—of *parrhesia*, of veridiction and all its associated forms of diction—is a form of *contre*-diction and *contre-conduite*, effectively placing the element of the *contre-* move at the very center of Foucault's thought. Balibar pointed us in particular to the *quatrième de page* of both Volumes 2 and 3 of the *History of Sexuality*, which reproduce the following quotation by René Char:

> L'histoire des hommes est la longue succession des synonymes d'un même vocable. Y contredire est un devoir.[20]

To *contre*-dict is a duty: for Balibar, this notion of parrhesiastic contradiction has within it the seeds of a counter-democratic principle, not in Pierre Rosanvallon's sense but as was exercised by certain parrhesiasts such as Socrates or Diogenes. This reflects an element of the *counter-majoritarian* in Foucault's work. And by means of the *contre-* move, Foucault's intervention and turn to parrhesia becomes an autonomous, independent theory based on a "contradiction" that is indexed but that we barely see.

In an essay titled "In Praise of Counter-Conduct," Arnold Davidson underscores how so many of the forms of resistance that we admire in Foucault's writings take us back to the concept of "counter-conduct":

> In a series of remarkable formulas concerning freedom, Foucault speaks of the "insubordination of freedom," the "rebelliousness of the will and the intransitivity of freedom," the "art of voluntary inservitude" and of "deliberative indocility" (Foucault, 2001b: 1056; 1990: 39). All of these phrases belong to the semantic field of counter-conduct and make evident the double ethical and political scope of this counter-conduct.[21]

One can hear, in Davidson's essay, a kind of admiration for the concept of counter-conduct. But it is important to emphasize that the *contre-* move is not always or necessarily progressive. As with concepts such as solidarity[22] or interior frontiers,[23] there is an equivocal nature to counter-concepts. They, too, can go a bit all over the place—and be deployed against the interests of a progressive agenda. This is reflected in what Robespierre would refer to as the "counter-revolutionary,"[24] or, depending on any given political interpretation, what Rosanvallon would refer to as "Counter-Democracy." I am here again in Balibar's *Equaliberty*—or rather, in his footnotes—always inescapably in Balibar's work.

Many of us bear an almost romantic attachment to the counter-practice itself. It feels so intimately linked to notions of disobedience, resistance, and countering power. But it is important not to get carried away.

Let me set forth as systematically as possible my central thesis. There is a particularity to the *contre-* move that distinguishes it from other political devices or mechanisms. It does not function like a dialectic. It is an opposition that leads not to a synthesis but instead to a stage of "perfection," in Conrad's terms, that (1) merely indexes its former counter-partner and (2) becomes a fully independent concept, all to itself, that does not incorporate its opposition and is no longer a reaction against anything. This is very different than the way that concepts generally work. It is markedly different, for instance, from the Nietzschean idea that concepts are the cumulative effect of dead metaphors, or that only when its history is forgotten can something become a concept.

It may be useful, then, to delineate three dimensions of the *contre-* move.

The first dimension distinguishes it from the more classic or simple opposition associated with the prefix "anti-." Adding the prefix "anti-" serves only to defeat or eradicate its object directly. For instance, antiterrorism aims to eliminate terrorism by stamping it out, in contrast to counter-terrorism, which uses the logic and strategies of terrorism to undermine it. The *contre-* move is more internal: It engages in a play, a movement, a dance with its object, using the force of the object against itself, in order to get beyond that game. It uses the energy of the object, and the internal logic of the object, to defeat it. It starts in a game with the object—as in chess, or fencing, or martial arts—but then transcends it.

There is, in this sense, some proximity between the *contre-* move and the term "against"—as in Paul Feyerabend's *Against Method*, or in *Against Prediction*.[25] "Against" is closer to "counter-" than to "anti-" insofar as it attempts to develop a new method in the oppositional work rather than simply to defeat its object.

In any event, the *contre-* move is different from the "anti-" move.[26] Returning to the example of security, specifically of counter-insurgency: Counterinsurgency uses the internal logic of Maoist insurgency to defeat the insurrection. It adopts and accepts the logic—in fact it fully embraces the logic—but it tries to do it better, to reappropriate it, to redeploy it even more aggressively. It does not rest on the idea that there would be two opposing views that are contrary to each other in a dialectical confrontation. Instead, it burrows into the logic and deploys it against its opponent.

The *contre-* move differs as well from the Socratic dialectic (the testing of an opposing view), the Kantian model of dialectics (thesis-antithesis-synthesis), and the Hegelian method (abstract-negative-concrete). It differs, in its very foundation, from an Adornian negative dialectics. It differs as well from Marx's dialectical materialism—which rests on a notion of direct opposition, as expressed in his *Capital*:

> My dialectic method is not only different from the Hegelian, but is its direct opposite. To Hegel, the life-process of the human brain, i.e. the process of thinking, which, under the name of "the Idea," he even transforms into an independent subject, is the demiurgos of the real world, and the real world is only the external, phenomenal form of "the Idea." With me, on the contrary, the ideal is nothing else than the material world reflected by the human mind, and translated into forms of thought.[27]

To be sure, there is of course a family resemblance among all these forms of opposition. Foucault was keenly aware of this and in fact suggested as much in an interview discussing what he called "countereffects," in which he added: "I dare not use the word *dialectics*—but this comes rather close to it."[28] The *contre-* move "comes rather close" to a dialectic but is not the same. It also comes close to the "anti-" move but, again, differs. One can hear that as well in Foucault's writing, with passages for instance in *Security, Territory, Population* that read as follows: "The first element of anti-pastoral or pastoral counter-conduct is asceticism."[29] Here and elsewhere, Foucault is struggling to pin down the conceptual move, using the term "anti-pastoral struggles" interchangeably with "pastoral counter-conducts" but trying to correct and replace the first with the second.[30]

A second dimension concerns the *internal* logic of the *contre-* move. It is almost an imminent form of critique: the object that is being opposed is taken as such, it already exists fully, and the *contre-* move effectively goes into the object to oppose it. Notice how the *Oxford English Dictionary* defines the term: "Done, directed, or acting against, in opposition to, as a rejoinder or reply to another thing of the same kind *already made or in existence*."[31]

Davidson points directly to this notion of immanence when he writes that, as in the interiority of the relationship between points of resistance and relations of power,

> in *Security, Territory, Population*, Foucault also emphasizes the nonexteriority, the immanent relation, of conduct and counter-conduct. The fundamental elements of the counter-conduct analysed by Foucault are not absolutely external to the conduct imposed by Christian pastoral power. Conduct and counter-conduct share a series of elements that can be utilized and reutilized, reimplanted, reinserted, taken up in the direction of reinforcing a certain mode of conduct or of creating and recreating a type of counter-conduct.[32]

There is, Davidson explains, a "tactical immanence" of counter-conduct to conduct. Counter-conduct is not "simply a passive underside, a merely negative or reactive phenomenon, a kind of disappointing after-effect."[33] In the words of Foucault, counter-conducts are not "les phénomènes en creux."[34] There is a "productivity of counter-conduct which goes beyond the purely negative act of disobedience."[35] It is in this sense that, for Davidson, "the notion of counter-conduct adds an explicitly ethical component to the notion of resistance."[36] As a methodological matter, the "counter-" element of "counter-conduct" works in a similar way as "resistance" to power does: as something internal, that does not reach beyond, that is not a gap or absence. Foucault talks about counter-conduct that is "used against and to short-circuit, as it were, the pastorate."[37] Notice the use of the term "against" and the idea of short-circuiting. The short circuit is tied to the internal dimension of the *contre-* move. It uses the circuit, the flow of electricity against itself. Davidson comes back to this in regard to homosexuality:

> Foucault describes these relations with the same expression, *court-circuit*, that he had used to describe religious counter-conduct: "these relations create a short-circuit, and introduce love where there should be law, rule, habit" (Foucault, 2001f: 983).[38]

A third dimension, and perhaps most important, is the ultimate emancipation of the *contre-* move, which goes beyond its oppositional object, is liberated from it, becomes autonomous. At that point, it is no longer "counter-." It is more like the Professor in Conrad's *The Secret Agent*: outside the game, outside the dance, beyond the counter-moves in the same game. But it always indexes the original opposing object. The Professor is perhaps the "perfect anarchist," but he is still an *anarchist*.

When the counter-move works, it gives rise to something that is neither the opposite nor even the dance partner but instead is perfectly autonomous and self-sufficient—a concept that functions all on its own. Counter-conduct is no longer conduct that resists something but conduct that has become its own form, a pure form of force, or disobedience, or of resistance.

Let me offer a more tangible or concrete illustration: the example of jujutsu (or Ju-Jitsu or Jiu-Jitsu), a form of judo. (I must emphasize up front that I am not a fan of martial arts, but I do believe the illustration is instructive here.) As I see it, jujutsu is the perfect illustration of the contre-move.

"Ju" stands for pliable or yielding to another. "Jutsu" means "techne" or "art." Together, the term signifies the art of yielding to the other's force. "The word jujutsu may be translated freely as 'the art of gaining victory by yielding or pliancy.'"[39]

The central idea of jujutsu is to use someone's own force against him or her. Rather than confront the other with one's force, the idea is to turn the force of the opponent into one's own weapon and use it against the opponent. In other words, to turn one's opponent's energy against the opponent, rather than trying to oppose that energy directly. In an article from 1887, "Jujutsu and the Origins of Judo," the authors explain that: "Its main principle [is] not to match strength with strength, but to gain victory by yielding to strength." And the first principle of the art: "not to resist an opponent, but to gain victory by pliancy."[40]

I would identify this as that first moment of the *contre-* move: to parry, to block, to ward off by a corresponding move. But what I would suggest is that forms of jujutsu as judo transcend that parry. The philosophy of jujutsu is that of the counter-move: to use the force of the attack and to transform it into something else, something that is neither an attack nor a block.

When the counter-move can exist on its own, without responding to its counter, always perhaps indexing it but fully unmoored, detached, independent, above its counter, doing what it does without responding to its counter, countering without reference to its counter—that, I take it, is the final productive moment of *contre-*.

The darkest illustration of the *contre-* move—one that demonstrates well its fullest potential—lies right before our own eyes in the United States. Over the course of the past two decades or more, a new form of governmentality characterized by counterinsurgency strategies has come to dominate our government. Developed as a counter-move that drew extensively on Maoist ideas of insurgency, this new form of governmentality has liberated itself from its oppositional object and become a form of governing *despite the absence of any domestic insurgency*. It has become an autonomous form of government.[41]

Since 9/11, the United States has undergone a dramatic transformation in the way it carries itself abroad and governs itself at home. Long in the making—at least since the colonial wars abroad and the domestic turmoil of the 1960s—this historic transformation has come about in three waves. First, militarily: in Vietnam and now in Afghanistan and Iraq, US military strategy shifted importantly from a conventional model of large-scale battlefield warfare to unconventional forms of counterinsurgency warfare. Second, in foreign affairs: as the counterinsurgency paradigm took hold militarily, US foreign policy began to mirror the core principles of unconventional warfare—total information awareness, targeted eradication of the radical minority, and psychological pacification of the masses. Third, at home: with the increased militarization of police forces, irrational fear of Muslims, and overenforcement of antiterrorism laws, the United States has begun to domesticate the counterinsurgency and to apply it to its own population.

The result has been radical: the emergence of a domestic counterinsurgency model of government, imposed on American soil, in the absence of any domestic insurgency. The counterinsurgency has liberated itself from its oppositional object to become a new and radical form of government. It is a *counter*-insurgency without an insurgency, an autonomous form of unconventional warfare unmoored from reality.

This illustrates perfectly the *contre-* move: Born in an opposition, it soon exceeds it. Neither inherently good nor bad, it can take us in multiple directions. It is not thesis, antithesis, synthesis. It is not "anti-." There is no inherent necessity to these logical steps. Counter can fail. But when it succeeds, it tends to be a powerful device, born of contestation.

In the end, the concept of the counter-move may bring us to the heart of resistance and disobedience, as well. It might be possible to develop a theory of the counter-move as one decisive form of critique. To draw on the energy and positivity of needing to counter. This is perhaps the counter-counter-revolution that Balibar had in mind in *Equaliberty*.

It is possible that, today, more than ever, we need to "go counter." Both in the sense of counter-play and in the sense of exceeding the ideology we counter, to achieve something autonomous. This is what happens when jujutsu becomes an art form. When the Counterreformation becomes something greater than a response to the Protestant reformation, but instead a new form of governmentality. When counterpositivism becomes a philosophical method that need not refer back to positivism anymore. When the Counterrevolution becomes a form of governmentality in the absence of any insurgency or revolution. Or when, in Joseph Conrad's book, the Professor becomes himself the "perfect anarchist" who has gotten past the play of the game of counter-moves. This is perhaps a model for resistance.

APPENDIX

My ambition and hope had been to write this essay with Étienne Balibar. We had often spoken about the idea but, as it so often happens, moved on to other collaborations. I will close then here with a memorable email from Balibar.

> Cher Bernard,
> Hier soir ma femme et moi étions à la très belle mise en scène de textes de Paul Celan que dit Nicolas Bouchaud, un des grands acteurs français actuels, au Théâtre du Rond-Point, et donc j'ai entendu (et ensuite retrouvé dans le texte) le passage suivant de son célèbre discours de réception du prix Georg Büchner en 1960 (connu sous le titre "Le méridien"):
> "Après toutes les paroles prononcées à la tribune (c'est ici l'échafaud sanglant), quelle parole! C'est la contre-parole, c'est la parole qui casse le 'fil,' la parole qui n'est plus la révérence faite 'aux badauds et à l'histoire sur ses grands chevaux,' c'est un acte de liberté. C'est un pas."
> Le mot allemand est "das Gegenwort," et il s'agit d'une allusion à l'exclamation de Lucile Desmoulins au pied de la guillotine, après l'exécution de son mari, provocation

destinée à lui permettre d'être exécutée à son tour pour le "rejoindre" dans la mort, dans la pièce de Georg Büchner, "La mort de Danton."

A mettre en réserve, pour notre essai à venir . . . (Foucault peut-être connaissait ce discours, qui a été édité d'abord de façon confidentielle en 1961 puis réédité en allemand en 1968, mais surtout traduit en français en 1967 par le poète André du Bouchet dans le premier numéro de la revue *L'Éphémère*, tout à fait le genre de choses que Foucault devait regarder; mais de toute façon l'important est la rencontre des mots).

Cf. Paul Celan, *Le Méridien et autres proses*, Edition bilingue, traduit de l'allemand et annoté par Jean Launay, Editions du Seuil 2002, page 63.

Bonnes fêtes et bonne année! Amitié, Étienne

NOTES

1. Étienne Balibar, *Equaliberty: Political Essays*, trans. James Ingram (Durham, N.C.: Duke University Press, 2013), 284.

2. Joseph Conrad, *The Secret Agent*, ed. John Lyon (Oxford, UK: Oxford University Press, 2008), 71.

3. Conrad, *Secret Agent*, 51.

4. Conrad, *Secret Agent*, 49.

5. Conrad, *Secret Agent*, 233.

6. Conrad, *Secret Agent*, 227.

7. Michel Foucault, *Mal faire, dire vrai: La fonction de l'aveu en justice*, ed. Fabienne Brion and Bernard E. Harcourt (Louvain, Belgium: Presses Universitaires de Louvain, 2012), 10.

8. *Oxford English Dictionary Online*, s.v. "counter-," https://www.oed.com.

9. Friedrich Nietzsche, *The Will to Power*, ed. Walter Kaufmann (New York: Vintage, 1967), Section 794, p. 419.

10. Michel Foucault, "Sur la justice populaire: Débats avec les Maos," in *Dits et Écrits*, vol. 1, *1954–1969* (Paris: Gallimard, 2001), 1234.

11. Michel Foucault, *"Society Must Be Defended": Lectures at the Collège de France, 1975–76*, ed. Mauro Bertani and Alessandro Fontana (New York: Picador, 2002), 79.

12. Michel Foucault, *Security, Territory, Population: Lectures at the Collège de France, 1977–78* (New York: Palgrave Macmillan, 2007), 211–12, quoted in Foucault, *"Society,"* 29.

13. Michel Foucault, "Sur la justice," 1235.

14. Michel Foucault, *The Birth of Biopolitics: Lectures at the Collège de France, 1978–1979*, ed. Michel Senellart, trans. Graham Burchell (New York: Picador, 2010), 137.

15. Michel Foucault, *The Order of Things: An Archaeology of the Human Sciences* (New York: Vintage Books, 1994), 379.

16. Balibar, *Equaliberty*, 205.

17. Balibar, *Equaliberty*, 284.

18. Balibar, *Equaliberty*, 159.

19. Balibar, *Equaliberty*, 159.

20. Michel Foucault, *Histoire de la sexualité*, vol. 2, *L'usage des plaisirs* (Paris: Gallimard, 1984), back cover; Michel Foucault, *Histoire de la sexualité*, vol. 3, *Le souci de soi* (Paris: Gallimard, 1984), back cover; Michel Foucault, *Histoire de la sexualité*, vol. 4, *Les aveux de la chair* (Paris: Gallimard, 2018), back cover.

21. Arnold Davidson, "In Praise of Counter-Conduct," *History of the Human Sciences*, 24, no. 4 (2011): 30.

22. See Jacques Lezra, "Relation," this volume.

23. See Ann Laura Stoler, "Interior Frontiers," this volume.

24. Balibar, *Equaliberty*, 316n7.

25. Paul Feyerabend, *Against Method* (New York: Verso, 2010); Bernard E. Harcourt, *Against Prediction: Profiling, Policing, and Punishing in an Actuarial Age* (Chicago: University of Chicago Press, 2007).

26. In this regard, I would contest Balibar's suggestion that Foucault's relation to Marx could be properly described as "anti-Marx," as Balibar titles his essay "L'anti-Marx de Michel Foucault." Especially in relation to the Foucault of the early 1970s, as I have argued, we are facing much more of a *contre*-Marx than an anti-Marx. The 1972 and 1973 lectures are determinative in this regard. Insofar as Foucault supplements, but does not displace, the accumulation of capital by the accumulation of docile bodies, what we face is a *contre-* move—at least in this most *Marxisant* period of Foucault. See Michel Foucault, *Théories et institutions pénales: Cours au Collège de France. 1971–1972*, ed. Bernard E. Harcourt (Paris: Gallimard, 2015), 262 ("Le contre-marxisme de Foucault n'est pas un anti-marxisme").

27. Karl Marx, "Afterword to the Second German Edition," in *Capital: A Critique of Political Economy*, ed. Frederick Engels, trans. Samuel Moore and Edward Aveling (Moscow: Progress, 1965).

28. Michel Foucault, "Sex, Power and the Politics of Identity," in *Ethics: Essential Works of Foucault 1954–1984*, ed. Paul Rabinow (New York: New Press, 1999), 167.

29. Michel Foucault, *Security, Territory, Population: Lectures at the Collège de France, 1977–78* (New York: Palgrave Macmillan, 2007), 208.

30. See also Foucault, "Sex, Power, and the Politics of Identity," 204.

31. *Oxford English Dictionary Online*, s.v. "counter-" https://www.oed.com.

32. Davidson, "Praise," 27.

33. Davidson, "Praise," 27.

34. Michel Foucault, *Histoire de la sexualité*, vol. 1, *La volonté de savoir* (Paris: Gallimard, 1976), 126.

35. Davidson, "Praise," 27.

36. Davidson, "Praise," 28.

37. Foucault, *Security*, 213, quoted in Davidson, "Praise," 29.

38. Davidson, "Praise," 33.

39. Jigorō Kanō and T. Lindsay, "Jujutsu and the Origins of Judo," *Transactions of the Asiatic Society of Japan* 15 (1887).

40. Kanō and Lindsay, "Jujutsu."

41. See a detailed elaboration of this argument, see Bernard E. Harcourt, *The Counterrevolution: How Our Government Went to War against Its Own Citizens* (New York: Basic Books, 2018).

CONVERSION

Monique David-Ménard

In Étienne Balibar's *Violence and Civility*, there are four affirmations that give us a fresh perspective on politics. The first affirms, by methodically distancing itself from Hegel's thought, that there is something inconvertible in the transformations that the classical theorists hoped for: social violence in right and in civility. The second affirmation is that we should have a resolutely nonmoral way of thinking about the foundations of the political. On this point, Hegel remains a decisive reference. The third affirmation, which links these first two seemingly unrelated affirmations, is that the diverse registers of communal life that the political unifies are organized in ways other than those that Hegel tells us about: the male subject—supposedly separated from the family—who assimilates [*inte'grer*] civil and political society and buys the right to desire by cutting himself off from the "affective substantiality" that linked him to the universal immediacy of mothers in fact commands the entire distribution of gendered roles in this construction. Now, this arbitrary construction leaves out other forms of separation, transitions, and exclusions that distribute genders in societies. Despite all of the readings of his reading of Antigone, Hegel's analysis makes of sexualities an essence instead of seeing in them, as in the analysis of the political, an occasion to think in nonessentialist terms, that is to say, an occasion to give a positive role to contingency: the contingent, in fact, is neither irrational nor an inferior form of rationality.

The fourth affirmation: the political is a domain of collective existence that, precisely, demands that we take leave from a fundamentalist way of thinking. Certainly, Machiavelli had said this but without making the link to the question of violence. Between the importance of contingent factors in which violence transforms into civility and the impossibility of founding the political on an essential truth that reality would accomplish, there is a mutual implication that particularly grabs my attention when I read the Wellek Library Lectures, which were recently published in English.[1]

STOP MEASURING THE REAL AGAINST THE IDEAL

It is in this respect that the texts published by Balibar over the past ten years are of particular interest to me, since I am working on showing that the same goes for psychoanalysis, this social practice that intervenes in the field of the sexuated unconscious. The relation between contingency and determination in the formation and the exercise of sexualities greatly resembles what Balibar describes: in psychoanalysis, we try not to measure the reality of the sexual against a norm, which would be the *telos* of treatment. We start from the impasses and the gaps in existence; the transposition of what is at stake in the unconscious into the very particular conditions of the treatment, as its function, has to loosen the grip of the vice by which symptoms, considered as a provisional style of life, are formed. We start from what isn't working [*ce qui ne vas pas*] and we undo the knots so that they can be formed differently. We don't know a priori what is good for such and such a patient. In the same way, Balibar no longer measures a state of nature that would be violent against its conversion into a civil state, as was the case in Hobbes and Rousseau. He no longer hopes, as did Hegel, that the negativity of violence will have by itself the ontological power to negate itself or that this self-negation of destruction will be the very process of History. The function of the topography of the two forms of extreme violence is to look at the reality of our political world from the epoch of nation-states, not with nostalgia but by giving itself the means to situate the dangers.

There are, even in Balibar's analysis, two uses of the topographical method that aims to be distanced from the idealization of the political while diagnosing (in Foucault's sense) where the risk that politics can no longer find a place comes into being:

> On the one hand, the calling into question of the primacy of the nation undoes the pertinence of the collective form of subjectivity that it had created: the "nation" interpellated individuals in order to inscribe them in the process of historical universality;

whence the importance of patriotism and citizenship. At the other extreme, the known fragility of nation-stations produces a family of comportments that are neither public nor private, but which are inscribed in a "gray zone in which recognition of individuality loses sight of its rules and norms. Peoples, subjects, citizens, territories."[2]

This topography of extremes concerns, then, the historical moment when nation-states lose some of their importance.

But the principal topography locates the risk of another short circuit between extreme forms of violence that, when each remains in its corner, so to speak, do not undo the political. The exploitation described by Hegel in his analysis of the populace, and by Marx in his analysis of the "reserve army of labor" in capitalism, extends to dimensions of globalization. In principle, this catalyst of the dissolution of political life has nothing to do with another extreme form of violence: the violence of the excluded who make of their exclusion an absolute incitement to self-hatred and hatred of the other in the name of an Idea of racial purity and religious election. The dissolution of what renders civility possible is what Kant, in his "General Remark on the Exposition of Aesthetic Reflective Judgments" (1790), analyzed as fanaticism, the diabolical combination of the sublime and enthusiasm: when sensibility finds nothing in front of it, it is ready to convert this nothing into the presence of the absolute in the sensible. In the same way, the confrontation with the abyss in conjunction with the sensible abolishment of the difference between an absolute that we believe to be realized and destruction multiplies a kind of radical evil of sensibility that tyrants and priests exploit. We would have to put Kant in dialogue with Lacan: the Thing of desire is so heinous that we make the other responsible for containing it. In certain historical conditions, racism, which is nourished by this abolishment of limits, leads to destruction. A fortiori, when extreme objective violence solicits without mediation this type of horror of the other and of the self, mixed with the adoration of the absolute, identified with everything by the intermediary of nothing. Absolute Truth.

DOES PROPERTY CONVERT THE VIOLENCE?

If there is inconvertible violence in social and political relations, it follows that the entire edifice or hanging-together [*étagement*] of different registers of human life that are capable of structuring themselves into a State is disrupted. I suggest here that another kind of challenge to this hierarchy internal to political philosophy is possible. I do so by distancing myself from Hegel, in accordance with Balibar's method, but on a different point. Balibar, emphasizing the anthropological presuppositions of the construction of the State, refers only to the third part of the *Elements of the Philosophy of Right*, which puts the family in relation with the society of labor and with the "properly" political relations that seem to result from it and that, however, support the family and the society of labor. Since Balibar's description of the political tends not to be derived from an ethics, we can also say that it takes into account the second part of the *Elements of the Philosophy of Right*, which treats "subjective morality," that is to say, the confrontation of a subject of desires and interests with the formal and categorical universality of the law.

But in this critical reading, curiously, the first part of Hegel's work, "abstract right," that is to say, the right of property, never enters into consideration. In the Hegelian and Marxist traditions, the critique of property is taken up again in the theory of civil society; it intervenes as the danger to the State posed by the formation of a common people [*plébe*] who have nothing and thus are no longer substantially involved in the political body. In Marxist terms, the incapacity of individual property to put into form the relations of production in the capitalist mode of production is one of the sources of the formation of the proletariat, that is to say, this social class that has nothing to pass along to its children and nothing for itself except its children. As such, property takes part in an objective violence, if not an extreme objective violence, that converts itself less and less into citizenship in our more and more unequal societies.

But there is another way to treat the right of property. Hegel's entire analysis shows the indigence of property, not only in its transformations in the heart of civil society: the confrontation of a will with a thing whose will affirms that it belongs to it and the act by which wills mutually guarantee this identity between wills and things shows itself to be inadequate. This very inadequation demonstrates the wealth (the concrete character, says Hegel) of social relations, which, precisely, do not result in a trickling down in the form of property. There is here a violence that likely is not an extreme violence but is certainly objective, in Balibar's sense.

We could even go so far as to say that this inability of property to produce the form of social relations simply proves that it belongs only to an inferior rationality, such as the still mechanical rationality of competition in the sphere of labor. But there is more. Is this confrontation of wills and inanimate things not precisely animist? Recall that in *The Savage Mind*, Lévi-Strauss sees a totemic ceremony in the visits that families make to an attorney's office following a death. What is inheritance if not a magic of things that is supposed to guarantee the persistence of a person by way of objects, even despite death?

And I'm here only evoking right as Giambattista Vico analyzed it: the magical repetition that contains in objects and in rites an interhuman violence is nowhere *aufgehoben* by the actions of the law. A third reference for reading the Hegelian theory of abstract right differently: at the end of his 1915 article "The Unconscious," Freud suggests that what remains of animism in our culture is to be found in our relation to others. Supposedly primitive people populate nature with spirits, but we scientists guard against doing such a thing, all while we continue to believe in the souls of others and thus of ourselves. Now, when Freud makes this unexpected reference, he also couples it with an allusion to Kant: the unconscious that is in us, this strange part of us that makes of ourselves an other, is perhaps less inaccessible than Kant's thing-in-itself is, he writes. Between alterity and strangeness, wherein we can longer tell whether it is ourselves or another, couldn't we say that property tries to and fails to ward off the threat? We would have there a less superficial view on the violence that inhabits social relations than the remark that Freud makes in 1930 in *Civilization and Its Discontents*, when he critiques socialism for naively believing that putting an end to private property would also mean putting an end to the mutual aggression of man in society. I propose that we reread the first part of the *Philosophy of Right* as a description of the savage magic of our relations to others that tries to contain our incapacity to recognize ourselves as at once linked and separated.

CONTINGENCY AND OVERDETERMINATION

Balibar's insistence on the role of contingency in the possibility or impossibility that violence converts into civility gives me the opportunity to put the concept of contingency, such as Balibar uses it, in dialogue with the concept of contingency that I tried to clarify in the field of psychoanalysis.

In *Éloge des hasards dans la vie sexuelle*, I maintain that psychoanalysis puts forward a specific concept of contingency that is impossible to inscribe in philosophical traditions, even in an "aleatory materialism." In the field of transference, contingent elements, picked up and/or invented by the analysand in a signifying relation very close to the elements of necessity, become capable of transforming what repeats itself with the necessity of the inexorable and to make of this repetition a reinvention of existence. We can employ in this way the Lacanian vocabulary that shows how transference transforms the symptom into a *sinthome*. But we can also describe this process in another way: so that symptoms are converted into the invention of a style of life instead of remaining an impediment to living, there have to be, thanks to the transposition of subjective impasses that make up treatment, new elements that intervene. Now, these new elements are contingent. Dreams made "in transference" and that remodel the signifiers of a history have this peculiar quality not only of being borrowed from the very materials of repetition but also of diverting from them. From the point of view of a solely formal logic, contingency is opposed to necessity. But from the point of a transcendental logic without a priori categories, contingency borrows from necessity, and this is why it can change the course of it. I have thus described at length a treatment in which a patient's dream, accusing the analyst of obstructing her from living, took the form of a "blue baby," which is in French a metaphor for a child whose existence is condemned. "This blue baby that I held in my arms is the possibility of a new love and you are like all the others, you want to prevent me from living," said this young woman. Because the blue is at your place [*chez vous*]: the blue of the child, she said, was the blue of a painting in my waiting room. This young woman—thanks to the blue of a painting—whose dream had invented the function was able to accuse me of preventing her from living and, from that moment, the episode of suicidal tendencies that crossed her mind became negotiable and permitted her to make a decision—which until that point had terrified her—about her love and sex life. The blue also belonged to the series of necessary elements, since much of the component parts of the life of this elegant, "neat and tidy" young woman were commanded by the love of *material excreta* [*des matières*] and of violent expulsion. Laurence's entire professional life was overrun by violence; she said with delight "I'm a killer." If blue and the blue baby had not been so close to the breeding ground of anal sexuality, then the dream would never have had this power of conversion. At the same time, nothing was more insignificant than a color when compared to the problematic of this woman: should I leave my husband, my kids, and the ideals of political power that bind me to my husband by giving myself over to the love of colors and of smells that awoke me to another man who was not even rich and powerful? Now, it is precisely the heterogeneity and the apparent insignificance of the day's residue—the color blue borrowed from the analyst's waiting room—that made it possible for this woman to be transformed, on the condition that she take the risk to experience a desire to throw herself out the window and that she can transform this experience in a dream addressed to the analyst. "This blue baby is the new love that you want to destroy." Contingency here is both the heterogeneity of the two series—the violence of power/love of colors—and the insignificance of the second—*jouissance* is not infrasignifying but beside or at the edge of signification.

Does the clinical field of transference where the particularities of the relations between the contingent and the necessary are knotted together have nothing to do with the logic of the political and of history? On the contrary! Balibar affirms that for a situation of political violence to "turn in civility," there have to be elements that are heterogeneous and exterior to violence itself. Hegel thought that the destructivity of violence negated itself immanently and that history was the very process of this conversion. Balibar thinks that violences do not have the immanent power to convert themselves. There must be measures or events or organizations that separate ultraobjective violence from ultrasubjective violence, and the putting into place of these organizations appeals to exterior, heterogeneous, and contingent factors. Politics is not rare, Balibar writes, but precarious.

Let's go over the history of these relations between the contingency and heterogeneity of factors that transform a political situation. We'll not go back to Epicurus, so let's stick to "Althusser 1967."

I have in mind the appeal that Althusser made to Freud's *Traumdeutung*, in the chapter of *For Marx* titled "Contradiction and Over-Determination." What interested him there was to understand with Lenin why the Bolshevik revolution had taken place in Russia and not in Germany, where everybody expected it. Germany was the most advanced country in the development of capitalism, the country where the principal contradiction of the mode of production was the most affirmed and where the political class struggle opposing the proletariat to the bourgeoisie had found a remarkable political expression. Now, these are precisely factors exterior to the so-called principal contradiction that rendered it politically efficacious: in exceptional sectors in which capitalism was established in Russia, the modernism of the system was all the more clear when it was a question of these exceptionally advanced sectors. For the rest, Russia was made up almost exclusively of peasants unscathed by capitalism. The Russian people were thrown onto the path of war by conflicts between the great powers, where they mixed with workers from these advanced capitalist sectors. And this contrast was a revolutionary catalyst, which rendered active a supposedly principal contradiction, if we speak in essentialist terms about historical movement. But the reality of history is precisely never the application of a truth. Such is the importance of the contingency that overdetermines that which we took to be essential.

Let's compare this to what Freud says: he introduces overdetermination in the chapter on "Dream-Work," which examines, starting from the practice of free association induced by transference, how we can conceive of the relation between the thoughts that the dream stirs up (the dream thoughts) and the dream story [*récit*] as it is first told. The dreamwork is the set of bridges that let us understand the relation between these two languages, which Freud says are like two foreign languages. Overdetermination can first be described from a structural point of view: between two dreams, latent and manifest, we do not have, Freud says, a biunivocal correspondence between terms. It is not only a question of replacing many ideas, image, or elements with only one in the manifest content. The correspondence between manifest and latent content is organized system by system: if we start from an element of the manifest content, then it leads to a plurality of elements of the latent content, but ones that are linked in turn to a plurality of relations of elements of the manifest content, whose link we didn't grasp at the beginning. Overdetermination is the set of relations of relations between the two registers of the dream. But this description is provisional: overdetermination has to do with the question of what is important and what is of little interest in the dream—that is to say, it has to do with intensities. The latent dream is "differently centered"[3] than the manifest dream. What shows itself to be decisive in the analysis had first appeared secondary in the telling of the dream. Instead of seeing this displacement of intensity in a negative light, Freud locates there the expression of a power to put into form, which makes possible the event of the dream by circumventing the "censor": "It thus seems plausible to suppose that in the dream-work a psychical force is operating which on the one hand strips the elements which have a psychical value of their intensity, and on the other hand, *by means of overdetermination*, creates from elements of low psychical value new values, which afterwards finds their way into the dream-content."[4] Overdetermination is the creativity of elements that are unimportant or that seem at first to be unimportant. Their creativity stems precisely from the apparent heterogeneity of these entities and their apparent insignificance with respect to the "essential." Exteriority, causal independence with respect to the "line of force" of a principal phenomenon: contingency thus allows for the formation of a dream by creating multiple intermediary threads between what is to be produced and what must be left out. The dream is possible thanks to the day's residues. It never goes directly to the essential, but rather it creates detours. Overdetermination is the textual inventiveness of these detours, commanded by an ambiguous power: "If that is so, *a transference and displacement of psychical intensities* occurs in the process of dream-formation, and it is as a result of these that the difference between the text of the dream-content and that of the dream-thoughts comes about."[5] The dream is the audacity to think what the night watch would never let pass through, but at the same time, it is by inventing multiple threads that both link together and mask the "most intense,"[6] the excess, the unbearable, that this latter manages to become an almost calm manifest dream. Overdetermination is the textual way of negotiating a relation of powers between the drive's expression (*darstellen*) and a fear or a prohibition of it.

Althusser sometimes says, and Balibar says it more clearly, that there is no principal contradiction; rather, it is always a contingent event that makes what is given play the principle role, and this is especially pertinent for extreme violence, which does not convert immanently into civility. And it is indeed on this point that it is worth being distanced from Hegel, despite his genius, since it is on the subject of violence that he affirmed the capacity of negativity to transform itself.

BY WAY OF CONCLUSION

The question I would like to pose to Balibar, then, is the following: I said that in psychoanalysis, the contingent is made of a near-transposition of the very materials of the necessary. Transposition, which gives a chance to elements apparently without importance. They become decisive precisely because their being of little importance introduces play by thwarting [*déjouer*] resistances, whereas overdetermination produces its work of subtle weaving between the insignificant and the decisive. Does the same go for political initiatives that can thwart the short circuits between extreme objective violence and extreme subjective violence? How can we invent subtle swerves in relation to the necessary in politics?

Translated by David Maruzzela

NOTES

1. Étienne Balibar, *Violence and Civility: On the Limits of Political Philosophy*, trans. G. M. Goshgarian (New York: Columbia University Press, 2015).

2. Balibar, *Violence and Civility*, 69.

3. Sigmund Freud, *The Standard Edition of the Complete Psychological Works of Sigmund Freud*, vol. 4, *(1900): The Interpretation of Dreams (First Part)*, ed. and trans. James Strachey (London: Hogarth Press and the Institute of Psychoanalysis, 1953), 305.

4. Freud, *Interpretation of Dreams*, 307.

5. Freud, *Interpretation of Dreams*, 307–8.

6. Translator's note: See Freud, *Interpretation of Dreams*, 330: "The most intense elements are also the most important ones."

> For reasons of accuracy, the director of news at Al Jazeera English, Salah Negm, has decided that we will no longer use the word migrant. . . . We will instead, where appropriate, say refugee.
>
> Migrant is a word that strips suffering people of voice. Substituting refugee for it is—in the smallest way—an attempt to give some back.
>
> —Al Jazeera

COSMOPOLITICS

Emily Apter

COSMOPOLITANISM/COSMOPOLITICS

In 2015, the news network Al Jazeera removed the term "migrant" from its coverage and proposed in its place "refugee" to refer to persons in transit, specifically those fleeing from regions of war, ethnic cleansing, religious persecution, and economic and environmental catastrophe.[1] Al Jazeera's action recognizes that the lexicology of migration is fraught with linguistic racism, the politics of exclusion, and imperial violence, all themes of Étienne Balibar's formative work on cosmopolitics. Balibar's broadside, *Europe, crise et fin?*, articulates the urgent need to reinvent political concepts and minoritized names. "Political categories," he affirms, "need to be changed; the old ones have changed in meaning: notions of 'migration,' borders, territory, population, cannot be used as before (as we've seen already with terms like money, citizenship, work)."[2] For Balibar, righting the language of migration (in the sense of putting it back on political course, restoring political rights to those whose language is treated as suspect or whose claims remain unlanguaged in any tongue) belongs to a larger project of rethinking what Europe is as a territory of cosmopolitical right (defined in Kant, as Balibar reminds us, as a universal system of juridical norms and a "meta-political point of view based on the idea of a moral destination of humankind, according to which the ultimate moral end or purposefulness of reason will transcend the simple sphere of positive law"), and beyond that, of translating "Europe" by means of a political philology of statelessness, detention zones, camps, settlements, and unsettled existence.³ Balibar's earlier interventions in debates around border politics and cosmopolitanism were of course crucial to orienting these concerns.

In the late 1990s and early 2000s, pursuant to and following the fall of the Berlin Wall and the post-Maastricht moment in which the ascendant prospect of a "United States of Europe" within a globally networked neoliberal economy prompted appeals for a different order of philosophical politics (from Jacques Derrida, Jean-Luc Nancy, Balibar, and others), there was an efflorescence of cosmopolitan theory, buoyed by Derrida's writings on unconditional hospitality and forgiveness, by Balibar's seminal book *Droit de cité: Culture et politique en démocratie* (1998), and by the collective volume *Cosmopolitics: Thinking and Feeling beyond the Nation* (1998), edited by Pheng Cheah and Bruce Robbins (which included Balibar's indispensable essay "The Borders of Europe"). This body of writing, though hardly uniform in its purview, built on the premise that cosmopolitanism could no longer rely on Enlightenment notions of freedom, reason, autonomy, individual interest, and national self-sovereignty. Nor could it leave unquestioned statutes of human rights protected by universal declarations, international treaties, universalist models of international civil society, world trade agreements, and free markets issuing from a Kantian ideal of mutually respecting federated nations equilibrated in perpetual peace. The cultural model of cosmopolitanism was, for these thinkers, equally obsolete, resting as it did on what I would be tempted to call a detachment theory of the subject divested of the primordial claims of ontological nationalism, as well as on a precomprehended notion of the human and the cultivation of the old humanisms within the disciplinary humanities.

Cheah and Robbins's *Cosmopolitics* departed from the premise that, since Goethe's time, worldliness and ramified notions of cultural belonging and identification were predicated on a concept of the human as that which overcomes the limitations of immediate existence. The human derived from the universal feeling of sympathy (Kant), from the intrinsic value of communication (translatability), and from the belief in a common cultural compact. The editors critiqued this humanist tradition from the standpoint of "actually existing practices of cosmopolitanism," characterized by "fragility of collectivity"; "long-distance nationalism" (Benedict Anderson); "Trojan nationalisms" (Arjun Appadurai); and conflictual identity politics in the place of a "gallery of virtuous, eligible identities."⁴ For Cheah, cosmopolitics was deputized to take on capitalist cosmopolitanism by pointing to "mass-based emancipatory forms of global consciousness, or actually existing imagined political world communities."⁵

By the mid-2000s, cosmopolitan theory had all but vanished in the shift from critiques of the humanist human to theories of "planetarity" that were aligned with translative encounters and non-Eurocentric ecological movements (Gayatri Chakravorty Spivak), "slow violence" (Rob Nixon), and an "indigenous alter-anthropology" that was inclusive of "Amazonian cosmopolitics" and composed of *interspecies perspectivism*, *ontological multinaturalism*, and *cannibal alterity* (Eduardo Viveiros de Castro).⁶

In an interview referencing his book *Inhuman Conditions: On Cosmopolitanism and Human Rights* (2006), even Cheah would take aim at cosmopolitanism, pointing out how its most recent iterations were compromising human rights by implicating them in global NGOs and the biopolitical management of human capital and resources. He maintained that the human was embedded in a language of right that was itself a juridical translation that obfuscated the effect of biopolitical technologies on bordered subjectivities.

> But if we approach human rights in terms of a biopolitical analysis, you can argue that what produces humanity and all its capacities such as needs, interests, the capacity to labor and so on, are biotechnologies that have now become globalized. Human rights or human-rights instruments are the codification of these capacities in a juridical discourse, that is to say, in the language of right. Hence, we don't begin with the human being who has rights, but with the production of fundamental human needs and capacities, which we subsequently understand in terms of rights that we can claim for ourselves or on behalf of others. But we can only claim these rights in the first place if the needs and capacities that these rights seek to protect were synthetically produced in us by biopolitical technologies. . . . if you look at the new cosmopolitanism in this way, then things become more complicated.⁷

Cheah underscored how countries in the global south, as part of the effort to attract capital investment, essentially subcontracted their citizens to countries abroad. In the name of developing their capacities as human resources through education and professional training, they ended up outsourcing their bodies for cheap labor. Cheah's insight—that the language of cosmopolitan right *produces* forms of labor injustice—may hardly be a revelation, but it reinforced the need, already well articulated by Balibar, to revive cosmopolitics as a term accountable to the fallout of economized existence, and to the necessity for a language of rights to have rights capable of doubling down on the politics of the global south within Europe. Cosmopolitics in this ascription would curtail the baggy "cosmopolitanism" set loose in the 1980s (identified by Robbins and Paulo Lemos Horta in their introduction to *Cosmopolitanisms*) with "a plural descriptive understanding" comprising "any one of many possible modes of life, thought, and sensibility that are produced when commitments and loyalties are multiple and overlapping, no one of them necessarily trumping the others,"[8] by aligning itself with "a cosmopolitanism of the poor,"[9] associated with "non-elite collectivities that had cosmopolitanism thrust upon them by traumatic histories of dislocation and dispossession."[10]

In a more recent piece titled "From Cosmopolitanism to Cosmopolitics," Balibar extends the cosmopolitical remit to a "philological model of political space" contoured by a "phenomenology of the border."[11] Here translation proves paramount, for the move entails attending to the specific idiomaticities of border language (noting where translation is impossible and where it contributes to structural cultural inequality) and working the interactivity of language multiplicities. Translation, as Balibar marks it, and as we know from his manifold contributions to theorizing in untranslatables (particularly his entries to Barbara Cassin's *Dictionary of Untranslatables: A Philosophical Lexicon* and his subtle dilations on the reciprocal transferences of *conscience*/consciousness in *Identity and Difference: John Locke and the Invention of Consciousness*), is no ancillary quilting point of politics and philosophy but a praxis essential to political theory. As a medium of linguistic exchange and a mediator of "cultural determinations and institutional power relations," translation lies at the crux of Balibarian cosmopolitics.[12] Cosmopolitics *is translation* insofar as it effects the depredication of universalism (casting the universal as an effect of the languages and idioms in which it self-enunciates) and insofar as its politics are flush with acts of translating, of translating the language of emigration and citizenship divested of usufruct, of occupation and real estate, of territorial and philosophical borders.[13]

UNTRANSLATABLE "EUROPE"

Ransomed, deported, parked in transit camps or abandoned in the no-man's-land of train and port zones, sometimes shot or robbed of their life savings, they die or give up before one barrier or another, but obstinately, from henceforth on, they are there.[14]

Balibar's "righting" and rewriting of the construct "Europe" never allows us to forget the a priori of the refugee's *thereness* within Europe. Accounting for thereness (an affront to what Condorcet, as Balibar notes, termed *adunation*, referring to a people's unitary self-image, protectively shielded against the prospect of "foreign" arrivals) is crucial to his project of reinventing the idea of the border as a cosmopolitical concept.[15] To available models of worldwideness (Jean-Luc Nancy's phenomenological coordinates for a *regard au loin*, a gaze trained on infinite horizons and the contemplative expanse of transfinite worlds), jurisdictional circumference, continental identity, integrity of perimeter, or the imaginary of a partitioned territory within a larger global cartography, Balibar adds "Europe" as the name for a border that misrecognizes itself, fails to see the "thereness" of who is there within actually existing cosmopolitanisms.[16] For Balibar, the stakes of this misrecognition are high: either Europe will remake itself by revolutionizing its territorial *nomos*, or Europe will destroy itself in denying reality and staying fixated on fetishes of the past. Europe, he argues, may think that it possesses integral borders, but in this it is wrong. In fact, Europe *is* little more than a complex of overlapping borderlands, displaceable boundaries, and disparate modes of governance. In "The Borders of Europe," Balibar coined the synthetic expression "the European triple point," harking back to *la voie romaine* and the transnational map of papal sovereignty in medieval Europe, creating territories of "conflictual cultural overlaps in and through the identification of the religious and the symbolic."[17] Now, these "conflictual cultural overlaps" have produced (in the place of the papacy) transversal forms of supranational sovereign power characterized by militarized borders—the policing of everyday life—and modes of governance in which the state of exception is permanent, effectively unexceptional.

Balibar emphasizes that Europe as such corresponds, technically speaking, to no unique territorial identification: the EU coincides neither with the Council of Europe (which includes Russia, Ukraine, Turkey, and most of the Balkan states) nor with NATO (which includes the United States, Norway, and Turkey, and which is charged with protecting European territory) nor with the Schengen (which includes Switzerland but not the United Kingdom) nor with the Eurozone (which still includes Greece but not the United Kingdom, Sweden, or Poland).[18] As there will never be congruent delimitation, Europe is simply not definable as a discrete territory.

Undermined as a univocal, absolute idea by the lack of a stable definition of inside and outside, European as a cosmopolitan ideal is further undone by the effects of an inherited vocabulary of colonial cartography, a skein of words bearing myriad forms of violence sanitized by bureaucratic usage or adminspeak. Let us think of these words as active, personifiable technicians of dominance—terms such as *outremer* (overseas), "non-European," or *indigènes* (natives) that, since the colonial period, have maintained their traction as terms of recolonization applied to Europe's internal boundaries.[19] "North" and "south" are similarly violent markers. As Balibar notes, there are increasingly shifting lines of global south and global north within smaller and smaller states of Europe, each unit improvised (almost like theatrical scaffolding) by the construction of walls erected in the hope not of arresting the influx of displaced people but of redirecting it elsewhere.[20]

The architect Léopold Lambert documented the remapping of Fortress Schengen, materialized through ad hoc barbed-wire fencing along the border between Slovenia and Croatia (the latter a member of the European Union but not yet of the Schengen countries). Lambert tracks the strange effects of small doors and apertures erupting inside townscapes and along riverbanks. He zeroes in "on the small Croatian town of Bregana, in the direct vicinity of the highway custom station between Ljubljana and Zagreb, [which] extends a small part of its urbanity in Slovenia, on the other side of the thin river sharing the same name."[21] Noting that the river border has been substituted by a small fence on a single street, Lambert discerns that "this street happens to be on the separation between Fortress Schengen (a 4 million square-kilometer area) and . . . the rest of the world. . . . The smallness of the door (Fortress Schengen's back door) accommodated in the fence [not] only attests [to] the past domesticity of this street but reinforce[s] the absurdity of the wall's spectacle."[22]

The proliferation of microborders, captured in images of fences running up against kitchen gardens and the back doors of local homes or in obscured views of the militarized border that serve, nonetheless, as projected virtual borders or battlements of rumored borders, underscore the extent to which borders may be fabricated from immaterial material but are no less politically functional for it. Fences and gates rezone Europe in ways that are only further rezoned by the attitudinal de-Europeanizing of European countries by other European countries. As Balibar reminds us, for France the global south is Italy, for Britain it is France, for Germany it is Hungary, and for Hungary it is Serbia, Macedonia, Greece, and Turkey. Who stops whom in this case? Who serves as border guard for whom?[23] It is always a matter of that other state, the one treated as more to the south or the east. The point here is that in place of a border, there is *rebordering in real time*, inclusive of those intangible "atmospheric walls" (as Sarah Ahmed defined them) produced by differential modes of existence across regions of economic and technological inequality.

Brushing each other, yet divided, there are those who live in planes, airports, shopping centers, and conference halls, and those who go by foot or truck, holding children and belongings (thereby instantiating what Balibar in "The Borders of Europe" calls "the empirico-transcendental question of *luggage*"), and those who navigate the seas on creaky boats and leaking container barges.[24] This state of affairs describes an *inverted cosmopolitanism* because it inverts our understanding of the relation between fixed territories and flux populations.[25] It is a condition characteristic of the post-Westphalian world in which cosmopolitan right and international law can no longer assume a one-to-one correspondence between legitimate states and sovereign nations. In the face of the newly arrived, Balibar asks, what is Europe? What is Europe hobbled by identitarian insecurity, galloping nationalism, and the destitution of the idea of itself set against the backdrop of a generalized condition of civil war?[26] What will be left of Europe in the wake of the migrant state of exception, which propels it back into old internecine conflicts and forces it to abandon the ideological fiction of a common European project?[27] To avoid the path of becoming a space of "managed inhospitality" (to borrow the term of a special issue of *Near Futures Online* by Zone Books on "Europe at a Crossroads"[28]), Europe must rebecome Europe, de-translating itself, so to speak—as in the "New Keywords of 'the Crisis' in and of 'Europe'" proposed by Martina Tazzioli and Nicholas De Genova—the stated aim of which is "to effectively 'hijack' the dominant discourse superintending how we speak and think about the conjunctures of 'Europe' and 'crisis.'"[29]

To effect the de- or retranslation of Europe essential to a cosmopolitics worthy of the name, one must recover the emancipatory force of its etymons—*demos*, ipseity, *hospites*, *sens communis*, *peuple*, *maidan*, *Gastrecht* (the right of residence), *refuge*—along with placeholders for the articulation of persons currently lacking in statehood, the so-called virtual Europeans. In *We, the People of Europe?: Reflections on Transnational Citizenship*, Balibar echoed Umberto Eco in designating "translation" as the name for the "language of Europe," conceived as "the concrete metalanguage made up of all the equivalences and all the attempts to overcome the 'untranslatable' between idioms," and an "unevenly developed practice." In *Europe, crise et fin?*, he points to the urgency of positioning Europe as a site for retranslating the language of rights and obligations: *droit*, *loi*, liberties, privileges, the right to. . . .[30] The predicates for this glossary subtract from Europe's crisis now, a crisis precipitated by the loss of a constitutional tradition of "conflictual" and "expansive" democracy, by the Schengen (whose accords fail to extend to refugees), by the delusion that wars (in Syria, Afghanistan, Africa) are not also Europe's wars, by the illusion that austerity politics could be imposed without effecting the demise of European consensus over democratic values and economic policies, and by the belief that Europe can call itself democratic while employing discriminatory and violent techniques of population control.[31]

Balibar does not focus on Turkey in *Europe, crise et fin?*, but it arguably serves as a potent mediator of "untranslatable" or "detranslated" Europe for a sum of reasons: (1) Turkey has played and continues to play a historically critical role in the fate of Europe, especially the Europe of antiausterity movements or Brexit-style secessionism; (2) it typifies the cynical bartering of refugees as a medium or language of political *chantage* built on preexisting categories of targeted minorities (Kurds, Armenians); (3) it is a mobile counter in the fallout of Middle East politics within Europe (the displaced iterations of the Israeli-Palestine conflict and the Sunni/Shia proxy wars); and (4) it reveals the contradictions and aporias underpinning the language of cosmopolitics and exilic destination. This last harks back to Turkey in the 1930s, when Erich Auerbach, along with other German and Austrian professors forced to flee after the institution of the Nuremberg laws, found themselves conscripted for a Kemalist project to de-Ottomanize Turkish education. By helping to invent and diffuse an order of vernacular *Öffentlichkeit*, these exiled Europeans made internal exiles of a prior generation; the irony was not lost on them. And one could say that Turkey remains a singular "translation zone," mediating fractious Europe/non-Europe modes of mutual un-understanding (*Unverständlichkeit*), operating diplomatically, if contentiously, as an east-west bivalve, and "translating," in a loose sense, not only what Europe currently is (Fortress Europe) but also what it can no longer become (a zone of cosmopolitan hospitality, open borders, perpetual peace).

The dialectics of mimesis, carrying faint but distinct echoes of the title of Auerbach's celebrated magnum opus of literary criticism *Mimesis: On the Representation of Western Reality* (composed between 1942 and 1945) structures the defeat of the cosmopolitical paradigm ("L'Europe en panne," in a state of breakdown, as Balibar will put it).[32] According to this scenario, Turkey is ambivalently cast as both a refugee sanctuary (an estimated three million Syrians), and a place of brute repression that subjects its own citizens to internment and military abuse. Reciprocally, Europe emerges as a region of political dysfunction, unable to deal with the *sans-papiers* within the shifting borders of its self-sovereignty even as it clings to the myth of itself as a beacon of universal human rights. Europe and Turkey, caught between aggressive if uneven policing and both in a defensive crouch toward radicalized religious factions, are in this sense joined at the hip, both unable to translate themselves as *îles de refuge* or conduits of safe harbor. Both may be seen as in the grip of resurgent Orientalisms (as postcolonial readers have consistently underscored, Edward Said, Azade Seyhan, Aamir Mufti, Kader Konuk, Nergis Ertürk, and Efe Cakmak among them) that exploit the tenuousness of secular humanism in a non-Euro context even as they sustain fictions of a Euro-Turkey.[33]

Balibar's *Europe, crise et fin?* brings out the structurally mimetic and destabilized Euro/non-Euro relation not so much in light of the nonequivalence between Ottoman and Muslim cultural heritage and Judeo-Christian cosmopolitanism, which has preoccupied scholars from Leo Spitzer and Auerbach to writers such as Ahmet Hamdi Tanpınar, Nâzim Hikmet, and Orhan Pamuk, but more in terms of the identification of Europe with nonsites that spell the negation of Europe: *ports* of exit and entry (Calais, Lesbos, Malta, Catania), *routes* (Somalia to Tangier, Istanbul to Algeciras, Yemen to Djibouti, Syria to Greece, Albania to Germany, Tripoli to towns in the west Balkans, Algiers to Spain), and *straits* (Gibraltar, Bosporus, Messina).

TRANSLATION ZONES: STRAIT/*STREIT*

A cosmopolitics of the border, tasked with translating zones of peril and traumatic detachment, brings us to a new functioning of "strait" as a term of charged conjugation—one resulting in a heterotopia of treacherous passage, a liquid border, a sieve of human triage, legislative and facultative conflict, and a protean site of affect in translation, to mention just a few of its proliferating referents. One might start with the colloquial sense of "being in dire straits," conjoining a body of water fraught with distress and the names for fear in every language. Hailing from the Old French *estreit*, "strait," which denotes difficulty, defilement, narrow stricture, isthmus, or narrow passage of water, extends into the modern French *étroit* (from Latin *strictus*) and comes to subsume a range of concepts associated with tightness and close-fittingness. The cognate in Middle English, *streit*, meaning "narrow" or "strict," moves on a parallel track toward the German *Streit*, signifying conflict, quarrel, dispute, or fight, as in Kant's *Der Streit der Fakultäten* [*The conflict of the faculties*] (1798). Here, one could say, a philosophical border politics of the *Streit*/"strait" stands behind its contemporary traction as function of the cosmopolitical lexicon.

Kant wrote the work after being censored by Frederick William II, King of Prussia, for his treatise *Religion within the Limits of Reason Alone*. As has been noted many times, Kant's defense of the "lower" faculty of philosophy (lower with respect to the "higher" faculties: theology, law, and medicine) was hardly a challenge to the right of government to sanction the doctrines that should be taught. Although Kant endorsed state control over education, he believed that a government's interests were best served by a philosophical faculty accorded full power to reconcile the tenets of ecclesiastical faith with reasoned moral law. The ability of the lower philosophical faculty to derive normative moral principles from a priori rather than empirical or mystical orders of experience, together with its philosophical techniques for rationalizing theological precepts, were grounds for ensuring its disciplinary autonomy. This position of course was unacceptable to the theology faculty who relied on forms of historical criticism deferential to the principle of divine revelation. A turf battle was inevitable, and Kant lost. In this context, *Conflict of the Faculties* must be read as a pushback document, a vindication of the right to philosophy, and the right of philosophy to self-legislate, to embed itself within the university while preserving its outlier status.

Kant coded *der Streit* within the political "strait" of the university, associating it with the jockeying for power between the upper and lower faculties. This historical context of pitched internecine institutional battles and struggles for subregional constitutional authority add philosophic substance to routine identifications of the "strait" as the space between Scylla and Charybdis, associated with clichés signifying "choosing between two evils" or finding oneself "between a rock and a hard place." Scylla and Charybdis, the mythical sea monsters of Greek mythology situated on opposing sides of the Strait of Messina (between Sicily and the Italian mainland), respectively named the treacherous rock shoal on the Italian side and the churning whirlpool off Sicily's coast. Their proximity foretold the zero-sum logic of navigating hazards; avoiding Charybdis meant passing too close to Scylla, and vice versa. Famously, in Homer, Odysseus must choose between monsters: he opts for skirting Scylla and losing only a few sailors over sacrificing his entire ship in the whirlpool.

The strait became a favored trope of political caricature from the eighteenth century on. William Pitt is seen in James Gillray's 1793 caricature "Britannia between Scylla and Charybdis" aboard the ship *Constitution*, which also carries "an alarmed Britannia, between the rock of democracy (with the liberty cap on its summit and the whirlpool of arbitrary power (in the shape of an inverted crown) to the distant haven of liberty."[34] John Tenniel's 1863 caricature for *Punch* magazine shows Prime Minister Lord Palmerston steering the British ship of state between Scylla (depicted as a craggy rock with the face of a grim-visaged Abraham Lincoln) and Charybdis (depicted as a whirlpool whose foam and froth assume the guise of Jefferson Davis). A shield emblazoned "Neutrality" hangs on the ship's thwarts, referring to how Palmerston avoided taking sides in the US Civil War. The American satirical magazine *Puck* also used the myth in a caricature dated November 26, 1884, in which the unmarried President-elect Grover Cleveland rows desperately between two snarling monsters, one captioned "Mother-in-law" and the other "Office Seekers."

This politics of the uncertain middle, of danger in the suspension of an outcome associated with the imagery of the strait (however satirical it might be), is given full thrush as a Balibarian figure of "inverted cosmopolitanism" in the work of two contemporary artists, Antoni Muntadas and Yto Barrada. Muntadas's video *Jauf/Miedo* (2007) investigates how words for the affect of fear and words describing the perilous physical journey across the Strait of Gibraltar become geophilosophically intertwined. Enabling the speakers, in the very fact of their speech, to affirm the right to have rights in and through their own languages, the work's medium is built from interviews conducted in Arabic, Spanish, English, and French. Part therapeutic session, part official inquiry into the relationship between sovereign inhospitality and translational violence, *Jauf/Miedo* presents the strait as a utopic landscape luring the touristic gaze that turns into a deadly corridor of fears, harboring human traffickers and piratical economies.[35]

In Yto Barrada's *The Strait Project: A Life Full of Holes* (1998–2004), the "holes" in question hark back to the mythic void that opened when Hercules separated Europe from Africa and reference, analogically, the treacherous deserts that separate Mexico and the United States. As Kristin M. Jones notes,

> Just as the Sonoran Desert has been a deadly lure for countless Mexican "illegal" immigrants looking for greater economic opportunity in North America, so the Strait of Gibraltar, closed since 1991 to passage by Africans without visas, has a larger-than-life presence for those suffering globalization's fall-out. Noting that in both French and Arabic the word for "strait" connotes constriction or distress, Barrada has written, "I try to expose the metonymic character of the strait through a series of images that reveal the tension—which restlessly animates the streets of my home town—between its allegorical nature and immediate, harsh reality."[36]

In *Le Détroit—Avenue d'Espagne (The strait—Spanish avenue*, 2000), there is an associative fusion of street and strait. The street, whose very name, "Avenue d'Espagne," evokes Europe, is mesmerizing in its emptiness and resemblance to a rushing river. The vantage of this image communicates disembodiment, ungrounding, spatial insecurity and perceptual disorientation. In his essay "Life Full of Holes," T. J. Demos notes that Barrada represents the Strait "less as vivid geography than as zone of imagination and desire, one split between the would-be émigré's longing for escape . . . and expatriate homesickness, gazing back with irrepressible memories of an intimately familiar place irrevocably lost."[37] For Demos, the work calls up Giorgio Agamben's dictum (in *Means without Ends*): "Rights are attributed to the human being only to the degree to which he or she is the immediately vanishing presupposition . . . of the citizen."[38]

Whereas in Muntadas's work the strait's imaginary is built from discrepant orders of affect among the terms *jauf/miedo/peur/*"fear," in Barrada's it belongs to a greater infrastructure of political vanishing points and barred representation. In both cases, the strait is a gate: a liquid gateway to another world, a stricture or blockade, and a trial, one that tests persistence in the face of failure. This is precisely the irony contained in the famous biblical line of Matthew 7:14: "Because strait is the gate, and narrow is the way, which leadeth unto life, and few there be that find it."[39] Werner Hamacher seems to have embedded this biblical portent of the strait in his idea of philology, which he characterized as a "question detained at the border, the drawbridge, the portico, that does not enter its interior and does not know its law."[40]

FRONTIER

For Geoffrey Bennington, extending border discourse to philosophy rather than philology, "frontier" is the premier philosopheme not only of a form of politics—the "end of history," the "end of ends," the endlessnessness of post-Kantian teleology—but also of the concept of the concept as such. In *Frontiers: Kant, Hegel, Frege, Wittgenstein*, precursor to the more recent *Kant on the Frontier: Philosophy, Politics and the End of the Earth*, "frontier" in his ascription redounds to Derrida's handy notion of "non-synonymous substitutions" glossed as "the name of a problem," namely, what determines the substitutions

> if the terms are not synonymous (i.e., interchangeable *salva veritate*, in Leibniz's definition). There seems to be good reason to think of Derrida here, not only in that he makes abundant use of this vocabulary but because these words or concepts or terms (frontier, border, etc.) seem to share with others, such as difference, the complication involved in also saying something about what it is to be concept, a word, or a term. The term "term," at any rate, means just that: "boundary," "border," or "frontier" or "territory." A term can be a stone or post (traditionally carved with the image of Jupiter Terminus, god of boundaries) marking the limit of possession of a piece of ground. In one conception of philosophy at least, it would be our task to establish as precisely as possible the frontiers between these various concepts—and the establishment of precise frontiers between them would be a condition of their conceptuality. Frege famously suggested that if a concept does not have precise boundaries, then it is simply not a concept.[41]

Bennington alludes here to Frege's assertion that "the law of the excluded middle is really just another form of the requirement that the concept should have a sharp boundary."[42] The law of the excluded middle (either a proposition is true, or its negation is true, no third way being admissible), much like Aristotle's law of noncontradiction (holding that where one proposition is the negation of the other, one must be true and the other false), reveals the extent to which cosmopolitics *qua* border politics encompasses the larger stakes of conceptual possibility. In this picture, every name for "border" becomes a placeholder for an excluded middle that makes possible conceptualization as such.

And yet this abstracted landscape of pure thought in no way precludes the frontier from signifying materially, from delineating the stakes of politics on the ground. As Bennington reminds us, the frontier is also a stone, a marker, a way of staking claim or possession to a piece of territory. And when that stone is rubble, rubbish, or rabble, it may take on the character of an unsettled settlement, the remnants of a neighborhood that has otherwise been transformed by gentrification or urban redevelopment, or that persists as a remnant or ruin of a town after it has been strafed or broken up by an occupying force. From Balibar's reflections on the crisis of inverted cosmopolitanism amid the flux of European borders, passing through the conflict zone of the "strait," we move inexorably to settlement politics in the Middle East.

In *Pastoral in Palestine*, a personal chronicle written in 2011, Neil Hertz works the slippages among "rubbish, rubble, and rabble," drawing out the social and architectural syntax of retaining walls and other urban morphologies that speak to the "gravitational pull that has to be constantly counteracted," recalling for Hertz what the poet Robert Lowell called "the downward glide and bias of existence."[43] The book is an observation of Palestinian ways of survival in the Occupied Territories and a stock-taking of the encroachment of extremist settlers on Arab neighborhoods. Hertz prompts us to interrogate fully—to translate—the ambiguous meanings accruing to the term "settlement," as concept, as literally "grounded" principle of the territorial claim, and as a set of differential typologies of living on according to conditions of provisionality, exclusion, and survival. Even the word "pastoral," a term borrowed from William Empson's *Some Versions of Pastoral*, is drawn away from its gentle associations with natural settings, the georgics of shepherds, and Romantic Lake District poets and into the vortex of Arab-Israeli settlement politics. Teaching at Al-Quds University in the Occupied Territories under the auspices of the University and Bard College, and directly inspired by the local topography of neighborhoods, building sites, and landscapes encountered daily, Hertz undertakes a census of the signage of settlement. In a formerly middle-class Palestinian neighborhood of West Jerusalem, advertisements (in English) boasting "Arab-style" rustication on the facades become a marketing tool of Israeli real estate developers ("fossilized forms of biblical authenticity," Arab style without the Arabs) that are aimed at Jewish clients from North America and Europe.[44] Hertz includes within "pastoral" the violent renaming of contested spaces: the "Seam" harks back to the "Green Line," so named because it was traced in 1947 by a wide green crayon. Now a six-lane highway connecting Jerusalem to the settlements, the Green Line has been euphemistically rebranded as "Peace Way"; the urban thoroughfare thus remakes the "seam" as an ethnic unifier that, as Hertz sees it, unthreads and excludes Palestinian life from the "urban web."[45] A "settlement" means something specific in the Occupied Territories. It is first and foremost a religious "colony," a colonizing populace whose mission is to reclaim "the Biblical Heartland of Israel" according to their literature.[46] Occupation is made possible by means of preferential rules of engagement on the part of the Israeli police force. As Hertz remarks on one of his photos of a settlement in the eastern part of Jerusalem where Palestinians once lived, it is not a matter of inserting single dwellings in a Palestinian neighborhood but of implanting entire gated communities into Arab areas of Jerusalem.[47]

PHILOLOGY OF THE SETTLEMENT

If, as Derrida argued and Bennington reconfirms, it is "the indecision of the frontier between the philosophical and the poetical that most provokes philosophy to think," we might imagine Balibar's *frontières-mondes* as cosmopolitical aporias that inaugurate a translingual rethinking of *what a settlement is* by means of acts of political philology.[48] Consider in this regard Ozen Nergis Dolcerocca's commentary on the term "settlement" in Turkish, which underscores the politics of linguistic cosmopolitics:

> Settlement in Turkish is *yerleşim* (pronounced "yérléshimme"), usually followed by *yeri*. Yer-leş-im is literally "getting a location." The Jewish settlements in Israel are referred to as *Israil'de Yahudi yerleşimi*, which registers as "location-getting." By contrast, camp is *kamp* in Turkish, a loan word from French, (with the same dual meaning of "camp" and *camp de détention*. *Kamp* signifies a temporary arrangement, as opposed to *yerleşim*, which denotes a settlement of greater permanence. Detention camp is *tutuklu kampı*, and refugee camp is *mülteci kampı*, as in *Suriyeli mülteci kampı* (Syrian refugee camp). The principle semantic difference between *yerleşim* and *kamp* rests on differences of temporality.[49]

The differences between "camp" and "settlement" in Turkish, hinging on temporal duration, give way to the larger cosmopolitical problems of duration, endurance, and traumatically intertwined yet morally incommensurate histories of "the camps."

The term for "camp" in common currency in Arabic, *Mintaqat al-I'tiqal* (منطقة إعتقال), is approximatively translated as "district of arrests," according to Hannah Scott Deuchar.

> *Mintaqa* means "district," "quarter," "area"—it's most often used for area or quarter of a city, but in recent years it has taken on the legal and military connotations of "zone": *Mintaqat al-Ihtilal* expresses "occupied territory" or "occupied zone." Unlike "zone," however, it is still also used colloquially to mean "area," without the threatening connotation. The word *mintaqa* derives from the triple-consonantal root *na-ta-qa*, "to utter" or "[to] articulate," of which the second form *na-tt-a-qa* also means "to girdle" or "[to] mark out" [according to Hans Wehr]. Related words are *nataqiyy*, ("phonetic"), *mantaqiyy* ("logical"/"dialectical"), and *nitaq*, ("girdle," "limit," "belt," or "boundary"). *Mintaqa* is a noun of place (like *mustawtana*, "settlement"—the *m* at the beginning denotes place), so it can be taken to signify a space that has been marked out, delineated, encircled.
>
> *I'tiqal* is the common word for arrests, military or criminal, and it is the verbal noun of the Form VIII verb for the root *'a-qa-la*. Interestingly, this root has two main meanings, one being "to arrest" and the other "to speak." The first meaning, then, is "to hobble," from *'iqal* (a tie for hobbling camels' feet), clearly a derivation for the modern meaning of "to detain," "to arrest," etc. According to Edward Lane (2166, C19 classical English-Arabic dictionary) the camel would be restrained with the *'iqal* in the yard of the abode of the heir/next of kin, hence the association of *'a-qa-la* also with paying blood money. Lane connects the sense of *aqala* (as "restraint," extended to "restraint from what is incorrect or immoral") to its second usage as "to reason," "to realize," or "to comprehend" [according to Wehr]. In *Lisan al-Arab* (C13 dictionary) it is noted that a man who is *'aqil* has constraint over himself and specifically over his tongue (Lisan 3046), which he can *i'taqala*, "arrest" (the Form VIII verb is used here).[50]

Deuchar brings into relief conceptual amphibolies of police restraint (physical arrests) and philosophic reason, consistent with Balibar's amphibolies of "ground" (mapped and materially sited) and "ideality" (border imaginaries, the question of "*being*" a border).[51] Rich associative valences are also drawn out of the word for "settlement" in Arabic—*mustawtana* مستوطنة—a noun drawn from Form X of the verb *wa-ta-na*, وطن, meaning "to dwell/live/reside/stay in a place." Hans Wehr's modern *Arabic-English Dictionary* offers an etymological juxtaposition rich in geopolitical implications, a link between *mustawtana* (colony) and *mustawtana zira'iya*, ("agricultural settlement" or "kibbutz").

COSMOPOLITICS 109

Noting the heated debates among Wikipedia Hebrew editors about the proper word for Jewish settlements in the Occupied Territories, Ophir parses its political usages exegetically and historically:

> The debate concerns the current use of the word and reflects the clear split between left and right Zionists in relations to Jewish colonization in the Territories. Historically, two terms were used by Zionists to designate Jewish settlements: ישוב, *yeshuv*, and תולחנתה, *hitnakhalut*. The first comes from the root ישב, y.sh.v, "to settle," but also, according to its conjugations, simply and generally, "to sit" or, specifically, "to sit down." The second comes from the verb לחנ, n.kh.l, which connotes taking possession, acquiring, or inheriting. *Nakhala* is a piece of inherited or possessed land. The second term is biblical and has a clear colonial connotation. The Pentateuch (Numbers), for example, describes in great details the distribution of the land of Israel among Israel's tribes, each with its own *Nakhala*, a land designated as belonging to this tribe by virtue of a divine promise even before it has been possessed.
>
> Interestingly enough, most Zionists before 1967, and certainly before 1948, used *yeshuvim* for Jewish settlements, and the term designated not only specific villages and towns but, more generally, the product and goal of the Zionist colonial activity. The colonization effort was always called *hityashvut*; "village," כפר, *kfar* in Hebrew, was mostly used as a generic name for any Palestinian locality, except for the cities such as Jaffa or Jerusalem, whereas Jewish sites were called according to the type of their cooperative arrangement—*kibbutz, moshav, moshava*, etc.
>
> After 1967, the new settlements in the Occupied Territories were called *hitnakhluyot*. I do not know how soon the political split appeared, but certainly after a few years the Left insisted on this term to distinguish the illegitimate colonial project from the legitimate one within the Green Line, in "Israel Proper," Ophir explains, where all localities are called *yeshuvim*.[52] For Zionists, no matter how leftist they are, this chapter in the history of Zionist colonization has never been understood as colonialist. The settlers themselves (*mitnakhalim*) rejected the term and insisted on *yeshuvim* and *hityashvut*. The main organ of the Jewish agency working on constructing and developing new settlements in the Territories is called "the department for *hityashvut*."[53]

Ophir sets in motion a chain of untranslatables, each word appositionally activated with reference to a situated politics and governed by relations of nonequivalence. The chain highlights *yeshuv* (settlement), *Nakhala* (inherited land possessed by right of divine claim), Palestinian *kfar* (village), Israeli *kibbutz* (literally "cooperative arrangement"), and *hityashvut* (new settlements in the Occupied Territories). Ophir alerts us to how semantic shifts of emphasis among "wandering," "standing still," "sitting down," and makeshift "sojourning" condition how we read the contextual politics of settlement/unsettlement. He notes that in the Bible, the verb *yashav*, usually meaning "to dwell," "is often opposed to travel, going from one place to another, or wandering. When one stops walking one is described not as standing but as sitting/dwelling. The native peoples of Canaan are said to dwell/sit in the land."[54] Ophir distinguishes, in the interstices of the opposition between wandering and staying, the Hebrew term *khana*, חנה, "camp." The noun for "camp" is *makhane*, מחנה, the overnight place of stay for the traveling tribe or army. In Modern Hebrew, "detention camp," like "concentration camp," "labor camp," "practice camp" (in sports) or the "death (or annihilation) camp" are all *makhane*. The term does not connote dwelling in a Heideggerian sense but designates, rather, "a site for temporary stay." Ophir's languaging of *yashav* and *makhane* arguably approach them to Derridean *mouvance*, meaning not simply "the fact of moving or of moving oneself or of being moved" but also a state of being that is between active and passive, that is in-différance in Derrida's sense of being in-between differing and deferral, beyond the sensible and the intelligible.[55] Though wary of overphilosophizing regional politics, Ophir nonetheless draws out critical etymologies to clarify dimensions of the settlement conflicts in Israel-Palestine, exposing ways in which the language of entitlement to land—the right to occupy or the conditions of dwelling somewhere—are forensically "grounded" in historical etymologies.

Ophir will have recourse to Agamben's "zones of indistinction" and "states of exception" to hone the distinction between "camp" and "zone of detention" in Hebrew.

> The equivalent of detention—or any form of exception—would not take place in the camp but outside of the camp, by an act of exclusion. See for example Exodus 33:7; Leviticus 13:45–46. It is interesting that Priestly sources of the Pentateuch conceive the camp of Israel as mostly impure, and purity—hence sacredness (*kdusha, kadosh*), too—is something that can be achieved only outside the camp, while Deuteronomist sources speak about the Israeli camp itself as a site that must remain pure. The sacred in the Hebrew Bible connotes exceptionality, like in Agamben's reading of the Latin term, but it is not a hybrid term that designates a zone of nondistinction. It is that which belongs to God or that which must remain pure to tolerate the proximity of God's presence. Sacred is the time and space where God dwells. The term for dwelling in this context is *shachan*, שכן, hence the feminine name of God—*shchina*, שכינה.[56]

Ophir's attention to philosophical and theological nuances in situ within "zone," "dwelling," "camp," "settlement" is consonant with the broader Balibarian project of a cosmopolitical philology. It is at the border or in those spaces of the *frontières-monde* that compel, as Balibar insists, "a confrontation with the impossible limit of an autodetermination, a *Selbstbestimmung* of thought. It implies an effort to conceptualize the line on which we think, the condition of possibility or the 'hidden art' of distributions and delimitations."[57]

Cosmopolitics in its Balibarian usage traces the history of how the philosophico-juridical discourse of sovereign right to a territory legitimates the violence of border policing and foretells the blocked or impossible translation of universal citizenship and cosmopolitan compossibility. It points to the problem that "philosophizing in languages," to use Cassin's phrase, poses to the institution of philosophy, such that philosophies of gnomically articulated truth may no longer comfortably position themselves above the fray of linguistic contingencies but find themselves subject to *différance*, to discrepant orders of grammar and diction, and to the dictates of ontological nationalism. It denotes a political philology encompassing the solemn, tremulous theology of the "strait (underwriting all treacherous maritime passages by immigrants)," the raced and ethnocidal nominalisms of "refugee," "camp," "detention zone," "rabble," and "settlement," as well as First World categorizations such as "beneficiary," recently unmoored as the solid signature of the privileged metropolitan by Robbins, who repurposes it to designate "something between a recognition of global economic injustice and a denunciation of it."[58] Cosmopolitics acts as a clarion call for a new material grounding of what is free and unfree in any neoliberal accounting of "free speech." And perhaps, at the farthest reach, it may be taken to designate the sublation of inverted cosmopolitanism by a global politics of real estate. Here, I would propose the rather unorthodox gesture of putting Balibar's political philology of the border (including internal and psychic borders, as addressed by Ann Stoler in her essay in this volume) into dialogue with Fredric Jameson's contention that "today, all politics is about real estate." For Jameson, the charged philology of real estate cuts across the dealmaking of global finance capital, the refugee crisis, and the "postmodern" geopolitics of unsettlement and occupation.

> Postmodern politics is essentially a matter of land grabs, on a local as well as a global scale. Whether you think of the question of Palestine, the settlements and the camps, or of the politics of raw materials and extraction; whether thinking of ecology (and the rainforests) or the problems of federalism, citizenship, and immigration; or whether it is a question of gentrification in the great cities as well as in the *bidonvilles*, the *favelas*, and the townships, and of course the movement of the landless—today, everything is about land.[59]

Balibarian cosmopolitics, crossed with Jameson's structural model of a postmodern politics of real estate, brings focus to translational praxis addressed to those made stateless by war, unlanded by comprador economies of development, taxed by terrestrial spoliation wrought by the extractive industries, and afflicted by what Balibar has characterized as "the equivocity of the category of the stranger and its tendencial reduction to the figure of the enemy."[60] Within the broad parameters of what I have construed as Balibarian cosmopolitics the philology of unsettled estates is imbricated in a political ontology of *being-bordered*, a mode of existence qualified by Balibar as "an *internal, quasi-transcendental* condition of possibility for the definition of the citizen and the community of citizens . . . [a] *Zwischenraum* of political action and contestation, where the right to have rights becomes formulated."[61] Cosmopolitics in this ascription is not so much a keyword amenable to any singular definition or geotopic *Weltanshauung* as it is a function of a distinctive form of philosophic politics, at once translational and phenomenological, at once a mode of production particular to site-specific material borders defined by quarantine and exclusion, and a question of the citizen subject as a right or claim affirmed in the face of capitalism's powers of eminent domain, territorial reset, and incursion.

NOTES

1. Barry Malone, "Why Al Jazeera Will Not Say Mediterranean 'Migrants,'" *Al Jazeera*, August 20, 2015, http://www.aljazeera.com/blogs/editors-blog/2015/08/al-jazeera-mediterranean-migrants-150820082226309.html.

2. Étienne Balibar, *Europe, crise et fin?* (Paris: Broché, 2016), 144; my translation.

3. See Étienne Balibar, "Citizenship of the World Revisited," in *Routledge Handbook of Cosmopolitanism Studies*, ed. Gerard Delanty (New York: Routledge, 2012), 295. In this important essay, Balibar raises a number of intractable problems, such as the quandary that arises when it becomes clear that cosmopolitics lends itself just as easily (if not more easily) to empire and capitalist markets as it does to the sway of the multitude. Another such problem is that the ideal of civic or republican principle, infused in global citizenship, remains institutionally resistant to definition. Additional problems include the limitations on instituting the political inhering in Kant and Marx: "Although Kant's cosmopolitical right appears as a dialectical overcoming of the traditional distinction between civil society and political community, itself rooted in the 'Roman' opposition between public and private realms, and Marx's proletarian internationalism as its disqualification, both leave obscure and uncertain the question of how to *institute the political* outside the State, beyond the State as institution" (Balibar, "Citizenship," 298).

4. See Bruce Robbins, "Introduction, Part I: Actually Existing Cosmopolitanism," in *Cosmopolitics: Thinking and Feeling beyond the Nation*, ed. Pheng Cheah and Bruce Robbins (Minneapolis: University of Minnesota Press, 1998), 10–12.

5. Pheng Cheah, "Introduction Part II: The Cosmopolitical—Today," in *Cosmopolitics: Thinking and Feeling beyond the Nation*, ed. Pheng Cheah and Bruce Robbins (Minneapolis: University of Minnesota Press, 1998), 32.

6. Eduardo Viveiros de Castro, "Cannibal Metaphysics: Amerindian Perspectivism," *Radical Philosophy* 182 (November/December 2013): 21.

7. Pheng Cheah, "Interview with Pheng Cheah on Cosmopolitanism, Nationalism and Human Rights," interview by Yuk Hui, *Theory, Culture and Society* (March 17, 2011), https://www.theoryculturesociety.org/interview-with-pheng-cheah-on-cosmopolitanism-nationalism-and-human-rights.

8. Bruce Robbins and Paulo Lemos Horta, "Introduction," in *Cosmopolitanisms*, ed. Bruce Robbins and Paulo Lemos Horta (New York: New York University Press, 2017), 3.

9. See Silviano Santiago, "The Cosmopolitanism of the Poor," trans. Magdalena Edwards and Paulo Lemos Horta, in *Cosmopolitanisms*, ed. Bruce Robbins and Paulo Lemos Horta (New York: New York University Press, 2017), 21–39.

10. Robbins and Lemos Horta, "Introduction," 3.

11. The heading is borrowed from the title of a lecture by Étienne Balibar delivered at the Birkbeck Institute for the Humanities, Birkbeck College, University of London, November 6, 2007, "From Cosmopolitanism to Cosmopolitics." A revised version was given at the Center for Ideas and Society, University of California, Riverside, January 23, 2008. Balibar was kind enough to share a typescript of the lecture and to allow permission to quote.

12. Balibar, "From Cosmopolitanism to Cosmopolitics."

13. In "A New Querelle of Universals" (a condensed, English version of an essay in *Des universels: Essais et conférences* [Paris: Galilée, 2016]), Balibar explains how any attempt to think the concept of the universal gives way to a translational problematic involving the contradictions that arise from any "saying" of universalism in a specific language or idiom. "My latent idea is that the universal is not really a concept or an idea, but it is always the correlative effect of an *enunciation* that, in given conditions, either asserts the differences or denies them (or even *prohibits* them), therefore leading to a *conflictual* modality of internal contestation of itself. But enunciations are always made *in a specific language*—an idiom—and idioms exist only in the form of a *multiplicity* of languages that are never isolated from one another, but continuously interacting, therefore inducing transformations within one another. 'Translation' is the general name for this interaction, which as we know takes a number of different forms, involving cultural determinations and institutional power relations" (Étienne Balibar, "A New Querelle of Universals," *Philosophy Today* 61, no. 4 [Fall 2017]: 941).

14. Balibar, *Europe, crise et fin?*, 142.

15. Condorcet's signature concept is hailed as an astonishing term for the reaction-formation of popular self-identity in the face of newly arrived strangers. Se Étienne Balibar, *Europe, constitution, frontière* (Bègles, France: Editions du Passant, 2005), 102.

16. Jean-Luc Nancy, "Euryopa: Le regard au loin" [1994], *Cahiers de l'Europe* 2 (Spring/Summer 1997): 82–94. See Georges Van Den Abbeele, "Lost Horizons and Uncommon Grounds: For a Poetics of Finitude in the Work of Jean-Luc Nancy," in *On Jean-Luc Nancy: The Sense of Philosophy*, ed. Darren Sheppard, Simon Sparks, and Colin Thomas (New York: Routledge, 1997), 19–31; and Rodolphe Gasché, "Alongside the Horizon," in Sheppard, Sparks, and Thoms, *On Jean-Luc Nancy*, 140–56. See also Rodolphe Gasché, *Europe, or the Infinite Task: A Study of the Philosophical Concept* (Stanford: Stanford University Press, 2009); and Samuel Weber, "Europe and Its Others: Some Preliminary Reflections on the Relation of Reflexivity and Violence in Rodolphe Gasché's *Europe, or the Infinite Task*," *CR: The New Centennial Review* 8, no. 3 (Winter 2008): 71–83.

17. Étienne Balibar, "The Borders of Europe," in *Cosmopolitics: Thinking and Feeling beyond the Nation*, ed. Pheng Cheah and Bruce Robbins (Minneapolis: University of Minnesota Press, 1998), 223.

18. Balibar, *Europe, crise et fin?*, 146.

19. Balibar, *Europe, crise et fin?*, 147.

20. Balibar, *Europe, crise et fin?*, 149–51.

21. Léopold Lambert, "Fortress Schengen: Report of the Wall as a Spectacular Rumor," *The Funambulist*, February 26, 2016, https://thefunambulist.net/architectural-projects/fortress-schengen-report-of-the-wall-as-a-spectacular-rumor.

22. Lambert, "Fortress Schengen."

23. Balibar, *Europe, crise et fin?*, 150

24. Étienne Balibar, "Borders of Europe," 219.

25. Balibar, *Europe, crise et fin?*, 151–52.

26. Balibar, *Europe, crise et fin?*, 160.

27. Balibar, *Europe, crise et fin?*, 170.

28. Michel Feher, William Callison, Milad Odabaei, Aurélie Windels, eds., "Europe at a Crossroads," *Near Futures Online* no. 1 (March 2016), http://nearfuturesonline.org.

29. Martina Tazzioli and Nicholas De Genova, "Europe/Crisis: Introducing New Keywords of 'The Crisis' in and of 'Europe,'" in "Europe at the Crossroads," *Near Futures Online*, http://nearfuturesonline.org/europecrisis-new-keywords-of-crisis-in-and-of-europe/#europe-crisis.

30. Étienne Balibar, *We, the People of Europe?: Reflections on Transnational Citizenship*, trans. James Swenson (Princeton: Princeton University Press, 2004), 177, 178.

31. In *We, the People of Europe?: Reflections on Transnational Citizenship*, Balibar

COSMOPOLITICS 115

discusses the concepts of "conflictual democracy" in which "heterogeneous constitutional principles are combined," thereby "contributing to a revival of the old notion of the 'mixed constitution'" and "expansive democracy" (a Gramscian notion referring to a politics that "remains open to the integration of new elements into the 'common part' of mankind, and there can be no 'end of history'") (224).

32. See Balibar, *Europe, constitution, frontière*, 25–47.

33. For the discussion of how secularism is instrumentalized in these conflicts, see Stathis Gourgouris, "Crisis and the Ill Logic of Fortress Europe," *Uppsala Rhetorical Studies* 6 (2017): 40–41.

34. Caption from frontispiece image, James Gillray's "Britannia between Scylla and Charybdis" (June 1793), in *The Impact of the French Revolution: Texts from Britain in the 1790s*, ed. Iain Hampsher-Monk (Cambridge, Mass.: Cambridge University Press, 2005), iv.

35. If I make the case here for attending to the particular valences of the strait as a geotopic translation zone of peril, trauma, and border-crossing, it is clear that much of what is ascribed to the strait is extendable to ocean crossings by emigrants the world over. In the ever-growing series of art projects dealing with refugee crossings, I would signal Manthia Diawara's *An Opera of the World* (2017), a documentary "chaos-opera" based on *Bintou Were, A Sahel Opera*, which premiered in Bamako, Mali, in 2007. I would also signal Richard Mosse's *Incoming* (exhibited at the Barbican's Curve Gallery in London in February 2017), a remarkable large-scale, three-channel video that sutures footage of refugees on boats or idling in camps such as Calais's "Jungle" and uses a thermal military camera to hologrammatic effect; the spectral bodies, like photographic negatives, capture the flux and presence of visitants traveling across and trying to survive the seas and ports of Europe.

36. Kristen M. Jones, "Yto Berrada," *Frieze* 101 (September 2, 2006), https://frieze.com/article/yto-barrada.

37. T. J. Demos, "A Life Full of Holes," *Grey Room* 24 (2006): 74.

38. Giorgio Agamben, quoted in T. J. Demos, "A Life Full of Holes," *Grey Room* 24 (2006): 74.

39. King James Version.

40. Werner Hamacher, *Minima philologica*, trans. Catherine Diehl and Jason Groves (New York: Fordham University Press, 2015), 120n.

41. Geoffrey Bennington, *Frontiers: Kant, Hegel, Frege, Wittgenstein* (self-pub., 2008), 4–5.

42. Gottlob Frege, *Grundgesetze der Arithmetik*, vol. 2, *Translations*, § 56, 139, quoted in Bennington, *Frontiers*, 5.

43. Neil Hertz, *Pastoral in Palestine* (Chicago: Prickly Paradigm, 2013), 12–13.

44. Hertz, *Pastoral in Palestine*, 70–71.

45. Hertz, *Pastoral in Palestine*, 96.

46. Hertz, *Pastoral in Palestine*, 98.

47. Hertz, *Pastoral in Palestine*, 101.

48. Geoffrey Bennington, *Kant on the Frontier* (New York: Fordham University Press, 2017), xxvi.

49. Ozen Nergis Dolcerocca, email exchange with the author, June 17, 2017.

50. Hannah Scott Deuchar, email exchange with the author, June 17, 2017.

51. Balibar, "Borders of Europe," 217.

52. Adi Ophir, email exchange with the author, June 15, 2017.

53. Adi Ophir, email exchange with the author, June 15, 2017.

54. Adi Ophir, email exchange with the author, June 15, 2017.

55. Jacques Derrida, *Margins of Philosophy*, trans. Alan Bass (Chicago: University of Chicago Press, 1982), 9.

56. Adi Ophir, email exchange with the author, June 15, 2017.

57. Balibar, "Borders of Europe," 216.

58. Bruce Robbins, *The Beneficiary* (Durham, N.C.: Duke University Press, 2017), 6.

59. Fredric Jameson, *An American Utopia: Dual Power and the Universal Army*, ed. Slavoj Žižek (New York: Verso, 2016), 13.

60. Balibar, "From Cosmopolitanism to Cosmopolitics."

61. Balibar, "From Cosmopolitanism to Cosmopolitics."

In the practice of philosophical writing, the words and propositions around which aporias crystallize and inventions take place always belong to long signifying chains; most often they constitute its element of *Unruhe*, of uneasiness or uncertainty. . . .

INTERIOR FRONTIERS

Ann Laura Stoler

AN "ASTONISHING" CONCEPT

This moment in which I write is one for which we should have been prepared:[1] Donald Trump, Marine Le Pen, and Geert Wilders are no longer on distant dark horizons: they are dead center in forging the political cleavages of our times.[2] They are singular crusaders, but they are not alone. They operate through racialized distinctions and fears to which we might have been more attentive. These are divisive cuts through our social, political, and affective landscapes that are not eruptions, as they are so often described. Rather, these figures register deep tectonic shifts not readily visible with the conceptual tools at hand, nor by the metrics we have used to measure durable sensibilities or to capture sonics to which we are so adverse, askew to our shared radars. Prevailing political categories and concepts may now seem inadequate or inoperative. But there are some with which we could do more, with which we might rethink and rework to track the claims (and panics) raised to condone and fortify amplified inequalities, with which we might crush their appeal so as to be equipped to respond differently and perhaps better.

"Interior frontiers"—Johan Gottlieb Fichte's early nineteenth-century concept, reanimated by Étienne Balibar some thirty years ago—long has informed my own thinking about the racialized forms in which colonial governance operates, as well as about both the unspoken and implicit distinctions in which racisms invest today.³ If Balibar has repeatedly directed us to its nuanced qualities and contemporary relevance, there are features of the term and the practices that it inhabits that deserve further examination now. What he has not sought to make explicit is why and how this term serves as a political concept to displace/replace/stand in for more typical conceptions of social difference and the legislation of fear that is animated to circumscribe person and polity.

"Interior frontiers" is a political concept to which we could turn to understand what sorts of sensibilities are recruited to produce hardening distinctions between who is "us" and who is construed as (irrevocably) "them"—features of governance, as we shall see, that work on multiple sentiments and across sliding scales. The term "interior frontiers" (*inners Grenzen*) first appeared in the thirteenth Address of Fichte's 1808 *Addresses to the German Nation*.⁴ Balibar consistently has rendered it in French as *frontière intérieure* and in English translations as "interior frontier" but also as "interior" or "internal border" or "boundary," as well.⁵

This "astonishing expression," as Balibar called it in a 1990 essay in which he focuses primarily on this term, derives its force from the "condensation of contradictions" that it offers; the term is "itself a symptom" of those very contradictory qualities. The border, he writes, is what encloses, imprisons, and puts in touch. It is a "site of passage," both an "obstacle" to movement, and the "starting point of expansion."⁶ We might specify that list of contradictions further: as sites of arrest and attenuated movement, of transgression and exchange.

But *internal* borders occupy more ambiguous and less visible sorts of spaces. They may divide the "interior of a territory or empire," "isolate" and thus "individualize it," and serve "as *expressions of the very constitution of the subject*."⁷ The oblique phrasing of that final clause (equally opaque in French and in English) is difficult to grasp, in part because it anticipates a fundamental feature of "internal borders." The clause bears vital weight, pointing us, still only implicitly, to the changing scale on which internal borders constitute subjects who do and will invest individually and collectively in them. If Fichte played skillfully on the term's multiple connotations, as Balibar suggests, then the latter has, as well. The politically affective charge of "interior borders" seems almost to suspend and secure the framing of a political condition in that very ambiguity.

Taking analytic advantage of this slippage between what becomes internal to both the person and the polity is a key to the term's diagnostic capacities and its incisive opening to political effects. "Interior frontiers" are malleable, situated, and responsive and have opaque power. The term itself, Balibar claims, embodies "the non-representable limit of every border, as it would be seen 'from within' its delineation."[8] This is not a bird's-eye view but a multiplex optic, a proximate and intimate one. It is a view from those hugging a border's edges and excluded from its protection—but, more pointedly, it is a view from those seeking security and refuge in its sheltered space.

Both elements of the concept—"interior" as modifying adjective, and "border" as mobile noun—gain their force from their polyvalence, from their variant referents. As such, the analytic challenge is to make room for both the tightening parameters of inclusion that such a term announces and the mobile practices to which it refers—exercises that a community and individuals practice on themselves. Potentially, the making and assertion of those interior frontiers confer belonging for some, estrangement for others—conjoining, adherence, and exclusions—neither sequentially in fixed order nor necessarily at the same time. Ambiguities about the sites, milieus, persons, and investments that "interior frontiers" seek to delineate and protect are themselves key features of the political, affective, and epistemic qualities that such a political concept may highlight and afford.

As we shall see, "interior frontiers" will provide a succession of vantage points from which to identify the making of the "stranger" in the matrix of citizen and subject formation. Not least, the concept blurs the distinction between political rationalities and the affective economy in which these designations of belonging and exclusion are lodged. Interior frontiers hover in the grey zone that makes the personal fundamentally political—fortifying the tenuous attachments that allow a "me" the sense of being part of a "we," an elemental feature in recruiting that "me" to invest in distinguishing between "us" and "them."

"Interior frontier" is more than a commanding concept in Balibar's work; he draws on it for decades (sometimes with similar emphasis, at times with different, even equivocal inflection in a score of texts). But even *prior* to its use as a political concept—and to even passing reference to the term itself—the problematic ambiguity that it addresses provides a thick thread through recurrent concerns in his work. One finds it invoked with respect to (1) the *dispositifs* that maintain inequalities; (2) the delineations of difference that inform the racialized issues and political "accents" on which he continues to press; and (3) the political logics that scramble citizen, stranger, enemy, and foreigner while they make securitization and fear more unreasoned if legible for us.[9]

Tracking the appearance of "interior frontier" in his talks and texts between 1984 and 2015 provides an occasion to situate the purchase that the concept's ambiguity yields, to identify the seemingly disparate scales that its filiations between person and polity make hard to untangle.[10] It disrupts any easy rendering of that which marks off an interior from an exterior, accentuating their conflation. For Balibar, "it brings to the fore . . . the classical aporias of interiority and exteriority." An "interior frontier" repeatedly raises not only the problematic of "purification"—and therefore a vigilance around the perceptions and practices that might lead to contamination—it foregrounds the very "uncertainty" of the distinctions on which those identities, precariously wrapped around a purest reasoning, so often depend.[11] These issues permeated Balibar's work before his use of the term, evident in the mid 1980s, when he was already working through what distinguishes "the interior" from "the "exterior," and why it politically mattered to pose the question: his trajectory is one that consistently probes the state's investment in casting the interior differentials of rights to the exterior frontiers that ricochet back to the interior again.

But earlier still, in 1981 (a time when racism was virtually banned from the French lexicon), he was on the track of a racism that was central to the making of modern France. Writing in *Nouvel Observateur*, he did more than condemn an endemic racism in the French Communist Party (of which he was a member until officially expelled, on the day after his text appeared). He called out an endemic racism in France, intimately tied to its colonial history and the resurgence of nostalgia for a "France for the French," just one symptom of what he was to call a "racist syndrome."[12]

BEWARE THOSE "INVISIBLE BONDS"

We might think to draw on the concept of "Interior frontier" with respect to the work it does: as a *political concept* whose fluctuating parameters mark diffracted histories of the present; as a *dispositif*, intangible and invisible but a viscerally central matrix of racialized states; and not least as a *diagnostic* of where and how sites of anxious *over*identification emerge. "Interior frontiers" is a concept that seeks to identify the conditions that depend on nurturing the intimately and fiercely held dispositions that those conditions solicit and on which they repeatedly call. As such, an interior frontier has a corporeal and affective quality. It is of body and mind: how one's body is disposed, where disgust is directed, shaping comportment and (dis)taste for what is imagined to make one discomforted and dis-eased.

How these "interior frontiers" are positioned—and where individuals fall vis-à-vis their gated space—marks some of the most consequential and violently guarded racial fault lines in our world today. For some, ready inclusion is easily conceived; for others—foreigners, those deemed "strangers," immigrants, children of immigrants born in France, and any persons at that moment defined as "dangerous"—those borders are checkpoints, and those checkpoints are for others trespassing warnings. No official papers are ever enough to guarantee passage, for interior frontiers are not secured by barbed wire but by unarticulated and often inaccessible conventions that grant no entry.

Those conventions may be boldly advertised, with easily decoded terms such as "family values" used in the service of police who "know" what family is, what kind of families count, and what living arrangements are considered abhorrent to (and beyond) any valuation. But paradoxically and crucially, whether invisible or displayed, the attributes of "interior frontiers" are made hard to decipher. They may be experienced as amorphous, narrow, and petty by those excluded, instilling more than *ressentiment*; rather, they can instill a categorical refusal to accept the required compromises demanded by what, in the end, will never really become the assurance of equity or of a refuge at all.

FICHTE'S USE OF THE TERM—AND BEYOND

Fichte developed the concept of "interior frontiers" at a specific moment and in a despairing context: as a summons to the defeated German nation on the brink of ruination following the Napoleonic Wars. Given as a series of lectures in Berlin in the winter of 1807–8, *Addresses to the German Nation* was a provocative call to take up moral arms rather than the militarized deadly weapons of war. Central to his visionary program, "interior frontiers" was to be a unifying concept, an enabling intervention, and indeed, by Balibar's account, a potentially radical one.

If in Fichte's hands, an interior frontier was a fortifying moral barricade against the erosion of the nation and self, one could be just as struck by its dark underside, by the raw and visceral and passionately protected distinctions that it has the potential to activate and install. I think here of racisms' intimate and surreptitious dwellings—bodily, affective, and in the flesh. Fichte's "Thirteenth Address to the German Nation" provides some sense of these multiple possibilities, which are worth attending to in his extended description and in his own words.

> The first, original, and truly natural boundaries of States are without any doubt their *internal frontiers* [*ihre inners Grenzen*]. Those who speak the same language are immediately and naturally linked by the very many *invisible bonds* to each other, prior to any human artifice [*kunst*]; they understand each other and are capable of continuously developing this understanding; *they belong together and are naturally one, an indivisible whole*. A people like this cannot desire to absorb [*in sich aufnehmen*] and integrate [*mit vermischen*] another of a different heritage [*abkunft*] and language

without at least initially confusing themselves and without profoundly disturbing the regular development of their culture. The outer demarcation of residence [dwelling] only follows as the consequences of this inner frontier, which is drawn by the intellectual nature of man himself.[13]

Italics may not really be needed here, but some of the claims are so strikingly dissonant with any notion of an inclusive polity that they seem to warrant added attention. (German) salvation here is sought in a nationalism generated out of this "multitude of invisible bonds."[14] A people is constituted for Fichte not by the borders of the territory they inhabit but because "they speak the same language."[15]

Balibar disrupts a facile reading to underscore two of Fichte's bold "displacements": one, Fichte's refusal to reckon descent through blood, and two, a rejection of language as a historical artifact. The strength of Fichte's insight, he insists, is that belonging is not derived from "the objectivity of language" in its originary cast but rather from how a language is "lived," "in the subjectivity of speech," coalescing in an "ethical attitude" and "reciprocal belonging."[16]

Balibar's interpretation of Fichte's "interior border" seems to take sustenance from the future possibility that it offers for fortifying moral responsibility, an internal "invincibility" that can forge "a new history."[17] It is here where the concept of the "interior border" holds political promise for him, describing this possibility as "its most profound import."[18] It is here where language is conceived as the "essence of the social bond." It not only provides the fabric of enduring connection: it "speaks in the first person" and, not least, embodies a spiritual training and moral education in which "an individual's interiorization of the patriotic community" is animated and lodged.[19] For Fichte, sensibility and feeling are linguistically tethered, ancestrally generated, nurtured in speech that adheres to the person and is community bound.[20]

But there is nothing inherently positive or inclusive about such attachments. On the contrary, Balibar halts here before the paradox that the internal border produces, entailing both "division and unity," "closure and opening." For the "border is no longer marking territorial spaces but a newly "constituted time" of "projection" and "the future." Warily, he notes that new "internal borders" emerge for Fichte in an educational system that "suppresses the differences between conditions" as it creates another "critical kind of internal border."[21]

And then on a more somber, prescient note, Balibar seems to hesitate; he asks "whether the whole education process does not tend to substitute for the historical division of social conditions, another division between the good and the wicked [*méchants*], an invisible border *between two species* of men."[22] That last sentence is chilling. We have moved from a utopian, unifying project to the potential for a racially defining, violent one. Balibar's cautionary observation might be considered anticipatory, as it remembers those categories of persons who are designated as disposable, exterminable, dangerous to the defense and well-being of society and the security of the state.[23] Even a passing familiarity with the racial inequalities both in French and US educational systems, employment, and housing leave little doubt where and how the racial geopolitics of these internal borders are drawn. *Homo academicus* displays its foundational grounding not only in a figure of *homo hierarchus* in bold relief; here, it portends one powerful Nietzschean installment of unequally valued human—and not-quite-human—kinds.

COLONIALISM, RACISM, AND INTERIOR FRONTIERS

So interior borders bear equivocal potentialities. They mark restrictive exclusions and new divisions, hierarchies of worth and privileged moral affiliation. Balibar's reanimation of the concept exceeds the prompt that Fichte provided, in part because of the ever more immediately divisive and discriminatory contexts in which he chooses to examine its contemporary application, consequences, and racialized effects.

The text published in 1990 is where the concept of "interior frontiers" is given its most analytic due, but he invokes the links between racism and "interior frontiers" five years earlier in two telling contexts: in a discussion of colonialism as an integral internal feature of French society and the French state, and in a discussion of the "interior" features of citizenship (in "Les habits neufs de la citoyenneté"), where it is prominently featured as a subtitle in a discussion of citizenship as a "property" in the double sense of the term, as "intimate character" of the person and as a legal disposition. In these discussions, citizens and subjects are distinguished not only legally but by "these interior frontiers" whose layout and outline" (*le trace*) is at once "mobile" and "constantly overdetermined": "The distribution of male and female roles, social rights, and distinctions between a national and foreigner" are all implicated in defining where the private begins and the public ends.[24] The domains that "interior frontiers" cover are illustrations. There is no analysis or explicit definition of the term.

"Interior frontier" appears again in 1985, but here with reference to an "interior *political* frontier" (*la frontière* politique *intérieure*) undergoing a critical historical shift on two fronts: it marks the distinction between citizen and subject and those kinds of people considered dangerous.[25] Balibar seems to invoke the term as if it were itself a political *dispositif* that creates new distributions and divisions: the "laboring classes" replaced by a category of *étrangers* (foreigners), of immigrants and colonized subjects, making race the divisive wedge.

But something else is afoot here, as well: the connotation of "interior" moves out (to describe segments of the population) and then is drawn in again to speak to character traits and characteristics of those personhoods that make them up. Tying these—if still obliquely—is a formulation of racism as the "psychic structure of the state."[26] For these are racialized identifications on which governance seizes and amplifies and through which states manage their microsites of control. If conceptualization emerges with the problematic in formation, the conceptual and political coordinates of interior frontiers are still subjacent, *avant le lettre*, an exacting examination of Fichte's use of the term.

It is no surprise that in 1987, in "Racism as Universalism," as Balibar's writing compresses more around racism and subcitizens, we find less an endorsement of the felicitous possibilities of "interior frontiers" than a dis-ease; as he notes, the "radicality" of Fichte's address "does not protect him against the more than ambiguous political implications of his doctrine."[27] For if racism is understood not as an additive or complement to nationalism but its product and fundamental infrastructural support, then the concept takes on another valence, one dependent on institutionalized inequalities and discriminations that internally divide not only subject and citizen but each among and within themselves.

"Double consciousness" in such a political frame may not only be the fate of those who are explicitly raced, as Du Bois argued.[28] A quite distinct double(d) consciousness may be the condition of those who endorse racism's unmarked signs to secure themselves. Europeans in the colonies were not unique in practicing a "politics of disregard," trafficking between claims to "ignorance" and practices of ignoring, accentuating the unease that comes with subscribing to the fictive worth of those distinctions.[29]

On first reading "Fichte et les frontières intérieures" in 1991, I was struck by its resonance with the colonial lexicons in which I worked: virtually every line of the text evoked what constituted the "invisible bonds" of white colonial privilege, the moral distinctions, and privileged cultural competencies that European colonials awkwardly relegated to and reserved for themselves.

The concept of *frontière intérieure* captured, in its almost oxymoronic quality, the sort of unspecified moral criteria used to distinguish which colonial subjects merited European equivalence in a court of law. That "merit" was fashioned by a particular kind of familiarity and comfort in European surroundings, one aided by child-rearing, schooling, domestic management and architecture, and Dutch proficiency, criteria deployed to bar those who did not display and could not sufficiently demonstrate that they felt adequately "at home" in a European milieu.

As striking as Fichte's very emphasis was in describing this intangible belonging as *les liens invisibles*, the very same phrase was used recurrently in Dutch and French colonial documents to assert who would be accorded the privileges of a white European status and who should not. These were part of an everyday that could be touched though unnamed, named but unseen.

The concept of "interior frontier" seems to reach equivocally for something more than mere affiliation: more an interior landscape of personhood responsive to—as it shapes—one's dispositions, one's "most private feelings," as Fichte put it, and attachments in the social world. The French and Dutch colonial archives seemed alive with animating and bounding those European interior frontiers at every turn. Thus, a colonial judge in Saigon could determine that a *métis* mixed-blood boy in the 1870s be tried (more severely) in a native rather than European court of law (despite having a European father) because he did not demonstrate the sort of visible and interior qualities that showed his love of country and moral respectability: he was illiterate in French, demonstrated no distaste for Germans (!), and seemed to speak only a few French words, with the added slur that his intimate relationship with his "alleged" French father of lowly origin may have been not parental but that of a sexual partner.[30] At issue is not the deed at all but the kind of person charged.

The convergence between Fitchte's aim to fortify these interior frontiers was based in part on the ethical qualities of participating in a speech community, and colonial projects designed to secure racialized governance were probably not as similar as I imagined them to be at the time of that first, startling encounter with the concept so many years ago. But one could also imagine the opposite: that the colonial archives offered unusual clarity on a historical and academic artifice in which metropolitan and colonial social grammars of exclusion could not be viewed on common ground. Contrary to that convention, both were powerful "interior frontiers" in the making: the category of European embellished for and by imperial pursuits, the category of internal enemy emerging out of those racialized frontiers.

But perhaps as much insight into the political critique that Balibar deploys the concept to do takes us back to those earlier 1985 texts in which he describes how citizenship operates to insure and then declare a whole range of people, mostly from former French colonies and protectorates, "inassimilable," differences created and maintained between "real French stock" (*Français de souche*) and *les immigrés*, despite the fact that most of the latter had and have long been legally French. He asks whether, if citizenship is based on a principle of exclusion, it is not only a *right* but a *status*, neither fixed nor permanent, present "by degrees."[31] Here, the term *frontières intérieures* of citizenship does some of that work to account for this process of granting and withholding the tools for acquisition, incremental success at mastering and/or succumbing to conventions, by "degrees."[32]

A BORDER IS NOT A LINE

Two moves add further ballast to the term, intensifying its relevance as a concept in its own right for contemporary political thought, as Balibar elaborates it in an even more compelling direction. Several years after "Fichte et les frontières intérieures," he makes a striking move, invoking the observations of the well-known (renegade Lacanian) French psychiatrist André Green's understanding of what constitutes a border in the treatment of madness.[33] In a bold, astute, and somewhat precarious leap of imagination, Balibar draws on Green's psychoanalytic treatment of "limit cases" and "borderline patients."

Balibar seizes on Green's observations about "the border" and the "line," recognizing an indubitable insight that makes another kind of sense. In Green's rendition, a border is a "line of demarcation that is never a 'line'" but "a vast territory where no precise division allows for the separation between what is [madness] and what is not."[34] In Balibar's rendering, the concept of "interior frontier" does away with what he rightly has called the "state fiction" that a border is a "line." There are no clearly demarcated or fixed lines to cross, where the "other side" provides immunity. An interior frontier depends on a messier set of attributes and occupies a less identifiable place. It bridges and makes a case for plural interior borders of person and polity.

Conceptually and concretely, an "interior frontier" defines the contours of a protective and precarious threshold more than it does a line. Instead of a border as a "line," we might think instead of thick and narrow corridors (replete with compartments, sensibilities, sensory aversions, dress, and speech) ill-perceived and unarticulated but not ill-defined—where the standards of normalization and defiance are at war and, as it were, on the line.

With intangible sensibilities and immeasurable measure, interior frontiers seem to share some kinship with that to which Raymond Williams once sought to turn our collective attention, namely, to those inchoate "structures of feeling" at "the very edge of semantic availability"—where feeling (experienced as fear, humiliation, threat, longing, or shame) is not opposed to political thought but indexical of a positioning in the making. Structures of feeling are not fixed in ideology but in solution, emergent in a space (like that of interior frontiers) that is intimate and political, active in the making of personhood, social complicity, and political affiliation.[35]

"INTERIORITIES" AND PERSONHOODS ON THE LINE

> One can be a citizen or stateless but it is difficult to imagine that one is a frontier.[36]

Dismantling the state fiction that borders are clear-cut lines reorients Balibar's analysis. But the second insight that he amplifies about one of Green's most striking and prescient statements is more profound: As Green writes, "One can be a citizen or stateless but it is difficult to imagine that one is a frontier." In this single stark phrase, Green shatters the parameters of the term. "Having a frontier" is not the same as "being one."

Balibar astutely attends, asking whether it is in just such a condition, in what Green calls a "no-man's land" where so many people live, "that affect up close their 'being' in as much they are subject to being neither in a physical, legal, and psychic space that is neither 'this nor that [*ni ceci, ni cela*]'".[37] And then with the clarity of that insight in hand, he poses rhetorical political questions: Is it really only on the margins of society, the *banlieue*, where this frontier is recognized and drawn? Or is it more so that "the parties, the nations, the regions that we have habitually come to consider as *having* borders, themselves are ones?"[38]

What is actually "interior" and "internal" about an "interior frontier" remains intentionally ambiguous and an open problematic in Balibar's writing: not least because it serves as a critical diagnostic of how persons are shaped into political subjects, as well as serving as a *dispositif* of governance. Circling cautiously around these issues, he both addresses and skirts how states harness individuals' affective ties and marshals the distinctions that make up who they imagine themselves to be, who they need to be to secure presence and dwelling, what they need to master to know they belong in their surroundings, and, not least, what they need to master in themselves.

In returning to the adjective "internal" or "interior," the "internal" moves analytically again and its political potential transforms. More demands are put on other "polysemic" features of the internal with a slight shift of political grammar: "interior" slides from adjective to an active verb, a set of practices and affective attachments imposed on and embraced by those precariously perched or comfortably settled on this toxic frontier. Of more issue is what is "interiorized by individuals" and "internalized" in citizens, subjects, and the stateless, who are never completely managed by the institutions of the state.[39]

With this semiotic shift, the internal border is rendered with more substance, equally shaped by and defined through the dispositions and habits of those who relish its delineations and by those who are relegated to its outside and on whom it bears. The "border" neither looks nor feels the same for the two. Relations of power and asymmetrical force assure that interior landscapes are implicated in the emotional economy on which enmity and fear are animated and secure their central place.

"Frontiers of Europe" (1993) marks a return to *frontière intérieure*, called out here as one of Fichte's "decisive formulations."[40] Two alternative formulations (offered in parentheses) suggest further rethinking about how to render what transpires in this space. The first is *frontières intériorisées*—by now a familiar if slightly variant formulation. The second, *frontières pour l'intériorité*, is awkwardly phrased.[41] What work might these supplemental recastings of the concept do that requires these two seemingly distinct qualifications? The first turns us to how persons in a polity construe these treasured delineations and *take them in as features of themselves*. But in the second, "frontiers for interiority," the "for" suggests another charge: an "interiority"—that is, a sense of one's worth that invokes the boundary/border as a stabilizing force, providing the psychic ballast that one might not otherwise have the means to garner. This is what Balibar seems to be reaching for when he writes more incisively several years later of "the subjective interiorization of the idea of the border—the way individuals represent their place in the world to themselves . . . by tracing in their imaginations *impenetrable* borders between groups to which they belong."[42]

Here, the imagined protective border joins the cultivation of a body politic that is secured through a "cultivation of the self." Such "symbolic differences" (as Balibar calls them) are not in the service of flourishing communal well-being (as Foucault described those of ancient Greece).[43] This is rather what I call a "circumscribed civility" whose participation for some people is categorically foreclosed.[44] "Impenetrable" seals too dark a fate. It is not a community to which anyone should wish to belong.

AT THE HEART OF CIVIC SPACE

Such a regime of truth has ugly consequences: Balibar will now, in 1996, identify these effects as "ultra subjective forms of violence," nourished in this darkened space. In these corridors of *la limite* and its "extreme" forms of expression, blockades are installed.⁴⁵ Specific institutional installations of violence remain central. But Balibar will once again call on Green to identify them more ominously again where an "idealization of hatred," as he understands Green to be suggesting, prevails:

> a process of psychotic cast, that, at the level of collective behavior, is integrally bound up with the fluctuating representations of the enemy, who is both potential victim and mimetic persecutor, or the fetishized Other (this also holds for imaginary constructs of the "races," whether superior or inferior).⁴⁶

In this vision, those expulsed are rendered as "disposable waste," whereas the "fetishized figure of 'us'—embodied in interior frontiers—is reduced to a fiction of 'absolute homogeneity.'" This socially damaging vision is not the making of those diminished by precarity and of weakened will alone. Interior frontiers gain their leverage because they are inscribed in the "naturalization of domination," a formula that Balibar attributes to the joined lexicon of Marx and Foucault.⁴⁷

One might think here with Edward Said's political concept "imaginative geography," which so productively and emotionally bifurcates what is deemed a threat (in his case, Islam) and what is not, a formulation of space and a "method," as he puts it, "of controlling what seems to be a threat to some established view of things."⁴⁸ This "imaginative" geography should be specified further: it is an affectively inscribed and ultimately violent material, one that distributes what I can care about, what invokes my moral disgust, and what and who falls outside the reasonable purview of my morally founded concerns.

On the cusp of the twenty-first century, Balibar accelerates and intensifies his condemnation of the political work done by the border. It is further indicted and renamed.⁴⁹ Nowhere has he stated it so boldly: the border, *la limite*, is "the wholly nondemocratic condition of democratic institutions." A key displacement is underscored: the border is "accepted, sanctified and interiorized" and transported from the exterior "to the *middle of political space*."⁵⁰ One is reminded of Nicos Poulantzas's 1978 treatment of "the internal enemy" as that which is amplified when and where the "frontiers of the national space" are "internalized" and "at the heart of that space itself."⁵¹

Note here that the making of "interior frontiers" can never be just a state project and a manipulation on high alone. Emerging at the "*heart of civic space*," they may create an invisible geography, marking out who can walk which streets without feeling "out of place," who can stand on a street corner without being suspect, narrowing down the spaces that one has the right to inhabit or in which one can feel "at home." In the United States, racecraft, as Barbara and Karen

Fields describe it, shapes the places where one is rendered "unsafe"—or is considered "unsafe" for others.[52] Selective surveillance and racialized punishment precede incarceration. Loïc Wacquant puts it precisely and takes it further, arguing that in the United States, "race is a civic felony."[53]

The analytic traction of attending to "internal borders" reappears with new force as Balibar sets out not only to mark Europe as itself a borderland but also to point to a hardening of internal borders threatened by the prospect of European citizenship, such that

> the category of the "national" (or the *self*, of what it requires to be the same) also becomes split and subject to the dissolving action of "internal borders" which mirror the global inequalities [with] disturbing resurgences of traditional patterns of exclusion.[54]

There are not only those who are unassimilated but increasing numbers who are rendered unassimilable (as if all want to be): on the one hand, with the designation of "foreign" and the category of (forever) foreigner assigned by those making an effort to bolster traditional "interior frontiers"; on the other hand, those demanding equal citizenship rights in law and in the everyday, which may manifest as the right to remain different (and defiantly indifferent) to the normative regulations of cultural and nationalized convention.

The lathe of the concept is turned once again to ask whether the "marks of belonging" that are "retrieved in the individual" and "interiorized by him" produce a "countereffect" or what we might describe as the underside of those designations.[55] Interiors and exteriors are turned inside out. That "countereffect" of belonging is "the *stranger* as *other* within[,] . . . an intruder, out of place." This *internal other* provides negative contour in everyday life to "interior frontiers."

But we should not imagine that what is rendered as "foreign" and "strange" and unseemly is always raced, or only so. There are "different modalities of *'contradicting' the norm*, i.e., of destroying normality or deviating from it."[56] In turning from Fichte to Foucault, the "interiorized border" between the criminal and deviant, between being socially wayward versus physically homeless, being "at risk" or "a risk" is made into a moral and dangerously political space. The potential criminal is deemed deviant, mobilizing a surveillance and security regime sanctioned by the legitimized mandate, as Foucault put it, to defend society (against itself).[57]

ON VISCOSITY AND "INTERIOR FRONTIERS"

Balibar's relentless efforts to identify the "extraordinarily viscous" and potentially vicious features of interior borders stop somewhat short of at least one of

Green's observations about such borders. In "The Concept of *La Limite*," Green asks what the limit of a person is, conjuring the intrusions and transgressions that racialized relations inflict on those subsumed by them, by those on whom they are imposed, and by those who claim their truths. Green makes no reference to Fanon as far as I know, but his conclusions are not that different from what Fanon saw as the psychic scars of a racial colonial machine burned into the future of Europe, and into the permeable membrane that is the flesh.

When we imagine the limit of a person, Green writes, it is the envelope of the skin that immediately comes to mind.[58] But no, he reminds us, the skin is discontinuous and porous. The tissue of flesh is interrupted by other tissues, it is full of holes (*il est troué*) that act as gates or better as custom inspectors, he writes: "eyes [the suspicious gaze]," "ears [unwelcome music as irritant/noise]," "nose [cooking smells rendered repugnant]," "mouth, anus, genitalia." At issue for Green are two problems: the "consistency and the structure of the border" and "circulation in and out of its gates." "But what are the frontiers of my psyche?" he asks.

Several types of borders are encountered in nature: lines or surfaces with or without circulation through the frontier, or an osmotic membrane, which affords communication with an adequate selection of what has to be taken in or kept out, or, if there is trouble, what has to be rejected, what is unwelcome inside, and finally, a blurred division in some state of intersection, a border resembling the meeting of two clouds. In case of danger, an osmotic border can open up to unburden the inside from the troublesome stimuli. But other measures are possible: for instance, the stultification of the line, a kind of mortification, or the blurring of the border, creating instead a fragile limit, a no-man's-land.[59]

In attending to "rigidification," "sclerosis," "the jamming of frontiers," Green seems to be anticipating what has become our collective, securitized present, speaking as though in a future conditional tense. His observation forebodes and offers more to reflect upon:

> To be a borderline implies that a border protects one's self from crossing over or from being crossed over, from being invaded, and thus becoming a *moving border* (not *having*, but *being* such a border). This in turn implies a loss of distinction between *space* and *time*.[60]

This is a disturbing passage on many counts, not only because it revamps the work that this making of an interior border does—it does not entail work *on* a body but rather *through* one. Bodily exposures are part and parcel of the interior frontier as a *dispositif*. And what of this "loss of distinction between space and time"? Does submission to the command compress into a transgression of my body and senses? One might think with Jacques Rancière here about *la partage du sensible* (the distribution/division/sharing of the sensible)[61]—or of Judith Butler's senses of the subject, the invocation of partitions, impingements, willfully and unwillingly imposed on a subject, reminding us that no selves can be fully subsumed or hermetically sealed.[62] If Green leans on the metaphor of territorial borders to make his case, he does so to emphasize permeabilities, invasions, contaminations, fissures, penetrations from which one has no ready exit and from which one cannot be immune.[63]

It is obviously not only in our present moment when interior frontiers are fortifying at the expense of others. Still, what Mbembe might consider as part of the "inversion" of democracy is occurring on a new globalizing imperial scale.[64] We live in a racial emporium that both exceeds nation-states as it instills ever-more expansive and intimate xenophobias. At issue is what forms of sociality might produce common refuge rather than anxious retrenchment. For no matter how well understood the conceptual matrix in which these internal and internalized distinctions are drawn, we are still left to learn more about their vernacular making. They inhere in things, feelings, infrastructural arrangements—in visual images, decibel levels, and aesthetic conventions and in what is misconstrued as the innocuity of common sense.

The colloquial form that these battles take are deceptively straightforward: there is a "we" who no longer feel comfortable and feel safely "at home," a *nous sommes plus chez nous* heard on the lips of more than *Front National* supporters. "We are where we belong and at home" (*nous sommes chez nous*), the response of a defiant citizenry born in North Africa and in France.[65] "Home" is invoked or rather erupts again with *pas de jungle chez nous* (no refugees, no squatter/refugee/gypsy encampments in our backyards) when the Calais refugee camp was dismantled in fall 2016. Not least, it reverberates among the well-mannered populace in small Dutch towns, in Iowa's high school hallways, on the wrestling team of a prestigious New York City university (Columbia), and at a self-declared poorly endowed progressive one (the New School). In each of these locations, some students felt licensed and emboldened to shout (as the French would put it, with no compunction, *decomplexifié*) "Go home where you belong."

Home figures again and again for those who spend so much of their lives in passage, pretending to want to "pass" just to be able to get through a frontier or guarded zone. As Balibar notes, "passing and repassing" occur "at the mercy of expulsions and familial regroupings" through this "viscous spatio-temporal zone."[66] With homing in and closing in such distinctive features of interior frontiers, their mirror image is dark. It is no surprise, then, that those frontiers can emerge as such a hollow space, as Balibar comes to understand: it is "almost a home—a home in which to live a life which is a waiting-to-live, a non-life."[67]

These designations and demarcations of what is and who can be at home are colloquial and familiar, but they have a history that is colonial through and through. The entire French military security apparatus conceived in the 1950s to control an "inferiorized" internal population, as Mathieu Rigouste argues, has now been imposed on an inferiorized interiorized immigrant population, most of whom are not immigrants but French citizens.[68] But the colonial figure of the "undesirable element," as the Dutch called those colonized, seen as a threat, or potential threat to colonial authority, and that of the "internal enemy," as the French called them, have a much longer history. That we know.

Note how the distinction between the terms, which are mutually defining, superimposed, overlapping, are hard to maintain: "Internal enemies" are figured on the qualities that make for "internal frontiers"; the "stranger" and the "enemy," as Balibar notes, are dangerously confused.[69] "Internal strangers" are a threat to "interior borders"; there is "growing confusion," as Balibar puts it, between the "internal stranger [and] the "internal enemy," and between the "internal stranger" and the "foreigner."[70] Each of these figures (and they are figures fashioned of fear) is traced out by the movement of what a citizenry takes to be its indubitable and defining features.[71]

What we seem to know less about are the ruinous qualities of life that these interior frontiers foster—the ultimate *pharmakon* of curative and corrosive, protective and poisonous qualities that they are. Although altered in density, composition, and form, they are spaces of refracted ruination, the dark, infrared corridors on which divisions rely. In *Let Us Now Praise Famous Men*, James Agee described impoverished white tenant families in the American South in the 1930s for whom there was no possibility of a buffered self—persons assaulted and slandered by a system that produced "slendering of forms of freedom" over the course of their lives.[72]

We might consider whether such "slendering" degrees of freedom in our hypercommodified world of fictive choice may manifest in the negative space of "interior frontiers." Are such frontiers given sustenance among those who experience the obscene inequalities in which we live as providing fewer buffers, and no buffered self? Interior frontiers puncture possibilities by assuring that the *unheimlich*, the strange, the stranger, the not familiar, too familiar, is an assault or potential assault on "feeling at home," and that no matter where one falls in this space, there is no safety or security. It is buttressed by a vicious fantasy that freedom comes from stronger barricades rather than the embrace of what Hegelians would call a radical dependency of us all.

NOTES

1. The epigraph to this essay is from Étienne Balibar, "The Infinite Contradiction," trans. Jean-Marc Poisson and Jacques Lezra, *Yale French Studies* 88 (1995): 147; it was originally presented at the jury for promotion to Research Director, January, 16, 1993.

I thank Jay Bernstein, Michel Féher, Lawrence Hirschfeld, Adi Ophir, Richard Rechtman, Mathieu Renault, and Diogo Sardinha for their queries as I prepared this essay, as well as those offered at the occasions where this essay was presented: the Political Concepts Conference, "Balibar Edition," Brown University, November 2016; the History of Science Department, Harvard University, November 2016; Bertrand Oglivie's philosophy seminar at Paris 8, March 8, 2017; and Journée d'Études on "Race et Migration," Sorbonne, April 2017.

2. On the fact that the Front National in France, and the Le Pen "phenomenon" were not "marginal" twenty years ago, nor was he *nul* (a hopeless nothing, of no import) but already recruiting political sensibilities and xenophobic dispositions that were already entrenched and firmly French, see Ann Laura Stoler, "Racist Visions and the Common Sense of France's 'Extreme' Right," in *Duress: Imperial Durabilities in Our Times* (Durham, N.C.: Duke University Press, 2016), 269–304.

3. My first use of the term is in Ann Laura Stoler, "Sexual Affronts and Racial Frontiers," *Comparative Studies in Society and History* 34, no. 3 (1992): 514–51; revised and published in Ann Laura Stoler, *Carnal Knowledge and Imperial Power: Race and the Intimate in Colonial Rule* (Berkeley: University of California Press, 2002). Balibar's most extensive engagement with the term appears in "Fichte et la frontière intérieure: A propos des *Discours à la nation allemande*," *Cahiers de Fontenay* 58/59 (June 1990): 57–81, repr. in Étienne Balibar, *La crainte des masses: Politique et philosophie avant et après Marx* (Paris: Galilée, 1997), 131–56. For the English translation, see Étienne Balibar, "Fichte and the Internal Border: On *Addresses to the German Nation*," in *Masses, Classes, Ideas: Studies on Politics and Philosophy before and after Marx*, trans. James Swenson (New York: Routledge, 1994), 61–84.

4. Throughout this text, I will refer to Johann Gottlieb Fichte, *Addresses to the German Nation*, trans. Isaac Nakhimovsky, Bela Kapossy, and Keith Tribe (Cambridge, UK: Hackett, 2013). However, other (earlier) translations have been consulted and are mentioned, as well.

5. It should be noted that "border" and "frontier" are used interchangeably for the thirty years of Balibar's texts covered in this essay. One could imagine a generative distinction with use of "frontier" marking a more intensely racialized imperial history than "border" usually invokes. But our concern here is with the "interior" and

"internal" qualities of these divisions, and that is where the analytic traction lies, to my mind. In any case, as late as 2014, the two terms are not distinguished, even as he turns to an explicit conceptualization of the "phenomenology of the border" most recently to date in "At the Borders of Europe: From Cosmopolitanism to Cosmopolitics," *Translation* (Spring 2014): 83–103.

6. Balibar, "Fichte and the Internal Border," 63.

7. Balibar, "Fichte and the Internal Border," 63.

8. Balibar, "Fichte and the Internal Border," 63.

9. This is not to suggest a deliberate calibration on each of the inflections that he has given to the term. Nor does it matter to my task. I am more interested in the richness of the concept as a political one that slips between the political and psychic spaces of power, as it reflects the actual quotidian ways in which racialized differences envelop the social relations and personhoods through and on which they work.

10. In dating his use of the term, I often refer to the date of presentation of the text rather than to its final publication or later translation.

11. The full quotation reads as follows: "This expression [interior border] brings to the fore all the classical aporias of interiority and exteriority. In the context of a reflection on the identity of a people, of a nation . . . it necessarily refers to a problematic of this identity, the way in which the 'inside' can be penetrated or adulterated by its relation with the 'outside' which here we will call the foreign" (Balibar, "Fichte and the Internal Border," 63).

12. Étienne Balibar, *Les frontières de la démocratie* (Paris: Découverte, 1992), 19–34; Étienne Balibar and Yves Benot, "Suffrage universel!," *Le Monde* (May 4, 1983). "Suffrage universel!" was published in response to the *Front National*'s "break through" in regional elections.

13. Fichte, *Addresses to the German Nation*, 158; my emphasis. Other translations give a slightly different sense to this last sentence. Thus a 1923 translation reads: "From this internal boundary, which is drawn by the spiritual nature of man himself, the marking of the external boundary by dwelling-place results as a consequence; and in the natural view of things it is not because men dwell between certain mountains and rivers that they are a people, but, on the contrary, *men dwell together . . . because they were a people already by a law of nature* which is much higher" (Johann Gottlieb Fichte, *Addresses to the German Nation*, trans. R. F. Jones and G. H. Turnbull [Chicago: Open Court, 1922], 224; my emphasis).

14. The extensive debates among French and Anglophone political theorists on the nature of Fichte's brand of nationalism as chauvinist or cosmopolitan, are only broached in this essay with respect to the concept of "interior frontiers." See Isaac Nakhimovsky's Introduction to Fichte's *Addresses to the German Nation*, in which he presents Fichte's proposals as a salutary set of "moral limits on power politics" (xxvi); for a review of the arguments, see Arish Abizadeh, "Was Fichte an Ethnic Nationalist?:

On Cultural Nationalism and Its Double," *History of Political Thought* 26, no. 2 (Summer 2005): 334–59.

15. Balibar, "Fichte and the Internal Border," 78.

16. Balibar, "Fichte and the Internal Border," 78–79.

17. Balibar, "Fichte and the Internal Border," 66.

18. Balibar, "Fichte and the Internal Border," 81.

19. Balibar, "Fichte and the Internal Border," 82–83.

20. This affective charge is even more pronounced in Fichte's Fourth Address: "This language goes deep into *the most private feelings of the individual's thoughts and wishes*, limiting or giving them free rein; it binds together all those who speak it into one common understanding; it is the *true mutual junction of the world of sense and of spirit*, merging them into one such that it is *no longer possible to say to which it belongs*" (Fichte, *Addresses to the German Nation*, 55).

21. Balibar, "Fichte and the Internal Border," 82.

22. Balibar, "Fichte and the Internal Border," 83.

23. On persons made disposable, see Bertrand Ogilvie, *L'homme jetable: Essai sur l'exterminisme et la violence extrême* (Paris: Editions Amsterdam, 2012). Somewhat surprisingly, Balibar does not take that racially inflected direction as he does in so much of his writing before and after 1990. In fact, he names those "two species of men" as "those who live in egotism and those who live in the realm of the spirit" (Balibar, "Fichte and the Internal Border," 83). I would draw on his phrase "two species of men" more literally, as he himself does a decade later, when he writes of racial discourses as attempts at interpreting "differences within the human species" and at defining what and who is "properly human" in relation to "the possibility of the inhuman." See Étienne Balibar, "Election/Selection" (keynote speech, tRACEs: Race, Deconstruction, and Critical Theory conference, University of California Irvine, April 10–11, 2003, https://vimeo.com/album/1631670/video/25691025 published as Étienne Balibar, "Election/sélection," in *Derrida*, ed. Marie-Louise Mallet and Ginette Michaud (Paris: L'Herne, 2004), 226–31.

24. Balibar says, "On voit que la notion juridique et para-juridique de citoyenneté est indissociable non seulement d'un espace constitutionnel (territoire, souveraineté) relativement clos, mais aussi de ses frontières intérieures, dont le tracé, mouvant, est constamment surdéterminé. La limite du 'public' et du 'privé' telle que la dessine la distribution des rôles masculins et féminins, la zone névralgique du 'droit social' . . . opposition du 'national' et de l'étranger" (Balibar, *Frontières de la démocratie*, 105).

25. Balibar, *Frontières de la démocratie*, 93; in this instance of the term's appearance, Fichte is not cited.

26. The French reads, "une structure psychique d'Etat" (Balibar, *Frontières de la démocratie*, 87).

27. Étienne Balibar, "Racism as Universalism," *New Political Science* 8, nos. 1–2 (September 1989): 9–22; this essay was originally delivered in 1988 at the New School for Social Research.

28. W. E. B. Du Bois, *The Souls of Black Folk*, ed. Brent Hayes Edwards (1903; Oxford, UK: Oxford University Press, 2007), 8–10.

29. This point is elaborated in Ann Laura Stoler, *Along the Archival Grain* (Princeton: Princeton University Press, 2009), 236–78.

30. On this case, see Ann Laura Stoler, "Sexual Affronts and Racial Frontiers: Cultural Competence and the Dangers of Métissage" [1992], in *Carnal Knowledge and Imperial Power* (2002; Berkeley: University of California Press, 2010), 79–111.

31. Balibar, *Frontières de la démocratie*, 113.

32. Balibar, *Frontières de la démocratie*, 109–23, 113.

33. Balibar, *Crainte des masses*, 381–95; see also André Green, *La folie privée: Psychanalyse des cas-limites* (Paris: Gallimard, 1990), which was published in English as *On Private Madness* (London: Hogarth Press, 1986).

34. Green, *Folie privée*, 104, 105.

35. Raymond Williams, *Marxism and Literature* (London: Tavistock, 1973), 134.

36. André Green, "Le concept de limite," in *La folie privée*, 107, quoted in Balibar, *Crainte des masses*, 383.

37. Balibar, *Crainte des masses*, 383. The French anthropologist Gérard Althabe made a similar observation with respect to the relationship between the rise of the FN, the precarity of "popular classes," and the racism directed at those designated as "the Maghrébins" when he wrote in *Production de l'étranger, xénophobie et couches populaires* (1985; Paris: Sorbonne, 2017) that, turned out from French society, they "camped at [its] doors, and constituted its frontier" (31).

38. Balibar, *Crainte des masses*, 383.

39. Balibar, *Crainte des masses*, 374.

40. Balibar, *Crainte des masses*, 388.

41. Balibar, *Crainte des masses*, 388.

42. Étienne Balibar, "At the Borders of Europe" [1999], in *We, the People of Europe?: Reflections on Transnational Citizenship*, trans. James Swenson (Princeton: Princeton University Press 2003), 8; my emphasis.

43. Balibar, *Crainte des masses*, 389; see Michel Foucault, *The Government of the Self and Others: Lectures at the Collège de France 1982–1983*, ed. Frédéric Gros, trans. Graham Burchell (New York: Picador, 2010); and Michel Foucault, *History of Sexuality*, vol. 2, *The Use of Pleasure*, trans. Robert Hurley (New York: Vintage Books, 1990).

44. Balibar, *Crainte des masses*, 389.

45. Étienne Balibar, "Émancipation, transformation, civilité," *Les temps modernes*, no. 587 (May 1996): 438.

46. Étienne Balibar, *Violence and Civility: On the Limits of Political Philosophy*, trans. G. M. Goshgarian (New York: Columbia University Press, 2015), 60–61. This text is based on his 1996 Wellek Library Lectures, delivered at the University of California, Irvine.

47. Balibar, "Émancipation, transformation, civilité," 439.

48. Edward Said, *Orientalism* (New York: Random House, 1978), 59.

49. Étienne Balibar, "World Borders, Political Borders," trans. Erin M. Williams, *PMLA* 117, no. 1 (2002): 71–78.

50. Balibar, "World Borders, Political Borders," 71–78.

51. Nicos Poulantzas, *State, Power, Socialism*, trans. Patrick Camiler (London: Verso, 1978).

52. Barbara and Karen Fields, *Racecraft: The Soul of Inequality in American Life* (New York: Verso, 2012).

53. Loïc Wacquant, "Race as Civic Felony," *International Social Science Journal* 57, no. 183 (March 2005): 127–42.

54. Étienne Balibar, "Europe as Borderland" [2004], *Economic Planning and Social Space* 27, no. 2 (2009): 201.

55. Étienne Balibar, "Civic Universalism and Its Internal Exclusions: The Issue of Anthropological Difference," *boundary 2* 39, no. 1 (2012): 215.

56. Balibar, "Civil Universalism," 212.

57. Michel Foucault, "About the Concept of the 'The Dangerous Individual,' in 19th-Century Legal Psychiatry," *International Journal of Law and Psychiatry* 1 (1978): 1–16; Michel Foucault, *Il faut défendre la société: Collège de France lectures* (Paris: Gallimard, 1976).

58. Indeed, that the skin not only is a "physiological envelope" but "has a psychological function which permits containing, delimiting, putting in contact and inscribing" is the insight of Didier Anzieu in his *Le moi-peau* (Paris: Editions Dunod, 1985). As Guy Lesoeurs wrote in his brief introduction to Anzieu's book, "the skin, through its sensorial properties retains a determinant role in the relationship to the other" (62).

59. Green, *On Private Madness*, 63.

60. Green, *On Private Madness*, 63.

61. Jacques Rancière, *Dissensus: On Politics and Aesthetics*, ed. and trans. Steven Corcoran (London: Bloomsbury, 2010), 44.

62. Judith Butler, *Senses of the Subject* (New York: Fordham University Press, 2015).

63. See Ann Laura Stoler, "Introduction: The Dark Logic of Invasive Others," *Social Research* 84, no. 1 (Spring 2017): 3–5; see also the essays in this special issue of *Social Research*, "Invasive Others," edited by Arien Mack and Miriam Ticktin.

64. Achille Mbembe, *Politique de l'inimités* (Paris: La découverte, 2015), 62.

65. See also Thomas Chatterton Williams, "The French Origins of 'You Will Not Replace Us': The European Thinkers behind the White-Nationalist Rallying Cry," *New Yorker* (December 4, 2017): 24–30, https://www.newyorker.com/magazine/2017/12/04/the-french-origins-of-you-will-not-replace-us.

66. Balibar, *Crainte des masses*, 379.

67. Balibar, *Crainte des masses*, 379.

68. Mathieu Rigouste, *L'ennemi intérieur: La généalogie coloniale et militaire de l'ordre sécuritaire dans la France contemporaine* (Paris: La découverte, 2009.)

69. Étienne Balibar, "Strangers as Enemies: Further Reflections on the Aporias of Transnational Citizenship" (working paper, Institute on Globalization and the Human Condition, McMaster University, March 2006), https://globalization.mcmaster.ca/research/publications/working-papers/2006/ighc-wps_06-4_balibar.pdf.

70. Étienne Balibar, "Can We Say: After the Subject Comes the Stranger?" (lecture, Thinking with Balibar, Columbia University, November 2014), https://www.youtube.com/watch?v=ACaXH-WW6Fo.

71. Akeel Bilgrami's insight that subjective identity is that without which I would no longer be whom I conceive myself to be, something that "one ought not to revise," sets out a moving target and complicates the temporality of subject formation with respect to interior frontiers (Akeel Bilgrami, "Identity," *Political Concepts: A Critical Lexicon* [New York: Fordham University Press, 2018]), 1. As Judith Butler will claim, identity is responsive to changing notions of whom I think I am in a present that is shaped by what I had wanted to be and could have been, and in relation to what acts upon me (Judith Butler, *Senses of the Subject* [New York: Fordham University Press, 2015], 8).

72. James Agee, *Let Us Now Praise Famous Men* (1939; Boston: Houghton Mifflin, 2001), 96.

MATERIALISM

Patrice Maniglier

The concept I have chosen is not just one political concept among others; it is the concept of the politicality of concepts in general. This concept is *materialism*. Some might object that it is not a political but rather a metaphysical concept, and even that it is not a concept at all but rather a doctrine that is a system of concepts, or maybe just an Idea or an orientation of thought. I argue that materialism is a political concept precisely because it bears on what is political in metaphysics in general, metaphysics being understood here and elsewhere in this essay as the exercise in constructing and exploring conceptual consistencies.

There has been renewed interest lately in the notion of materialism in the wake of what is now called "speculative realism." Notably, Quentin Meillassoux's own expression for his philosophical position is not speculative realism but "speculative materialism"; and the recent interest in François Laruelle's work is because of his attempt to formulate a materialist position.[1] That interest flows mainly from Meillassoux's argument that pure speculation (the mere use of concepts) is, in spite of Kant's critique, capable of saying something objectively true, and this truth would establish the independent existence of something radically alien to thought (i.e., matter). Some have lamented the apolitical dimension of this new philosophical fashion.[2] They might be right, but I think they miss the deeper problem raised by materialism, which the very notion of speculative materialism erases, namely, the problem of the role of metaphysics in politics in general. More specifically, that we cannot do away with metaphysics, and metaphysics cannot do away with politics. This is what should be at the heart of any form of speculative materialism properly understood.

The importance of Étienne Balibar's work in contemporary philosophy is, in my view, to have constantly maintained those two requirements, and the following lines are an attempt not to comment on Balibar's thought generally but to characterize the problematic within which his work, precisely, *works*.

These preliminary remarks also answer, I hope, the worry that materialism might not be a concept. Materialism is the concept of a *task*. Identifying clearly this task is, I believe, urgent, if we want to know where we are going. Concepts matter for practice, because they help diagnose our problems.

DOGMATIC MATERIALISM

The idea that materialism has something to do with politics might seem obvious to many of us, since the notion was used by Marx as well as many others in the history of Marxism and of the communist regimes (in particular through infamous expressions such as "dialectical materialism" or "historical materialism"). However, we should refrain from taking this connection for granted. It is far from being universally accepted. For instance, the entry "materialism" in the *Encyclopedia Britannica* contains not one mention of the word "politics." The *Britannica* defines "materialism" as a synonym of physicalism, and does so through the following proposition, which I will from now on call the Materialist Credo: "All facts (including facts about the human mind and will and the course of human history) are causally dependent upon physical processes, or even reducible to them."[3] Materialism is here opposed to idealism, which would argue, in one way or another, for the autonomy of concepts with regard to nonconceptual or physical processes. This autonomy is both *causal* and *explicative*, that is, ontological and epistemological: idealism states (1) that concepts can be *causes*, either because they can trigger other concepts or because they can have an effect on the nonconceptual realm; and (2) that they can account for themselves. Ideas can be self-explanatory; ideas can change the world.

Materialism defined in this way, however, immediately encounters a serious problem, since the definition implies that the very "idea" we are expressing when we utter the Materialist Credo is itself dependent or even reducible to physical processes. The concept of "physical" is itself "physical," or at least the work that it does in the world does not originate in the concept but in some physical process behind or under it. But if that is true, it means that the Materialist Credo simply indicates a particular physical situation. To assess it in a materialist way, to judge whether I should hold it or not, I should try to see whether I am in a situation that contains the kind of physical processes that cause the Materialist Credo. However, this is not what materialist philosophers do: they *argue* in favor of their credo; they produce concepts and try to relate already-accepted concepts to the ones they want us to accept. And they are right. Because if they did otherwise, they would be taken in an infinite regress: the perception of that-physical-state-being-the-case is itself a judgment and should itself be assessed on materialist grounds, etc. In other words, materialists are caught in a pragmatic contradiction. They do the contrary of what they argue for.

The argumentative strategy I have just sketched is typical of the entire "idealist" tradition since at least Descartes. It became dominant with Kant and then, later, after Husserl. The success of phenomenology (at least in France) can be largely imputed to the fact that it provided a strong argumentative strategy against materialism, appealing to consciousness as that which must be presupposed even when one tries to get rid of it. One of the clearest versions of the argument, however, might be found in Cassirer's introduction to the *Philosophy of Symbolic Forms*, which makes Plato a *critical* philosopher.[4] On Cassirer's account, then, idealism lays claim to the power of critique, whereas materialism would be necessarily dogmatic.

CRITICAL MATERIALISM (MARX AND ENGELS)

I have no doubt that those who subscribe to the Materialist Credo, even in its apparently most vulgar versions, have the means to defend themselves. However, I want to recall another version of materialism that is not only itself critical (in the sense that it performs the same sort of operation as the one we saw at work against the Materialist Credo, which consists in drawing our attention to the unapparent or suppressed conditions of possibility of the very action we are performing) but is actually critical of the very conception of critique that we just saw, that is, the idealist critique. This version is the one that Marx and Engels introduced and illustrated in various places. Indeed, their argument in defense of materialism is precisely that its opposite, idealism, is not critical enough, precisely because it presupposes that to be critical is exclusively a matter of speculative or theoretical decisions.[5] (For instance, in order to correct the mistakes that materialists are supposed to have made, one only needs to point at their conceptual inconsistency—and this is critique.) As we all know, Marx famously reminded us that some ideas do not change simply because they are criticized on intellectual grounds. Typically, for instance, religious ideas have roots in the reality of our existence—and the real critique of those ideas would be actually to change the world, that is, to bring about revolution itself. Hence the famous line: "Philosophers have hitherto only interpreted the world in various ways; the point is to change it."

What is preserved here of the definition of materialism found in the *Britannica* is the notion of the *heteronomy of concepts*. This heteronomy, however, is expressed, as it were, for itself, instead of being reduced to another plane of already identified entities (say, "physical" objects) that can only be accessed through concepts anyway (thus generating the vicious circle we just saw). Furthermore, this heteronomy is not conceived as a purely speculative observation but as putting in question the very possibility of such speculative concerns as to the autonomy and the heteronomy of concepts. In other words, the very possibility of having a discussion about materialism relies on nonconceptual presuppositions.

We need to be blunt here, since something unwelcome necessarily intervenes at this point to interrupt our conversation and alters it in unpredictable ways. Let's say, then, that I am merely referring to the fact that if I hadn't had anything to eat today, if I hadn't been allowed to sleep in a bedroom protected from the cold, if I hadn't had a computer to write these lines, etc., I would not be able to have this conversation. *We can care for ideas as ideas because our lives are taken care of by others*. The materialist intuition has to do with the old word: *primum vivere, deinde philosophari* (before thinking, one has to survive). Philosophers cannot live on concepts, while many entities of the world can live without concepts. This raises not only epistemological and metaphysical issues but also problems pertaining to the order of justice. As Althusser put it in his letter to Jean Lacroix (his former philosophy professor), philosophers receive their world and their life from some of their fellow human beings, and they give them concepts in return. This is why, Althusser continues, we must "accept sharing their language and their truth as [we] share their bread."[6] But bread is only one of those "materialities," that is, those nonconceptual *conditions* of conceptual activity. Gender, race, class, diets, health, etc., are others. And this is not only true of philosophy; it is true of thought in general. Thought emerges and reemerges constantly out of concerns that are not intellectual concerns. Philosophy consists in testing the conceivability of a thought for itself, but this conceivability does not account for this thought in any sense.

This might sound all too trivial. It is not. It is one of the deepest thoughts one can have, so deep that it actually challenges the very notion of depth itself. What this version of materialism (i.e., *critical materialism*) comes down to is this: thought comes second. This is actually the exact summary that none other than Lenin gave of his definition of materialism, using a quotation that he took from Engels: "While for the materialists nature is primary and spirit secondary, for the idealists the reverse is the case."[7] But specifying *what* is primary is already to cross the limits allowed by critical materialism. All we can say is that whatever is primary is heterogeneous to thought as well as the cause of thought. Critical materialism only says that spirit (mind, thought, concepts, etc.) comes second. Or, as it could be put in an inverted version of Descartes's cogito: I come second, *ego secundus*, or *a me sequitur*. This is what I would like to call the Materialist Postulate (not to be conflated with the Materialist Credo).[8] The secondariness of what we are doing when we affirm this secondariness is the core of materialism.

A few remarks are necessary in order to understand the many displacements made by this simple claim.

First, to be a materialist is thus not to say anything about *what is to be thought about* (Being, Reality, Objectivity, Matter, as one wishes to call it)—for instance, that it can only be accessed through sensations, or that it is made ultimately of nonexperiential realities such as atoms, space, or forces (to mention two interpretations of materialism that have been illustrated in the history of philosophy). It is to say something about the very *being of thought itself*, that is, of this element within which any claim whatsoever is made about matter: it is to say that it comes second.

Second, what comes first is the *cause* of thought. The problem is not whether it exists prior to and independently from the mind (or concepts in general) but how it causes the mind (or concepts in general). Materialism does not answer the same question as idealism. It doesn't ask about the object of thought ("What is really the case out there?"). To suppose that thinking is representing an object is an idealist supposition, even if this object is argued to be "matter." Materialism claims, rather, that thinking is continuous with Being—in a sense, it is a function of something else (what you might call "matter," if you refrain from qualifying it further than "that which comes first and has some causal power"). Thought is not only *about* something; it is first *within* something. Or maybe, more minimally, thought is embraced within something larger than itself, something that it is not the measure of, something that is not "object-like." Idealism makes the opposite claim, namely, the claim that thought embraces everything, since whatever there is, for it to be, it has to be the object of thought. Being, whatever that is, is what is *expressed* through thought as by its *effect*, that to which thought contributes, not what needs to be *represented* by thought.[9] Being is not what we think *about* but what *makes us think*.

Third (and consequently), materialism immediately includes a critical element, if critique means playing the suppressed or unapparent conditions of an operation against its purported outcome. Indeed, materialism here is not a philosophical doctrine but a strong relativization of the very importance of defending such philosophical doctrines in general, since they can only be *effects* and never causes. Materialism, therefore, is not a philosophical doctrine but rather a modification in the very *practice* of philosophy in particular, and of all intellectual disciplines in general.

When we bear these three claims in mind, we are immediately faced with this question: What is the rationale for what I am doing here right now, namely, trying to understand materialism philosophically or to clarify the *concept* of materialism? Shouldn't we drop philosophy altogether and not even bother approaching materialism as a philosophical position?

The question is twofold. First, is philosophy worth practicing or not, according to the Materialist Postulate? Second, what does the Materialist Postulate contain in terms of positive claims about the realm of causes that would help us assess the worth of philosophy (i.e., the mechanisms by which speculation changes the world)? In other words, we need to build a particular concept, the concept of materialism, but it can only be one that at the same time criticizes the very possibility of such an endeavor. Critique and construction here must come hand in hand—and this is specific to materialism.

Since we must not presuppose anything that would be incompatible with the critical power of materialism itself, we can only proceed in the following way: the minimal requirements that make the *content* of the Materialist Postulate must not contain more than what is necessary to criticize *themselves*. In other words, we mustn't say more about the concept of materialism than what is at the same time necessary to criticize the very gesture of explicating a concept in general. Materialism is here nothing more than the power to criticize materialism as a concept.

SPECULATIVE MATERIALISM (LENIN)

We have to start with the question: Why would materialism as a practice, as a way of life, as a "material" reality, need any conceptual clarification or speculative construction? What does the concept of materialism add to materialist practices?

The only way to answer to such a question is to look at materialist practices and see when, where, why, and to what effect they have met the necessity or simply the effect of conceptual clarifications. We can think of some cases in which speculative interventions have been made in the name of critical materialism in the sense that I have just defended. Just to mention a few: Marx in his *Theses on Feuerbach*; Engels when he invents "dialectical materialism" at the end of the nineteenth century; Lenin in *Materialism and Empirio-Criticism*, which is a rectification of certain misunderstandings of "critical materialism"; Gramsci in many places of his intellectual adventure; Althusser throughout his entire work; Balibar more recently; and so on.

Let's start with Lenin's *Materialism and Empirio-Criticism*, since it may be the most unexpected of the works I have mentioned. Here is undoubtedly a very speculative book, dealing with the most metaphysical issue one can think of, the issue of the "thing in itself." Its entire point is to show that, although the definition of matter can vary along with scientific discoveries, the fact that matter precedes and determines thought can be posited as an "unconditioned" and "absolute truth"[10]: "The mutability of human conceptions of space and time no more refutes the objective reality of space and time than the mutability of scientific knowledge of the structure and forms of matter in motion refutes the objective reality of the external world."[11] This absolute truth is what we identified as the kernel of materialism, the priority of nonthought over thought. It is the only positive content that can be posited in a speculative way, but it has necessarily to *be* posited: "The antithesis of matter and mind has absolute significance only within the bounds of a very limited field—in this case exclusively within the bounds of the fundamental epistemological problem of what is to be regarded as primary and what as secondary. Beyond these bounds the relative character of this antithesis is indubitable."[12] Materialism thus requires a leap into the speculative, since nothing but an act of thought can posit the existence of something that is *absolutely and indeterminately* beyond and prior to human experience.

But why does Lenin feel the necessity, in the midst of his numerous political activities during the year 1908, to respond to those philosophers who believe they have found in Mach and Avenarius (that is, in some form of pre-Husserlian phenomenology or what I am tempted to call *Third-Way metaphysics*) some good foundational grounds for Marxism? The first paragraphs of the preface to the first edition made it very clear: because those Marxists were in fact "proceeding fearlessly to downright fideism."[13] "Fideism" is a word that Lenin used because censorship prevented him from using the word that he had chosen: "clericalism." "Clericalism," however, makes clear that the problem here is not one of faith or belief; it is a problem of power: the question is how to get rid of the Church as an instrument of power, an institution that uses the idea that there is another world after death where injustice is abolished to secure obedience and resignation in this world. Materialism thus has to go speculative if it wants to live on, because the question as to whether matter is everything is at work in some power relations (we might say in passing that religion construed this way might be defined as that place where speculative issues are *directly* political).

The argument to this point is not satisfactory, however, since Lenin has not explained why fighting ideas might help in fighting powers. He seems to take it simply for granted. This blind spot is one in which idealism can easily reconstruct itself: if we hold that ideas matter simply because, as it is well known and easy to experience in our everyday life, the way that we think has an effect on what we do, then we have an idealist understanding of why materialism matters!

One might object: Maybe we don't need such a clarification! After all, since there is no reason for conceptual clarification in general, since the will to knowledge is no longer justified in principle, the question of whether this blind spot in Lenin's speculative materialism matters at all is an open question. It is not enough for a doctrine to be incomplete or incoherent to be wrong: that it is wrong has to matter for its main purpose, or not at all.

But it should matter to Lenin at least—and for the very same reason that fighting empirio-criticism matters. Indeed, if fighting the wrong ideas helps in fighting the powers that use them, then we must not accept an understanding of this relation between speculative ideas and life-changing activities that might be based on those wrong ideas. We need to undermine them everywhere, including in the way that they account for our very effort to fight those ideas in view of fighting those powers. It is true, however, that Lenin does not content himself with saying that fighting clericalism requires chasing idealist notions away from even our most metaphysical intuitions. Clericalism is not only, for Lenin, a matter of ideas; it is also a way of approaching problems in general, including the problem of clericalism. It is, in fact, a *style* of intellectual intervention. The Third-Way materialists, tempted by Mach and Avenarius, are wrong about materialism not only because they introduce false ideas but also because they approach problems as pure intellects, as *professors*, as if the problems were interesting *in themselves*. On the contrary, the true materialist should approach them as a *revolutionary*, with one question in mind: how does this help build a powerful working-class organization? This difference transpires in the way that professors write about those problems, as opposed to the way that Lenin does: while professors are trying to make a problem subtle and are attracted by conceptual complexity for its own sake, as an object of contemplation and aesthetic pleasure (which it is, undoubtedly), the revolutionary looks for clear directions, does not hesitate to trivialize the arguments when necessary, tries to assess the difference in terms of consequences, and so on. Whereas professors claim only to assess ideas and to confront propositions, Lenin is not afraid of *ad hominem* arguments: indeed, the question asked here is not only whether what is said is true or false but what sort of life is promoted through this or that expression.

Materialism, in other words, is for Lenin not only a question of content, it is also a question of style, of writing style and of lifestyle. By "life," we must understand all those networks that sustain the existence of the one who speaks. The way in which professors *live* makes it impossible for them to convey materialism *in fact*: they can mean it, but not contribute to it as a mode of life. Indeed, they are paid to think: their identity as intellectual workers implies that intellectual work is separated from nonintellectual life, as if they didn't have to take part in other aspects of life in order to *think* properly. They contribute to clericalism not because of the indirect implications of what they say but because of the very way that they *live*: they live as clerics, and clericalism is neither a doctrine nor an institutional structure; it is the name of this state of separation between thought and life in which the division of labor makes of intellectuals specialized workers. Materialism would thus require much more than possessing or producing the right ideas; it would require a different connection of intellectual activity and other activities, a connection whereby the former is not separated from the latter, and it would require a different *practice* of theory, both in the sense of the way that theory is inserted in the web of life connections and in the sense of the style in which it is delivered.

Are we supposed to discard any contribution made by professors? This would disqualify immediately almost all of us here, starting with myself. Besides, is it not imprudent to dismiss the separation, or the autonomy, of thought, in general, and to reduce the interest of an idea to its function in some political struggle? The disastrous episode of Lysenko's "proletarian science" is here to remind us of the ravages that this idea might cause in our intellectual and political lives alike. We could push the point a little further and argue that stressing the *gratuitousness* of some parts of human labor in general and of intellectual labor in particular is actually a political point, and one that might not be so incompatible with communist values, in particular with the notion of *free work* or emancipation. Pointless expenditure (in the sense of Bataille, if you wish) might be considered a communist value, and speculation might be precisely the best example of gratuitousness.

However, to attribute to Lenin a position similar to Lysenko's would be a straightforward misreading. Indeed, it is not all intellectual activity that has to be uncovered as serving this or that political party; it is only philosophy. Scientific practices are relatively independent from this fate. Lenin makes it very clear in a short but very significant passage of *Materialism and Empirio-Criticism*:

> *Not a single one* of these professors, who are capable of making very valuable contributions in the special fields of chemistry, history, or physics, *can be trusted one iota* when it comes to philosophy. Why? For the same reason that *not a single* professor of political economy, who may be capable of very valuable contributions in the field of factual and specialised investigations, can be trusted *one iota* when it comes to the general theory of political economy. For in modern society the latter is as much a *partisan* science as is *epistemology*. Taken as a whole, the professors of economics are nothing but learned salesmen of the capitalist class, while the professors of philosophy are learned salesmen of the theologians.[14]

How are we to understand this statement? Why are sciences relatively immune to political struggle? Why is philosophy, on the contrary, necessarily a "partisan science"? Lenin does not give us much of a hint here. He suggests that it is the difference between a "special" and "general" science that is at stake here. But how does this help us understand the issue? Why are specialized claims more independent from material conflicts than general ones are?

Lenin leaves us with a certain number of questions. We will focus on two:

(1) Do we have a good materialist concept of the *relative autonomy* of science with respect to political struggle, by comparison with philosophy?
(2) Why is it philosophy that bears the weight of class struggle in theory? And do we have a good materialist account of the way that conceptual thought contributes to class struggle?

The importance of Althusser's intervention in the history of materialism is to have faced those issues. We will now turn to his contribution.

STRUCTURAL MATERIALISM (ALTHUSSER)

The question of the role and position of philosophy in and for materialism is the running worry of Althusser's entire body of work. It would be easy to show that Althusser's adhesion to the French Communist Party in 1947 is a consequence of his most consistent decision: that philosophy must become the world, which is, as Sartre argued, what happened with Marxism. For the sake of our purposes, we will summarize Althusser's contribution in two theses:

(1) Sciences are relatively autonomous (as all structures are), but they are characterized by the way in which they internalize their own structural finitude in their very mode of production.
(2) Philosophy is precisely the point where scientific activity meets political issues, for reasons that have to do with the very nature of politics (i.e., with its materiality).

As we will see, the responses to these two theses all have to do with the notion of *structure*, true materialism being thus ultimately revealed as *structural materialism*.

(1) Let's start with the first point. Sciences cannot escape from the general law of human practices: they are just one of them. If they can be relatively autonomous, it is not thanks to some kind of miraculous property of theirs but because practices in general leave room for autonomy. The general reason for this autonomy holds to the fact that practices are *structured*. The concept of structure comes into play here for the first time to account for the autonomy of what Althusser calls "levels." Structure refers here to the fact that a certain number of aspects of some human practices can only be explained by other aspects of the same practice. Language is a good example. The very existence of a phoneme depends on the existence of other phonemes. We have difficulty not just in first understanding but in first perceiving, for instance, a name in a foreign language because this perception is differential. Linguistic sounds don't simply exist as isolated physical signals; they perceptively emerge from the background of the play of differences that we call our language. Let's emphasize the fact that we are here talking of the very existence of a linguistic entity: structures are not principles of the organization of already-given entities but principles of constitution for entities that only exist in relation to one another. Let's note also that this does not mean that languages are immune either to all nonlinguistic influences or to history. It means that whatever forces are exerted in language will have to go through the filters of systems. For instance, factors of social distinction might explain why, at a certain point in its history, speakers of French muted the final *e* but didn't anticipate and could not escape the systemic consequences of this "choice," which is that the entire conjugation system had to change.[15]

To construct this concept of autonomy, Althusser introduces a certain number of theses that give his "structuralism" its distinctive flavor.[16]

First, structures must be defined in such a way that they can be reduced neither to some general human *praxis* (as in the humanist version of Marxism that, for Althusser, was embodied primarily by Sartre's *Critique of Dialectical*

Reason), nor to any specific structure, in particular not to economic processes (as in economism, which goes hand in hand with humanism). That implies that structures must each have their own logic (i.e., their way of being systematic) that cannot be superimposed on the logic of other ones in any isomorphic way—hence the importance of the concept *décalage*.

Second (and for the same reason), the existence and nature of those structures are not transhistorical facts, since that would imply the possibility of identifying one general entity unfolding itself in history under its variations. In other words, not all societies have been layered in language, economy, kinship, religion, politics, etc., as ours seems to be. History is not only about what happens on those different layers but also about their very existence. Religion, politics, ideas, etc., are necessarily equivocal notions that need to be redefined in the context of their structural relations (i.e., in a *critical* way).

Third, this autonomy is only relative—not because its scope would extend only to certain number of actions and stop at a certain point but because it is itself contingent on one particular "layer," the layer of production, on which the variation of structural layering (stratification) is governed. In fact, truly speaking, it is not a layer, since it does not exist separately but only as the principle of layering in each case. The difference between structural materialism and dogmatic materialism is precisely that the former avoids *reductionism*, because it does not identify the primary cause (i.e., matter) as belonging to any particular substantial plane of reference, as if we knew already where to look for the heteronomy of our practices and by what means this heteronomy operates; it rather makes of it the very reason why we always need to investigate afresh. It is *critical*, in the sense that it must relativize the supposedly universal categories used to study history (including the notion of history itself).

Fourth, this relative autonomy means that those layers are not simply independent from one another; they exist *differentially*, in the system of their contrasts (*décalages*). Religion exists through the set of the differences by which it distinguishes itself in one particular society from politics and family, etc. The structural cause is not any particular substantial level of reality but the system of intervals, disparities, differences, which keep one structured layer at a remove from another. In other words, Althusser uses the Saussurean concept of structure to think not only of the systematic organization of each layer but also of the relation *between* structures—and this is why he can avoid both reductionism and idealism. The concept of structure provides the notion of cause that the materialist tradition needed: the cause can be said to be "absent" simply because it cannot be identified with any particular substantial being, but it is nonetheless a cause.

For all those reasons, we can say that the notion of structure, far from being deterministic, is the concept of the deeper contingency of the very layers of practice. This finitude is itself marked within each structured system in the blanks that it is surrounded by, that is, in that for which it cannot account. Events that have no room in the systematic space opened by a structure can indeed occur, but they will go unremarked: they will act as elusive and vanishing events. Althusser gives many examples of this sort of situation in Marx's own corpus, but it is a general property of structures. It is through those elusive points that alternative structures communicate with one another.

As impressive and convincing as all this might be, however, it has not allowed us to start answering our question: If all structures are relatively autonomous, what is specific to scientific practices? Why would they be more "immune" to class struggle than philosophy or religion are, which after all are also structured practices? It is here that the (in)famous "epistemological cut" makes its appearance. Although Althusser will vary in the precise construction of this concept, he will never abandon it (as he makes it clear in his "Autocritique"[17]). To summarize brutally what would require a very complex development, we can say that the difference between ideology and science for Althusser is that the first one is aimed at locking or foreclosing artificially the space of its problematic (the space of possibilities that it constitutes, which, as we have seen, necessarily includes marks of its own finitude), whereas the other not only acknowledges its finitude (which is, at the same time, its openness) but strives to *do something with it*. Science is a practice that constantly tries to let itself be altered by its own structural finitude. Science is thus defined not by the fact that it represents anything adequately but by the mode of production that characterizes it, a mode of production that constantly relativizes its own working system within itself. It is in this sense that it is materialist, and not in the sense that it would hope to reduce everything eventually to one substantial plane of reference.

(2) Now, what about philosophy? Here, Althusser's position varied significantly. At first, he basically argued that philosophy was a way to accompany radical changes, either in politics or in science. He implied that philosophy could not take any initiative. However, in the last period of his work, he revised this doctrine and redefined philosophy as "class struggle in theory."[18]

A large part of Althusser's work is of course devoted to correcting the mistaken philosophical views that Marxist materialism had of itself, through producing a materialist concept of contradiction (which appeals to structuralism), thus completing the task of articulating a coherent *speculative materialism*. But we might accept that the Hegelian concept of contradiction is indeed incompatible with materialist premises (contradiction being a logical concept; to claim that something is self-contradictory is to claim that it can be resolved in logical relations—and thus to be arguing in favor of idealism). We may even recognize that Althusser's conceptual system is the ontology that the idea of materialism required. We will still ask, why does it matter? How do concepts have an effect on how we do things (including how we try to produce a science of history)? On this, Althusser hesitates. It can even be argued that this question is the central impetus and the running thread of his entire work, that which makes it stall and start again. The suspicion that the philosopher's life is lived for nothing (the life of a parasite, a life in debt, and even a risible life), as well, however, as the determination to do justice to the importance of speculation for revolution itself, is the constant worry of Althusser's philosophical and personal adventure. Consequently, it is possible to find traces of this effort in Althusser's entire corpus.

I think the last word of this untiring effort is to be found in a posthumous text only recently published, *Philosophy for Non-Philosophers*.[19] Nowhere else, perhaps, do we find so complete and detailed an account of Althusser's entire philosophical system taken as a response to the question: why does speculation matter? The gist of his position in *Philosophy for Non-Philosophers* can be summarized as follows: (1) philosophy is speculative in the sense that it is the bricolage of totalizing views—discourses on *everything* that include both existent *and nonexistent* objects—itself accomplished by totalizing means, namely, by means of conceptual *systems* or, rather, Althusser says, structures; and (2) philosophy matters because practices, although diverse, need to be unified, since each practice comes with its own ideological apparatus, thus making it difficult to ensure the *hegemonic* function of ideology, namely, its capacity to secure the domination of one class over the other ones by way of including the latter ones within the worldview of the former one. The important category is thus the category of totality. Philosophy is identified by Althusser with a certain idea of metaphysics or, at least, with speculative thought.

Speculation does not appear as any specialized and optional activity that would come on the top of other ones but as something that is already distributed in the masses and that belongs to the very existence of all practice as one of its conditions. Althusser thus does justice to the fact that *everybody thinks*: speculation is not an arbitrary whim but an activity deeply rooted in the necessities of our life. However, unlike the entire idealist tradition, he does not ground speculation in some metaphysical need but in the logic of class struggle, itself rooted in the necessity of practical life (first because production requires exploitation and, hence, conflict, and second because exploitation ultimately requires a form of hegemony in the Gramscian sense). But philosophy is not speculation in general: religion is another sort of speculation—it could even be shown that myth in the Levi-Straussian sense has the same unifying function! Philosophical speculation has, argues Althusser, two specific features: (1) it is professionalized to a certain extent, since it is entrusted to a group of experts to forge conceptual propositions that, in one way or the other, contribute to the unification of practices—which means that it is a form of conscious and reflective speculation; and (2) it responds to the appearance of scientific practices that challenge the established order, says Althusser, "because [these practices] offered people proof that 'absolute' knowledge of things could be provided by their own scientific practice rather than divine revelation."[20] Speculation thus tries to repair the breaks made by scientific practices in the fabric of our ideological life.

A materialist account of the necessity of speculation thus appeals to the fact that practices are diverse (relatively autonomous) but need to communicate, not because of any natural need for unification in the human mind but rather as a consequence of the *hegemonic* nature of class struggle, which requires that the dominant class rule over all the aspects on the human life in order to secure its domination in the productive process. All philosophy has thus a *comparative* dimension, since it tries to negotiate the heterogeneity of ideologies because of the heterogeneity of the practices they contribute to.[21]

This, then, is materialism: here, the concept of the cause of conceptual thinking in general (i.e., speculation) is exactly coextensive with the relativization of philosophy. Class struggle is both that which is repressed from the dominant philosophical tradition (idealism) and that which causes speculation in general (the reason why it does have an effect on the world). Materialism, however, cannot be any particular theory of speculation; it is the *practice of philosophy that lets itself be altered by the realization of both its necessity and its heteronomy*. To be a materialist in philosophy, for Althusser (as for Lenin and, later, for Balibar), is not (only) to articulate a materialist worldview (including a materialist theory of the role of philosophy) but rather to practice philosophy in a specific way. Which way, exactly? First, it is a way of practicing philosophy that accepts its conflicting nature as well its partisan logic, which means that philosophical ideas do not matter only because some individual consciousness can consider them true or false but because of the way that they contribute to some collective body of power (as organic intellectuals, in Gramsci's sense). Second, it does not try to provide ultimate justifications for practices but instead tries to liberate new inchoate practices from the ideological (i.e., political) obstacles that impede them. Third, and correlatively, although involved in the exercise of totalization that defines speculation in general, materialism uses it to expose that which needs to be repressed for the dominant totalizing view of a time to constitute itself. Althusser mentions these as examples: matter, work, body, gender, age, prisoners, savages, madmen and -women, power relations, and so on.[22] These are the *materialities*. They are not mere objects that would wait out there to be accurately represented by us; they are critical elements that cannot be taken on board without changing the very way in which we represent things in general, and altering the very position of the activity of representing things in the balance of our practices. They can be said to exist in the exact measure as they change us, that is, as they operate a *structural variation* within our speculative systems. This is not to say that they exist only for us. We are not the measure of their existence; on the contrary, this measure is provided by our own finitude or, more precisely, by the fact that changes can make us vanish. They are outside of us, although it would make no sense to posit them as objects of representation. This position is the only one that avoids both idealism and dogmatism. Eventually, a materialist practice of philosophy will constantly articulate the professional and technical aspect of philosophy (philosophers are professors who study already-existent philosophical systems or fabricate new ones) and the savage speculation that it is distributed in the masses ("Every human being is virtually a philosopher"[23]), which implies (as Lenin already argued) a particular *style* of writing (and Althusser does illustrate this style in particular in his late work). In other words, materialist philosophy requires much more than a modification of either the contents or the styles of philosophers; it requires a new alliance between academics and activists or, more precisely, between academics and those who fight at the heart of the productive process ("workers").

Materialism thus appears to be critical, speculative, and structural. Of course, much more would have to be said in order to articulate this concept of materialism fully. But enough, I hope, has been offered to make clear why a concept of materialism matters: it matters because it tells us why speculation, in general, matters. Indeed, we need both to acknowledge the necessity of speculation in our life in general, and to resist the very unrealistic account of speculation generally given by philosophers (including the "speculative materialists" of our time).[24] We need to do with regard to philosophy what Bruno Latour has argued was the aim of anthropology in general, that is, to send back to those who are involved in a particular practice (say, the sciences) an image of their practice that corrects the fantastic story they tell themselves about it, while doing justice to its power and significance.[25] In our time, one work has continued this secular endeavor to contribute to materialism understood not as a philosophical doctrine but as a transformation of the practice of philosophy—that of Étienne Balibar. The preceding lines have no other purpose than to introduce his work and to suggest that the reader approach it while keeping in mind the problem of materialism as I have defined it here—in other words, they are meant to argue why and where Balibar's work matters.

NOTES

1. See Quentin Meillassoux, *After Finitude: An Essay on the Necessity of Contingency* trans. Ray Brassier (London: Continuum, 2008); François Laruelle, "The Generic as Predicate and Constant: Non-Philosophy and Materialism," trans. Taylor Adkins, in *The Speculative Turn: Continental Materialism and Realism*, ed. Levi Bryant, Nick Srnicek, and Graham Harman (Melbourne: Re.Press, 2011), 237–60; and Ray Brassier, *Nihil Unbound: Enlightenment and Extinction* (London: Palgrave Macmillan, 2007).

2. See, for example, Catherine Malabou, "Le vide politique du réalisme contemporain, ou pourquoi je suis matérialiste" (lecture, Choses en Soi conference, Paris, November 19, 2016), https://www.youtube.com/watch?v=EZyUVgV_u5A.

3. John Jamieson Carswell Smart, *Encyclopedia Britannica*, s.v. "materialism," https://www.britannica.com/topic/materialism-philosophy.

4. Ernst Cassirer, *The Philosophy of Symbolic Forms*, vol. 1, *Language*, trans. Ralph Manheim (New Haven: Yale University Press, 1965), 73.

5. On this, see Étienne Balibar, *The Philosophy of Marx*, trans. Chris Turner (London: Verso, 1995); and Pierre Machery, *Marx 1845: Les "Thèses" sur Feuerbach* (Paris: Editions Amsterdam, 2008).

6. Louis Althusser, *Écrits philosophiques et politiques* (Paris: Le Livre de Poche), 1999, 313; my translation. The French reads: "accepter de partager leur langage et leur vérité comme vous partagez leur pain."

7. V. I. Lenin, introduction to *Materialism and Empirio-Criticism*, trans. Abraham Fineberg, vol. 14 of *Lenin: Collected Works* (Moscow: Progress, 1972), https://www.marxists.org/archive/lenin/works/1908/mec/intro.htm. The original quotation is from Friedrich Engels, *Ludwig Feuerbach*, in Karl Marx and Friedrich Engels, *Selected Works* (Moscow: Progress, 1958), 2:369–70.

8. Althusser speaks of the "opacity of the immediate" as the core intuition of materialism, which he sees first represented in Spinoza ("From *Capital* to Marx's Philosophy," in Louis Althusser, Étienne Balibar, Roger Establet, Pierre Macherey, and Jacques Rancière, *Reading Capital: The Complete Edition*, trans. Ben Brewster and David Fernbach [London: Verso, 2015], 8).

9. One might recognize in the opposition between representation and expression formulations that are very close to those used by Deleuze throughout his entire work,

starting with the very first published text he acknowledged (Gilles Deleuze, "Review of Jean Hyppolite's Logique et Existence," in *Desert Islands and Other Texts 1953–1974*, ed. David Lapoujade, trans. Mike Taormina [Los Angeles: Semiotext(e), 2004]). Althusser will prefer the word "production" to the word "expression," but the general move is the same.

10. See Lenin, *Materialism and Empirio-Criticism*, chap. 2, §5, chap. 3, §1.

11. Lenin, *Materialism and Empirio-Criticism*, chap. 3, §5.

12. Lenin, *Materialism and Empirio-Criticism*, chap. 3, §1.

13. Lenin, *Materialism and Empirio-Criticism*, Preface to the First Edition.

14. Lenin, *Materialism and Empirio-Criticism*, chap. 6, §4.

15. For more about this, see my book on Saussure: Patrice Maniglier, *La vie énigmatique des signes: Saussure et la naissance du structuralisme* (Paris: Léo Scheer, 2006); for a summary in English, see my essay "Signs and Customs: Lévi-Strauss, Practical Philosopher," *Common Knowledge* 22, no. 3 (September, 2016), 415–30.

16. I draw here freely from Althusser's *For Marx*, trans. Ben Brewster (London: Verso, 2005); and from Althusser, Balibar, Establet, Macherey, and Rancière, *Reading Capital*.

17. Louis Althusser, *Éléments d'autocritique* (Paris: Hachette, 1974), 17; Louis Althusser, *Essays in Self-Criticism*, trans. Grahame Locke (London: Humanities Press, 1978).

18. For this last definition, see Louis Althusser, *Réponse à John Lewis* (Paris: Maspero, 1973); repr. in "Reply to John Lewis," in *Essays in Self-Criticism* (London: Humanities Press, 1976), 35–77.

19. Louis Althusser, *Initiation à la philosophie pour les non-philosophes* (Paris: Presses Universitaires de France, 2014); Louis Althusser, *Philosophy for Non-Philosophers*, trans. G. M. Goshgarian (London: Bloomsbury, 2017).

20. Althusser, *Philosophy for Non-Philosophers*, 170.

21. It is worth noting that this conception of philosophy is remarkably similar to the one recently defended by Bruno Latour in his latest masterpiece, *An Inquiry into Modes of Existence* (trans. Catherine Porter [Cambridge, Mass.: Harvard University Press, 2013]), that is, philosophy as diplomacy. On the notion of philosophy as a form of radical comparatism, see Patrice Maniglier, "Manifeste pour un comparatisme supérieur," *Temps modernes*, no. 682 (July 2015): 86–145.

22. Althusser, *Initiation à la philosophie*, 100–2.

23. Althusser, *Initiation à la philosophie*, 385; my translation.

24. I have exposed the reasons why I believe the notion of "speculation" found in Meillassoux, for instance, is unrealistic in Patrice Maniglier, "Manifeste pour un comparatisme supérieur."

25. Latour, *Inquiry*.

THE POLITICAL

Adi Ophir

Halfway through his argument in "The Proposition of Equaliberty," precisely in the middle of the text, Balibar writes,

> There will be *a permanent tension between the conditions that historically determine the construction of institutions that conform to the proposition of equaliberty and the excessive, hyperbolic universality of the statement*. Nevertheless, it will always have to be repeated, and repeated identically, without change, in order to reproduce the truth-effect without which there is no revolutionary politics. There will thus be a permanent tension between the universality of the political signification of the rights of man and the fact that their statement leaves the task of producing a politics of the right of man entirely up to practice, to struggle, to social conflict.[1]

In what follows, I argue that this tension, so central to Balibar's conception of the various kinds of politics driven by the proposition of equaliberty, is not unique to this kind of politics. I argue that if equaliberty is a binding principle of modern politics, it has found its rival and Other in a no-less-powerful binding principle, one that consists of an explicit and systematic negation of the universalist dimension of equality and liberty. This other principle binds what I propose to call "a politics of purity." I show that it has a structural similarity to the principle of equaliberty, and look for the common ground that accounts for this resemblance. Juxtaposing these two antagonistic forms of politics and explicating their common ground helps articulate (albeit briefly and schematically[2]) an outline for a concept of the political that does not exclude one type of politics in favor of the other but is rather realized equally in both. The two types (and their opposite binding principles), I show, are symmetrical in certain respects that make them equally (and especially well) equipped to demonstrate basic aspects of the political event, and of the political *as* an event.

A STRUCTURAL TENSION

There are several aspects to the tension that Balibar underlines in the opening quotation, but the most basic, I believe, and the one I will be mostly interested in is the following: On the one hand, the "statement leaves the task of producing a politics of the right of man entirely up to practice, to struggle, to social conflict." On the other hand, the very act of institutionalization—with respect to the governed community and the ruling power alike—sets limits on both liberty and equality, and even with the best of intentions, it exerts a toll that gradually accumulates. Balibar is occupied with the history and logic of these constraints. He reconstructs the institutionalization of equality and liberty as mediated by property rights and by a political community, each setting its own boundaries and structural constraints and embodying conditions that constrain the ability to realize equaliberty, even under the most fortunate circumstances. This institutionalization, Balibar seems to believe, must also confront two irreducible differences, of gender and of mental competence, which are responsible—both historically and logically—for renewed forms of inequality.

Hence the repeated abstract claim implied in the proposition exceeds any concrete institutionalization and must be constantly renewed, as well. The proposition of equaliberty is not merely a descriptive assertion regarding the nature of politics but a principle and an imperative that must be reinserted into the political struggle by those committed to "revolutionary politics" (or "a politics of emancipation"). The immanent tension between the concrete conditions and institutionalization of equaliberty and the hyperbolic universality of its proclamation should not be taken as a given. It should be enacted and performed, and repeatedly so. Otherwise "no revolutionary politics" would become possible.

"Revolutionary politics" is a term that Balibar gradually abandoned. In an important essay first published in 1996, Balibar distinguishes and discusses three kinds of politics: of emancipation, of transformation, and of civility.[3] The aim, he says was to confront a major problem: the aporias of a reduction of *extreme violence*, "which led [Balibar] to suggest . . . that the two critical concepts which continue to inspire much political philosophy in the progressive tradition (*emancipation* and *transformation*) should be rounded off (but certainly not replaced) by a third one, for which I borrowed the old concept of *civility*."[4]

Even before introducing the last concept, "revolutionary politics" had been replaced by two of its moments, emancipation and transformation, which are carefully distinguished, and transcended. "The progressive tradition," it is safe to assume, is the one committed to equaliberty, whereas the urgency of confronting extreme violence may come from two opposite directions of the struggle for equaliberty. On the one hand, civility, which is the political response to extreme violence, implies a struggle for making politics—any kind of politics—possible. This includes a recognition that the struggle for equaliberty has to give way, temporarily at least, to the exigencies of the efforts to curb extreme violence, and do that in coalition with forces that may not be committed to equaliberty, to one's interpretation of equaliberty, or to one's means of achieving it. On the other hand, extreme violence may originate from an overzealous revolutionary struggle to achieve equaliberty.[5] In both cases, violence must be tamed at the expense of the revolutionary struggle, adding another crucial reason for the need to repeat, perform anew, the hyperbolic, universal claim of equaliberty. The proposition itself, however, and the claim and the imperative that it encapsulates, will be articulated anew according to the terms of each one of the three kinds of politics. The tension between the enunciation of the statement and its institutionalization pervades all three of them. Each kind of politics is engrained in the same structural tension between concrete institutionalization and a surpassing, hyperbolic, universal proposition that serves as a binding principle, a guide, and a moral-political imperative.

Balibar has never claimed to exhaust the spectrum of possible kinds of politics. He sometimes speaks of politics in general as a sphere of action and institutions dedicated to "community building, regulating social conflict[s], defending the public interest, taking and exercising power, governing the multitude, transforming social relations, [and] adapting to change."[6] But all the kinds of politics he studies are those committed to equaliberty; they are different versions of the struggle to realize it, or at least (in the case of civility) they create the conditions for such politics. Balibar focuses on those not only because this is the politics to which he is committed but because it is a politics of a special kind. Its uniqueness is at once conceptual and historical: conceptual, because the intricate and multidimensional dialectics of equaliberty could be extended to cover the entire history of politics, and of politics *tout court*, and suggest its general outlines and inner logic;[7] historical, because the modern event of equaliberty has become "irreversible." It is irreversible not because the proposition has been universally accepted and its history completed but rather because it has set the terms of the political debate, such that even "its opponents found themselves obliged to criticize . . . [it] in its own language, based on its own implications."[8]

The irreversibility of the proposition of equaliberty is a historical claim that should be questioned today on historical grounds. I am afraid that the answer would be mixed, at best. It seems to me quite obvious that not all the opponents of equaliberty find themselves today "obliged to criticize . . . [it] in its own language, based on its own implications." The reverse may also be true; there are enough cases, I believe, to show how the advocates of equaliberty work hard to criticize their opponents but find themselves obliged to use the latter's language and follow the implications of their political proposition. This does not mean that one should be less committed to the principle and the imperative, only that the terms of the struggle have shifted. My point is not only that the effect of the event of equaliberty has not eclipsed altogether other, regressive or counterprogressive, and explicitly antiuniversalist forms of politics, but rather that some of those forms are structured by the same structural tension that generates the recurrent renewal of radical politics, a politics guided by, articulated in terms of, and legitimized and judged by an appeal to a hyperbolic proposition of its own. In what follows, I would like to examine one such hyperbolic proposition that consists of an explicit negation of universalism in politics and an active struggle to inverse the advance of equality and liberty for the sake of equaliberty's radical other. This is a politics guided by a proposition that does not simply negate liberty or equality under particular circumstances but calls to overrule universal principles of any kind in the name of a certain hyperbolic particularity.

The opposition is symmetrical, however, at least with respect to the tension produced by the attempt to transform or invent political institutions so as to realize a hyperbolic particularist proposition. Whether this other hyperbolic statement gives rise to another revolutionary politics or is only responsible for its simulation, even to the extent that it is no longer possible to distinguish the true revolutionary politics from its counterfeit, matters little in this context. What matters is that the political materialization of this principle has already changed the contemporary conditions of the struggle for equaliberty and seems no less "irreversible" than does the proposition of equaliberty. This struggle is shaped today not only by the aporia of equaliberty, its mediation through property rights and political communities, and the irreducible differences responsible for the introduction of inequality. The struggle is also, if not especially, shaped by the presence of active counterforces that seek to exalt a certain principle of particularity, the particularity, exceptionality, or chosenness of one political entity at stake—be it one people, one state, a republic, an empire, or a race—and subsume all their politics under the reign of that principle. The condition of equaliberty as an ongoing project, like the very concept of the political, must be reinterpreted in light of the recurrent event—and the new advent—of this politics of particularity, which I would like to name and interpret here as *a politics of purity*.

THE POLITICS OF PURITY

Balibar was not oblivious, of course, to the counterforces that I have in mind here. A little more than a year before the presentation of the first version of "The Proposition of Equaliberty,"[9] as part of his collaboration and constructive dialogue with Immanuel Wallerstein, Balibar published his now classic analysis of "Racism and Nationalism."[10] With the progressive domination of the system of nation-states over other social formations, racism has been intimately linked to nationalism, "constantly emerging out of [it], not only towards the exterior but towards the interior," functioning as its internal "supplement . . . always in excess of it, but always indispensable to its constitution and yet always still insufficient to achieve its project."[11] The forces at stake have been formidable and persistent, starting long before the biological racism of the nineteenth century and lasting long after the Second World War, "since the time of the Reconquista in Spain" down to contemporary Europe, where "'the dangerous classes' of the international proletariat tend to be subsumed under the category of 'immigration,' which becomes main name given to race within the crisis-torn nations of the postcolonial era."[12] This racism, which "first presented itself as a *super-nationalism*," has been "*a supplement of particularity*,"[13] has repeatedly undermined any institutionalization of the nation (through the nation-state and its universalist conception of nationalism, including the recognition of the equal national status of other nations). Notwithstanding the universal aspect of nationalism, racism—its indispensable excess—pushed other groups of humans, both internal and external, to positions of radical inferiority, as subnational and subhumans.

This inferiority has been nothing but the other side of the "excessive particularity" of the nation. The institutionalization of the nation cannot be separated from "the excess of purism" and "the obsessional quest for a 'core' of authenticity that cannot be found," and this dialectic "shrinks the category of nationality and de-stabilizes the historical nation" or forces phantasmatic history, vocation, and destiny as well as the engineering of its population so as to create it in line with that phantasmatic model.[14] One can hardly fail to notice the structural similarity between this dialectic of excess and institutionalization ("Every historical racism is both institutional and sociological"[15]) and the one that Balibar developed soon after with respect to the principle of equaliberty. But as far as I am aware, the analogy has never been drawn explicitly, and the notable differences between the two have not been discussed. These differences are significant. Neither racism nor the idea of "excessive particularity" have ever been associated with an event that has become "irreversible," and, more importantly, perhaps, the excessive element that racism introduces into every form of nationalism, as "a necessary tendency" and an "indispensable, internal supplement," *has not been studied or even articulated as a binding principle of politics.*

Racism, for Balibar, is "a social relation," an ideological "configuration," a fundamental operator of classification, "a philosophy of history, or, more accurately, a historiosophy," "one of the most insistent forms of historical memory of modern societies," and a force endowed with "a structuring dimension" that functions as "supplement of [nationalist] particularity."[16] This impressive reading of racism, its history, discursive structure, and ideological configuration is not wrong, but it is decisively symptomatic. Racism's "excess" and "obsessions" are read as symptoms of its distinct discursive structure but not so much as principles and operators in and guides for political action, or as a politics that deserves a place of its own in the typology of political formations that Balibar would propose about a decade later.[17]

In what follows, I propose a fuller analogy between the proposition of equaliberty and a proposition encapsulated in racism, and look for the common ground of the two opposing types of politics. This principle, I contend, enables a straightforward account of racism as politics, a lively mode of political belonging, irreducible to any given social structure, political institution, or phantasmatic subjectivity, but one that is actively involved in their formation. The principle is that of purity. As I mentioned briefly above, Balibar recognizes its operation at the heart of racism:

> Racism constantly induces an excess of "purism" as far as the nation is concerned: for the nation to be itself, it has to be racially or culturally pure. It therefore has to isolate within its bosom, before eliminating or expelling them, the "false," "exogenous," "cross-bred," "cosmopolitan" elements. This is an obsessional imperative.[18]

Obsessive or not, this imperative should be recognized as a principle of political action, whose logic is not limited to the formation of the nation and the nation-state, and whose operation precedes that of modern racism in much the same way that the principles of equality and liberty precede the event of the

French Revolution. Like equality and liberty, purity, too, should be recognized as an affair of antiquity. In fact, the principle of purity is as old as politics in the West. I will take my example from the Hebrew Bible. A typical formulation of a hyperbolic statement guiding a politics of purity is presented as a concise imperative in the book of Deuteronomy:

> Your camp must be holy (*ve-haya makhanecha kadosh*). (Deut. 23:14)

As old as the book of Deuteronomy is, I do not refer to it because it is an originary or founding moment but because of the context in which that imperative appears: a straightforward conjunction of hygiene and strategy, biopolitics and security. Cleanse your camp of the impure stuff that your body discharges, the text says, so that God, which is also your sovereign, can reside in your midst and protect you from your enemies:

> With your utensils you shall have a trowel; when you relieve yourself outside, you shall *dig a hole with it and then cover up your excrement*. Because the Lord your God travels along with your camp, to save you and to hand over your enemies to you, *therefore your camp must be holy*, so that he may not see anything indecent among you and turn away from you. (Deut. 23:13–14)

Purity is a means of survival when living too close to God. Closeness to God and, hence, degrees of purity are also a status, authority, and capital distributed unequally among priests, Levites, and the rest of the Israelites. For all of them, purification is an ongoing practice that needs to be resumed periodically and occasionally. The encounters with the impure cannot be exhausted by any final list of impurities, and hence the imperative anticipates and seeks to encompass what it cannot articulate, but it also calls for ongoing practice. Living bodies, people on the move, with their numerous and unpredictable forms of intercourse, constantly produce impurity. The line needs to be repeatedly redrawn. During the Second Temple, the question concerning what and who must be considered impure was up for grabs, and since then it has never ceased occupying Jewish sectarian politics and, later, the rabbinic circles that revolutionized Jewish life in the early centuries CE. It is an open question that must be repeatedly posed, because the realm of the impure always exceeds what the imperative of purification can articulate, and nothing and nobody can be purified once and for all. More importantly, ever since the emergence of sectarian politics in the fifth or fourth century BCE, the boundaries of the "camp" itself have been questioned. The boundaries were questioned, but not the basic idea of a separate camp actively separating itself from the realm of the impure: "the camp" has always designated the community—at once territorial, ethnic, religious, and political—that must purify itself. The politics of purity is, first and foremost, a politics of belonging, a way for articulating belonging, drawing its boundaries, and setting its conditions. Whoever knows the secrets of purity and purification exerts political power; whoever is authorized to separate the pure from the impure enjoys a certain degree of sovereignty; whoever questions this authority and proposes alternative boundaries or principles of purity takes part in a politics of purity.

The biblical imperative of purity has been repeatedly proclaimed in many languages and various political contexts, with considerable "truth effects." Numerous repetitions and variations of the statement can be found throughout history and across different cultures. It is also in this form that the imperative produces the permanent tension Balibar describes between the hyperbolic statement and its institutionalization. With slight adaptation, this description (presented in the opening quotation) may be paraphrased thus:

> There is a permanent tension between the conditions that historically determine the construction of institutions that conform to the proposition that constitutes the purity of the community and the excessive, hyperbolic purity (and exclusivity) that the statement seeks to establish. Therefore, it will always have to be repeated, though repeated differently, with respect to the ever-changing mélange of the governed, in order to reproduce the truth effect, without which there is no racist, nationalist, chauvinist, or fundamentalist politics.

Clearly, the proposition of equaliberty and the imperative of purity are different in many respects, in both form and content, and involve very different regimes of truth. Most importantly, the extraordinary *elenchus*, or proof by double negation, which Balibar reconstructs with respect to equaliberty cannot be found in the imperative of purity. Obviously, the mediating role played by property and community has no equivalence here; the political community is the direct object of the imperative, and property is nothing but a set of objects, including land that may be impure and may or may not be "purifiable." Concerning equaliberty, Balibar writes, "There are no examples of restrictions or suppressions of freedoms without social inequalities, nor of inequalities without restrictions or suppressions of freedoms."[19] The case of purity is more simple and straightforward. Questions of the equality and the distribution of freedom or power among members of "the pure camp" are secondary to the very act of separating—and the lines that separate—the pure from the impure. It is assumed that purity is always violated, threatened, and undermined; impurity is both structural and occasional, and the only question is how to identify the impure elements and get rid of them, or at least separate from them. But this does not mean that the hyperbolic element is not at work here. The negation of purity is caught in an infinite regress—the means of purification need to be purified by people, who need to be purified in their turn, and so on. The imperative generates a project without end, a perpetual movement of exclusion. Thus, both claims—for equaliberty and for purity—exhibit a highly productive tension between the institutions that realize the proposition and the enunciation of the statement that sets their principle and grants their legitimacy.

The history of citizenship, Balibar reminds us, "is open, just as the history of equaliberty is open. They have a past before modernity and its bourgeois or socialist revolutions, declarations of rights, etc., [and] . . . certainly also have a future after modernity."[20] This history should include a politics of equality articulated in terms of a hegemonic regime of purity. There are many examples of this. I take mine, once again, from the Hebrew Bible. There, we find the claim that the community of the pure must be a community of equals. This claim is raised by a rebel named Korah. Readers who remember Walter Benjamin's single, paradigmatic example of divine violence may remember his story and fate. Korah's claim was addressed to Moses, challenging his leadership:

> Now Korah son of Izhar son of Kohath son of Levi, along with Dathan and Abiram sons of Eliab, and On son of Peleth—descendants of Reuben—took two hundred and fifty Israelite men, leaders of the congregation, chosen from the assembly, well-known men, and they confronted Moses. They assembled against Moses and against Aaron, and said to them, "You have gone too far! *All the congregation* [or community, *edda*] *are holy, every one of them, and the Lord is among them. So why then do you exalt yourselves above the assembly of the Lord?*" (Num. 16: 1–3)

This was the beginning and the end of a politics of equality in the Hebrew Bible. Korah and his company were consumed by divine fire (Num. 16:35), and the politics of equality with him, but not without leaving a clear mark—equality pertains to those deemed holy; it can be formulated only on the basis of a prior principle that separates the holy congregation. A politics of purity may be inflected so as to produce a community of equals, as long as holiness—and the purity associated with it[21]—are equally distributed. A politics of purity may but need not involve a proposition of equality.[22] Its imperative to separate precedes and overrides other principles. Here is the most dramatic episode, played out by

Ezra, a leader of the Judeans who, under the auspices of Cyrus, King of Persia, had returned to Jerusalem from the Jews' exile in Babylon:

> After these things had been done, the officials approached me and said, "The people of Israel, the priests, and the Levites *have not separated themselves from the peoples of the lands with their abominations*, from the Canaanites, the Hittites, the Perizzites, the Jebusites, the Ammonites, the Moabites, the Egyptians, and the Amorites. For they have taken some of their daughters as wives for themselves and for their sons. Thus *the holy seed has mixed itself with the peoples of the lands* [i.e., the indigenous population], and in this faithlessness the officials and leaders have led the way." (Ezra 9:1–2)

The elite of "officials and leaders" are not condemned for seizing power or property that they do not deserve but for being leaders in profaning "the holy seed." The story of the expulsion of their foreign wives in the Books of Ezra and Nehemiah has become a paradigm of segregationist, supremacist politics and was used repeatedly from antiquity to our present, from Palestine to Nazi Germany, and to the American Bible Belt.[23] It is often used by Christian American fundamentalists to support white supremacism.[24] Then and now, the call to purity seeks to limit the freedom to interact, intermarry, and cohabit on the same piece of land and to undermine any claim to equality between indigenous residents and returning newcomers who quickly became colonizing settlers. Thus, when commanded to expel their wives and children, the people of the Judean community dared not question either the imperative to purify or the impurity of their wives. The terms of the imperative were taken for granted. Their strategy of resistance, in fact their politics of purity, was based on a series of postponements. Instead of resisting the expulsion, they tried to postpone it, reaffirming the irreversibility of the imperative while undermining its efficacy: "But the people are many, and it is a time of heavy rain; we cannot stand in the open. Nor is this a task for one day or for two, for many of us have transgressed in this matter" (Ezra 10:10–14). And when Third Isaiah, a prophet who was more or less Ezra's contemporary and who rejected Ezra's segregationist position, offered an inclusive understanding of YAHW's worship, he was able to do so only by extending the boundaries of the sacred and including members of other nations among the priests and Levites (Isa. 66:18–23).

In light of this call and within the framework of its consequent institutionalization, whoever wished to ease restrictions on the freedom to intermarry, question the inequality of status between Israel and others, or open the gates of the Jewish community to newcomers has had to do so by rearticulating purity and interpreting or manipulating its internal logic, extending its realm and relaxing the practices of purification. When doing so, however, the hyperbolic particularistic principle still reigns over any universal claim. Membership in the political community still implies purity, a radical distinction between members and nonmembers, institutionalized inequality, and a slippery slope from denying nonmembers' rights to forsaking their lives.

Biblical anecdotes cannot replace the historical study and conceptual analysis necessary here, and examples from past and contemporary Jewish politics might seem too esoteric to teach us any lesson of a wider scope. But such anecdotes and examples do indicate both the antiquity and the persistence, or at least recurrence, of a politics of purity. This politics has had many ideological variations—religious, sectarian, nationalist, racist, and racist-nationalist—and several institutional frameworks, including monarchial and tyrannical; imperialist, colonialist, and totalitarian; and populist and democratic. The politics of purity does not die in democratic water, which it constantly pollutes (just as a politics of equaliberty can survive in autocratic regimes as long as a window for democratization is still open). Its principle is more basic and cannot be reduced to any specific ideology. Its known racist and nationalist versions do not exhaust its spectrum, for it can thrive without them, as it did in eras and cultures where both modern terms had no equivalence (as the Books of Ezra and Nehemiah, the apocryphal Book of Jubilees, or the scrolls left by the Qumran Sect exemplify). Moreover, there have been revolutionary, socialist, and communist, not only fascist, versions of this politics, such as the terror of the French Revolution and the Stalinist and Maoist purges throughout the twentieth century.

The total collapse of Nazism—arguably the ultimate paradigm of a politics of purity[25]—and the disintegration of Stalinism were conceived, for a certain historical moment, at least, as an ultimate defeat of the politics of purity itself. This defeat was marked after the Second World War by a universal consensus and global treatises condemning anti-Semitism, racism, and apartheid, and was seemingly sealed with the fall of the apartheid regime in South Africa in the early 1990s. But this account appears today as shortsighted. Balibar's essays on racism showed clearly, in the 1980s, how shortsighted this view was in postwar, "postcolonial" Europe. Looking at some of the current models of the politics of purity, among Indian nationalists, Pakistani Muslim fundamentalists,[26] Jewish Zionists, French or Hungarian neofascists, or American white supremacists (a partial list), one must admit that the forces animating the politics of purity are alive and well and that, far from being defeated, the modern forms of this type of politics seem no less irreversible than do the truth effects of "the event of equaliberty" produced by bourgeois revolutions of the eighteenth century.

THE LIMITS OF THE POLITICAL

This kind of politics is precisely what has been relegated outside of the very realm (and concept) of the political by at least one influential political thinker, Jacques Rancière.[27] For him, the purity of the political is established by an explicit denial of the possibility of a politics of purity.

> Politics doesn't always happen—it actually happens very rarely.... Politics only occurs when these mechanisms [the apparatuses of power] are stopped in their tracks by the effect of a presupposition that is totally foreign to them yet without which none of them could ultimately function: the presupposition of the equality of anyone and everyone.[28]

Disruption of the mechanisms of power, of the everyday functioning of governmental practices would be considered political only when carried out on the basis and in the name of the assumption of "the equality of anyone and everyone."

Disruption—or the attempt to disrupt—the mechanism of power is indeed crucial for anything to become political. For even power itself—governmental or otherwise, let alone the forces that collaborate with or oppose it—would assume a political dimension only once the acts and functioning of power are disrupted, when a gap is opened between its taken-for-granted presence and its factual operations, on the one hand, and its legitimization, or simply the possibility of these operations to be otherwise, on the other. This disruption should not be conceived necessarily in the form of a popular resistance, mass demonstrations, or a general strike. Even a poem or graffiti would suffice, even a naïve but hitherto-silenced observation of the kind offered by the little boy in the Hans Christian Andersen story *The Emperor's New Suit* can sometimes constitute a disruption and turn anything it touches—the king's body and clothes, his entire entourage, the two swindlers, and the whole cheering crowd—into a political matter.[29] The political moment is this event of disruption that problematizes power in public, deprives power of its seeming naturalness and inevitability, and introduces the possibility of change, of a different way to be governed, a different form of government, different relations between rulers and ruled, a different distribution of power and access to power, and different boundaries to the political community.[30]

Like Arendt, though with some differences, Rancière sets the bar for the disruption of the political much higher than what I am proposing here, closer to Balibar's own account.[31] Rancière turns the political moment into a rare and quite radical event. Politics, for Rancière, is separated from most human affairs; the numerous moments in which power has been questioned, problematized, disrupted, and resisted without invoking radical equality unjustifiably shrinks the history of politics. But the real problem with Rancière's concept of politics is not a matter of degrees of radicalness or comprehensiveness of the disruption but that only one kind of disruption is allowed. That which decides the political moment for Rancière is the eruption of radical equality of those subjected to a rule in which they do not take part, and this eruption is at one and the same time a radical opening of the closure of the political body and a leveling of all hierarchies within it. In this sense, Rancière's concept of politics is precisely a negation of the politics of purity. For a politics of purity closes the political community, redefining its terms and imposes metrics of legitimation for the hierarchies within it.

It would be a gross mistake to equate the politics of purity with what Rancière calls "the police." The call for purity has all too often been the principle underlying radical disruption to the order of that "police" and the many governmental apparatuses associated with it. The disruptive intervention in the state apparatus and its violent restructuring may be orchestrated from above, by the highest authorities, as clearly demonstrated by the transformations of the state in Nazi Germany, in Stalin's USSR in the 1930s, or today in Turkey under Erdoğan. But it may also come from below, carried out by the individuals and groups who take active part in reiterating and enforcing the imperative of purity, using it precisely to criticize power and defy it in the name of a higher power. Is there a reason to exclude these moments and those movements and forces from the history and theory of politics, or even to collect them under the heading and logic of racism? Is it right not to include in this history the many versions of sectarian politics, with their transformative potential and revolutionary fervor, which, from time immemorial, have acted on the principle of purity, performed ever-new modes of closure and exclusion, transforming modes of political belonging while invigorating hierarchies and restructuring them? The imperative of purity can be the binding principle of a politics that involves the people, the masses, while bypassing or undermining many of the formal institutions of government. Such a politics includes grassroots organizations, public gatherings, and the political actions carried out in the public sphere. In the course of these actions, power structures and the boundaries of the community (of those entitled to benefit from the power's protection and of those entitled to share it) are questioned more and less radically. Obviously, this politics has its own tension between the visionary and idealist elements and the more pragmatic, corruptible, or utterly corrupted elements. It is a politics like any other, it is as ancient as the politics of equaliberty, it has had its ancient, medieval, modern, and postmodern phases, and its specter, by which Europe has been haunted for so long, is looming large today over the entire global horizon.

Once the imperative of purity is understood as a political proposition, the concept of the political cannot be conceived from the perspective of equaliberty or that of democracy. Unlike Rancière's theory of *mésentente*, the proposition of equaliberty does not prevent us from thinking the two kinds of politics together despite, or precisely because of, their radical opposition. The comparison is worth making, for they oppose each other not as the core of the political versus the political's Other but as two extremes within a spectrum of political possibilities. Let me examine them briefly.

THE TWO EXTREMES AND THEIR COMMON GROUND

The hyperbolic statement of equaliberty is a proposition of democracy as an ever-renewable and ever-repeatable process of democratization. A struggle for equaliberty may survive in a nondemocratic regime, but the only regime that it is compatible with is a democracy in which democratization is an ongoing process. The imperative of purity, however, does not preclude any regime found on Plato's, Aristotle's, Montesquieu's, or Arendt's lists of political regimes. Rather, it inflects each of these in a specific way. In this sense, the imperative of purity inflects citizenship, too, and, as stated above, must be considered part of its history. Like equaliberty, purity is a principle that *precedes* the division between the political community and its ruling power, *demos* and *archē*, and gives these distinctions their distinct forms. These forms may change according to the type of liberty/equality—or purity—at stake. Various types of equaliberty are responsible for expanding and extending the bounds of the political community differently, but in each case, such restructuring is both a goal and an ongoing project; various types of purity are responsible for drawing the boundaries of the political community differently, but in each case, closure is both a goal and an ongoing project. In a politics of equaliberty, the closure of the community is both inevitable *and* an obstacle to be resisted, negotiated, and constantly removed; in a politics of purity, universalizing tendencies play a similar role.

Equaliberty is horizontal: the principle of a relation between anyone and everyone. Its questioning of boundaries is always a matter of time and circumstances, never of principle, whereas the principle that imposes closure on the political body is always foreign to it, or at least potentially so. From the perspective of equaliberty, citizenship is always expandable, its limits temporary and contingent. The struggle for equaliberty can neither constitute nor presuppose the identity, boundaries, or essence of the community in which it is taking place—it can only undermine and deconstruct them. Purity is vertical: the principle of a relation to a transcendent, salvific element, whether a god or an idea (of a superior race, class, or nation or of the mode of purification such as the revolution, the party, and so on). The imperative to purify does not simply contradict the universal claim of equality and liberty. Because it is always addressed to a particular group, to a distinct, special, if not divinely chosen camp, which it presupposes and constitutes at the same time, purity endows that political community, imaginary as it is, with an absolute privilege that negates universality *tout court*.[32] From the perspective of the imperative of purity, citizenship is not the ground for power's legitimization but a privilege derived from a principle and a source higher than both power and its subjects. This source, from which the imperative of purity emanates, is responsible for the fact that citizenship is always erodible, and that shrinking its scope and meaning is a recurring political project, carried out through or along with various forms of exclusion, dispossession, and oppression of the impure.

In much of modern and contemporary politics, certainly in the United States today, the purity of the camp and universal equaliberty are not simply contradictory but actively antagonistic positions.[33] If these two forms of politics are indeed opposite extremes within a spectrum of possibilities, it may be useful to look again at their common ground. This common ground, I believe, is that permanent tension about which Balibar speaks in the text that opens this essay, the tension between the institutions of power and the hyperbolic statement that sets the principle that these institutions are supposed to embody. The political emerges through this tension, whereas the performance, the enacted statement, and the institutions simultaneously assume their "politicality." Only when directed at a certain always-already-existing order of power does the performance of the statement assume or reveal its political nature. And only when addressed by a claim that problematizes their logic or practice do institutions of power lose their self-evident nature, assume their politicality, and reveal their potentiality for politics.

Most of Balibar's work vacillates in the space opened here, being interpellated by this tension between hyperbolic political statements and their aporetic encounter with, and embodiment in, political institutions. He would never fix his thinking on one of these poles without immediately referring to the other, always struggling to articulate the many and various historical and theoretical manifestations of the tension, and to reconstruct the dialectics unfolding between the opposing poles. I would like to take the liberty of interpreting this tension in which Balibar is so thoroughly engaged as a manifestation of the basic structure of the political event—and of the political *as* an event. This tension and this gap between the institutions of a ruling power and the acts that actually or virtually—but always publicly (a point we must return to)—challenge them is precisely where the political resides.

The hyperbolic principle of equaliberty and the obsession of purity are two opposite modes of challenging institutionalized power according to its own principles. Challenging existing institutions of equaliberty on the one hand and of purification on the other, they introduce gaps in the interstices of power that feed off the logic of that very power they publicly call into question. The ruling power can always be questioned in its own terms and the opposition between the poles is never played out fully, never creates an unbridgeable split, as is the case, for example, in a slave rebellion or a struggle against a foreign tyranny. This strange dialectics make these rival types of politics especially adept for demonstrating the nature of the political. In both, the interruption brought about by the problematization of power takes place in the *medias res*, with respect to an always-already-institutionalized power, on the one hand and, on the other, an excess of particularity or hyperbolic universality that, when called into present, is always-already remembered, if only as forgotten, concealed, or repressed. And even when a phantasy of a constituent foundation is violently sought, the struggle to achieve it interrupts an existing power structure while reiterating some of its elements and relying on various performances in which precedents are reiterated (as clearly demonstrated in the establishment of a community of purity in Ezra and Nehemiah or in the emblematic case of the French Revolution).

These two extreme forms of problematizing power are special even though they may not introduce forceful interruption into schemes of power relations, and even when they have little effect on the excess of particularity or universality in the political event (the failure to interrupt or achieve an excessive effect is always an option). The two opposite types of politics are special because the problematization of power's institutionalization is built into their logic. Without being necessarily democratic, they are open to the *demos*, which, however it is defined, can be called into question. Without a necessary figure of a Hobbesian or Schmittian sovereign, they recognize a political authority whose grip on power can always be challenged. The most radical political question, the relation between the political authority and the many—who is supposed to recognize the political authority and be bounded by it, who has access to it, and who is entitled to challenge it—can never be settled, because of the obsession with interpreting and applying the principle that binds this authority.

THE POLITICAL

We may now address the political more generally. There are many types of politics, of course, and not all of them manifest the political with the same degree of clarity. To understand this, one must draw a decisive distinction between politics and the political and allow for a politics that is hardly political, and for a political event that does not translate into politics. The political is any event in which a ruling power is problematized in public. A binding principle in the name of which power is problematized may be implied in or ascribed to the problematization—but the problematization may be carried out without it, in a silent refusal or a scream of protest or grief, for example. An interruption in the operation of power may follow the problematization—or not. What counts is the public problematization itself. This is the political event. It may take place even when a ruling power publicly defends one of its own acts or principles without being directly challenged, for this means that the possibility of such a challenge is publicly acknowledged (i.e., that an order of power has been denaturalized). An act, a person, a monument, policies and procedures, patterns of exchange and interrelation, space and time, gods and animals—any of these *becomes* political by taking part in the public problematization of an existing power, being drawn into the space opened in public between the problematizing act and the problematized authority, act, actor, etc. A thing becomes political because it becomes integral to such a challenge or its suppression. When this space of public contention shrinks, the political shrinks with it.[34] The political event is always also the event of becoming political, or of reasserting the politicality of whatever is publicly problematized in the event.[35]

The political cannot take place without an actual confrontation between the two parties to this tension, hence their copresence in some actual or virtual space. The political is distributed between these two poles, as the confrontation grants "politicality" to each. The political does not emanate from either of them; it resides in between. The universality of equaliberty and the exclusivity of "the pure camp" are two opposing forms this "in between" might take. The distinctly modern event of equaliberty is the historical moment in which the two forms appear as the exact inversion of each other, even when they defy and problematize the same power.

Hence, "the political" is not an idealized realm or a set of transcendental principles that precedes or conditions politics, grounds its autonomy, or sets its ultimate goals. The political is an event that takes place *by* publicly problematizing a certain order of power, a form of rule or a mode of government. When power is problematized with respect to principles that should allegedly bind it, when such principles are named, articulated, and questioned *in* the space created by this problematization, the political event can be prolonged, reiterated, and disseminated. But even without such articulation, the gestures expressing refusal, shock, unbearable grief, as well as ridicule or disdain, can be imitated and no less if not more widely disseminated.

The political event takes place through concrete performances of problematization of power and politicization of what power strives to naturalize, regardless of the nature of the "part" that defies power and questions its principles. The nature and scope of this event determine what is being politicized. Nothing is politicized *avant la lettre*—that is, prior to the performance and outside the scope of some such performance—and nothing *remains* political without reiterating this problematization, or at least without the ghostly presence of its suspended repetitions. This means, among other things, that the question of the autonomy of the political—which concerns Balibar a great deal—must be recast.

The political event is one in which a certain portion of politics' "other scene" is put on display. That another scene always accompanies politics, both preceding and following it, that the political struggle is both displaced from other spheres of actions and continues through other means, and that forces working in those other scenes (for there are always more than one) prepare the ground for and shape the stage of the political performance—all this, and the importance of all this for political theory, cannot be denied. If autonomy has any meaning here, it is because none of those forces and structures at work behind the political scene can determine the political event. How and what would be problematized, resisted, defied can never be foreclosed, no matter how totalitarian an order of power might become.

The problematization of power, however, need not be performed as defiance, disobedience, or anarchy—these may be merely invoked or alluded to as possibilities at the moment power is denaturalized. One only has to look through the open cracks to see the abyss, as Balibar shows convincingly when reading Arendt's essay on disobedience:

> We must say that, strictly speaking, human beings *are* their rights, or exist through them. But this notion covers over a profound antinomy, for we are forced to note that the same institutions that create rights—or, better still, by means of which individuals become human subjects by reciprocally conferring rights on one another—also constitute a threat to the human as soon as they destroy these rights or become an obstacle to them in practice.[36]

This immanent instability, reversibility, of political power, with its irreducible elements of unpredictability, cannot be dissociated, however, from the immanent potentiality of human beings to disobey.

> At the origin of political institutions—or better, in the indeterminate neighborhood of this origin—[there is] an imperceptible moment of anarchy that has to be constantly reactivated precisely if the institution is to be *political*. . . . Without the possibility of disobedience, there is no legitimate obedience.[37]

We should add, however, that the potentiality of disobedience does not depend on whether rights have been granted or deprived, whereas obedience necessitates the possibility of disobedience. Power is embedded in and exists through a set of institutionalized apparatuses because of the disruptive potentiality of individuals to disobey its decrees, whereas individuals obey because power is both regular and reversible, because it can smash their rights even when pretending to protect them, because *there is always more* it can take from them, unto death, and beyond—the death of their loved ones, the destruction of their world, the erasure of their memory. This is also, at the same time, a proof that their obedience can never be guaranteed.

When power is performed by those ascribed with agency and authority—the policeman, the tax collector, the streetlight with its camera, the talking head on the television screen—each of its agents may invoke the imaginary perpetuity and ubiquity of the ruling power and the supremacy of its authority. When power is disrupted and problematized, the individuals who bring the possibility of disobedience to the surface or actually perform it may pierce this image and seek to reinaugurate power. And both kinds of performance, it should be noted, by surrogates of a ruling power and by those challenging it, enact and imply suspensions of certain violent acts. But (contrary to Arendt, as Balibar understands well) it is not violence itself that is suspended, only *more* violence. At the end of the slippery slope of violence stands the violence that would eliminate the space in which the political resides.[38] This violence cannot be monopolized, not even by the state apparatuses of an effective sovereign power, and it might come from both sides of the barricades, no matter how asymmetrical the power relations seem to be. Furthermore, this violence may be integral to many forms of politics, including (if not especially) those we find at the two ends of the spectrum—equaliberty and purity. In and of itself, sheer violence, no matter how massive and excessive, does not put an end to the political; the political is doomed only when the space for the public problematization of power is closed or, more accurately, as long as no one dares to occupy it, fearing the forces that systematically prevent the subjects of power from reintroducing publicly the gap between the seeming naturalness and inevitability of power and its legitimacy or its alternative modes of operation. Excessive violence should be directed toward this goal, but it is only one way of achieving it; there are today several other, more gentle ways of doing so—you may recognize them immediately when looking at your laptop, iPad, or iPhone screen.

Although violence itself does not put an end to the political, politics does not ensure it. Not all politics is political. Whatever goes on behind closed doors, concealed from the public, cannot involve public problematization of power and is a power struggle that fails to become political. The same is true more generally for the institutions of power and authority. The state and its apparatuses are not political merely by virtue of being involved in the more or less institutional exercise of power for more or less collective ends, not even because they concern the lives of the governed and the consistency and boundaries of the community. They become political and are endowed with a politicizing force when they are split by the acts that call into question, in public, what they do, how they are structured and legitimized, and how they are affected by forces beyond their control. Similarly, terrorist organizations don't cease being political because they use brute force, and are not baptized into the political sphere once they start to negotiate; they are political as long as their acts of terror force the public problematization of power.

This lack of overlapping between politics and the political goes both ways. A public reading of a poem, graffiti drawn on a wall to be seen by many, a defiant speech in a graduation ceremony—all these may be political even without any affiliation with any of the institutions of a recognizable, organized politics. Even when not entirely institutionalized in parties, blocks, and social movements, politics requires a continuity of affiliations and bonding—persistent patterns of reiteration of principles, claims, and demands—and the political event may take place without any of these. When it is conceived in relation to a recognizable politics, its potential disruption has already been reduced to the terms, coordinates, expectations, and horizons of what is possible in that particular politics. Politics is a particular mode of performing the political that realizes and conceals it at the same time. No matter how power is problematized, there is always much that remains unsaid, unthematized, and ignored; there is always more ruling and governing than the political event can articulate and problematize. When demanding not to be governed thus, that much, or like this, those defying power leave in the dark, unarticulated, inexistent perhaps, other possible modes of rule and governing that lie between what has been problematized and the anarchy that the political act could have brought into existence.

The political event happens in public, but its disruption of power is limited by the way "publicness" is institutionalized. Like any other institutions of power, those through which a public comes into being and persists can be called into question by a political event. With the help of figures such as camp, community, the people, the nation, and the working class, the public is imagined more clearly than it can ever be grasped or experienced. Lately, the public is simulated by opinion polls and replaced by devices such as "people meters" and metaphors such as "base." Neither an imagined nor a simulated public can stand for the public that a political event presupposes. This public appears when some people—and it does not matter how many or who they are—are capable of responding to power by saying not "we, *the* people" but rather "*we, those people* affected by this power." This response, always contingent, insecure, and unstable, not the institution of the power that invokes it, is the inaugural moment of the political. Once this moment comes into being, it immediately calls for its own reiteration; it cannot survive without it.

An actual ruling power precedes the political community and is the first thing that community has in common. This commonality of a ruling power always exceeds—but is also far less than—the imaginary community envisaged or called for by any specific politics. From opposite directions, and for opposite purposes, the politics of equality, just like the politics of purity, throws into relief the irreducible incongruity between these two commonalities, one projected through the imagined unity of a ruling power, and the other ascribed to the imagined community under its rule.

NOTES

1. Étienne Balibar, *Equaliberty*, trans. James Ingram (Durham, N.C.: Duke University Press, 2014), 50; my emphasis.

2. The first version of this essay was written in the dark shadow of the recent elections. A certain theme, on which I did not intend to dwell, has become irresistible. As a result, the constructive part of my essay will be sketchy and fragmentary.

3. See Étienne Balibar, *Politics and the Other Scene* (London: Verso, 2002). To these three, Balibar later added his interpretation of the politics of human rights, which he presents as "a politics of the second order" or "a politics of politics," a politics that concerns decisions related to the tension itself, "reflecting the consequences of its insurrections and resisting the modalities of its perversions." At stake in this politics are decisions regarding "which compromises or articulations of rights must be left to authorities [i.e., the current form of the institutionalization of equality and liberty] and which ones must be elaborated by the people themselves [i.e., those committed to the hyperbolic principle and to following its call] in the form of intellectual debates and social movements" (Étienne Balibar, "Politics of Human Rights," *Constellations* 20, no. 1 [March 2013]: 20, 23).

4. Balibar, *Politics and the Other Scene*, viii.

5. The two directions are implied but not explicitly addressed in Étienne Balibar, *Violence and Civility: On the Limits of Political Philosophy*, trans. G. M. Goshgarian (New York: Columbia University Press, 2015).

6. Balibar, *Violence and Civility*, 20.

7. The dialectics of equality and liberty and "their realization in the forms of property and community . . . [allow] us to set out successively three ages in politics," an ancient one, a modern and a postmodern" (Balibar, *Equaliberty*, 65; see also 127–28).

8. Balibar, *Equaliberty*, 119–20. This is a milder version of a stronger claim made in the original essay, "The Proposition of Equaliberty," published in 1989. There, Balibar underlines "the revolutionary moment of the *Declaration* and its *uninterrupted efficacy* in the course of sociopolitical struggles"; he argues that by linking the struggle against tyranny with the struggle against injustice, the Revolution of 1789 brought about "an *irreversible mutation* in the very meaning of the term [revolution]," and he ascribes to the current, postmodern age of politics the most advanced form of equaliberty that goes "beyond the abstract or generic concept of man on the basis of generalized citizenship" (Balibar, *Equaliberty*, 42, 47, 65; emphases mine).

9. The paper was first presented at Le Petit Odéon, November 27, 1989, and first published as Étienne Balibar, "La proposition de l'égaliberté," *Les conférences du perroquet* 22 (November 1989); translated into English as "'Rights of Man and Rights of the Citizen': The Modern Dialectics of Equality and Freedom," in *Masses, Classes, Ideas: Studies on Politics and Philosophy before and after Marx*, trans. James Swenson (New York: Routledge, 1994), 39–59.

10. Étienne Balibar, "Racism and Nationalism," in Étienne Balibar and Immanuel Wallerstein, *Race, Nation, Class: Ambiguous Identities*, trans. Chris Turner (London: Verso, 1991), 37–67; originally published as *Race, nation, classe: Les identités ambiguës* (Paris: Découverte, 1988).

11. Balibar, "Racism and Nationalism, 53, 54.

12. Balibar, "Racism and Nationalism," 52.

13. Balibar, "Racism and Nationalism," 59; my emphasis.
14. Balibar, "Racism and Nationalism," 59–61.
15. Balibar, "Racism and Nationalism," 39.
16. Balibar, "Racism and Nationalism," 54–60.
17. Balibar, *Politics and the Other Scene*, 1–39.
18. Balibar, "Racism and Nationalism," 59–60.
19. Balibar, *Equaliberty*, 49.
20. Balibar, *Equaliberty*, 127.

21. The relations between purity and holiness unfold differently in different layers of the Bible and are widely disputed. See for example M. J. H. M. Poorthuis and J. Schwartz, eds., *Purity and Holiness: The Heritage of Leviticus* (Boston: Brill, 2000). In the rabbinic tradition, purity came to be equated with holiness and even replaced it altogether. See Yair Furstenberg, *Purity and Community in Antiquity: Halakhic Traditions between Second Temple Judaism and the Mishna* (Jerusalem: Magnes, 2016) [in Hebrew].

22. Balibar underscores the need to account for "egalitarian" racist societies as part of "the structural conditions . . . of modern racism" ("Racism and Nationalism," 49). What is modern here, however, is racism, not the egalitarian element associated with the hyperbolic principle of purity.

23. See Donald P. Moffat, *Ezra's Social Drama: Identity Formation, Marriage and Social Conflict in Ezra 9 and 10*, Library of Biblical Studies (London: Bloomsbury, 2013), 81–82; see also the works cited in Moffat, *Ezra's Social Drama*, 81n56; Wilhelm Rudolph, *Esra und Nehemia samt 3: Esra* (Tübingen, Germany: Mohr Siebeck, 1949), 89; Jacob M. Myers, *Ezra, Nehemiah*, 1st ed., Anchor Bible Commentaries (Garden City, N.Y.: Doubleday, 1965), 77; and Joseph Blenkinsopp, *Ezra-Nehemiah: A Commentary*, The Old Testament Library (London: SCM Press, 1989), 176.

24. Recently another, related episode from Ezra and Nehemiah, the building of a wall around Jerusalem, was invoked in a sermon delivered by Robert Jeffress, senior pastor of First Baptist Church in Dallas, Texas, during the morning worship service of Donald Trump's inauguration day (Sarah Pulliam Bailey, "'God Is Not against Building Walls!': The Sermon Trump Heard From Robert Jeffress before His Inauguration," *Washington Post* [January 20, 2017], https://www.washingtonpost.com/news/acts-of-faith/wp/2017/01/20/god-is-not-against-building-walls-the-sermon-donald-trump-heard-before-his-inauguration). Jeffress, who had previously spoken about Obama as "antichrist" and about Islam as an "evil religion," and who described the lifestyle of gays as "miserable" and "filthy," told Trump that Nehemiah built a wall around Jerusalem "to protect its citizens from enemy attack." But when placed in context, the notion of the enemy would include Mexican migrants, "filthy" gays, and even Catholics "led astray by Satan," and the real danger these enemies pose is degradation to a "blessed—great—. . . nation whose God is the Lord." Hence, this reference to "the Wall" is but another expression of a politics of purity, as it is indeed in the biblical story.

25. See, most adequate for the point I am trying to make here, Philippe Lacoue-Labarthe and Jean Luc Nancy, "The Nazi Myth," trans. Brian Holmes, *Critical Inquiry* 16, no. 2 (Winter 1990): 291–312; and Jean Luc Nancy, "Eulogy for the Mêlée," in *Being Singular Plural*, trans. Robert D. Richardson and Anne E. O'Byrne (Stanford: Stanford University Press, 2000), 145–58.

26. By virtue of its name, Pakistan is a particularly apt example. See Mohsin Hamid, "In the Land of the Pure, No One Is Pure Enough," *The Guardian* (January 27, 2018), https://www.theguardian.com/books/2018/jan/27/mohsin-hamid—exit-west-pen-pakistan.

27. Rancière is the clearest voice of an approach shared by many who question and explicate the political only or mainly from the perspective of some kind of radical democracy, with strong commitment to equality—that is, from the perspective of the politics they prefer. Rancière also brings into relief the strong Eurocentric bias common to many of these thinkers.

28. Jacques Rancière, *Disagreement: Politics and Philosophy*, trans. Julie Rose (Minneapolis: University of Minnesota Press, 1999), 17.

29. In Andersen's tale, the Emperor understands the message but decides to "bear up to the end," and the procession continues as "the chamberlains walked with still greater dignity, as if they carried the train which did not exist" (Hans Christian Andersen, *Fairy Tales and Stories*, trans. H. P. Paull [1872], http://hca.gilead.org.il/emperor.html). Only now everyone knew who the real stupid person was and who collaborated with that stupidity, and with the scam that allowed it to be shown in public.

30. For a systematic account of the political moment, of which this section is a fragment, see Adi Ophir, "The Political," *Mafte'akh: Lexical Review for Political Theory* 2 (Summer 2010), http://mafteakh.tau.ac.il/issue/2010-02/ [in Hebrew].

31. See the opening of this essay and note 6, above.

32. The superb analytics of universals and universalization recently proposed by Balibar and the pluralization and differentiation of universalism that this analysis entails would seem irrelevant from the point of view of a politics of purity. For Balibar's analysis, see Étienne Balibar, *Des universels: Essais et conférences* (Paris: Galilée, 2016).

33. The tension may take many forms. But even if the antagonism of equaliberty and purity dominates the political scene today, it by no means exhausts the diversity of the forms of politics at play.

34. Arendt explained this in detail, taking totalitarianism as the paradigmatic, albeit not the only, case in which the space that enables political events is reduced or eliminated. The Frankfurt School thinkers addressed a similar problematics with respect to liberal democracies, and later critics as different as Baudrillard and Brown have extended this analysis. See Jean Baudrillard, *In the Shadow of the Silent Majorities: Or, the End of the Social, and Other Essays*, trans. Paul Foss, John Johnston, and Paul Patton (New York: Semiotext(e), 1983); and Wendy Brown, *Undoing the Demos: Neoliberalism's Stealth Revolution* (New York: Zone Books, 2015). The list is long;

besides being brilliant, these two works represent two different and influential trends of the same problematization that span over four decades. Most of these thinkers, however, thought about the shrinking of political space in terms of diminishing freedom and growing inequalities. They missed the other option, namely, that the political space might be reopened—and not only closed—by a claim to purity embedded in a very powerful and dangerous politics of its own.

35. Therefore, a struggle in which nothing is at stake except for a sheer will to dominate, on the one hand, or an arbitrary, whimsical expression of individual freedom, on the other hand, is not political. When this text was written it was still unclear who won the last election—the politics of purity or the party whose only principle is both to eliminate the role of principles in the use of power, including the very distinction between true and false, and hence to eliminate the political. Sooner or later, the coalition between the two ought to break down. See Marian Constable, "When Words Cease to Matter," *Amor Mundi*, Hannah Arendt Center, November 20, 2016, https://medium.com/amor-mundi/draft-c-when-words-cease-to-matter-fe71c3637099.

36. Étienne Balibar, "Hannah Arendt, the Right to Have Rights, and Civic Disobedience," in *Equaliberty*, trans. James Ingram (Durham, N.C.: Duke University Press, 2014), 173.

37. Balibar, "Hannah Arendt," 175.

38. One may be tempted to read this excessive violence as referring to Balibar's concept of extreme violence (Balibar, *Politics and the Other Scene*, 23–35, chap. 7; Balibar, *Violence and Civility*, chap. 1, 127–28). The overlap is only partial, however. As the critics cited above (see note 34, above) show, it does not take a genocide to eliminate the political. And even in the midst of a genocide, a space for challenging power may emerge.

PUNISHMENT

Didier Fassin

Is punishment a *political* concept?[1] Indeed, as a concept, it has been mostly discussed by moral philosophers and legal theorists who have defended the importance of distinguishing between definition (supposedly value-neutral) and justification (definitely value-laden), between the institution in general (viewed as justified) and the act in particular (possibly subject to criticism), between backward-oriented considerations (deontological or retributivist) and forward-oriented arguments (consequentialist or utilitarian).

In fact, there are two sorts of reasons why the concept should be politicized—rather than being contemplated only from moral and legal perspectives. The first reason is structural: punishment largely has to do with a particular arrangement of power, sovereignty, authority, repression, violence, and the state. Of course, it can also be inflicted by a father on his disobedient child or by a teacher on an unruly student, but the remarkable fact in that regard has been the contrast between the increase in the intolerance toward physical and even moral retribution in the family and at school and the acceptance of ever-tougher public policies against offenders, a contrast that attests to the expansion of the state monopoly over the legitimate use of punishment. Significantly, on July 1, 2016, the day when France established a new record for peacetime regarding the demographics of its imprisoned population, its Parliament passed a law prohibiting spanking. The second reason is historical: in recent decades, most countries in the world have gone through a unique punitive moment. I use the term "moment" in reference to a period during which a spectacular extension of the domain of punishment has occurred independently of a rise in crime rate, as well as to a dynamic, as suggested by the etymology of the word that has been maintained with the term "momentum." What characterizes the punitive moment is this singular configuration in which punishment, the putative solution to the problem of crime, has increasingly become the problem itself because of its consequence in terms of social exclusion, community destructuring, soaring incarceration costs, and, ultimately, increased crime recidivism. With almost seven million people under the supervision of the correctional system—more than two million of those imprisoned, and this number having been multiplied by eight over thirty years—the United States offers the most extreme illustration of this phenomenon, but statistics collected since the 1990s at a global level indicate that the trend is worldwide (notably in France, where for ten years I have conducted ethnographic research on the police, the justice system, and the correctional institution) with only few exceptions, such as most Scandinavian countries. In light of these two reasons—structural and historical—the concept of punishment can be deemed intrinsically and circumstantially political.

In "Violence, Ideality and Cruelty," a lecture delivered in a seminar at the Collège de France in January 1995, Étienne Balibar notes that one German word, *Gewalt*, ambivalently corresponds to both power and violence, this conflagration of meanings being revealed by the translation in other languages.[2] In the same way, I suggest that the English term "punishment" equivocally refers to what the French would express with three notions: *punition*, which is the most mundane and generic form; *châtiment*, which has a religious or literary connotation; and *peine*, which belongs to the juridical and technical language. Here again, the translation unveils the polysemy of the term. This polysemy should not be seen, however, as an obstacle to the comprehension of punishment but, on the contrary, as a condition to it. My critique of the prevalent liberal theories of punishment, whether by philosophers or jurists, precisely resides in the fact that this foundational ambiguity is rarely acknowledged. This oversight allows most authors to limit "punishment" implicitly to its legal sense of the French *peine* and, thus, to adopt a normative approach at the expense of a critical one. Reciprocally, it is their tacit use of this restrictive sense that generates their misunderstanding of my alternative reading of "punishment," which they consider too inclusive.

The most widely accepted definition of "punishment," derived from H. L. A. Hart's famous 1959 "Prolegomenon to the Principles of Punishment," provides five decisive criteria: (1) the infliction of a pain or of an unpleasant equivalent (2) to an actual or supposed offender (3) in response to an offense against legal rules (4) that is intentionally imposed by a legal authority and (5) administered by human beings with appropriate roles.[3] Although the definition is said to be independent of any justification, it assumes that punishment is both legitimate since it sanctions an offender for the offense he has committed and legal since it is applied under the law for a violation of the law. Actually, Hart himself had called attention to the risk of what he described as a "definitional stop" that would restrain our questioning of punishment, but his important caveat has not been really taken into account by philosophers and jurists, who have mostly focused on the justification while simply using this definition as their starting point. Even social scientists have often adopted it for methodological reasons perfectly grounded but problematically exclusive.

For my part, I want to challenge this definition on three counts: first, it purposely ignores nonlegitimate and extralegal expressions of punishment; second, it questionably takes for granted the centrality of suffering in the administration of punishment; and third, it wrongly presupposes a just and fair distribution of punishment. These three criticisms are crucial for the apprehension of punishment as a political concept. But this discussion of the commonly accepted definition stems from a more general epistemological position regarding the relation of the social sciences to their objects. Indeed, when studying a social fact, one option consists in circumscribing it precisely from the outset through a definition so as to try to recognize it in the real world, whereas the other conversely privileges its progressive emergence from fieldwork through conversations with actors and observation of action. In the first case, the social fact is thus constructed a priori from the author's viewpoint, while in the second it is established a posteriori from the agents' perspective. One may call the former approach Durkheimian and the latter Weberian. The choice of one method rather than the other may have significant political implications. In my view, a critique of punishment definitely implies a comprehensive perspective based on empirical work allowing for an understanding of punishment as it is rather than as it should be.

So what is in a definition? The typical situation that moral philosophers and legal scholars have in mind when they use their definition of "punishment" is that of a judge deciding in court the sentence to be given to an offender as a retribution for his offense, which is thus established and punished under the law. It corresponds to the official version of punishment as legally grounded, legitimately imposed, and fairly distributed. This is certainly a common configuration but far from the most frequent. Let us consider an institution that does not have as its mission punishment but does punish routinely and extensively: the police.[4] In quantitative terms, their punitive actions are decidedly more numerous than are those of the justice system: as an example, in France, there are one hundred thirty-five thousand arrests for use of cannabis but nine thousand prison sentences, and to use an even more telling illustration, in the United States, the number of individuals killed by law-enforcement agents is forty times higher than the number of persons executed as a result of a legal process. Actually, as I realized while carrying out an ethnography of anticrime brigades on the outskirts of Paris for fifteen months, policing has become the most ordinary mode of retribution experienced by many individuals, especially those from ethno-racial minorities belonging to the working class and living in disadvantaged neighborhoods. Punishment by law-enforcement officers takes multiple forms: harassment through stop-and-frisk, bullying via insults and threats, humiliation by offensive comments and public handcuffing, gratuitous arrests and taking into custody, and physical brutality and moral violence. It involves presumed offenders as well as mere bystanders, in large part on the basis of ethno-racial profiling. In other words, it is not necessary that the persons punished be guilty of any specific violation of the law: their culpability is assumed based on generic features such as appearance and residence. Two telling illustrations of the disconnection between criminal activity and retributive action are punitive expeditions and random punishment, especially frequent in response to an offense committed against the police. In the first case, it is the whole group—for instance, the inhabitants of an apartment block in a housing project who are the victims of the excessive use of force, being pushed, thumped, or pinned to the ground, and when a house search is conducted, have their doors broken and furniture overturned. In the second case, it is anyone in the group, usually the slowest runner or the least lucky passerby, who is beaten up, arrested, and indicted in place of the culprit.

One could dispute the fact that these acts are considered punishment. Are they not plain abuses of power, sheer domination, pure repression? When it is in response to an offense against the police, is it not simply reprisal? Some have tried to differentiate these terms, often with good theoretical or moral reasons. Thus, Robert Nozick establishes a clear distinction between retribution and revenge.[5] The distinction is analytically valuable, with five proposed criteria for differentiating the two, while also ideologically oriented, as it separates us (the civilized who punish) from them (the barbarians who avenge). But empirically, the distinction is often difficult to establish and ultimately serves to legitimize or delegitimize the infliction of pain. How to decide, then, when a given practice can be regarded as punishment? Two kinds of arguments may be used: one, subjective, refers to the meaning given by the agents to their action; the other, objective, concerns the interpretation that the analyst can make of the course of action. In the case of the aggressive behavior of the police toward given publics, both arguments speak strongly in favor of punishment.

First, the agents consider it as such. This is true in particular of the officers themselves. It is not only that they would try to mask reprehensible practices of vengeance with fear of consequences from their hierarchy or from the justice system: they do find rational justifications for their acts. On the one hand, they indiscriminately regard those they handle in this way as actual enemies and potential criminals: mistreatment is therefore just deserts. On the other hand, they systematically view judges as being too lenient toward the suspects whom they arrest: justice in the street becomes a substitute for the magistrates' supposed indulgence. However, neither justification is factually grounded, since opinion polls indicate that a majority of people, including those in housing projects, have favorable views of the police and even try to collaborate with them, whereas penal statistics show that judges are increasingly severe in their sentencing, especially with respect to the petty crime typically committed by lower classes. Notwithstanding these discrepancies, for law-enforcement agents there is a moral justification to what they deem just punishment. Although most people would describe it as violence, this justification serves to cover up racist prejudices and discriminatory practices.

Second, the institution also participates in this interpretation. Especially revealing is the fact that over the past two decades, the number of offenses of insulting an officer and resisting arrest has skyrocketed. As the agents and their superiors admitted to me, this incrimination corresponds to situations of police misconduct, either through verbal provocation or use of excessive force. In particular, when the individual is injured, the accusations of insulting an officer and resisting arrest become a legal instrument for a preemptive counterattack in case of complaint for police violence. During the trial, it is the word of the sworn-in agent against the word of the alleged suspect. There is therefore a double punishment, first physically, on the spot, and then legally, in court. The institution forcefully backs this practice as the Ministry of the Interior encourages officers to file complaints and request financial compensation (it even pays attorneys' fees for officers who file such complaints). This is part of a broader policy that uses law enforcement as an instrument to enforce a social order in disadvantaged neighborhoods and among low-income populations in the name of the war on crime. Such illegal, illegitimate, and unfair practices serve to inculcate the concerned individuals into their place in society. They simultaneously produce political subjection and subjectivation. The state of emergency declared after the 2015 Paris attacks has extended the discretionary power of the police for these targeted punitive practices.

If we accept these premises, such police interventions involve an institution that has no legal authority to punish and yet does punish outside the law using ethno-racial profiling for stop-and-frisk or unjustified and disproportionate physical force for arrests. Moreover, they affect individuals who are at most suspects, and frequently not even so. They simply belong to stigmatized and dominated social groups, and they often do not have the pretext that an offense has been committed, since it is merely routine behavior. In other words, most of the criteria defining "punishment" in the legal tradition are absent from the actual practices of punishment by law-enforcement agents. Of course, such practices are specific neither to the French police nor to the police in general. A more systematic examination of the multiple expressions of state violence exerted against certain individuals or groups in various countries with retributive intentions would show that punishment often considerably exceeds its classic definition. In fact, only one criterion of the latter seems to resist the empirical test: the infliction of pain as a retribution for something that does not have to be an offense but can simply be what those targeted represent, that is, the form of otherness that they embody and the suspicion associated with it.

That punishment would, in the final instance, be reduced to the imposition of suffering—be it through flogging, imprisoning, or shaming—is probably the least questioned fact about punishment among theorists as well as laypersons. The avoidance of this questioning comes down to a denial of two crucial facts: far from being universal, this *reductio ad dolori* is temporally and spatially circumscribed, and far from being accidental, it is telling of profound truths rarely acknowledged.

First, punishment has not always and everywhere corresponded to the infliction of pain. In most societies, until a recent period, the commission of a reprehensible action called for a collective response in terms of compensation, generally material. Etymologically, as has been shown by Émile Benveniste, the Greek *poinē* and the Classical Latin *poena*, from which the word "punishment" stems, referred to the debt that had to be paid to atone for a crime; only in Late Latin did the connotation of torment appear; it remains explicitly present in the word "pain."[6] Similarly, Latin *retribuere*, which later yielded the noun "retribution," meant "to give in exchange" and "to restitute what is owed," whether it implied recompense or penalty; interestingly, at the time of the Renaissance, under a differentiated religious influence, the English "retribution" came to have the negative sense of punishment for a wrong, whereas French *rétribution* took the positive meaning of fair-salary rewarding work. Beyond this philological discussion, it is notable that historical findings from ancient worlds as well as ethnological accounts from precolonial societies attest to the generalized practice of reparation. Thus, Georg Simmel discusses *wergild*, which was the sum required to repay a crime, in Anglo-Saxon England.[7] Similarly, Claude Lévi-Strauss mentions practices in the form of reparation among contemporary Plains Indians.[8] For the Western world, Christianity at the end of the Middle Ages, and for traditional societies, colonization in the modern era, radically transformed the moral economy of punishment from a dominant logic of exchange into a dominant logic of suffering. In response to the crime committed, the pain inflicted on the offender replaced the debt owed to the offended or his relatives. Most importantly, whereas the payment of the debt previously involved a collective obligation for the clan or the family, the infliction of the pain henceforth signified the individual liability of the culprit.

Second, the fact that punishment amounts to the imposition of suffering suggests more troubling truths. As noted by Émile Durkheim, the act of punishing often seems to include "an additional torment that serves no purpose," whose "motivating force is entirely emotional."[9] But why would that be? Why should the judge humiliate the accused with hurtful remarks and embarrassing lectures before sending them to jail, to the point that when I would meet one of them later in his prison cell, he would tell me that in court he could not wait for the end of the trial, even when he knew this meant his incarceration? Why would police officers purposely put handcuffs on a suspect they have arrested incorrectly so as to painfully twist his arms and make fun of his complaints while taking him into the precinct for questioning? Why would a corrections officer refuse a shower to an inmate and ostensibly let another take one as they return from the yard where they have played sports? I intentionally use mundane illustrations here, avoiding much more dramatic or tragic cases that result in the death of an individual in the hands of police or corrections officers. This excess in the practice of punishment has been interpreted by Nietzsche in the most explicit and powerful manner as "the voluptuous pleasure *de faire le mal pour le plaisir de le faire*."[10] In the assimilation of punishment with suffering and, even more, in the unnecessary torment that is added to it, one cannot not recognize the manifestation of bare cruelty. Such ruthlessness is not, as is often argued, the fact of outliers, of cynical judges or sadistic officers. It is not the exception: it is part and parcel of retribution. In fact, society delegates to certain institutions and certain professions the power to mete out punishment so as to be in excess of what it is supposed to be. Typically, a prison sentence is never only a deprivation of liberty: it is also a deprivation of autonomy, of privacy, of affective and sexual life, of the right to decide on one's most personal facts and ordinary events of life, and ultimately, in most cases, for lack of work, education, and rehabilitation, it is a deprivation of the very meaning of the sentence.[11] The culmination of cruelty is solitary confinement, which is a punishment within the punishment, an unbounded torment added to the normal infliction of pain, which concerns eighty thousand inmates on any given day in the United States.

To understand how punishment can escape its official definition and exceed its determined limits, how extralegal and nonlegitimate retribution is normalized, how suffering is imposed with little restraint, one has to take into account a dimension that has not received the attention it merits in classical theory: the distribution of punishment. It is because certain individuals and certain groups are more easily targeted that, for them, such exceptions may become the rule, that policing may be an ordinary mode of punishing them, and that the infliction of pain may seem justified in their case as a form of retribution.

The distribution of punishment across society is, however, obscured by the fact that the differentiation of offenders appears to be a mere differentiation of offenses. It is not that African Americans are more harshly punished, the champions of law and order policies contend; it is that they commit more crimes deemed punishable. Indeed, the question "Who is punished?" is strictly linked to another: what is punished? As shown by Michel Foucault, the distribution of punishment is the consequence of the differentiation of illegalisms.[12] Not all offenses are treated in the same way. Today, in France, tax evasion is better tolerated socially than shoplifting is, and in the United States, financial crime is settled through negotiations leading to fines for the company, whereas petty crime is settled through plea-bargaining leading to prison sentences for the accused. The explicit differentiation of illegalisms is itself in large part conditioned by an implicit differentiation of populations in terms of their punishability, that is, the social inclination to punish their deviant practices. But whereas Foucault tends to link the selective severity in the eighteenth and nineteenth century with the economic effect of illegalisms, robbery being apparently more damaging to capitalism than fraud is, I would argue that in contemporary society it is rather the moral evaluation of perpetrators that is at stake, the undesirability of ethno-racial minorities, immigrants, and the poor, rendering them definitely more punishable a priori. More than the quality of the offense, it is the quality of the offender that explains the intolerance of society toward certain illegalisms rather than toward others.

Dominated categories are, thus, those deemed punishable. They are also those for whom punishment can be something different from what it is supposed to be and imprisonment more than the deprivation of freedom. In the French short-stay prison where I conducted an ethnography, black and Arab men represented two thirds of the inmates, half of whom declared themselves unemployed. During the four years of my research, the number of prisoners increased by one fifth as the facility became more and more overcrowded. In contradiction with the centennial legal principle of single-cell housing, cells were occupied by two inmates, although their nine square meters were designed for one person. The indignity of the prison system reflects the assessment of their occupiers' worthiness. Translated into a hierarchy of illegalisms, the hierarchy of populations ultimately produces an unequal distribution of punishment not only in quantitative terms (the overrepresentation of ethno-racial minorities and socioeconomically disadvantaged) but also in qualitative terms (the carceral condition being an indication of it).

Punishment is not what it is said to be. Both common sense and theoretical discourses tend to represent it in a way that not only justifies it on utilitarian or retributive ground but also legitimizes it as an institution that is necessary for the common good and the social fabric. The empirical examination of punishment does not confirm this representation. Without adopting a normative stance regarding the justification or legitimacy of punishment, I argue that what is assumed in order to justify and legitimize it is simply unfounded. The critical approach I have tried to develop has therefore proceeded in two steps. First, the confrontation of the norm, along with its implementation, revealed the discrepancy between the two: punishment exceeds its definition, its illegal use is trivialized, its social distribution is unfair, its equivalence with the infliction of pain is problematic. Second, the interpretation of this discrepancy unveils its logics: the determination of punishable populations has for its counterpart the impunity of others, both processes being made opaque via an apparently neutral hierarchy of crime; punishable populations correspond both economically and ethno-racially to undesirable social categories, whose alleged unworthiness renders possible their mistreatment by the repressive institutions; punishment is therefore better understood not in terms of justice but in terms of unequal allocation of power relations and social resources.

NOTES

1. Didier Fassin, *The Will to Punish*, ed. Christopher Kutz (2017; Oxford, UK: Oxford University Press, 2018).

2. Étienne Balibar, "Violence, Ideality and Cruelty," in *Politics and the Other Scene* (1997; London: Verso, 2002).

3. H. L. A. Hart, "The Presidential Address: Prolegomenon to the Principles of Punishment," *Proceedings of the Aristotelian Society* 60 (1959–60): 1–26.

4. Didier Fassin, *Enforcing Order: An Ethnography of Urban Policing* (2017; Cambridge, UK: Polity, 2013).

5. Robert Nozick, "Retributive Punishment," in *Philosophical Explanations* (Cambridge, Mass.: Harvard University Press, 1981), 363–97.

6. Émile Benveniste, *Dictionary of Indo-European Concepts and Society* (1969; Chicago: HAU Books, 2016).

7. Georg Simmel, *The Philosophy of Money* (1907; London: Routledge, 1978).

8. Claude Lévi-Strauss, *Tristes tropiques* (Paris: Plon, 1955).

9. Émile Durkheim, *The Division of Labor in Society* (1893; New York: Free Press, 1984).

10. Friedrich Nietzsche, *On the Genealogy of Morals* (1887; New York: Vintage Books, 1989).

11. Didier Fassin, *Prison Worlds: An Ethnography of the Carceral Condition* (2015; Cambridge, UK: Polity, 2016).

12. Michel Foucault, *Discipline and Punish: The Birth of the Prison* (1975; New York: Pantheon, 1977).

RACE

Hanan Elsayed

In 1992, Étienne Balibar participated in a colloquium devoted to the question "Is the term *race* unnecessary [*de trop*] in the French Constitution?"[1] The colloquium was itself part of a national debate over the question of whether the term "race" should be removed from the article in the Constitution that guaranteed the "equality of all citizens before the law, without distinction of origin, race or religion."[2] Those in favor of its removal argued that race was now generally recognized as a fiction founded on discredited scientific notions whose function was to perpetuate the subjection of racialized populations. To retain the term in the Constitution, they argued, would be to permit the continuation of "racial thinking" and, by extension, the racist attitudes that inevitably arise from it.

Balibar's response contains the lines of argumentation that continue to define both his conception of racism and the place of race within it, beginning with the postulate that racism both precedes and exceeds every notion of race as its condition of possibility. First, Balibar warned against the danger of a purely political elimination of the word "race" in the name of the scientific evidence. To deduce the disappearance of racism from the invalidation of the biological concept of distinct human races is to deny the very real modes of exclusion operating around a social construction that is anything but a mere illusion. The concept of race as it functions in biology and the concept of race (which may exist and function in the absence of the word) in social sciences and even popular culture are not the same. The refutation of one concept may have little effect on the other. The proposal to delete the word from the French Constitution fails to recognize the different meanings of race as a concept and its different functions in the biological and social realms. It is an empty gesture that can neither banish the concept that designates the ongoing processes of racialization nor diminish their practical existence in the world today. On the contrary, to render it invisible is to allow it to operate more effectively: "The word *race* in the Constitution is not unnecessary. It would rather be *insufficient* for what we have to face."[3]

In what follows, I will briefly explore the three nodal points of Balibar's analysis of race and racism:

1. The relation between race and racism, on the one hand, and nation and nationalism, on the other, both grounded in what Balibar calls "fictive identity"
2. The relation between race and racism and the theory and practice of universalism, the definition of the human through the identification/production of anthropological differences, and the tendency of equality (a notion central to any universalism) to become confused with similitude and likeness
3. The process by which the foreigner becomes the stranger, who will in turn become the enemy. The essentialization of language and culture and its relation to the production of the inassimilable and incompatible that underlie many of the contemporary forms of racism.

THE RELATION BETWEEN RACE, RACISM, AND THE NATION

For Balibar, the current and potential objects of racism paradoxically require a signifier, however "impure," to make visible the very real and material forms of their subjection and exclusion, and to formulate claims and demands for an equality, freedom, and dignity that is real and not simply formal or symbolic.[4] Like the concept of citizenship, too, both as a principle of inclusion and a principle of exclusion, it is difficult to disentangle from notions of nationality (and natality), the people (as a biopolitical entity) and ethnic identity (understood as a historical construction). Thus, notions of race that may be only distantly related to the now discredited biological concept continue not only to exist but in some cases to proliferate. "Race" in its nonbiological sense has proved remarkably resilient and able to adapt; it often works more effectively through convenient substitutes and euphemisms, that is, through a process of delegation. This gradual drift is a strategy that corresponds not only to the relations of political necessity but also to a subjective need that is tied to these relations ("The term *race* has become difficult to assume by the mass of racists themselves"[5]). Balibar underscores the tendency in French political discourse to circumvent prohibitions and taboos by resorting to the notions of ethnicity, culture, identity, or immigration, understood as a violation of national integrity, if not sovereignty, which are becoming the assumed "names of race"; it is therefore necessary, affirms Balibar, to call things "by their name."[6] To remove race from a constitutional text is therefore not to accede to scientific truth; rather, it is to deny the effectiveness and historical reality of fictive ethnicity as well as the bodily projection of social differences as a factor in racism.[7]

Balibar emphasizes the impossibility of isolating questions of race even from racisms that no longer invoke race as such, as well as from nationalism: the concept of race is linked to a somatic imaginary in which are projected the perceived or instituted differences in the "human species" that go back to the beginning of the nineteenth century at least—that is, since the predominance of nation-states. He also emphasizes that race is a conflictual, "ambiguous" expression of national identity and nationalism—in the interest of a restriction, a "purification," or a "selection" from which identity is established.[8]

What theoretical racism calls "race" or "culture" (or both together) is therefore a continued origin of the nation, a concentrate of the qualities that belong to the nationals "as their own"; it is in the "race of its children" that the nation could contemplate its own identity in the pure state. Consequently, it is around race that it must unite, with race—an "inheritance" to be preserved from any kind of degradation—that it must identify both "spiritually" and "physically" or "in its bones" (the same goes for culture as the substitute or inward expression of race).[9]

Race has not "disappeared," insists Balibar, but, instead has undergone a radical polarization: The color bar today is inextricably intertwined with the criteria of "cultural" difference—a modern "color barrier" that is global and crosses all "national" social formations.[10] More than ever, there are, in the strong sense, only "two races," which are socially constructed: whites (or "Northerners") and nonwhites (or "Southerners"); no one really knows exactly what a "white" is or what a "nonwhite" is.[11] Moreover, the line of demarcation separating the two, whose presence is perceptible everywhere, has not faded with the global movement of populations and, consequently, the diffusion of physical types made possible by the intensification of global communications and migrations.[12]

Is the return of race, asks Balibar, a continuation of the past history or the beginning of the mutation of the structures of hatred? Alongside the return of race, another return occurs, that of the theory of racism. Although the origins of race go back to the end of the Middle Ages and the beginning of modernity, the concept of racism is recent; its crystallization dates from the 1940s and 1950s—a conjuncture of three historical and geographical problems whose unity is not a given: the problems of European anti-Semitism, of colonialism, and of the segregation of people of "color."[13] According to the official declarations made by UNESCO and a group of prominent scholars in 1950 and 1951 regarding the notion of racism, although "races do not exist," it is nevertheless the case that "racism exists."[14] Balibar warns, however, against the tendency to "naturalize" racism itself by looking for the sources in the natural and therefore transhistorical tendency of cultures (ethnic or class related) to perceive "the other" as interior or exterior to the "self" as non- or infrahuman.[15]

ON "FICTIVE ETHNICITY," INTERPELLATION, AND LANGUAGE

In *Race, Nation, Class: Ambiguous Identities* (1991), coauthored with Immanuel Wallerstein, Balibar points out that "the discourses of race and nation are never very far apart."[16] As national/cultural identity becomes increasingly decisive, he sheds light on the constitution of a people by developing a notion that captures the historical association of nation, people, and race: "fictive ethnicity." Balibar demonstrates that the myth of the national identity inevitably refers to a factitious, imaginary, but material construction that is produced and lived as reality. In this way, race is both displaced and, through the very act of displacement, preserved. In "The Nation Form: History and Ideology," Balibar pinpoints the continuity that characterizes the narrative of national origins, even when historians themselves do not agree on the various claims concerning origins. The origins of France, for instance, have been traced to the Gauls, the Capetian monarchy, and even the 1789 Revolution.[17] The "illusion of national identity" encompasses both the project and destiny of the nation: On the one hand, the "formation of the nation appears as the fulfilment of a 'project' stretching over centuries"; this "retrospective illusion" consists in the belief that the successive generations presumably share an "invariant substance" handed down over centuries. On the other hand, there is the belief that the "process of development from which we select aspects retrospectively, so as to see ourselves as the culmination of that process, was the only one possible, that is, it represented destiny."[18] However, the prehistory of the nation differs in essential features from the nationalist myth of a linear destiny;[19] moreover, the "French" of 1988—one in three of whom has at least one "foreign" ancestor—were only collectively connected to the subjects of

King Louis XIV (not to speak of the Gauls) by a succession of contingent events, the causes of which have nothing to do either with the destiny of "France," the project of "its kings," or the aspirations of "its people."[20]

Balibar further underscores the illusion of national identity:

> No nation possesses an ethnic base naturally, but as social formations are nationalized, the populations included within them, divided up among them or dominated by them are ethnicized—that is, represented in the past or in the future as if they formed a natural community, possessing of itself an identity of origins, culture and interests which transcends individuals and social conditions.[21]

Fictive ethnicity is necessary to nationalism's attempt to create an "imaginary unity" and a homogenous sense of nation. As Balibar notes, without fictive ethnicity, the nation would appear as an idea or an arbitrary abstraction; ethnic identity constitutes the people as a fictively ethnic unity against the background of a universalistic representation.[22] He thus argues that "nation" in any other than as purely juridical sense is as socially constructed as race or ethnicity are, and every attempt to assign to any of these notions a permanent or essential character is an example of what Georges Canguilhem calls "scientific ideology"; it accurately reflects the fact that scientific work is not isolated from technical practices, political, or social ideas, nor does it consist of fantasy elaborations of identity and otherness.[23]

More recently, in *Des Universels*, Balibar emphasizes the articulation of race and nation, arguing that race is a "privileged aspect of the process by which nations represent their own 'election' to themselves, that is, the mission which they believe has been assigned to them of saving, or through governing, liberating the world of the evil with which it is afflicted."[24]

The progress of nations is typically measured by the nature of the "values" they hold and promote: today, above all, those of democracy and individualism. Whether we are speaking of the forms of colonial domination or of the coercive assimilation (if not expulsion) of immigrant populations in Europe and North America today, these values take on the practical and institutional forms by which nonnational communities are subject to a "decomposition" that will permit their successful assimilation. As Balibar notes, the decomposition of foreign communities—or communities of foreigners that are created through "the interpellation of individual as subject, as Althusser said"—as well as their recomposition through the acts of "reciprocal inclusion and exclusion, recognition and discrimination" take place through the materiality of institutions and apparatuses.[25]

Balibar's condensed presentation of Althusser's theory of interpellation here draws on Pierre Macherey's recent extended analysis of interpellation and race through a comparison of Althusser and Fanon. Macherey argues that interpellation is performed or enacted by means of language, which plays an essential role in the different forms of interpellation. But language, he insists, is not to be understood as representation but rather as "an ordering [*agencement*] of elements, words, for example, that are not substitutes for things but are themselves things."[26] Language in interpellation is not a means of communication or a repository of meaning but "acts directly on bodies."[27] Macherey points out the strangeness of Althusser's well-known formula *Hé, vous, là-bas* (Hey, you there!). It is a kind of demand or command but one that is empty and indeterminate: it does not ask the person to whom it is addressed what he or she is doing or thinking of doing. The "you" at which the utterance is directed is *a* you, not a specific person selected by virtue of certain actions or thoughts but "a subject determined by the absolute, prior to any specification."[28] It is both a person and *personne* (anybody and nobody), just as the statement does not issue from a specified subject but functions like voice-over narration or a voice from offstage. For Macherey, Althusser's interpellation is precisely universal: every individual is recruited as subject, every individual is universally addressed with the formal *vous*. Even as interpellation separates individuals in their identities as subjects, it renders everyone like every other one. What is missing is an account of the way in which interpellation simultaneously assigns to different registers the individuals whom it recruits and orders them hierarchically. Macherey turns to Fanon for a theory of the differential effects of interpellation.

In opposition to the anonymity and abstractness of Althusser's allegory (his "little theater of theory"), Fanon, in *Black Skin, White Masks*, writes in the first person of his own experience, or rather of an experience in which, as a black man, a "subject of color," he participates: the experience of being exposed at any moment to the interjection—"Look, a negro!"[29] This interjection marks him "not as a subject like all the others" but as a subject "with something more than the others, or perhaps, more accurately, with something less."[30] In the colonial context, "color" is the sign of deficiency in relation to the norm of whiteness. White in this scheme is not a color but a blankness, the absence of color, "as if it fulfilled a function similar to that of zero in a system of numeration."[31] Macherey notes that the interpellation that Fanon experiences occurs through "face to face encounters": the fact that he is interpellated through the voice of a small child held in the arms of a mother who is clearly embarrassed by her child's words, makes the exchange all the more devastating. Fanon is confronted with the fact that the supplement of blackness or even simply "color" that defines him as not-white is not merely a matter of individual prejudice on the part of *petits blancs* but is irreducibly bound up with his body and its visibility. It is not the child in person who speaks here; he is "the spokesperson or echo of a discourse of which he himself is not the author and that does not come out of his mouth in a spontaneous fashion but is dictated to him by another voice that has remained silent."[32] Fanon is condemned to be "the representative of an essence that bears the mark, the stigma of a foreignness [*étrangeté*], that is, of an absolute, irremediable alterity."[33]

Interpellation plays a key role in the production of the fantasy of a homogeneous nation by sorting the subjects it constitutes into those who take their place *là-bas*, that is, among their fellows, those who are like them and those whose alterity is defined as irreducible and may at best be tolerated and at worst rejected or eliminated. In this way, to return to Balibar's formulation, "the national institution," or set of institutions, "reproduces the 'fictive ethnicity,' that is, the racial signifiers that permit the marking of the border . . . between nationals and non-nationals, or between 'true' and 'false,' or 'illegitimate,' nationals."[34] Both Balibar and Macherey have discussed the role of language in the reproduction of the paradoxes of national identity. The imposition of a national language on the individuals or speaking subjects who constitute the nation in one sense guarantees their mutual intelligibility, a common medium through which democratic deliberation takes place. Furthermore, "schooling is the principal institution which produces ethnicity as linguistic community."[35] But, as Balibar has observed in his discussion of Fanon in *Citizen Subject*, there exist alongside this tendency at least two countertendencies that reproduce the distinction between true and false nationals: "the colonizer's institution of norms of pronunciation that make it possible to mark creole or 'negro' speech and to relegate it to the status of an infantile or barbaric subhumanity."[36] Following the end of colonization and the reversal of population flows, the constant adjustment of phonological and syntactical norms—both at the level of state apparatuses, such as the educational system, and "spontaneously" in patterns of speech that are never entirely codified or institutionalized—become the means by which "native speakers" are distinguished from all others. Similarly, modes of address, from personal pronouns and honorific titles to official and quasi-official designations such as "undocumented," "unauthorized," or "illegal" (that work to stigmatize those to whom they are applied) are determined by constantly shifting in response to power relations. The colonial relation dictated the use of the informal *toi/tu* when addressing members of the colonized population, another form of interpellation that placed them outside of the "universal" constitution of individual subjects addressed as *vous*. Furthermore, as Macherey, following Fanon, notes, the colonial authorities ordered the use of a crudely simplified version of French, invented just prior to the First World War by a French commander of Senegalese troops, from which articles and most verb tenses were eliminated, for use among African conscripts.[37] They were forced to express themselves not only in the language of the colonizer but in a version that immediately and indelibly marked them as inferior, unable to master the complexities of standard French. Thus, the individuals who made up the colonized populations in sub-Saharan Africa were allotted subject positions but on the condition that their inferiority to the authentic speaker of French was institutionalized. This invented language was then imposed on them a second time (the delayed effect of the first) as the idiom in which any person of African ancestry, irrespective of his or her command of French, should be addressed. Fanon evokes the example of a passenger on a train asking for the location of the dining car, only to be answered with an imitation of an artificially degraded language: "Sure, fella. You go out door, see, go corridor, you go straight, go one car, go two car, go three car, you there."[38] The nonmutual *tutoiement*, lost in the English translation, also expresses the hyperbolic separation and subjection imposed by the colonial regime.[39] As the auditory accompaniment to visible "blackness," Petit-Nègre was an essential element in the fabrication of a fictive French ethnicity, of which it represented the inferior complement.

RACE, RACISM, AND UNIVERSALISM

Balibar's most original and provocative contribution to our understanding of race and racism undoubtedly lies in his argument that racism (together with nationalism, to which it remains closely tied) and universalism cannot be understood as opposites or contraries. From the concrete historical development of universalism, that is, from the moment universalism "ceases to be a mere word, a would-be philosophy, and becomes an effective system of concepts, it necessarily incorporates in its very center its opposite."[40] More recently, Balibar abandoned even this limited conception of an initial exteriority of racism to universalism (overcome at the moment of the incorporation of the former into the latter) to speak of a mutual "intrinsic determination"[41] of universalism and racism, according to which they are intelligible only to the extent that they are understood as logically and historically inseparable and reciprocally constitutive. From the beginning of his analysis of the relation between racism and universalism, Balibar has repeatedly insisted on drawing a distinction between a more or less conscious and cynical "use" of universalist themes as an element in a strategy of domination, which undeniably took place, above all, in the colonial empires, and a profoundly unconscious racism proper to universalism as such, not simply contingently—a result of its historical existence up to this point—but structurally.

It is perhaps easier to grasp the universalist element intrinsic to racism: racism must exist in the paradoxical form of a local or tendential universalism. A particular racialized population or community can invent and then progressively magnify the differences that separate it from the other races only to the extent that it simultaneously eliminates or diminishes the socially and politically meaningful differences within the racial community itself, dismissing them as extrinsic and foreign to its essential racial truth. It is a universalism that extends only to the limits of the race as such, whether it is understood as a biological or cultural entity.

The case of the racism internal to universalism is more complex and, as a concept, has engendered far more resistance, undoubtedly because it forces us to confront the constitutive and politically decisive contradictions of the European Enlightenment. The declaration of human rights (or *les droits de l'homme*) in the US and French constitutions, rights possessed by every human being as such, irrespective of nation, status, and finally gender, and thus rights understood as imprescriptible and inalienable, were necessarily founded on a particular concept of the human. Such a concept involved establishing a border or limit between the human and nonhuman and, therefore, a definition of the human species that in turn made possible an interpretation of human history as progress understood as the appropriation of the "*normative essence of the human, or the final goal of humanity's development* (for example, 'rationality')."[42] The identification of a "normative essence of the human," however, necessarily included a hierarchical differentiation "between the human, the more than human and the less than human"[43] within the boundaries of the human species. The crucial distinction might be based on what today we call phenotypical characteristics (e.g., skin, eye, and hair "color," and facial features such as, above all, the shape of the nose and lips) but also on cultural practices or systems of belief that, "by means of a process of naturalization," tended to be seen as fixed and unchangeable.

> Culture is the new name under which the conception of "the diversity of the human race" and their inequality is perpetuated and adapted to a new conjuncture, even as the conception's central notion is disqualified, or it shows, retrospectively, that "race," a pseudo-biological notion founded upon natural history and evolutionary theory combined with the eugenic program of European nationalism, was never anything but a naturalist projection of a "cultural" concept or a historical myth.[44]

These factors allowed both for the sorting of individuals into groups, communities, and collectivities and for the arrangement of the resulting entities into a hierarchy whose order was determined by the degree to which these collective forms realized the normative essence of the human. From these notions emerged the very concept of race and an apparatus of arguments for the modern forms of colonialism and slavery.

The recrudescence of racism or racisms in Europe and North America—cultural, above all, rather than biological racisms—that derive more or less directly from Enlightenment themes, has both confirmed Balibar's analysis and permitted him to extend it to the phenomena of anti-immigrant racism and Islamophobia in their conjunctural specificity. Although it is tempting to assign this horror to dark pre-Enlightenment ideologies rooted in religion rather than reason, which by their nature excluded any genuine toleration of differences, Balibar argues that one of the most fundamental points "for the analysis of the contradictions of universalism" is the "notion and institution of equality."[45]

A significant part of Balibar's work is devoted to an examination of the contradictions proper to the notion of equality as it emerged in the seventeenth and eighteenth centuries. The primary focus of one of his recent works, *Equaliberty*, is in part what we might call the extrinsic contradiction between freedom and equaliberty based on the assumption, which he will deconstruct, that there exists between them a zero-sum game in which the increase of the one signals a decrease of the other. But Balibar also takes up the contradiction intrinsic to any notion of equality, a contradiction between a symbolic or formal equality, that is, equality before the law, and what in the years following the Russian Revolution of 1917 was called "real equality," an equality of the material conditions that allow individuals to participate in political life (not only housing, sustenance, and income but access to the means of communication and the ability to take part in decision-making through the forms of direct democracy). In his work on racism and universalism, however, Balibar identifies a second contradiction intrinsic to the notion of equaliberty, perhaps now—that is, in the present historical conjuncture—its primary contradiction. To make this contradiction visible, he turns to the German term for equaliberty, *Gleichheit*, which offers the advantage of signifying both equaliberty and sameness, equivalence and uniformity. On the one hand, it refers to the condition of individuals in relation to the law, to the fact that every individual is treated equally and can claim the same rights as every other individual. Equaliberty here is the relation of individuals to rights and obligations imposed on them from without, to be precise, by the state. On the other, it is in practice difficult to disentangle equality before the law from the idea that the individuals who possess the same rights must in certain essential ways be the same, connected by the fact of their similitude, each in fundamental ways resembling every other in appearance but also, and more importantly, by virtue of language, customs, and values. At this point, one might object that the resolution of this contradiction lies in the universalization of equality, its extension to the entire of humanity in all its admitted diversity.

The effect of such normativity is not the creation of a homogeneous humanity; on the contrary, it is the means by which humanity is divided into a hierarchically ordered sequence of races, nations, cultures, or religions. Groups that are genetically very diverse may be racialized, and their deviation from a norm or set of norms "naturalized," that is, regarded as part of an invariant essence, through a process that is, nevertheless, not without paradoxes. Those groups charged with refusing to recognize human equality are by that fact declared unequal and deprived of the rights that belong to humans as such. Muslims in Europe may be denied the right to an education, the right to enjoy public facilities, and even the right of asylum in the face of war on the basis of the assertion that they do not accept the principle of gender equality, for example. Modes of dress (the hijab), traditional dietary practices (halal), and etiquette (whether individuals shake hands in greeting each other), even the Arabic language (which is assumed to be resistant to secularism) are identified, generalized to the entire population (contrary to empirical evidence), cataloged, and assigned a function in the Muslim community's deviation from secular Enlightenment values. To this is added the attribution to this community of a cultural tendency to violence, naturalized, and generally regarded as both obvious and unchanging, of which the riots in the *banlieue* (a response to police brutality) and the attacks on *Charlie Hebdo* and the Bataclan are equally the expression. Fanaticism, violence, and misogyny are projected on a racialized Muslim community in Europe. Refugees fleeing war and destitution who succeeded in reaching Europe have become its internal enemy. The stranger is now conceived as an existential threat to Europe.

THE PRESENT CONJUNCTURE: THE TRANSFORMATION OF STRANGER INTO ENEMY

In some of his most recent work, Balibar has sought to describe the historical process by which the "foreigner" has become the "stranger," who is in turn increasingly regarded as the "enemy." The notion of foreigner was once a primarily juridical notion designating the individual who is a citizen of another nation-state, without regard to race or culture. But the very definition of "foreigner" changed with the emergence of the concept of the internal border, a border that is precisely not a juridical demarcation but an authentic border within the artificial border, existing not through treaty or agreement by nature, that is, by race, culture, or language. Part of the nation was revealed to be "inner foreigners,"[46] whose alterity has proven irreducible and to whom a different and always at least potentially antagonistic fictive ethnicity is ascribed. The strangers who dwell among us may be defined as such by linguistic difference (not a difference between languages but the more subtle and not-easily-detected differences within a given language: phonological, lexical, etc.), by religious practice or customs. Although the racism that accompanies the categorization of part of the population of a given nation-state as strangers is primarily "cultural" (through the naturalization or essentialization of cultural practices), it may "coincide with other anthropological differences."[47] Unlike the foreigner, the stranger through this otherness makes visible the identity of the nation to which he does not belong and, by this fact, poses the problem of his assimilation and even more his assimilability: Can those who are essentially different be assimilated into the national identity? That is, can they, and also are they willing, to lose their otherness, to give up that which sets them apart from the true nation? The overriding concern to create and maintain the homogeneity and purity of a people sets into motion a politics of either forced conversion and coercive assimilation—the aim of which is to strip the stranger of every removable mark of difference—or—in the case of those who have proven inassimilable through resistance or because of the marks of difference that they bear, which are now invested with meaning and which cannot be removed—a politics of exclusion and even elimination. The latter are transformed into enemies.

What is remarkable in this transformation is the fact that the populations of strangers in some of the most prominent cases—the United States, France, and Germany—have been present in the nation for generations or even centuries. In some cases, the fact of their alterity was only discovered (that is, produced in order then to be discovered) relatively recently, whereas in others such populations were marked in some important sense as "alien" and, as such, contained through processes of legal or extralegal segregation and containment. In every case, however, these populations were and are minorities who pose no serious threat to the existence of the nation. The walls and fences erected to prevent an "invasion" of refugees are in some sense, as Balibar notes, a fantasmatic projection of a fear of an "internal invasion," as are both the demographic threat posed by the supposed fertility rate among the others among us and the threat of the contagion of their religion or ideology.

The case of France is particularly instructive: The descendants of non-European immigrants are routinely designated as *immigrés* or as *issus de l'im-*

migration as opposed to the "true" French, designated as *Français de souche*, a phrase that evokes the "rootedness" of the "authentic" French while underscoring the artificiality of the "false nationals." The essentializing labels used to denote both groups point to their permanent and mutually exclusive status, despite the frequency of mixed marriages. So-called secular Frenchness is a priori deemed unattainable and hence is permanently denied to a sizable segment of the population who will always be labeled as *issus de l'immigration*.

Demographer Hervé le Bras has traced the evolution of the notion of *Français de souche* from the beginning of the nineteenth century: while, initially, the expression referred to the French who were born in France of French parents, it has changed to designate the French whose entire ancestry, or at least most of it, is French, as opposed to those whose ancestry has a significant foreign element.[48] According to le Bras, the expression has acquired a pseudoscientific legitimacy thanks to the research conducted in 1991 by the Institut National d'Etudes Démographiques (INED), which defines *Français de souche* as "résidu" not belonging to any immigrant generation post-1900, but without justifying this temporal barrier.[49] Such an expression is meaningless, argues le Bras, since a genealogy of every individual, both maternal and paternal, would reveal a multiplicity of origins; what this does, however, is qualify the other as other.[50]

In fact, the National Front has exploited the newly established pseudoscientificity of the notion of *Français de souche* and the high estimates of "foreigners" in the INED's findings, a category that includes generations of descendants of immigrants, to confirm the existence of a large number of "false" French whose presence threatens the cultural identity of the nation.[51] Le Bras argues that there was a strategic need to redefine the category of foreigner, by which is meant the production of figures significant enough to accentuate the fear of foreigners, to justify the mounting xenophobia in France and to sponsor a movement "against anti-French racism."[52] He challenges the INED's study by pointing to the impossibility of defining a population as "issue de la population étrangère," given that mixed marriages have taken place for generations and that descendants of those in mixed marriages, as a result, belong to both populations.[53] He further adds nuance to his argument by underscoring the impossibility of ascribing an exact generational number of the familial presence in France (such as second or third generations) because both the maternal and paternal sides must be considered.[54] Moreover, if the study accords dominance to the foreign lineage, then the latter acquires ascendance over the French lineage in a society that paradoxically privileges integration.[55] What is striking here is the fact that le Bras equates the dominant practice of institutional demography with racism not because, as he explains, the two are equivalent but because they both play the same role with the same tools in the service of nationalism.[56] Demography, however, provides an apparently more rational and less morally objectionable means to accomplish the ends of racism. The dominant demography, like the racist discourse, justifies its negative view of immigration in the postcolonial context by constituting arbitrary genealogies and attempting to "ethnicize" the French through a highly reductive view of the category of *Français de souche*.[57] This is an example of Balibar's notion of the fictive racialization of a segment of the population without ever using the word "race." By systematically avoiding any reference to race, demography becomes one of the effective means of producing a "racism without race."

In *Marianne and the Rabbits: The French Obsession*, le Bras examines the theme of an internal invasion by demonstrating the complex and close relationship between "natalism" and nationalism.[58] More precisely, he argues that the "politics" of "low" fertility in France—effected by pointing to the "problem" of a decline in fertility—was based on the INED's misleading use of statistics in order to play to the pronatalists' fears of a decline in the authentically French part of the population. He refers to a persistent "demographic anxiety," which amounts to a fear of "invasion" not only by Arabs (to which he devotes a chapter) but also by Russians, Poles, Romanians, and Turks, among others.[59] To illustrate how widespread this demographic obsession is, le Bras recalls the statements of such "legitimate" political leaders as François Mitterrand, who thought that "the population in due course is condemned to extinction," and Jacques Chirac, who declared, "In twenty or thirty years our country will be empty." He also points to social scientists such as Jean Fourastié, who predicted a "collective suicide."[60] These statements have had real effects, driving the pronatality and profamily legislation that has been adopted by the state.

Le Figaro Magazine, the weekly supplement of its eponymous right-wing newspaper, has long provided a platform for natalist views. In October 1985, the magazine published an article by Jean Raspail with the inflammatory title "Serons-nous encore Français dans 30 ans?" on its cover and featuring an illustration showing Marianne, the personification of the French Republic, with a bare chest and her hair and most of her face covered by an ornate veil. The image captures the sense that the true French risk extinction in the face of a tidal wave of Muslim immigration, and it nurtures racism and Islamophobia in particular. To create a fear of the imminent danger facing *douce* France and its cultural identity, Raspail cites highly questionable statistics from Gérard-François Dumont that provide a grossly inflated estimate of the Maghrebi fertility rate (4.69) alongside a much lower rate (1.25) for the French, in addition to an overestimation of the "foreign" population.[61] The *Figaro Magazine* article not only ignores naturalization in its projections but also engages in acts of denaturalization, according to le Bras.[62] Thirty years later, Hubert Huertas's article recalled Raspail's apocalyptic vision in order to challenge the unfounded premises that continue to inform the demographic fears of French Islamophobia.[63] Such developments confirm Balibar's hypothesis that the culmination of the complex discourse on race for the past three centuries is the production and reproduction, in constantly changing conditions, of the internal enemy. It is a biopolitical threat to the true nation, an alien presence whose putative ability to reproduce renders its actual numbers both irrelevant and misleading, and which threatens to impose its parasitic reign over all of Europe and North America.[64]

Balibar's work on race and racism over the last thirty years represents a relentless pursuit of theoretical racism through the mutations, adaptations, and resistances that characterize its conjunctural existence over a period of centuries. By insisting that racism survives and even flourishes in the interstices of universalism, a project once thought to be achievable only on the basis of racism's extinction, Balibar confronts us with the fact that it is exceedingly unlikely that racism will ever be finally defeated and that the belief that it can may be one of the most important reasons for its persistence. By tracing its pathways and identifying the tactics and strategies that racism employs, however, he opens the possibility of preempting and containing it, to diminish its power and the hatred that its power mobilizes. But what comes after or with the time when the stranger can only be seen as the enemy? Balibar has shown us that it is not a question of rejecting universalism per se but of fighting for a different universalism, a universalism of difference that is organized to counter the ever-present tendencies to both biological and cultural racialization, including those disguised as their contrary. He has made visible the lines of force and flight that disturb the concepts of race and racisms in their historicity and, in doing so, rendered them intelligible, placing before us the interminable task of challenging them.

NOTES

1. See Simone Bonnafous, Bernard Herszberg, and Jean-Jacques Israel, eds., "Sans distinction de . . . race," special issue, *Mots: Les langages du politique* 33 (December 1992).

2. "France shall be an indivisible, secular, democratic and social Republic. It shall ensure the equality of all citizens before the law, without distinction of origin, race

or religion. It shall respect all beliefs" (Article 1, *Constitution of October 4, 1958*, Republic of France).

3. "Le mot *race* dans la Constitution n'est pas 'de trop.' Il serait plutôt *insuffisant* pour ce que nous avons à affronter" (Étienne Balibar, "Le mot *race* n'est pas 'de trop' dans la Constitution française," *Mots: Les langages du politique* 33 [December 1992]: 256; my translation; emphasis in the original).

4. Balibar, "Mot *race*," 247.

5. Balibar, "Mot *race*," 247.

6. Balibar, "Mot *race*," 249.

7. Balibar, "Mot *race*," 251.

8. Balibar, "Mot *race*," 250.

9. Étienne Balibar and Immanuel Wallerstein, *Race, Nation, Class: Ambiguous Identities* (London: Verso, 1991), 59.

10. Balibar, "Mot *race*," 255.

11. Balibar, "Mot *race*," 255.

12. Balibar, "Mot *race*," 255.

13. Étienne Balibar, "Le retour de la race," *Mouvements*, no. 50 (2007): 167.

14. Balibar, "Retour de la race," 167.

15. Balibar, "Retour de la race," 167.

16. Balibar and Wallerstein, *Race, Nation, Class*, 37.

17. Balibar and Wallerstein, *Race, Nation, Class*, 86.

18. Balibar and Wallerstein, *Race, Nation, Class*, 86.

19. Balibar and Wallerstein, *Race, Nation, Class*, 88.

20. Balibar and Wallerstein, *Race, Nation, Class*, 86–87.

21. Balibar and Wallerstein, *Race, Nation, Class*, 96.

22. Balibar and Wallerstein, *Race, Nation, Class*, 96.

23. Balibar, "Mot *race*," 250.

24. Étienne Balibar, *Des Universels: Essais et conférences* (Paris: Galilée, 2016), 20.

25. Balibar, *Universels*, 23.

26. Pierre Macherey, *Le sujet des normes* (Paris: Editions Amsterdam, 2014), 62. All English translations of *Sujet des normes* in this essay are mine.

27. Macherey, *Sujet des normes*, 63.

28. Macherey, *Sujet des normes*, 63.

29. Frantz Fanon, *Black Skin, White Masks*, trans. Charles Lam Markmann (New York: Grove, 1991), 84; French original: "Tiens, un nègre!"

30. Macherey, *Sujet des normes*, 70–71.

31. Macherey, *Sujet des normes*, 72.

32. Macherey, *Sujet des normes*, 74.

33. Macherey, *Sujet des normes*, 70.

34. Balibar, *Universels*, 23.

35. Balibar and Wallerstein, *Race, Nation, Class*, 98.

36. Étienne Balibar, *Citoyen sujet et autres essais d'anthropologie philosophique* (Paris: Presses Universitaires de France, 2011), 284; my translation.

37. See Cécile Van den Avenne, "Bambara et français-tirailleur," *Documents: Pour l'histoire du français langue étrangère ou seconde* 35 (2005): 123–50.

38. Fanon, *Black Skin, White Masks*, 36.

39. See Olivier Le Cour Grandmaison, "Violences symboliques et discriminations raciales dans l'empire français," *Réflexions historiques* 36, no. 2 (Summer 2010): 24–38.

40. Étienne Balibar, "Racism as Universalism," in *Masses, Classes, Ideas: Studies on Politics and Philosophy before and after Marx*, trans. James Swenson (London: Routledge, 1994), 197.

41. Balibar, *Universels*, 20.

42. Balibar, *Universels*, 25; original emphasis.

43. Balibar, "Racism as Universalism," 197.

44. Étienne Balibar, *Citizen Subject: Foundations for a Philosophical Anthropology*, trans. Steven Miller (New York: Fordham University Press, 2017), 286.

45. Balibar, *Universels*, 27.

46. Balibar, *Citoyen sujet*, 287.

47. Balibar, *Citoyen sujet*, 287.

48. Hervé le Bras, "Les Français de souche existent-ils?," *Quaderni* 36 (Fall 1998): 83–96.

49. Le Bras, "Français," 92.

50. Le Bras, "Français," 93.

51. Le Bras, "Français," 83, 88.

52. Le Bras, "Français," 88.

53. Le Bras, "Français," 88.

54. Le Bras, "Français," 88.

55. Le Bras, "Français," 88.

56. Le Bras, "Français," 92.

57. Le Bras, "Français," 92.

58. Hervé le Bras, *Marianne et les lapins: L'obsession démographique* (Paris: Olivier Orban, 1991).

59. Le Bras, *Marianne*, 11.

60. Le Bras, *Marianne*, 71.

61. Le Bras has often problematized the expression of "personnes issues de la population étrangère" and underscored its inconsistencies, particularly in Hervé le Bras, "L'impossible descendance étrangère," *Population* 52, no. 5 (1997): 1173–85, 1180.

62. Hervé le Bras, "L'impossible," 1174.

63. Hubert Huertas, "Trente ans après?: Nous sommes encore français . . . ," *Mediapart*, October 28, 2015, https://blogs.mediapart.fr/hubert-huertas/blog/281015/trente-ans-apres-nous-sommes-encore-francais. Huertas writes,

> Trente ans après, les prédictions catastrophistes de Raspail et Dumont ressemblent donc à des superstitions. On y décèle des préjugés raciaux plutôt que des diagnostics. Ce qui apparaît dans ce fameux numéro du *Figaro Magazine* n'est pas le profil d'un pays malade mais bel et bien la permanence d'une France réactionnaire, recroquevillée sur ses peurs et sur ses préjugés.

> Thirty years later, the catastrophic predictions of Raspail and Dumont look like superstitions. They reveal racial prejudices rather than diagnoses. What appears in this infamous issue of *Figaro Magazine* is not the profile of a sick country but rather the permanence of a reactionary France, curled up on its fears and prejudices.

64. Balibar, "Retour de la race," 168.

[Marx's point in the sixth "Thesis on Feuerbach"] is to reject both of the positions (the *realist* and the *nominalist*) between which philosophers have generally been divided: the one arguing that the genus or essence precedes the existence of individuals; the other that individuals are the primary reality, from which universals are "abstracted." For, amazingly, neither of these two positions is capable of thinking precisely what is essential in human existence: the multiple and active relations which individuals establish with each other (whether of language, labour, love, reproduction, domination, conflict, etc.), and the fact that it is these relations which define what they have in common, the "genus." They define this because they constitute it at each moment in multiple forms.
   —Étienne Balibar, *The Philosophy of Marx*

RELATION

   Jacques Lezra

"Relation." Its genealogy is ancient, its uses today fractious—its adventures usually fought primarily on the scholastic terrains of epistemology or logic, with occasional important sorties into anthropology and, of course, diplomacy.[1] An etymological glance reminds us that the word derives from the Latin *re-* + *ferō* (to bear, to carry). "Relation" comes into English and the Romance languages from the Latin *relatio*, which, as Lewis and Short tell readers of their standard *Latin Dictionary*, means "a carrying back, bringing back" and also "throwing back, retorting."[2] *Relatio*'s first uses are juridical—one refers a case to a court or appeals a decision; one bears, translates, or carries a case or a decision to a court or a superior magistrate: *re* + *latio*, though the sense of bearing-to or bearing-back precedes the Latin. "Relation": *ta pros ti* (τὰ πρός τι), this toward that, or something we say about this inasmuch as we envision it toward or bearing-upon or bearing-back-to, *pros*, that. Thus Aristotle, describing one of the ten highest "kinds" or categories of predicates (at *Categories* 1b25; other kinds are substance, quantity, quality, and so on[3]). A companion, not entirely congruent tradition interprets "relation" as a synonym for predication generally—hence as a term covering any statements about substance, quantity, relation, quality, and so on, inasmuch as all these statements are kinds of emplacements of a subject toward a predicate.[4]

   In the pages that follow, I will gloss the *political* quality of the concept of relation. My stress falls on the formal defects of the concept. "Relation"'s incoherence and the unsettled relations among the techniques and institutions historically developed to address it are the conditions on which the term may be considered a political concept. For if there is a concept of *relation*, then it has this peculiar feature: "relation" serves to shape and regulate the field of politics, to shape and regulate the notion of the "concept," and also to shape and regulate the *relation* between "politics" and "concepts." Marilyn Strathern has drawn attention to the simultaneously holographic ("The relation models phenomena in such a way as to produce instances of itself. We could call it a self-similar construct, a figure whose organising power is not affected by scale"), scalar, *and* incomplete or other-requiring qualities ("The relation . . . requires other elements to complete it") that the concept of "relation" has in vernacular use and in the lexicon and disciplinary, institutional protocols of social anthropology.[5] What makes "relation" a political concept can be glimpsed—and takes its form of being, its ontology—just where its holography and its incompleteness *fail* to form a concept.

"Relation." The term's domain swells speciously: what is there that *cannot* bear a relation to something else? My horizon ranges from the relation that any thing has with what cannot on its face be related to it, to the relation of a thing with itself, its identity-with-itself. From one hand to another. That this *left* hand I hold out is not the crown of the present king of France means exactly that I extend them to you, like this: these are my examples of entities that are different from one another; they nevertheless bear to each other the double relation of not-being-identical each to the other, and of being, each, an example for me of something that is not identical to something else (even of things that can't obviously or conventionally be related to each other). On the other hand, my *right* hand is nothing other than my right hand: it, and only it, has just all the properties collected in the expression I offer you as the name that stands in for exactly these properties: "my right hand."[6] The two, "my right hand" and the set of properties the expression collects, are indiscernible. And now the notion that "my right hand's" being indiscernible from the collection of its properties is indeed a *relation* (of "my right hand" to "itself") serves to unhitch my metaphysics from the tautologies that it abuts. Definitions henceforth count as relations (the relation between a concept such as "my right hand" and the set of properties that uniquely correspond to it), and I'm no longer limited to considering the relation between the set of properties and the term's equivalent (another relation) as barren statements such as "my right hand is my right hand."

Self-identity, nonidentity, even nonrelation, are, on the inflationary view, relations; anything bears like everything else the weight of possibility, of possibly becoming an example of what is unrelated to another thing. All terms have, as one of their properties, that they not only are this or that but exist also in the modality of possibility: either of my hands can, in some possible world, bear a relation to any other term, and in this way minimally my hands, too, are related. In that way any thing can be, and thus is, related to any thing else.

"Relation." Can the term *be* deflated, though? We restrict its domain: it enters back into relation with bodies of knowledge we'd like to preserve from miscegenation. Remark the discomfort that the philosophical term provokes when it carries out other of its lexical duties. Consider *relativity*: "It's all relative." Here, "relation" comes into contact with the old philosophical problem of "relativism"—alethic, cultural, ontological. In the twentieth century and after, it will have brushed against the physical problem of relativity—with the effect, for instance, of reconfiguring the asymmetrical relation between causes and effects relativistically. (A cause flies on time's arrow to its effect *for* an observer, emplaced—and differently for another, otherwise emplaced; it flies *in* a world with physical laws we recognize and differently in another world, say, one in which our miracles are commonplace, even normal, phenomena.[7]) Or recall that "relation" (in English, at any rate) indicates kinship, even consanguinity (my relatives: parents, siblings, extended family, uniquely mine; the standard unit of normative biopolitics), as well as a generalized principle of contingent emplacement. Here, as in the case of "relation's" relation to philosophical and scientific relativism, we ask: Does this coming-into-contact happen necessarily? Accidentally? Under what conditions does someone become my relative? Take for example what's usually thought as the human animal's first relation—to the person who bears us. Argumentative appeals *ad matrem* are as old as the city. (Recall the *Crito*, at 50d–e: Socrates imagines the state and the laws upbraiding him for a lack of respect to those who bore him, γεννάω.) The trope is on Aristotle's mind in a passage from the *Politics* that I'll return to in brief, bearing "for instance" on what brings into relation the "union of female and male for the continuance of the species . . . and the union of natural ruler and natural subject for the sake of security."[8] In Castilian Spanish, my mother tongue or one of them, we say "Madre no hay más que una," there is only *one* mother. It's understood that this means that each human animal has just one mother, but of course that's not what the privative Castilian sentence says (and it's certainly not what the laws and the state argue in the *Crito*)—of "mothers," it says there's only one, and yours and mine, our mothers, cannot be she, since there's more than one of them, yours and mine. Well, what are they then, and what unique relation might this animal I am bear to my mother, whatever she is? Even the seemingly unobjectionable proposition that any human animal *has* a mother is too strong—as the developing kinship among biological reproduction, capital, and technology makes ever-more clear. And consider what else I mean when I say that I have a mother. That my mother is a mother is not a condition that my relation to her singularly establishes. (I have sisters.) Does her being-a-mother inhere in her, or in her-inasmuch-as-she-is-toward-me and, or, my-sisters? In her being-*relative-to*-me and my-sisters? What *tense* governs the relation I have to my mother? (I die, my sisters die. Our mother is no longer ours, but is she still a mother?) Others will have no biological siblings; the person I call my mother could have been not-a-mother: it could have been otherwise—the lemma of nondialectical materialism. There are elective mothers; there are families with more than one mother. And my mother is many other things, too, things definitive of her in ways sometimes more ample and thorough than the biological, even the familial, relations. (She is a writer, a musician.)

From the start, then, I have two quite contradictory intuitions about "relation." The first intuition: that "relation" is not self-evidently a *political concept—* it's a term we might use to give shape to logical worlds, to epistemological puzzles, that are *prior to* and more fundamental than political considerations. Furetière's *Dictionnaire universel* of 1684–85 calls "relation" in this sense "en termes de Logique, . . . un des accidents de la substance . . . le rapport qui est entre deux personnes, entre deux choses qui ne peuvent être conçues l'une sans l'autre, et dont l'une suppose l'autre."[9] Thus, he says, "il y a une *relation* entre le fils et le père, entre le maître et le serviteur, entre l'œil et l'objet." The relation between the son and the father, between the master and the servant, is given in the couple of terms alone. (We would say that "father" and "son," and "master" and "servant," are *correlative* couples of terms: one term implies the other. No son without a father and vice versa; no master without a servant. It's less clear immediately how the "eye" and the "object," or even "sight" and "object," might be correlative terms, or how each might sup-pose the other. We're handed over, by Furetière's analogy, to two presupposed, ultimately tautologous definitions of "eye" or "sight" and of "object," requiring that "eye" be an organ of "sight" for perceiving "objects," and "objects" be those entities perceptible to the senses, among them and primarily, the sense of sight and its organ, the eye.)

Think, more explicitly still, of the sense of the term "relation" that we find in Locke, and then of the list of examples we might derive from the *Essay Concerning Human Understanding*. Published in 1689, Locke's work is Furetière's almost exact contemporary: "Relation," Locke writes, is "the last sort of complex ... which consists in the consideration and comparing one idea with another." These compared "ideas," Locke says,

> how remote soever they may seem from sense, or from any operations of our own minds are yet only such as the understanding frames to itself, by repeating and joining together ideas that it had either from objects of sense, or from its own operations about them: so that those even large and abstract ideas are derived from sensation or reflection, being no other than what the mind, by the ordinary use of its own faculties, employed about ideas received from objects of sense, or from the operations it observes in itself about them, may, and does, attain unto.[10]

Our examples of "relation," understood in this strong, Lockean sense, will be for instance succession, distance, causation, and magnitude. On Locke's account, the understanding "frames" "relation" to itself. The scene is solitary, even Cartesian: the objects-of-sense before me are objects-for-my-sense; atomic ideas present themselves to my thought similarly. No consideration of other minds is entailed. I negotiate nothing with you—who are first, after all, an object-for-my-senses in the way that this chair might be. Not even with myself do I negotiate anything whatsoever. When I write an essay concerning human understanding, I take myself as the object of my thought or sight, and the appropriateness of taking-myself-as-object-of-thought-or-sight is given in myself: it is, as Furetière's definition would allow us to say, a definitive accident of my substance. Between substance and accident, hardly a shadow falls. At most, I "consider and compare" my idea of myself *before* I perceive this-or-that object-for-my-senses, and *after*—and from this "consideration and comparison" of myself *before* and *after*, I take myself to be, for my understanding, an idea in time, changing but furnished with an identity. My perception of myself changes me; the relation between this changed me and the "I" that I perceive is one of succession, perhaps even of causation. The claim in any case is metaphysical rather than historical. Whatever we call "politics" will or may supervene, in the shape of my negotiation with you or with myself of the conflict of different ideas, but it will stand on this prepolitical ground that I first form for and of myself, as the first identity to which ideas and sense-data can then be related. "Politics" as the negotiation of differends is, on this description and to use Gilbert Simondon's term, only the unfolding, the negotiation, the formalization and deformalization of interindividual relations.

But I have, simultaneous with my idea of this solitary scene, a second intuition about "relation," supported by and flowing from what I called, with Strathern, the term's other-directedness. I have a sense that "relation" is indeed a *political* concept, or that the idea *leads to* something other than the lonely scene of self-relation on which interindividual relations unfold, or indeed that the idea of "relation" may not just *lead to* but stand on something other than my empty first-identity with myself. What we have just heard Locke call "the consideration and comparing [of] one idea with another" involves minimally four parts, which might form a tight system: a judgment that *I* might make, *for* someone (a someone who may be myself, as we've just seen), concerning *this* idea or sense-datum, and *that* idea or sense-datum. I say "minimally," and I say that something tugs at the idea that my four-part scheme is indeed so closed, so systematic. I find that something like a circle, or like a sort of excess or compensation worries me here, in this Lockean field (as it does when I read Descartes). I find here that the idea of the un-divided, if not in-divisible, identity of every sense-datum is at once given in the senses *and* intuited a priori. My intuition that "relation" is indeed something other than an indivisible idea remitting to a solitary ontology expresses my uneasiness with this circle. And just what *is* this "uneasiness," this simultaneous and triple suspicion that the sense-datum is not clearly or immediately or singularly *given*; that it is never (for all appearances) undivided; and that "I" to whom the possibly-not-one sense-datum or idea is possibly-not-only-given, that this "I" similarly (but not identically) may possibly be other than clearly or immediately or singularly *given*?

One way to bring into explicit relation with one another these two intuitions concerning the political quality of "relation" is to return to the related usage of the term on which I opened from the sphere of the law. In classical Latin, "*relātiōn-, relātiō* [is the] action of laying a matter before the Senate . . . [or the] action of referring a case back to the original magistrate." In its nominal sense, *relātiō* is "the motion so introduced" (OED): we re-late, return, refer a matter to the magistrate; we tell him (yes, *him*) the story, the relation, once again. Furetière's *Dictionnaire universel* offers this definition: "Relation, en stile de Pratique, se dit d'un référé, du témoignage d'une personne publique. Dans tout les contrats en forme le Juge dit, Nous à la relation Notaires avons fait apposer le sceel du Chastelet à ces présents." By early modernity, a "relation" is also an account, a report—often referring (as in French, and even as the specific *Fremdwort Relation* in Germanic languages) to detailed narrative accounts of voyages or events. (The New World, battles, explorers' voyages: the *Dictionnaire* says that a "relation" is a "rapport, récit de quelque aventure . . . se dit particulièrement des aventures des Voyageurs, des observations qu'ils font de leurs voyages.") The drift of *relatio* from the juridical frame to broader, sometimes fictional narrative frames—with the consequent loosening or shifting of the relation between *relatio* and forms of truth-claiming—occurs differently and at different moments in European languages and nations, in which the juridical regimes are hardly identical; where the standing of "adventures" and of explorers' travels may have distinctly different relations to state, imperial or colonial institutions; where a testimony or the claim of *fact* may take its probative value from quite different popular, ecclesiastical, or state institutions. When the eponymous protagonist of the anonymous 1554 *Lazarillo de Tormes* sets out his life story for a nameless, perhaps juridical figure, a certain "Vuestra merced," Lázaro frames his tale as the response to a request that he "escriba y relate el caso muy por extenso," or that he "write the matter at length," as the first English translation (of 1586) has it.[11] We might better capture the legal sense of the Castilian *relatar* that's hidden cloudily in the English translation "[to] write the matter" if we said that Lázaro has been asked to "make a deposition regarding the matter"[12] or to "testify regarding the matter," and that his story or testimony, his *relación*, cheekily stands on the protocols both of legal affirmation or testimony and of fiction. The *relación* has standing as a case, a deposition; as legal, sealed, and binding testimony; *and* as a sort of poiesis, as a fiction or an invention; or even, as the literary critic Stephen Greenblatt might say, as a self-invention. "Relation" as *relación*, as "writing the matter." As testimony as well as fiction, as a report. "Relation" now works as a discursive mode shaping and regulating the *relation* between two sorts of life and two sorts of truth-claims *about* life, each made *as* or *in the form of* a "relation."

This may not be the semantic range that we first think of in English when the word "relation" crops up, but it bears importantly on the concept's *political* sense and value. When we underscore, of the definitional qualities indiscernible from "relation," its sense as "relating" or "deposing" or "fabulating," "relation" stands forth as an amphibious term unsettled between different forms of life and different sorts of truth-claims and remitting to the discursive, the imaginary, and, even more, the *temporal* frame of the term "relation."

It's not clear that even this second, supplementing sense of "relation" explains how it works as a political concept. We will need something more if we're to set aside a classic conception of individual needs, interests, rights, and responsibilities, and a classic conception of a *community*, or a *society*, or any aggregate or class composed of individuals who share needs, interests, rights, and/or, responsibilities. We will need a stronger way of relating relation and narration in order to think through "relation's" political ontology.

To this end, let me turn now to the analytic frame that has been keeping me company all along—Balibar's account of the "multiplicity of relations," the series of "transitions, transferences [and] passages in which the bond of individuals to the community is formed and dissolved, and which, in its turn, constitutes them."[13] For no one writing today has done more to shift our understanding of "relation," of "politics," and of "concepts" than Étienne Balibar has—to the degree that since 1993, and with a different inflection after 2014 (when the revised edition of *La philosophie de Marx* appeared), the term "relation" is definitively associated *with* Balibar's work and with his longstanding project to unsettle the various notions of "politics" to which Marx's project is most often attached today. In 1993, Balibar offered an interpretation of the sixth of Marx's "Theses on Feuerbach" that rejects "both of the positions (the *realist* and the *nominalist*) between which philosophers have generally been divided: the one arguing that the genus or essence precedes the existence of individuals; the other that individuals are the primary reality, from which universals are 'abstracted.'" Balibar here is seeking to understand how Marx is imagining "social relations," *gesellschaftlichen Verhältnisse*. Balibar continues:

> For, amazingly, neither of these two positions is capable of thinking precisely what is essential in human existence: the multiple and active relations which individuals establish with each other (whether of language, labour, love, reproduction, domination, conflict, etc.), and the fact that it is these relations which define what they have in common, the "genus." They define this because they constitute it at each moment in multiple forms.[14]

"Relations" define "what is essential in human existence . . . because they constitute it at each moment." The stakes could hardly be higher. What then are "relations" for Balibar?

We know from *La philosophie de Marx* that Marx's work provides an "ontology of relations," an "ontology" that "substitutes," in place of "the discussion of the relations between the individual and the genus . . . a programme of enquiry into th[e] multiplicity of relations [that] . . . exist between individuals by dint of their multiple interactions."[15] Balibar's readers associate the concept of an "ontology of relations" with the term "transindividuality," which Balibar elaborates from Gilbert Simondon's writing.[16] Here is Simondon on "relation." What *La philosophie de Marx* calls a "programme of enquiry," Simondon offers as a "method":

> The method consists in not trying to compose the essence of a reality by means of a conceptual relation [*relation*] between two pre-existing terms, but instead to consider every true relation to rise to the rank of being. Relation is a modality of being. It is simultaneous with the terms whose existence it insures. A relation must be grasped as

a relation *in* being, a relation *of* being, a *way of* being, and not a simple relating [*rapport*] of two terms which one could adequately know by means of concepts since they would have an effectively separate and prior existence. Relation [*relation*] is understood as a relating of terms [*rapport*] because terms are conceived as substances, and being is separated in terms because being is primitively, and before individuation is taken into account, conceived as substance. If, on the other hand, substance is no longer the model of being, it is possible to conceive relation as the non-identity of being with respect to itself: the inclusion in [the, a] being of a reality that is not only identical to it, to the point that [the] being as being, before any individuation, may be grasped as more than unity, and more than identity. Such a method makes an ontological claim.[17]

Stressing, with Simondon, that "substance is no longer the model of being," Balibar suggests that "relations" escape the Scholastic trap in which ontologies are generally caught—the conception of individual beings existing alongside other individuals to whom they may be brought into relation (into *rapport*: Simondon's subtle distinction between *relation* and *rapport* deserves underscoring) either on internal grounds (grounds intrinsic to their substance or to their definition) or external (accidentally related, through propinquities or inessential circumstances, or through a concept external to the *relata*).[18]

The trap: Are "relations" supervenient modes of substance, or do they have a being in themselves? If so, how should it be characterized, and how is it related to the way that other beings-to-be-related, other individual substances, exist? If "relations" are modes of substance, then they can be divided, critically, from the in-divisible "individual" who precedes them, logically if not chronologically. Their secondariness at this analytic level can be pressed into the service of institutions that administer "relations" inasmuch as they are secondary to the interests, needs, responsibilities, etc., of "individuals," here understanding "individuals" not as a logical but as a social term—individuals are subjects, selves, persons. If, however, "relation" is the a priori condition for our thinking what is "individual," if individual substance is a mode of relation, then it itself, "relation," cannot be *thought*, neither as an in-divisible object of thought nor in relation to other objects of thought. We may have an *intuition* regarding "relation," but as soon as our intuition rises to the level of thought its object is no longer the *a prioricity* of "relation." The unthinkability of "relation" at this analytic level can be pressed into the service of institutions that mystify the grounds on which they stand, cloaking them in tautology and in violence, reasserting as institutional principles, and as if in compensation, the principles of identity and noncontradiction threatened by the *a prioricity* of relation: "Matters are like this because they are like this," or "That's just the way things are," or "Make America great again."

The two expressions, "transindividuality" and "ontology of relation," do positive work as well as the negative work of setting aside substantialist ontologies: they redefine what a relation is in the first place. An ontology of relations offers us not only an account of beings understood as a nexus of relations (what we could call an ontology of social being) but a philosophy of the *being* of "relations" understood neither as qualities that are "ideally 'in' each individual" nor as qualities that "serve, from outside, to classify that individual."[19] (They will not be exhausted, then, by Strathern's "qualities": they are never simultaneously—or, as in sequence as episodes or as protagonists of a *relación*—either *holographic* or *other-directed*.) When *relata* are not substances, "relations" among them are "transitions, transferences or passages," a dynamic, non- or not-yet-substantial, reciprocal forming and dissolving of bonds between non- or not-yet-substantial individuals and communities. As to the phenomenal and logical relation of each to the other, of this sort of relation and these sort of *relata*—matters are sticky and urgent now, for on this question the political stakes of the being of relation intrude.

We may not short-circuit the question or evade the Scholastic trap by just defining "relation" and *relata* as correlative terms (as Furetière's definition does, though hesitatingly), since "correlation" is a sort of *relation*.[20] Neither may we relegate to the steppes of casuistry the question of how to relate an individual with that with which the individual is related: the question is as old as the city, and marks the horizon of politics for us still. The paths before us seem equally impassable. *Here*, social being is built on the accretion of individuals and stands on the priority of individual over relation. First Robinson Crusoe; then Friday; then their relation, master and servant. First my language, then yours, then a translation between them. Yes, Friday's footprint marks the solitary beach—but that mark is external to Crusoe's being, and Friday, though he is the condition on which Crusoe becomes a social being, is ancillary to him, supplementary. The asymmetry between master and servant beats at the insular heart of this city. *There*, social being flows indeed from a *relation*—naturalized, correlative to the expressive animals that we humans are, Aristotle says. The political animal emerges as such when individuals form part of a necessary "coupling": "necessity [*ananke*] gives rise" to the coupling "between those who are unable to exist without one another: for instance the union of female and male for the continuance of the species . . . and the union of natural ruler and natural subject for the sake of security" (*Politics* 1252a). A sequence of proportional relations leads from the minimum of relation, the necessary reproductive relation and the necessary relation of subjection for the purposes of safety, to the city and to the commonwealth. "The state" becomes "by nature clearly prior to the family and to the individual, since the whole is of necessity prior to the part; for example, if the whole body be destroyed, there will be no foot or hand, except in an equivocal sense, as we might speak of a stone hand; for when destroyed the hand will be no better than that."[21] "The state" here is prior to the family as the whole is prior to the parts, that is, on the basis of the priority of the characterization of the individual (here, the family) as a "part" definitionally in need of a correlative "whole." That minimal, prior logical relation subtends the whole eventual city, though its necessity becomes, step by step, episode by episode, story by story, clearly external to the *relata*, since the criteria "continuance of the species" and "security" are accidental aspects of these. (It is true that "Socrates is a man" or that *Socrates albus est*, whether the species "man" "continues" or not and whether Socrates, the city he's to honor even more than his parents, and the laws that tell him so are "secure" or not. Those considerations are of a different order from the ones that specify that *Socrates albust est* for or toward something or someone, relative to something or someone, *pros ti*.) But the disengagement—the exteriority—of these criteria from the original arrangement of terms—first Robinson, then Friday; my language, then yours—isn't yet poisonous. What follows in Aristotle as in Defoe is the unfolding, in relation to that originary, externally necessary relation, of the minimum of relation. This unfolding is also relational—a *relación*, an amphibian story that follows both necessary rules (rules of thought that lead from part to whole but which understand the whole to be definitive of the part) and contingent circumstances (for instance, the historical circumstances that lead one family or—in Crusoe's case—one solitary castaway to associate with another under certain circumstances, for protection from this or that concrete or imaginary threat, and these families or minimal pairs in turn to seek association with others and to draw up rules governing the administration of their different interests within the common project of the state or the city). That these two orders, the order of thought on which necessary relation necessarily unfolds and the contingent order of history in which events occur, are not identical does not keep us from seeking to relate them. We might, for instance, seek to bring the necessary unfolding of minimal relations into accord with the accidents of fortune by grounding human sovereignty in something we'd stipulate to be as universal as the "necessity of reproduction"—call it a generalized concept of reason, or call it natural law. (The claims that "reproduction" is "necessary," and that this putative necessity is "universal," are ideological: historical, emplaced, and emplacing, the tokens and causes of violence committed and to come.)

On Balibar's reading of Marx, though, the story shifts, and rather perilously—and a third path opens before us. One of the things that changes in Balibar's treatment of "relation" in the sixth of Marx's "Theses on Feuerbach" is his account of the *Fremdwort Ensemble*, which Marx uses to indicate the way that "social relations" (*gesellschaftlichen Verhältnisse*) are to be grouped. Here is the section of the sixth Thesis on which Balibar comments: "Feuerbach resolves the essence of religion into the essence of man. But the essence of man is no abstraction inherent in each single individual. In its reality it is the ensemble of the social relations" (Feuerbach löst das religiöse Wesen in das menschliche Wesen auf. Aber das menschliche Wesen ist kein dem einzelnen Individuum innewohnendes Abstraktum. In seiner Wirklichkeit ist es das Ensemble der gesellschaftlichen Verhältnisse). In 1993, Balibar remarks quickly that "il est significatif que Marx (lequel parlait le français presque aussi couramment que l'allemand) soit ici allé *chercher* ce mot étranger 'ensemble,' manifestement pour éviter l'emploi de *das Ganze*, le tout ou la totalité."[22] The insight bears on the *negative*: Marx wishes to *avoid* the implication of totality, of closure and completeness, that seems inseparable from *das Ganze*. The argument on this point is stronger and much more extended in 2011 and in 2014. Among what the twenty-year period has added to *La philosophie de Marx* is the consideration of the *positive* elements that Marx's choice of the *Fremdwort Ensemble* brings to the sixth Thesis, and this observation regarding the *effects* of these positive elements. When the word *Ensemble* steps in where, philosophically, we expect *das Ganze*, Balibar writes, "a performative effect of 'detotalization' is produced, deconstructing the *totality-effect* or . . . signaling that the new category of being or essence only works as a 'detotalized totality,' which is to say as a totality that 'detotalizes' itself."[23] Note here something specific to the conjuncture, to the moment of enunciation, we might say, of the 2014 complement. Consider, first of all, the articulation of the word—the practice, the program—of "deconstruction" with *translation*. It's only after, and in the context of, the project of the *Vocabulaire européen des philosophies* that this articulation takes shape—and *that* project takes shape in two informing contexts:

> —First, the political-economic conjuncture in which globalization and translation, even translatability, seem to go in hand, both inasmuch as natural-language translation is the instrument for globalization, and inasmuch as the economics of globalization depends upon the notion that the value of commodities is translatable across markets. Between these two senses of the relation of "translation" to globalization, we draw a system of mutual grounding whose closure seems irreducible: each is cause, and determinate *effect*, of the other. Here "translation" can *only* have the "performative

effect of 'detotalization'" or of "deconstructing the *totality-effect*" of the logic of global capital if "translation" retains and affirms its relation to an axiom of *untranslatability* that *weakens* the notion of "effect," both the "performative effect" and the "totality-effect." And here "weakens" means "renders indeterminate, or over- and underdeterminate." Deconstruction-as-translation renders indeterminate, or over- and underdeterminate, the reflexive relation between natural-language translation and the value of commodities.

—The functional primacy of "detotalization" in the articulation of deconstruction with translation doesn't occur in a vacuum, in the abstract. It occurs just where the closure, and the "totality," of one system of institutions is being debated most urgently, between 1993 and 2011 or so: on the frontiers of Europe, as the European union struggles, with increasing difficulty, to understand the nature of its frontiers and to enforce different principles of closure, coherence, identity, and continuity. It is in the context of "Europe's" deployment of the political and economic principle of translatability among national languages and national markets that the corresponding, critical, positive, "deconstructive" effect of translation can be envisioned. Where Europe wants to establish, through the paradigm, the principle, or the fantasy, of translatability, the commonality or incompatibility of the "individuals" whom it aggregates, *there*, just there, the critical articulation of deconstruction with translation can produce counterinstitutional effects, or institutions structured about and founded on different sorts of principles, and on a different understanding of the concept of "principle" than obtains within the closure of the circuit tying the value of translation to the translatability of value.

With this conjugation of "relation" as relating (narrating, deposing, fabulating) and as translating every form of "relation" comes into relation with others *as* the condition on which we have "individuals," and thus provides—beyond atomic, unrelated "individuals"—"what they have in common, the 'genus.'" Imagine, Balibar says, that the "transitions, transferences or passages" that we call "relations" have a way-of-being that is distinct from the way-of-being of those "individuals" and communities or classes that they serve to relate: "relation" as first ontology. (Where I put in Balibar's mouth the injunction "imagine," Simondon and Whitehead say "think": for them, relations are rather the a priori condition on which an individual can be thought as such—relations are what we *think* them *with*.) Even without settling what we mean by "first," the paradox appears profound. Affirming that "relation" is primary, that it is prior to substantial *relata*, that its way of being is distinct from the way that *relata* exist, is like saying that *translation* is prior to (or has a mode of being distinct from) whatever languages we translate between, from, or to. The beginnings of a disturbing logical-political supplement to this relational, *relacional*, sequencing of "first" and "then" are on show. "First" and "then" here *first* mean: occurring in sequence; *then* they come to mean "having more importance than; being more original than; mastering." That what obtains as *first ontology* is a "multiplicity of relations" means that we will never be able to bring this multiplicity into accord or into the closure of a classical concept, under the sovereignty of a guiding relation: no shaper shapes or regulates the multiplicity of relations. This isn't to say that all relations are equal, or that no relation can serve for a moment, through acts of violence, or love, or through miracles, to bring an evanescent, ephemeral order to a multiplicity of relations. It *is* to say that the necessity of this or that principle of order (for instance, the proportional order that flows in Aristotle from the correlation of male and female members of the species, or "natural" ruler and "natural" subject), of this or that guiding relation or hypothesis, of a relation that serves for now to shape and regulate the field of relations, cannot be derived from or made to cover without exception the multiplicity of relations. It's also to say that no relation can either last or prevail on immanent grounds. (It will require acts of force, institutions, the negotiation of sovereignties, a politics.) An ontology of relations is incompatible with *any* form of aristocracy, including aristocracies that install empty operators at their heart: operators such as the people, reproduction, "natural" sovereignty and "natural" subjection, the multitude, the *demos*, the "deplorables."

"Only connect!," E. M. Forster's character Margaret Schlegel infamously exclaims to herself. "Only connect the prose and the passion, and both will be exalted, and human love will be seen at its height. Live in fragments no longer. Only connect, and the beast and the monk, robbed of the isolation that is life to either, will die."[24] Forster cannot endorse his character's sentimental, and ultimately catastrophic, sermon—and yet the delirious exclamation to which Margaret hews with fatal and farcical results becomes a topos of modernist studies. "Only connect!"—Polonius nattering on about "modernism," the touchstone of popular platitude, the first relation among relations. "Only relate," or "only translate," or rather, *first* relate, *first* translate—by which we would now mean "Live in fragments, in relations, in incompatibly true and fictional stories, *relaciones*, in translations, henceforth." This claim regarding the primacy of relation is the color of modernism in the fabric of contemporary political philosophy.

"Relation," on this description, cannot lead, as Margaret Schlegel's injunction does, to catastrophe or to farce because the injunction to *relate* is never one for the "genus" constituted "at each moment" by "relation's" "multiple forms," as Étienne Balibar puts it. A fully and radically differentiated concept of the political (and thus of what constitutes a political concept) stands on the defectiveness of the concept of relation. The sovereignty of the defective institutions that "relation" in this sense entails (the family, the state, the school) is always divisible; the time and conditions of their emergence are never given in the axioms of other institutions, nor are the conditions of their continuity and disappearance. After and with "relation," defective institutions persist and decline according to discontinuous logics and times. They entail regimes of representation, police forces, pedagogies, rhetorics, and lexicons that do ephemeral work, with often reversible results, transparently. No one, no human existence, in the city or out can ever *only* relate—but all human existence, as such, stands on relation.

NOTES

1. My epigraph is from Étienne Balibar, *The Philosophy of Marx*, trans. Chris Turner and Gregory Elliott (New York: Verso, 2017), 32.

2. Charlton T. Lewis and Charles Short, *A New Latin Dictionary* (New York: Harper, 1891), s.v. *"relatio,"* http://www.perseus.tufts.edu/hopper/text?doc=Perseus:text:1999.04.0059.

3. Aristotle, *Categories*, 1b25: "Of things said without any combination."

4. Aristotle, *Categories*. On Aristotle and relation, see Anna Marmodoro, *Aristotle on Perceiving Objects* (Oxford, UK: Oxford University Press, 2014); and especially Pamela M. Hood, *Aristotle on the Category of Relation* (Lanham, Md.: University Press of America, 2004). Boethius's commentary on the *Categories* may, rather intriguingly, be considered a precursor of contemporary political ontologies of relation. He comments that "things toward something [or relations] cannot be grasped by the intellect by themselves or individually, so that we could say that things toward something exist individually. Whatever is known regarding the nature of a relation must be considered together with something else. For example, when I speak of a master, this by itself means nothing if there is no slave. The naming of one relative immediately brings with it another thing toward something" (Boethius, *In categorias Aristotelis*, in *Patrologiae latinae cursus completus*, vol. 64, ed. J. P. Migne [Paris: Vivès, 1860], 217). This English translation of Boethius and a substantive, clear account of the medieval treatment of "relations" are found in Jeffrey Brower, "Medieval Theories of Relations," *Stanford Encyclopedia of Philosophy* (Winter 2015), https://plato.stanford.edu/archives/win2015/entries/relations-medieval. A far-reaching, subtle approach to

what I'm calling the "emplacement" of predicate terms with respect to subject terms, in the discussion that Scholastic supposition theory offers about the function of the *copula* in atomic logical statements such as "Homo est animal" (Man [generic] is an animal). I accept Lambert Marie de Rijk's valuable argument that the term "is" in such expressions either stands for (*sup-poses*, signifies) the concept of an existing relation (Ockham's position), or effects the joining of "man" to "animal" and brings about the relating of one to the other (Abelard's standard interpretation of Aristotle). See de Rijk's *Logica Modernorum: A Contribution to the History of Early Terminist Logic* (Assen, Neth.: Van Gorcum, 1962); and the much more focused restatement of the argument in his "Semantics and Ontology: An Assessment of Medieval Terminism," in *Medieval Supposition Theory Revisited*, ed. Egbert. P. Bos (Leiden, Neth.: Brill, 2013), 13–59, especially 31–36. Still, to my mind, unassimilated to the discussion of the "ontology of relations" is Jacques Derrida's treatment (by means of Benveniste's analysis of the framework of Aristotle's *Categories*) of the "transcategoriality of being" that the "supplement" of copula radicalizes. See Jacques Derrida, "The Supplement of Copula: Philosophy before Linguistics," in *Margins of Philosophy*, trans. Alan Bass (Chicago: University of Chicago Press, 1982), 175–207.

5. Marilyn Strathern, "The Relation: Issues in Complexity and Scale," Prickly Pear Pamphlet, no. 6 (Cambridge, UK: University of Cambridge, Department of Social Anthropology/Prickly Pear Press, 1995), 17–19.

6. The right-hand argument is indebted to Max Black's very influential gloss of Leibniz's so-called Principle of the Identity of Indiscernibles throughout Leibniz's corpus but explicitly in *Discourse on Metaphysics*, Section 9, in *G. W. Leibniz: Philosophical Papers and Letters*, ed. and trans. L. Loemker, 2nd ed. (Dordrecht, Neth.: D. Reidel, 1969); see Max Black, "The Identity of Indiscernibles," *Mind* 61, no. 242 (1952): 153–64. My "right-hand" example of how self-identity is a relation amounts to an extension of the position that Black's "B" defends.

7. I'm thinking of the development of David Lewis's argument regarding the asymmetry of the causation-relation, as Lewis moves from his "Causation," *Journal of Philosophy* 70, no. 17 (1973): 556–67; to "Counterfactual Dependence and Time's Arrow," *Noûs* 13, no. 4 (1979): 455–76. Debate over the past fifteen years regarding so-called "weak discernibility" suggests that the question is very much alive as to whether the Leibnizian principle of the identity of indiscernibles survives the solvent of quantum physics. The debate generally follows Simon Saunders, "Physics and Leibniz's Principles," in *Symmetries in Physics: Philosophical Reflections*, ed. K. Brading and E. Castellani (Cambridge, UK: Cambridge University Press, 2003), 289–308; and Simon Saunders, "Are Quantum Particles Objects?," *Analysis* 66 (2006): 52–63. More recently, Dennis Dieks and Marijn Versteegh, "Identical Quantum Particles and Weak Discernibility," *Foundations of Physics* 38, no. 10 (2008): 923–34; and, for what he calls the "*metaphysical contribution of weak discernibility to the metaphysics of*

quantum mechanics," Jonas R. Becker Arenhart, "Does Weak Discernibility Determine Metaphysics?," *Theoria* 32, no. 1 (2017): 109–25.

8. Aristotle, *Politics*, 1252a, in *Politics: Aristotle in 23 Volumes*, vol. 21, trans. Harris Rackham (London: William Heinemann, 1944), http://data.perseus.org/citations/urn:cts:greekLit:tlg0086.tlg035.perseus-eng1:1.1252a.

9. Antoine Furetière, *Dictionnaire universel* (1684–85), s.v. "relation." The term "relation" is not defined in Furetière's first editions (Amsterdam, 1685, and The Hague, 1690). It appears first in the 1727 edition in the form that I cite: *Dictionnaire universel* (The Hague: Chez Pierre Husson, 1727), vol. 4. It seems likely that "relation" is among the terms added by Basnage de Beauval or Brutel de la Rivière, who review, correct, and enlarge Furetière's *Dictionnaire*. The 1732 Paris edition defines "relation" but, significantly, omits the examples of the eye and the master and servant.

10. John Locke, *An Essay Concerning Human Understanding*, ed. A. C. Fraser, vol. 1 (New York: Dover, 1959), 217.

11. *La vida de Lazarillo de Tormes*, ed. Asima F. X. Saad Maura (Miami: Stockcero, 2007), 2; published in English as Diego Hurtado de Mendoza, *The pleasaunt historie of Lazarillo de Tormes*, trans. David Rowland (London: Abell Ieffes, 1586).

12. This is Sebastián de Covarrubias's definition, from the 1611 *Tesoro de la lengua castellana española* (Madrid: Luis Sánchez, 1611): "RELACION, Latinê *relatio, à referendo, actus reserendi*. RELATOR, oficio en los Consejos o Audiencias, el que refiere vna causa bien, y fielmente, sin daño de ninguna de las partes."

13. Étienne Balibar, *The Philosophy of Marx*, trans. Chris Turner (New York: Verso, 2007), 32.

14. Balibar, *Philosophy of Marx*, 29–30.

15. Balibar, *Philosophy of Marx*, 31–32.

16. Gilbert Simondon distinguishes among "individuation," the "interindividual," and the "transindividual." A compact mapping of the relation between the three terms, in his *L'individuation à la lumière des notions de forme et d'information* (Paris: Presses Universitaires de France, 1964): "Mais le psychisme ne peut se résoudre au niveau de l'être individué seul: il est le fondement et la participation à une individuation plus vaste, celle du collectif; l'être individuel seul, se mettant en question lui-même, ne peut aller au-delà des limites de l'angoisse, opération sans action, émotion permanente qui n'arrive pas à résoudre l'affectivité, épreuve par laquelle l'être individué explore ses dimensions d'être sans pouvoir les dépasser. *Au collectif pris comme axiomatique résolvant la problématique psychique correspond la notion de transindividuel.*" And:

> L'être psychique ne peut résoudre en lui-même sa propre problématique; sa charge de réalité préindividuelle, en même temps qu'elle s'individue come être psychique qui dépasse les limites du vivant individué et incorpore le vivant dans un système du monde

et du sujet, permet la participation sous forme de condition d'individuation du collectif; l'individuation sous forme de collectif fait de l'individu un individu de groupe, associé au *groupe* par la réalité préindividuelle qu'il porte en lui et qui, réunie à celle d'autres individus, *s'individue en unité collective*. Les deux individuations, psychique et collective, sont réciproques l'une par rapport à l'autre; elles permettent de définir une catégorie du transindividuel qui tend à rendre compte de l'unité systématique de l'individuation intérieure (psychique) et de l'individuation extérieure (collective). (Simondon, *Individuation*, 12)

Balibar's account of "transindividuality," in his reading of Spinoza and of Simondon, may be found in his *Spinoza: From Individuality to Transindividuality*, Mededelingen vanwege het Spinozahuis (Delft, Neth.: Eburon, 1997). For an excellent, thorough treatment of Balibar's relation to Simondon, see Jason Read, *The Politics of Transindividuality* (Leiden, Neth.: Brill, 2016). See also the careful parsing of the concept of "ontology of relation" or "relational ontology" in Vittorio Morfino, "Spinoza: An Ontology of Relation?," *Graduate Faculty Philosophy Journal* 27, no. 1 (2006): 103–27. Morfino expands his argument and places the ontology of relation in the long line leading from Lucretius to Althusser and Balibar, in Vittorio Morfino, *Plural Temporality: Transindividuality and the Aleatory between Spinoza and Althusser*, trans. Jason E. Smith, Ted Stolze, Sara Farris, and Zakiya Hanafi (Leiden, Neth.: Brill, 2014).

17. Gilbert Simondon, *L'individuation collective et psychique* (Paris: Aubier, 1989), 23–24; my translation. The French is rather more subtle:

La méthode consiste à ne pas essayer de composer l'essence d'une réalité au moyen d'une relation conceptuelle entre deux termes extrêmes préexistants, et à considérer toute véritable relation comme ayant rang d'être. La relation est une modalité de l'être; elle est simultanée par rapport aux termes dont elle assure l'existence. Une relation doit être saisie comme relation dans l'être, relation de l'être, manière d'être et non simple rapport entre deux termes que l'on pourrait adéquatement connaître au moyen de concepts parce qu'ils auraient une existence effectivement séparée et préalable. C'est parce que les termes sont conçus comme substances que la relation est rapport de termes, et l'être est séparé en termes parce que l'être est primitivement, antérieurement à tout examen de l'individuation, conçu comme substance. Par contre, si la substance cesse d'être le modèle de l'être, il est possible de concevoir la relation comme non-identité de l'être par rapport à lui-même, inclusion en l'être d'une réalité qui n'est pas seulement identique à lui, si bien que l'être en tant qu'être, antérieurement à toute individuation, peut être saisi comme plus qu'unité et plus qu'identité. Une telle méthode suppose un postulat de nature ontologique.

18. A very influential account of the difference between "internal" and "external" relations, in the first section ("Appearance") of F. H. Bradley's 1897 *Appearance and Reality* (New York: Routledge, 2016), chaps. 2 ("Substantive and Adjective") and 3 ("Relation and Quality"). The disagreement over the status of "relations" between

Bradley (who moves from merely "apparent" relations to the hypothesis that relations are internal and inseparable from the substantive qualities of *relata*: an idealist solution, as he sees it) and Russell (who advocates for what he calls a "doctrine of external relations," laid out first in "The Basis of Realism" of 1911 and developed subsequently) has an intense, more-than-just-local history of sequels and developments in analytic philosophy—as in work by D. W. Mertz, Keith Campbell, and Hochberg; more recently, Fraser MacBride, "How Involved Do You Want to Be in a Non-Symmetric Relationship?," *Australasian Journal of Philosophy* 92 (2014): 1–16; Fraser MacBride, "On the Origins of Order: Non-Symmetric or Only Symmetric Relations," in *The Problem of Universals in Contemporary Philosophy*, ed. G. Galuzzo and M. J. Loux (Cambridge, UK: Cambridge University Press, 2015), 173–94; on to the indispensable, quite recent volume Anna Marmodoro and David Yates, eds., *The Metaphysics of Relations* (Oxford, UK: Oxford University Press, 2016); and Bertrand Russell, "The Basis of Realism," in *Collected Papers of Bertrand Russell*, vol. 6, *Logical and Philosophical Papers, 1909–1913*, ed. J. G. Slater (London: Allen and Unwin, 1992), 128–81.

19. Balibar, *Philosophy of Marx*, 32.

20. The impasses signaled by the ontologizing of "relation" are largely immune to the sorts of criticism that John Searle famously made of Culler's account of cause-effect relations in the early 1980s. Culler affirms, in *On Deconstruction*, that because deconstruction shows that "if the effect is what causes the cause to become a cause, then the effect, not the cause, should be treated as the origin. By showing that the argument which elevates cause can be used to favor effect," Culler continues, "one uncovers and undoes the rhetorical operation responsible for the hierarchization and one produces a significant displacement. If either cause or effect can occupy the position of origin, then origin is no longer originary; it loses its metaphysical privilege" (Jonathan Culler, *On Deconstruction: Theory and Criticism after Structuralism* [Ithaca, N.Y.: Cornell University Press, 1983], 88). Searle responds: "There isn't any logical hierarchy between cause and effect in the first place since the two are correlative terms: one is defined in terms of the other. The OED, for example, defines 'cause' as 'that which produces an effect' and it defines 'effect' as 'something caused or produced.'" (John R. Searle, "The World Turned Upside Down," *New York Review of Books* [October 27, 1983]: 74–79).

21. Aristotle, *Poetics*, 1253a12–14.

22. Étienne Balibar, *La philosophie de Marx* (Paris: Découverte, 2001), 31.

23. Étienne Balibar, *La philosophie de Marx* (Paris: Découverte, 2014), 232–33.

24. E. M. Forster, *Howards End* (New York: Penguin, 2000), 159.

RIGHTS

J. M. Bernstein

Étienne Balibar's political philosophy innovates a complex constellation of concepts aimed at reviving and renewing the great tradition of radical democracy. *Equaliberty, citizenship, intensive universality, civility, constituent power, structural violence, insurrection and transformation,* and the *democratizing of democracy* are all plausible candidates for concepts that leverage the constellation as a whole. Yet not only is Balibar's concept of *rights* the most exorbitant in his conceptual armory, but it is also the conceptual fulcrum on which his political philosophy pivots: without its particular normative insistence, the constellation falls to pieces.

In accounting for who we are, philosophy has proposed a bundle of familiar answers; rational animal, *zoon politikon*, soul, self, person, subject, self-consciousness, agent, and *Dasein* each intends a defining account of what it is to be human. If modernity is the discovery-invention of subjectivity in which one's relation to oneself precedes one's relation to the other, then for us moderns to be human is to be a subject. There is only a short distance from Kant's conception of the synthetic activity of the subject to Marx's conception of social labor as world making. Balibar argues that the Marxian correction is insufficient; knowingly or not, the French Revolution contested the claim that human being was subject; it *declared* that it was the *citizen* who composed the truth of human being: "The citizen (defined by his rights and duties) is that 'non-subject' who comes after the subject, and whose constitution and recognition put an end (in principle) to the subjection of the subject."[1] The citizen is "defined," that is, composed, constituted, and constructed by her rights and duties. If the citizen comes after the subject, displaces the subject, and the citizen is constituted by rights and duties, then the meaning of being human, the value of the human is given through the possession of human rights. Rights and duties are the normative materials out of which the human is made, or rather, they are the normative materials through which we make ourselves who we are and through which we come to recognize one another *as fully human*. Balibar takes the French Revolution as the original effort to create, invent, and install a radically new account of the being of the human as such: the citizen as one who is *constituted* through her rights and duties.

It will prove useful to place Balibar's conception of rights in a wider setting. I will thus begin my argument with a recounting of Hannah Arendt's critique of the natural rights position as a prelude to the idea of the right to have rights, which is one of the pivots of Balibar's account. I complete the first section by showing how Arendt's analysis of the wholly *constructed* character of human equality prepares for Balibar's epochal comprehension of the primacy of politics and citizen identity. In the course of elaborating Balibar's theory of equaliberty in the third section, I demonstrate how these ideas of equality and citizenship turn on the right to have rights and, by inference, the rights character of the human *überhaupt*. I conclude by arguing that Balibar's conception of equal liberty, equaliberty, requires a supplementation by the notion of equal dignity.

NOWHERESVILLE: OF NATURAL RIGHTS AND HUMAN RIGHTS

Chapter 9 of Arendt's *The Origins of Totalitarianism*, "The Decline of the Nation-State and the End of the Rights of Man," offers a withering critique of the thesis that human rights are moral rights. What makes the critique unanswerable is that, in the first instance, the verdict on the emptiness, futility, nonexistence, and even bad faith involved in the presumption of the existence of moral rights is offered not by Arendt's work of philosophical analysis and critique but by history, that is, by all the participants in the decimating history of minority peoples in Europe following World War I. The Minority Treaties, Arendt argues, by making the League of Nations responsible for protecting the rights of minority populations, made evident what had always been implicit in the practice of nation-states: "that only nationals could be citizens, only people of the same national origin could enjoy the full protection of legal institutions. . . . [The League treaties] took it for granted that the law of a country could not be responsible for persons insisting on a different nationality."² The consequence of the inability to resolve the problem of minorities led to increasing internal crises within states, to the growth of refugees from states where they were unwanted and without place, thus to increasing numbers of stateless people even in nontotalitarian nations, to the use of internment camps, and to the terrible events we know too well. In all this, the Jews were simply the exemplary minority: "Those whom persecution had called undesirable became the *indésirables* of Europe."³ Uncannily anticipating the crisis and European reaction created by refugees fleeing the war-torn, broken states of Syria and Afghanistan and parts of Africa today (September 2016), the Official SS newspaper, the *Schwarze Korps*, stated in 1938 that "if the world was not yet convinced that the Jews were the scum of the earth, it soon would be when unidentifiable beggars, without nationality, without money, and without passports crossed their frontiers."⁴ Here is the historical verdict being rendered:

> The incredible plight of an ever-growing group of innocent people was like a practical demonstration of the totalitarian movements' cynical claims that no such thing as inalienable human rights existed and that the affirmations of the democracies to the contrary were mere prejudice, hypocrisy, and cowardice in the face of the cruel majesty of a new world. The very phrase "human rights" became for all concerned—victims, persecutors, and onlookers alike—the evidence of hopeless idealism or fumbling feeble-minded hypocrisy.⁵

If the defender of universal moral rights thinks that these events and this verdict are insufficient to demonstrate the nonexistence of human rights, then it is unclear how philosophical argument can proceed: must not a priori theory give ground to empirical reality somewhere? And if not here, then where?

Arendt's philosophical analysis of the Rights of Man is intended as an explication of this historical verdict, as an attempt to understand how, in the moment when the possession of rights would have been most humanly important, they were perspicuous in their absence. She argues that the Rights of Man were aporetic in character because their very gesture of dignification was the *source* of their abrupt emptiness. In making rights *inalienable*, a permanent, unlosable possession, rights strip man of his actual placement in a world, making participation in worldly practices an afterthought with respect to his status as a bearer of rights: "From the beginning the paradox involved in the declaration of inalienable human rights was that it reckoned with an abstract human being who seemed to exist *nowhere*."⁶ In this respect, the fate of stateless persons is, at least in part, a working out of the paradox of inalienability:

> The Rights of Man ... had been defined as "inalienable" because they were supposed to be independent of all governments; but it turned out that the moment human beings lacked their own government and had to fall back upon their minimum rights, no authority was left to protect them and no institution was willing to guarantee them.[7]

Because rights were taken to be inalienable, their possessors effectively inhabited a terrifying Nowheresville.[8] What inalienability accomplished was to make the having of rights independent from their claiming; making the possession of rights the foundation on which the activities associated with them were to rest effectively emptied those activities of their political powers of claiming, invention, recognition, and authority. Inalienability, as a transcendental guarantee, *subjects* humans to their presumptive standing as rightholders.

The best explanation of why a transcendentally guaranteed moral possession does nothing is because considering rights as possessions is a category mistake.[9] Considering claims and rights possessions, nondetachable moral things, fixes them to us in a manner that makes them *practically unintelligible*. It is that precise unintelligibility that eventuated in the skeptical judgment of history that human rights represented a form of either hopeless idealism or feeble-minded hypocrisy.

For Arendt, the possession of so-called "human rights" in the absence of political community turns out to be a world without rights: "The calamity of the rightless is not they are deprived of life, liberty, and the pursuit of happiness, or of equality before the law and freedom of opinion ... but that they no longer belong to any community whatsoever. Their plight is not that they are not equal before the law, but that no law exists for them; not that they are oppressed but that nobody wants even to oppress them."[10] What happened to minorities in the interwar years is today a fundamental mechanism of capital domination: humans who are without a political place in the world are "superfluous" beings,[11] disposable, beings whose sheer naked humanity, their naked possession of human rights and nothing else, is the mark of their superfluousness and disposability.[12]

In claiming that natural inalienability is partly to blame for the human rights disasters of the interwar years and what immediately followed, in claiming that the consideration of human rights as inviolable moral rights strips humans of their political habitation in the world in the act of morally dignifying them, Arendt is arguing that only through a paradigm reversal, only through the contingent rights of the citizen becoming the ground of universal human rights can there be human rights at all. Arendt and Balibar are not moral skeptics; on the contrary, they contend that some version of the idea of the primacy of politics is a necessary condition for the possibility of human rights being both actual and effective. For a quick way into this thought, Arendt's brief remarks on equality will prove helpful. The equality of moral rights, the thought that each human being in light of her possession of human rights should be treated equally belongs to the great moral decency of modern morals. But that great moral decency erases not only the long and difficult history through which it came to be, turning social invention and construction into discovery, but it also obscures the obvious fact that each human being is empirically different from every other. Nor is it intuitively plausible to think that everyone should be treated the same since that would ignore manifest differences that *should* be considered morally salient, nor is it the case that all the practical inequalities in wealth, intellect, power, capacity, and status are wrong. Meritocracies depend on the idea that differences in status and power can be earned, and that meritocratic procedures are among the rational ways of distributing (some) goods and (some) statuses. If expertise and hierarchy are good for the ordering of science laboratories and business administrations, why are they not equally good for morals and politics? Equality is not natural.

The thought of a priori moral equality is just another version of universal natural rights. Against this, Arendt argues that equality, in the senses in which it matters to us, was an ethical invention of the Greeks.[13]

> Equality, in contrast to all that is involved in mere existence, is not given us but is the result of human organization insofar as it is guided by the principle of justice. We are not born equal; we become equal as members of a group on the strength of our decision to guarantee ourselves mutually equal rights.
>
> Our political life rests on the assumption that we can produce equality through organization, because man can act in and change and build a common world, together with his equals and only with his equals.[14]

Arendt is emphatic that rights are neither given features of the human world nor deposited from on high but items that we mutually give to one another. Rights, in this respect, are the stuff out of which mutuality amounting to significant equality is made. Rights are products of human activity; from guaranteeing one another rights, we manufacture significant human equality. Human equality is the product of an ongoing series of collective and intersubjective acts of equalization. Equality is a practical state of affairs that must be brought into being and sustained through acts of equalization. Our becoming equal is the result of a *decision* we have made about who we are. That decision, I shall want to say, is neither arbitrary nor fully determined. We are switching from the nominative to the verbal form, from equality as a moral property possessed by individuals to equality as a social status achieved through a series of rigorous practices of equalization: the active distribution and guaranteeing of rights. All actual moral equality is nothing but a time-slice portrait of the equalization processes constitutive of a given community.

THE PRIMACY OF THE POLITICAL

Arguing that equality must be conceived as a communal decision to undertake a process of equalization is a component of Arendt's general defense of the autonomy of the *Vita Acitiva* from the life of contemplation, that is, from theoretical understanding and explanation in general. Employing a method of historically informed phenomenology, Arendt demonstrates that the spheres of labor, work, and action have an internal logic that is not determined by, dependent on, or, in the final instance, under the guidance of theoretical truth. Action, she contends, is bound to an intersubjective space of appearances in which opinion, rather than truth, is the fundament of collective political action.

Balibar radicalizes the argument for the autonomy and primacy of politics from a phenomenological theorem to a constitutive historical political project—political action itself grounds the claim for the primacy of the political—that commences with a groundless act of declaration.[15] In Balibar's handling, the reversal from transcendence (theory) to immanence, from human rights as moral rights to political rights being the ground of human rights is initiated by three moments: (1) the political act of declaring of the *Declaration of the Rights of Man and of the Citizen*; (2) the identification of the rights of man with the rights of the citizen, or better, the inclusion of the rights of man in and as an element of the rights of the citizen; and (3) the material a priori truth of the theorem of equaliberty. These three moments are best considered as three aspects of a singular act of political founding in which modernity constitutes itself as a distinct form of human living in the long and discontinuous history of societal experiments on the meaning of being human. It is only in the light of these three moments that the universality of equal rights can come into view. Equal rights for Balibar will manifest a definition of the meaning of human being in general; it is that transfiguration in the meaning of the human that spells out the historically constitutive character of the primacy of politics. To put the thesis most broadly and crudely: only through the epochal reconstitution of the human as a creature composed of legal rights that are indefinitely politically implemented, sustained, invented and reinvented—the process through which "constitution" is continually created and recreated through insurrection—can we finally exit from the Nowheresville of theoretical transcendence, natural hierarchy, and social domination.

It is not uncommon to interpret the French Revolution as riven by the intention of founding history anew and its commitment to "the natural, inalienable and sacred rights of man,"[16] to men being "born . . . free and equal in rights,"[17] to "the preservation of the natural and imprescriptible rights of man,"[18] etc. Balibar fiercely opposes the natural reading of the *Declaration* as maneuvering the suppressed egalitarian tendencies of the classical natural-rights tradition in the direction of radical egalitarian political fulfillment. Nor does he accept the claim that the alignment of sovereignty in *Declaration*'s Article 3 with the nation operates a simple substitution whereby monarchical sovereignty is taken over by the sovereignty of the nation. With respect to the latter problem, Balibar insists that it is the thesis of an "egalitarian sovereignty" that is "practically a contradiction in terms" that enables the expulsion of "transcendence" and makes possible the inscription of "political and social order in the element of immanence, of the auto-constitution of the people."[19] Since this thesis will find its substantiation in the identification of man and citizen, I will leave it undefended for the present.

More troubling is the attempt to deny what appears on the surface level of the text as obvious, namely, that the *Declaration* affirms and relies on a broad transcendent conception of natural rights. It is the critique of this claim at which Balibar's three moments are directed. First is the thesis that the tradition of natural rights undergoes an emphatic sea change, an ontological transfiguration through its being *declared*. The speech act of declaration provides the determining framework through which what is declared takes on its specific salience and meaning. Roughly, it is through the political act of being declared here and now that the enumerated rights come to determine the fabric of a people's being together as men and citizens; hence, it is through being declared that those rights take on the mantle of actuality—an actuality that is politically constituted. If rights are to be effective, then the agents whose rights they are must actualize them. The first act by which they become actual *as their rights* is through the declaring of them. By politically declaring them, rights are deposited into a social space that is politically constituted, so a self-created political space. The declaring of those rights is, then, a claiming of them—an insisting upon them and a demanding of them—as what is fitting and proper to each, what "we" declare to one another about who "we" are, individually and collectively, endowing one another with the very rights being so declared. The declaring of the rights transforms all (natural/moral) rights into claim-rights, and makes claiming into the actuality of those rights.

All this I take to be what is implied by Balibar's statement that "the *materiality* of this act of enunciation was the anchoring point for a series of claims that, from the day after the *Declaration*, started to *claim it* in order to *demand* the rights of women, workers, or colonized races to be incorporated into citizenship."[20] Said differently, the materiality of the enunciation, our coming to perceive the depth and ineliminability of the performative character of the act of declaration, submits the contents of the performance to a transformation: whatever they once were and, indeed, however they were originally conceived by their framers, through being declared they have *become* immanent elements in our radical act of collective self-constitution. The afterlife of the *Declaration*—that it has been the political origin of the continuing demand for the rights of women, workers, and colonized races to be included in the scope of citizenship—reveals the significance of the materiality of the original enunciation. In retrospect, the materiality of the enunciation requires us to perceive the *Declaration* as, in Ayten Gündoğdu's limpid phrasing,

> a revolutionary speech act that transforms the organization of political community as well as the terms of human coexistence by constituting human being as the subjects with the capacity to declare rights and the objects to which the declared rights are addressed. Once we understand declaration as a practice of political founding and attend to its inaugural effects (i.e., constitution of rights, subjects, political community, humanity), we realize that what is at stake is not only justification or reason-giving but instead the *political invention and disclosure of a new world.*[21]

The brio of this statement accurately captures the trajectory of Balibar's argument. Nonetheless, there is a patent overreach in its conclusion: declaration on its own cannot have all the constitutive consequences claimed for it independently of the content of the rights claims made. If Marx is correct in his analysis that the *Rights of Man*, on the one hand, *and the Rights of the Citizen*, on the other, are separate and distinct bodies of right in which the former covers private man, man as an inhabitant of civil society, "[that is,] of egoistic man, of man separated from other men and community[,] . . . the right of the *restricted* individual, restricted to himself[,] . . . the right of self-interest,"[22] then the inalienability of these rights are for the sake of man opposing himself to political society, of having those rights independently of political society, and hence of relegating political society to the task of protecting rights that are taken as, precisely, natural and inalienable.

This is why Balibar quickly leaves off the discussion of declaration in order to defend his second thesis, namely, *pace* Marx, the identity of the *Rights of Man* with the *Rights of the Citizen*: "They are exactly the same. Nor, consequently, is there any difference between man and the citizen, at least to the extent that *they are defined practically by their rights to which they are entitled.*"[23] Balibar's argument proceeds cautiously in the first instance. He first offers the reminder that the rights noted in Article 2 of the *Declaration* (freedom, property, security, and resistance to oppression) are, finally, the rights that "the *Declaration* will show are organized juridically by the social constitution."[24] After noting that "resistance to oppression" acts as a "verbal trace" of the revolutionary struggle that makes the claim of freedom pivotal for the *Declaration* as a whole, Balibar returns his attention to the issue of juridical organization. Noting the absence of any mention of equality in Article 2, Balibar turns our attention to Article 6, in which it is stated, "The law is the expression of the general will. All citizens have the right to take part ... in its formation. It must be the same for everyone whether it protects or penalizes. All citizens being equal in its eyes ... [,] etc." Article 6 announces the juridical organization the state in which law is both the product of all in being the expression of the General Will, and, more emphatically, what determines the actuality of the equality of all citizens: To be equal is to be equal under the law, to be equalized by having fundamental possibilities of action determined by laws that are the same for everyone. The rule of law is being transformed into the rule of equality.[25] This is why Balibar contends that the formulations of Article 6 "do more than compensate for the absence of equality in the enumeration of Article 2; they reverse its meaning, *making equality the principle of right that effectively ties all the others together.*"[26]

Nothing about the concept of rights or the operation of law necessitates that rights must be equal for all (there can be special rights) or that laws equalize (there can be laws that insure relations of domination). On Balibar's reading, Article 6 performs a triple operation: it juridifies rights, making their possession a question of law, not morality; it subsumes law under right so that being a creature of law endows individuals with the power to claim rights; and it binds the operation of law as the expression and articulation of right to the principle of equality. Hence, the efficacy of law is at one with the actuality of equal rights—the creation of human equality. In this scenario, laws provide for the actuality of rights, and the rule of law is the operative mechanism of equalization: law rules rather than any man ruling over others—Rousseau's miraculous if plangent proposal. If rights are primarily for the sake of equalizing and dignifying—and that still needs to be shown—then rights juridification is the truth of right, the subsumption of law under right underwriting the ethical actuality of law, and their joint operation the historical coming-to-be of human equality. This begins to hint at what I claimed in my opening was the exorbitant status of rights in Balibar's political thought.

It is the thorough juridification of right as the work of equalization that allows for the "most precise identification of man and citizen."[27] But it is this very identification, under the umbrella of equal rights, that seems quietly to erase freedom and liberty, as least freedom and liberty as they appear in liberal thought. Is freedom not a human power, the power of self-determination? And if that is too strong, then at least a freedom *from* external interference, including the interferences of law? Isn't the ideal of negative freedom a reason why one might suppose that there is a distinction between the private rights of man and the political rights of the citizen? Isn't the power of negation, of saying "No!" forever outside the constitutive sway of political citizenship? Neither declaration nor the identity of man and citizen accomplished through the juridification of right is sufficient to institute the ontological primacy of the political unless freedom can be socialized. But it cannot be solely the socialization of freedom that is required but a socialization commensurate with the great project of equalization. Hence, the decisive third moment of Balibar's declension of the political: "The *Declaration* in fact says that equality is identical to freedom, is equal to freedom, and vice versa."[28] Balibar names this identity *equaliberty*. If equality is accomplished through the juridification of right, and freedom is identical to equality, then freedom is a social and political achievement of a certain kind rather than the limit condition of social immersion and social making.

There are normative analyses of the meaning of freedom that might be appropriate here, but this is not the direction of Balibar's thought. The proposition of equaliberty, that liberty and equality are equal ($L = F$), is not a conceptual matter, not the posing of an egalitarian theory of positive freedom (although such a theory is necessary for Balibar's analysis), but an empirical and experimental one. Freedom and equality are *extensionally* equivalent. Wherever there is a lack of freedom, then there will be a lack of equality, and wherever there is a lack of equality, there, too, will be a lack of liberty: "The (de facto) historical conditions of freedom are exactly the same as the (de facto) historical conditions of equality."[29] The proposition of equaliberty proposes an *experiment* in the idea of a form of life where it is taken to be the *material a priori* truth underlying our collective pursuits. For reasons that will become clear directly, the form of life projected by the proposition of equaliberty can only be a historical experiment because there are no obvious ways of demonstrating it directly. As Balibar underlines, part of the logic of the equaliberty is causal: the conditions in which there is debilitating inequality are ones that bring about or depend on the deprivation of some liberty, and wherever there is lack of needful freedom, this will cause or be caused by a lack of equality.

Because this is a social causality, whereby the phenomena are themselves socially constructed—the actuality of meaningful human equality through the juridification of right as an idea about the meaning of the human—then we have no definitive insight into the workings of this logic beyond naively hydraulic models. Rather, we come to understand what is meant by and wanted by the desire for freedom and the need for equality through the political practices in which their urgent demand is satisfied by the implementation or invention of an appropriate right. Learning, constructing, and/or inventing the appropriate rights necessary to satisfy particular exigent needs, and the even more exigent cases of domination and systematic humiliation, are how we come to understand what freedom and equality *are*. They are not Platonic norms or deontological principles but socially constructed ideas that govern specific forms of practice subject to indefinite determination and redetermination as those practices develop and unfold.

The material a priori truth of the proposition of equaliberty is what grounds the theorem of the primacy of the political: because the rights of man and the rights of the citizen are one, being a man and being a citizen are one. Even after the argument for the inclusion of the rights of man within the rights of the citizen, the further identification of the being of man with the being of the citizen can still sound blisteringly wrongheaded and exorbitant. Clearly, what makes the argument load bearing is the original identification of the *rights* of man with the *rights* of the citizen. Can the rights of the citizen intelligibly absorb the meaning of the human in this way?

THE RIGHTS CHARACTER OF THE HUMAN: THE RIGHT TO HAVE RIGHTS

In *The Origins of Totalitarianism*, Arendt offers an analysis of the destruction of the human in the camps, an account of how persons can have the very fabric of what makes them human undone while yet they remain alive. Humans can have their very humanity, their dignity, taken from them because what this destructive process revealed is that the human is a status that requires the work of an entire complex social world to hold it in place. Remove the fundamental structures of that world, the social practices and forms of recognition constituting that world, deprive individuals of all rights, all entitlements, strip them of their names and identities, subject them to fierce routines, brutal labor, and near starvation, and what remains is nothing human, nothing recognizable as human. In the camps, these beings were called *Musselmanner*. We don't yet have a general concept to cover the extreme of degradation and dehumanization; for these purposes, I have proposed the term "devastation."[30] What Arendt documents in *Origins* is that human beings are the kinds of being who can suffer devastation.

After bearing witness to Arendt's account of the destruction of the human, Balibar remarks that it is in light of this analysis that we must separate Arendt's critique of human rights—including her emphatic institutional thesis that only the juridification of right can generate rights that have enforceable corresponding duties—from the denial of natural rights that one finds in Burke, Bentham, and later legal positivism. She does indeed want to argue that if the destruction of civil rights entails the destruction of human rights, then in reality the latter rest on the former; that is her concession to the tradition of Burke and legal positivism. But hers is a "much more radical and philosophically opposite idea: outside the institution of community . . . there are no human beings. Humans do not exist as such, and thus they are not, strictly speaking."[31] If humans are destructible in their *being* human, then being human is a status and an achievement, not a theological, metaphysical, or natural fact about the world.

But this is not to surrender the claim of human rights; on the contrary, Arendt does not intend to relativize the idea of human rights but rather "to make it indissociable and indiscernible from a construction of the human that is an internal, immanent effect of the historical invention of political institutions. We must say that *strictly speaking human beings are their rights, or exist through them.*"[32] Elsewhere, Balibar states the thesis this way: "The recognition of social rights implies the emergence of a form of citizenship that makes their effective institution possible, and it is these rights that, as new fundamental rights, come to define the human."[33]

If we are not to disown or repudiate being human as a value concept, as idea and ideal, then the idea of human rights is "indissociable and indiscernible from a construction of the human" under conditions in which politics has become the primary form of collective self-interpretation and collective self-determination. The converse of this thesis also holds: we come to recognize the primacy of politics, the identity of the rights of man and the rights of the citizen, once we recognize the contingency of the human status is, *now*, dependent on the possession and recognition of political and civil rights (where once it was dependent on just community membership—being one of *us*). What other forms of collective self-interpretation ignored, the reason why they de facto installed humans in Nowheresville—a Nowheresville that became and has become again horrifically literal with the emergence of superfluous beings, beings stateless and rightless—was the indisputable discovery that being human is destructible, and what follows from that discovery: being human is a status whose achievement is contingent; for some beings with a human form, it may never be fully achieved, and even after it is achieved, the human remains subject to devastation.

Balibar parses this contingency and necessity of the rights character of the human in terms of Arendt's doctrine of the right to have rights. Balibar's deduction begins with the recognition of the contingency of right: "Rights are not properties or qualities that individuals possess on their own, but qualities that individuals confer on one another as soon as they institute a 'common world' in which they can be considered responsible for their actions and opinions." On Arendt's accounting, this recognition is, again, not a positivist critique of the metaphysics of natural right but an inference from the radical experience of the rightlessness of stateless persons. The right to have rights is consequent upon perceiving the connection between rightlessness as a work of exclusion and rights as a product of mutual bestowal because, quite literally, "among the rights individuals are thus deprived of . . . [is] the fundamental political right to demand or claim their rights, the right to petition in the classical sense." In the condition of statelessness and rightlessness, what becomes lost is the human power to claim as such, to make claims against others, to have one's claiming be a recognizable and meaningful intervention into social space that can set other events in motion. But to lack this singular possibility is to lack all that the possession of rights involves and entails. Thus, "the reciprocal thesis that follows from this is that the first right is precisely the right to have rights, taken absolutely or in its indetermination . . . and not some particular statutory right."[34]

If rights represent the condition for making meaningful and valid claims with the force of law behind them, then not all rights can be legal rights. The right to have rights, the right to make legal claims, is not itself a further legal claim, and hence not itself a statutory right; it is, precisely, its condition of possibility. There is a temptation here to suppose that the right to have rights is a moral right to have legal rights, but this cannot be correct because moral rights would here have precisely the Nowheresville structure of natural rights from which we are seeking to depart; a moral right to have legal and political rights is a way of being rightless. This is the opposite of Arendt's intent. Although I will want to say that ethical experience of a certain kind is integral to claiming rights, Balibar emphatically takes the right to have rights as an irreducible political moment, a moment of political decision in which *we* recognize our mutual dependence both on one another and on those whose refusal of equal rights first calls us to political claiming.³⁵ Balibar titles the eruptive acts of politically claiming the right to claim rights *insurrection*, or, in an equivalent if quieter locution, civil disobedience. In acts of civil disobedience those without rights, or without equal rights, or without the precise rights they need, claim that as beings whose humanity is equivalent to their possession of right, they here and now claim those rights. The right to have rights is the political premise of their action, the presumption of the extensional equivalence between self-respect and the right to have rights. The right to have rights is the rights character of the human in action. The right to have rights is thus the *political recognition* we bestow on one another as members of a rights community, a community composed not of likeness—of having the same ethnicity or skin color or religion or first language—but solely of mutual rights, hence, a community without community. Notice how here the concepts of "insurrection" and "community without community" that are integral to Balibar's political theory are simply a conceptual working out of the right to have rights as the nisus of the rights character of the human.

The political surplus beyond positive rights in the right to have rights is anyway patent once we remind ourselves that positive law has always operated simultaneously as a force of domination and the condition of emancipation, that even if the rule of law means the effort to overcome the arbitrary domination of the ruled by some ruler, nonetheless the positivity of law enables the normalization and consolidation of privilege and hierarchy. A particular regime of rights can be a regime of exclusion, discrimination, or domination; for this reason, the claim of right must exceed every particular regime for the distribution of rights—the heartthrob that, beginning with Plato, has always propelled belief in natural rights. There must be some ethical excess beyond statute; for Balibar, this is why the *declaration* of the rights of man and citizen exceeds whatever implementation is achieved through it: it proposes the proposition of equaliberty as a material a priori truth of the human. Political idea, promise, and project are the form of immanent transcendence necessary for finite creatures whose ethical existence is practically endowed not transcendentally guaranteed. Thus, even if it is true that the rights character of the human is the ethical realization of humanity, the process of realization is political, a political project in which humans undertake the political struggle to become (world) citizens.

THE RIGHTS CHARACTER OF THE HUMAN: EQUAL DIGNITY

The buoyant utopian phrasing of that last statement is patently unearned, and contrary to Balibar's tragic conception of the political. The political excess of the claim of right beyond every regime of rights is just the converse of the thesis that the authority of rights lives off the absence of right, the demand for rights the pained response to their even more brutalizing absence, the positive just the negation of a negation, hence the acknowledgement that the politics of right operates through a negative dialectics of right. Balibar likes to state this thesis as the *malgré lui* truth of Nietzsche's theorem that all morality is a slave morality. What is helpful in this statement is its joining of ethical authority to what has been negated, denied, excluded, discriminated against, undone, that is, to the condition of rightless lives, superfluous lives, disposable lives, and, finally, to the reminder that each of these formations of hollowed-out lives, lives that do not live, image, or presage what Arendt presents as the scene of the destruction of the human.

Nothing in this argument can hold without the acknowledgement of the destructibility of the human, and the consequences of that truth for understanding what it is to be human. Again, from the destructibility of the human it follows immediately that to be human is a status that is bestowed in accordance with local standards that are produced and reproduced through processes of socialization and social reproduction; that because being human is a status, it can come in increments and degrees—one can *be* less human than one's fellows; and because becoming and achieving humanity is accomplished in accordance with a local schema of collective self-interpretation, every appearance of the human is in reality an experiment in the meaning of being human—as a member of some enduring tribe, as a member of a people who are themselves parts of a wider nature, as creatures of a creator God, as citizens of some state. On Balibar's interpretation, the particular ethical thrust of the proposition of equaliberty is that it is meant as a historical project in which each human would finally achieve an equal standing or status with every other, that no human would be counted as worth less than any other human, that no differences in sex, gender, race, intellect, et al., would be grounds for lesser treatment or lesser standing as human. This idea of "worth" more or less, of having a higher or lower status in a way that matters to one's humanity, is the ethical stakes of the right to have rights. In a way that Balibar is fully aware of and repeats sufficiently often but without theoretical emphasis, we have come to call the idea of the *equal intrinsic worth* of all humans' *dignity*: "[Throughout the twentieth century,] 'multitudes'—'ordinary' citizens, classes, 'mass' parties—have come together to force the state to *recognize* their dignity, and to introduce norms of civility into public service or the public sphere."[36]

Because he rightly does not want to ground the possession of rights in an anterior moral principle, Balibar is cautious in the extreme in his employment of ethical and moral vocabulary; his claim that the truth of the proposition of equaliberty is material yet absolute is the perfect exemplar of his normative strategy. Nonetheless, if the human can be destroyed, and that matters, then something of *value*—either intrinsically or conditionally—has been destroyed. Although without emphasis, Balibar quietly accepts the idea that when humans are directly excluded from the human community, no matter how, they suffer a "wrong," a moral injury.[37] The most natural way to express that thought is to say they have suffered a violation to their dignity.

Here is my broad hypothesis: First, if the idea of dignity is the placeholder for the idea of the intrinsic worth of individuals, then when individuals are destroyed, it is their dignity that is destroyed, that when humans are excluded, discriminated against, or dominated by another, there occurs a violation of their dignity. When we perceive others treated with disrespect, we experience their intrinsic worth as human beings violated, their dignity being violated and, hence, at the same time, the worth of the human as such depredated. The destruction or violation of dignity is the ethically charged *negative* moment that is directly capable of being experienced. At the discursive level, this is equivalent to the thesis that has been repeated again and again in the course of moral history, that there are no moral grounds justifying a given range of discriminatory treatment. However fiercely abided by and brutally enforced, the vicious insistence that some others are of lesser moral worth and lesser human value is revealed as groundless; we *experience* the rational groundlessness of the presumptive claim of moral difference through an experience of moral injury—an experience of humiliation, degradation, violation, or devastation.

Second, since the human is destructible, we know that dignity is nothing metaphysical or natural; indeed, *we know that human dignity (now) is a status of being counted as being of equal worth with all other humans*. If dignity is a status that is destructible, then, for us, it will follow that *the possession of equal rights is constitutive of human dignity*, that, here and now, having equals rights is the necessary condition for possibility of achieving dignity in the modern world. If the possession of dignity expresses the intrinsic value of the human, and the possession of equal rights constitutes the possibility of achieving dignity, then the possession of equal rights is the constitutive condition for being human. QED.

We know that "full" participation in the life of the community means different things in different cultures, and in the light of what Balibar calls "anthropological differences"—differences in sex, gender, race, language, lineage, and the like, differences that do not carry in themselves any transparent indicator of rank, of higher or lower, but nonetheless have been used—almost everywhere and almost always—in order to create hierarchies of rank, worth, privilege, and status, then the idea of *full* participation in community has historically not entailed anything like *equal* participation. The *Declaration* of rights was, again, intended to signal a new, radical idea of equal participation, even as its announcement comfortably abided with the very inequalities that its *words* claimed were at an end. But the problem is even deeper than this; if real differences are ignored, then equal rights, the same for everyone, will brush past what is needful—maternity leave, child-care facilities, freedom of conscience, etc. This is part of the aporia of rights: equal rights should provide equal dignity, but they cannot do so if equal rights means precisely the same rights for everyone, independent of significant differences. To connect equal rights with equal dignity can help us begin to think about what the possession of equal rights involves, if not the possession of exactly the same rights for everyone yet sufficient for full and equal participation in social life.

I will take as evident that the primary social function of the concept of dignity is to signify the inherent, nonderivative worth of each individual human life. By "nonderivative," I mean only that the worth of a particular life is not derived from or dependent on the roles she plays or the social functions she serves in a particular community such that were she to become functionally useless, she would lose her human worth. Because dignity signifies the intrinsic worth of a human life, it has routinely been thought to entail a form of metaphysical individualism, but even the briefest reminder of the relation between the sociality of rights and their function as the ground of claiming obviates that thesis. The question that needs to be interrogated is how can dignity play the role of protecting and ensuring the intrinsic worth of each individual life?

Dignity has two distinct aspects, aspects that seem to correlate precisely with the two sides of the proposition of equaliberty; so convergent are the two aspects of dignity with the two sides of equaliberty, they might be taken as two versions of an underlying idea about the equal worth of every human life that requires both for its full expression. We can denominate the two aspects of dignity as the noncomparative and comparative aspects, respectively.[38] On the one hand, taking up the account of the mechanisms for the destruction of the human presented by Arendt, we can say that an individual's dignity is violated when she is treated in a way *not fitting* for a human being: when she is treated as a beast or thing, when she is denied proper control over her own body, when she is excluded from the surrounding community.[39] In each of these cases, we recognize different mechanisms for denying full participation in the life of the community. We may also say about each of these typical forms of infringement of dignity that they deny an individual basic liberties. On the other hand, we also take it as a violation of dignity when an individual is, comparatively, denied equal treatment with others, when women are offered less pay for the same work, or when individuals are prohibited from voting because of race or class, or when individuals, because of the color of their skin, are treated differently by the police. Such forms of unequal treatment are profound sources of humiliation and degradation—that is, such different treatments are not merely different but are experienced as moral injuries to the individual in herself because lying behind them is the implication that she is thereby of less worth than her fellow citizens.

Corresponding to the proposition of equaliberty, we should now be able to propound a proposition of equal dignity: whenever there is violation of the inherent dignity of individuals, there will be also a failure of interpersonal, comparative dignity, a failure to affirm their being of equal status, and wherever there is a failure to affirm an individual as possessing an equal status with surrounding others, there is an injury to her inherent dignity, some way in which she is not being treated as fully human in herself but dehumanized, instrumentalized, infantilized, etc. Although I do take the proposition of equal dignity to be a material a priori truth, we do have the beginnings of an explanation of why the two sides of equal dignity are materially joined in this way—namely, that being human just is a constructed status that comes in increments and degrees, and is further capable of destruction.

The difficult thought underpinning the proposition of equal dignity is that *to be human is to be (fully) recognized as (an equal) human*, where the necessary condition of being recognized as human in the modern world is being recognized as possessing equal rights. The difficulty in this thought is patent: even if it is true, as Balibar argues time and again, because no one can be *given* rights by another, and because rights are equivalent to capacities and entitlements to make claims, then having rights involves claiming those rights, that only in claiming them can they be actual, it nonetheless remains the case that we are forever dependent on our fellow citizens or the institutions of the state to recognize those claims; there is always an absolute and irrevocable dependence on all others to recognize whatever rights are claimed. And all too obviously, the intransigence or brutality of the other can decimate any rights claim. It is the radicality of our dependence on others that exposes each human to the multiple forms of actual and symbolic violence that effectively humiliate, degrade, violate, and destroy. *The possibility of dignity is simultaneously the possibility of the violation and destruction of dignity*. I take the sense of exposure intrinsic to the experience of having dignity to be difficult, even threatening; indeed, it is often experienced as so threatening that great efforts to deny dependence are put in place.

What is at issue here is "the admission of negativity into the field of political practices, in opposition to the normativity and normality toward which both juridical positivism and the dominant culture tend."[40] The destructibility of the human—"Humans do not exist as such"—and the moral primacy of the negative over the positive mutually entail one another. Often, the profoundest and deepest stakes in the preservation of hierarchy and privilege do not concern hierarchy and privilege at all: their furthest reach and deepest concern are the radicality and insuperability of *dependence*, where the felt fact of dependence on another demonstrates a level of exposure and vulnerability that can be experienced as decimating to one's very self-image as human. That this is acted out through the subsumption and expulsion of an other who can be symbolically represented as a protuberance of nature into the human—women, or the man of color as a splinter of nature in the flesh of culture—or as a being not itself fully human sublates both the other and nature at the same time, keeping the human "pure." Purity and some idea of "independence" typically hang together in ways that make purification an incessant work that is ready to topple over into violent repression and/or expulsion.

The experience of violation, repression, or expulsion, the *force of the negative*, must depend on some *indeterminate but determinable value ascription*: some sense that something of (intrinsic) value is being injured. Relationality in the human is *about* the meaning of the human, its existing as a status-conferring set of forms of practice and interaction.[41] The notion of "physical dignity,"[42] for example, by which I understand Balibar to mean some notion of actively achieved bodily integrity, some determinate ways in which an individual can determine her body as hers in relation to all others in her physical interactions with them, is not itself a priori determinate: our bodies touch, press, intrude, bump, and are entangled in all sorts of ways all the time with significantly different meanings, registers, and significances in different cultures. But to agree that what counts as physical dignity is not an a priori, transcultural, or natural norm does not entail that it is arbitrary. The history of violation in relation to the progressive history of universalism—the work of declaring rights—generates the possibility of determinate responses. For example, although it was breathtakingly late in coming—in France in 1990, in England in 1992, in Germany 1997—eventually each European nation dropped the marital exemption clause from laws prohibiting rape.[43] Does anyone really want to argue that prohibiting marital rape is *merely* customary, relative, a wholly conventional matter? That there is no logic of moral progress involved in enabling individuals to control which others are allowed to touch and penetrate their bodies? That some notion of moral individualism, individuals as irreducible objects of moral concern, is what the notion of dignity intended to bring into view?

At least in terms of public morality, there is nothing more to equal dignity than equal rights, and therefore nothing more to the possession of dignity than the possession of equal rights.[44] What I am calling the "rights character" of the human is, arguably, the essential and necessary ethical subtext to contemporary ethical and political struggles. Denying that dignity is a metaphysical essence (although the temptation to so believe is as deep as the repudiation of dependence generally), together with the widely shared yet wholly indeterminate moral intuition that every being with a human form should be taken as possessing human dignity, yields an experiential logic of dignity: dignity as the intrinsic value of the human exists only through its practical realization in each human; this is why any violation of the dignity of any individual human *can* be, is often, and should be felt as a violation of the human status itself. *Connecting the experience of the violation of any individual's dignity with the depredation of the human status as such is the experience of our undergoing an anthropological revolution through which the human comes to be ethically and normatively experienced as constituted through the possession of rights.* We only possess the dignity of humanity through realizing the dignity of each individual human through each human being recognized as having basic rights. The destructibility and contingency of the human status is the source of its ethical necessity: either dignity matters just here and now with this one vulnerable body, or the dignity of the human suffers a practical delegitimation.

The experience of the violation of dignity is the orienting ethical experience, the force of the negative, *necessary* for Balibarian insurrectional politics, the politics of the citizen. That is, only as the anthropological revolution borne of the advance in the recognition of the rights character of the human, the political actuality that has increasingly bound human rights and human dignity in the ethical depiction of humanity, could the negative experience of the violation of dignity and the absence of rights become ethically sufficient for the contemporary insurrectional politics of the right to have rights. This thesis requires one severe qualification: ethical sufficiency falters when it proves motivationally insufficient. Thus, we had better say that the ethical logic of dignity violation has sometimes proved ethically sufficient, but that sufficiency has and will continue to come under fierce denial. That said, I do want to argue that in implicit and explicit ways, equal dignity, more so than the inaugurating impulse of equaliberty, has been the ethical impulse and presupposition making formations of contemporary political radicalism possible. Hence my thesis that equaliberty demands equal dignity as its further articulation.

The fragility of human dignity, its existing through recurrent efforts of mutually endowing one another with it, each human deserving the protections and entitlements of basic rights, underlines both its contingency and necessity. Again, we experience that necessity through the experience of violations of dignity that manifest the absence of fundamental rights; Balibar construes this experience of necessity as a version of "intensive universality." However, if there is nothing more to dignity than equal rights, then for us here and now, the meaning of being human can be nothing other than having or struggling for, for ourselves and for all others, the rights of the citizen: "The *human subject* is able concretely to meet the essence of its 'humanity' only within a *civic*, or *political*, horizon in the broad sense of the term, that of a 'universal citizenship.'"[45]

NOTES

1. Étienne Balibar, "Citizen Subject," trans. James B. Swenson Jr., in *Who Comes after the Subject?*, ed. Eduardo Cadava, Peter Connor, and Jean-Luc Nancy (New York: Routledge, 1991), 38–39.

2. Hannah Arendt, *The Origins of Totalitarianism* (New York: Meridian, 1958), 275.

3. Arendt, *Origins*, 269.

4. Arendt, *Origins*, 269.

5. Arendt, *Origins*, 269.

6. Arendt, *Origins*, 291; emphasis mine.

7. Arendt, *Origins*, 291.

8. I am borrowing the concept of Nowheresville from Joel Feinberg, "The Nature and Value of Human Rights," *Journal of Value Inquiry* 4, no. 4 (Winter 1970): 243–57; he uses the concept to explicate the experience of a world without rights.

9. Feinberg, "Nature and Value," 253.

10. Arendt, *Origins*, 295–96.

11. Arendt, *Origins*, 457.

12. Rather than following Arendt on the idea of superfluousness, Balibar borrows from Bertrand Ogilvie the idea of "making of disposable man." See Étienne Balibar, *Politics and the Other Scene*, trans. Christine Jones, James Swenson, and Chris Turner (New York: Verso, 2002), 23–26.

13. Hannah Arendt, *On Revolution* (Harmondsworth, UK: Penguin, 1973), 30. For a further elaboration, see Étienne Balibar, *Equaliberty: Political Essays*, trans. James Ingram (Durham, N.C.: Duke University Press, 2014), 173–74.

14. Arendt, *Origins*, 301.

15. By "groundless," I do not mean "without reason": There were massive social transformations occurring in the eighteenth century that gave meaning, substance, and urgency to the French Revolution. But it is the Revolution itself, including the *Declaration of the Rights of Man and of the Citizen*, that gives these reasons that particular modern formation.

16. Preamble, *Declaration of the Rights of Man and of the Citizen* (August 26, 1789), Republic of France.

17. Article 1, *Declaration of the Rights of Man and of the Citizen* (August 26, 1789), Republic of France.

18. Article 2, *Declaration of the Rights of Man and of the Citizen* (August 26, 1789), Republic of France.

19. Balibar, *Equaliberty*, 42.

20. Balibar, *Equaliberty*, 42; my emphasis.

21. Ayten Gündoğdu, *Rightlessness in an Age of Rights: Hannah Arendt and the Contemporary Struggles of Migrants* (New York: Oxford University Press, 2015), 172.

22. Karl Marx, *Early Writings*, trans. Gregor Benton (Harmondsworth, UK: Penguin, 1975), 229.

23. Balibar, *Equaliberty*, 44.

24. Balibar, *Equaliberty*, 44.

25. For a detailing of this transformation in the European understanding of the rule of law—which emerged in the effort to abolish judicial and penal torture—see J. M. Bernstein, *Torture and Dignity: An Essay on Moral Injury* (Chicago: University of Chicago Press, 2015), chap. 1.

26. Balibar, *Equaliberty*, 44; my emphasis.

27. Balibar, *Equaliberty*, 45.

28. Balibar, *Equaliberty*, 46.

29. Balibar, *Equaliberty*, 48.

30. See Bernstein, *Torture and Dignity*, chap. 3.

31. Balibar, *Equaliberty*, 172–73.

32. Balibar, *Equaliberty*, 173.

33. Balibar, *Equaliberty*, 117.

34. Balibar, *Equaliberty*, 171.

35. "The 'right to have rights' clearly is not (or not primarily) a moral notion; it is a political one. It describes a process which started with resistance and ends in the actual exercise of a 'constituent power.' . . . It should therefore be called a *right to politics*, in the broad sense, meaning that nobody can be emancipated from the outside or from above, but only by his or her own (collective) activity" (Balibar, *Politics and the Other Scene*, 165).

36. Balibar, *Politics and the Other Scene*, 33.

37. The notion of "wrong" is Rancière's borrowing from Lyotard's conception of the differend. The concept of moral injury is mine.

38. In sketching out the claim of equal dignity in this way, I am following the lead of Allen Buchanan, *The Heart of Human Rights* (New York: Oxford University Press, 2013), 98–106.

39. Andrea Sangiovanni, *Humanity without Dignity: Moral Equality, Respect, and Human Rights* (Cumberland, R.I.: Harvard University Press, 2017), 74, lists five forms of treating as inferior: dehumanization, infantalization, objectification, instrumentalization, and stigmatization. Avishai Margalit notes just three, with slightly different phrasing: "treating humans as nonhuman, rejection" from the encompassing group that provides the forms of recognition of membership necessary for belonging and social participation, "and acts intended to lead to lack of control or to highlight one's lack of control" (Avishai Margalit, *The Decent Society*, trans. Naomi Goldblum [Cambridge, Mass.: Harvard University Press, 1996], 146). Sangiovanni seems unaware of Margalit.

40. Étienne Balibar, *We, the People of Europe?: Reflections on Transnational Citizenship*, trans. James Swenson (Princeton: Princeton University Press, 2004), 75; original emphasis removed.

41. Bernstein, *Torture and Dignity*, chap. 4.

42. Étienne Balibar, *Violence and Civility: On the Limits of Political Philosophy*, trans. G. M. Goshgarian (New York: Columbia University Press, 2015), 52.

43. Joanna Bourke, *Rape: Sex, Violence, History* (Emeryville, Calif.: Shoemaker & Hoard, 2007), 327.

44. For a thoughtful exposition of this claim, see James W. Nickel, *Making Sense of Human Rights*, 2nd ed. (Oxford, UK: Blackwell, 2007), 61–69; and, with a surprising acknowledgement of the primacy of negative, Jürgen Habermas, "The Concept of Human Dignity and the Realistic Utopia of Human Rights," *Metaphilosophy* 41, no. 4 (July 2010): 464–80.

45. Étienne Balibar, "Subjection and Subjectivation," in *Supposing the Subject*, ed. Joan Copjec (New York: Verso, 1994), 7.

SOLIDARITY

Gary Wilder

We might understand Étienne Balibar's work as an extended attempt to articulate Marx's critique of political economy with democratic political theory. He regularly treats the insights from one tradition to interrupt the conventional limitations of the other. This in order to develop a dialectical approach to historical contingency and political possibility (as well as a contingent approach to dialectical history and political determinations). From this perspective, his shift in the mid-1980s from analyzing capitalist structures to examining the conditions of possibility for democratic politics is not as striking as it might appear.

Already in 1965, Balibar argues against treating Marxism as a theory of universal history that proceeds through fixed evolutionary stages.[1] Similarly, in 1994, he argues that the possible transition from capitalism to communism marks not the necessary development *of* freedom but the beginning of struggles *for* a freedom that is never guaranteed.[2] Rather than simply critique Marxism from the standpoint of politics, he critiques one-sided approaches to both structural determinism and historical contingency from the standpoint of Marx's own attempts to transcend this dichotomy. Balibar thus calls for a "critical philosophy" that would treat historical change in ways that are "prospective and conjunctural," explaining that "*action in the present*" requires "*theoretical* knowledge of the material conditions which constitute 'the present.'"[3] And he reads Marx's understanding of praxis in frankly democratic terms, as a struggle for "socialization," or "the capacity for individuals collectively to control their own conditions of existence."[4]

I read Balibar's recent efforts to reenvision an emancipatory and egalitarian universalism that is rooted in, rather than abstracted from, what he calls "anthropological differences" as an attempt to think with and beyond Marx. I would suggest that he does so partly by thinking about politics with and beyond deconstructive criticism. Balibar's work develops a radical critique of economic and political liberalism. He attends directly to knowledge-power complexes and traces the profound dilemmas that confront democratic projects. But his task is never simply to unmask an emancipatory project for being complicit with power, burdened with tainted categories, or beset by formidable dilemmas. On the contrary, he attempts to reclaim and refunction foundational categories—liberty, equality, universality, democracy, justice—for our political present. If Balibar often starts with a deconstructive operation, he does so in order to elaborate the contradictory conditions under which political thinking and acting must necessarily proceed. It is never the aim of his analysis.

One thread running through Balibar's recent writings is the question of how, in the absence of the supposed certainties provided by universal history, mechanical materialism, class essentialism, ethnic unity, natural nations, or territorial fixity, a political subject and social collectivity manages to emerge, hang together, and act in the world, whether during or after struggles for emancipation and collective self-determination. "Citizenship" is one name that Balibar assigns to this political problem and phenomenon. But we might also locate the question of citizenship within the more general problematic of solidarity (and vice versa). In this essay, I have chosen to think with Balibar about the political prospect of being-in-common differently through this concept. "Solidarity" rarely appears explicitly in his work, but it seems to be implied everywhere. This concept also links political economy and political theory; in it, we can discern the intimate links that once existed, and should be reestablished, between Marxism and democracy.

"Solidarity" has long been central to Leftist discourse, but its significance is usually treated as self-evident. In the following, I discuss the consolidation of solidarity politics through the matrix of labor militancy, socialist mutualism, and Marxist internationalism. I suggest that this political concept has functioned as a relay point between anticapitalism and democratic politics through experiments in sociability that were both actual and anticipatory.

THE CONTRADICTORY LEGACY OF SOLIDARITY

The concept of "solidarity" developed simultaneously with the capitalist system and bourgeois society whose individualist and competitive logic it opposed.

From the French *solidaire*, it has long signaled the solid bloc of resistance, the forms of association and unity, that developed among modernity's dispossessed. Peter Linebaugh and Marcus Rediker, for example, use solidarity to describe the forms of autonomous self-organization and coordinated resistance that developed between the sixteenth and nineteenth centuries among sailors, slaves, pirates, dockworkers, peasants, religious radicals, and radical republicans across the Atlantic world.[5] Likewise, Thomas C. Holt uses solidarity to analyze forms of slave resistance and postemancipation revolts in colonial Jamaica.[6] Historians E. P. Thompson and William Sewell use the idiom of solidarity to trace how, following the French and industrial revolutions, European craftsmen and skilled workers mobilized existing forms of collective identification and corporate organization to resist processes of expropriation and proletarianization through mutual-aid societies, workers' associations, and strikes.[7] In northwest Europe, these resistant solidarity practices slowly crystallized into various political projects to reconstitute society on nonliberal foundations.

By the early nineteenth century, the term *solidarité* gained currency among French labor militants and republican socialists. The popular current of the 1848 Revolution in France fought to create a social republic that would assume responsibility for citizens' welfare by instituting social rights founded on principles of mutuality, reciprocity, cooperation, and collectivity. Pierre-Joseph Proudhon, the self-taught printer and revolutionary socialist who participated directly in this revolution, explicitly uses the concept of "solidarity" to describe his mutualist program for "socialist democracy" through the self-organization of workers into producers' cooperatives and the creation of a democratic system of banking and credit.[8] "Equality in exchange," he argues, would serve as "the basis of the equality of labour, of real solidarity."[9] Likewise, a Bank of the People would "[organize] workers' mutual solidarity" in the service of a democratic socialist republic based on nonexploitive relations of exchange.[10] Proudhon believed that cooperative labor and democratic credit would allow the "democratic and social creed" to triumph on larger and larger scales, moving from workers' associations to collective ownership of small farms and firms, to large scale property and industry, to massive ventures such as mines, canals, and railways.[11] These would be "handed over to democratically organised workers' associations" that would serve as "the pioneering core of [a] vast federation of companies and societies woven into the common cloth of the democratic and social Republic."[12] Proudhon remarks that in such an "anti-governmental" society, "the centre is everywhere, the circumference nowhere."[13] Accordingly, he believed that these practices would create "real solidarity among the nations."[14] He thus viewed mutualism and internationalism as two sides of the same coin; solidarity would guide relations within and between social formations.

Marx's thinking was also inflected by 1848. He, too, however deep his disagreements with Proudhon, regarded social solidarity as both a means and end of anticapitalist struggle. Between the 1840s and 1870s, Marx regularly critiqued industrial capitalism, liberal democracy, and the bourgeois state from the standpoint of "association." For him, this term was an analog to "solidarity." In one register, Marx uses "association" to describe the forms of sociality, organization, and unity practiced by workers in everyday life, in the workplace, and through labor struggles. *The Communist Manifesto* thus describes how "the advance of industry . . . replaces the isolation of the labourers, due to competition, by the revolutionary combination, due to association."[15] Workers "club together in order to keep up the rate of wages; they found permanent associations in order to make provision . . . for these occasional revolts."[16] Through this "ever expanding union of the workers," local class conflicts coalesce into a common national and general political struggle.[17]

Marx treats association as both a method of labor militancy and its aim; it would allow workers to enjoy the kind of cooperative sociality that competitive capitalism had obstructed. In his 1844 manuscripts, he writes, "When communist *workmen* gather together, their immediate aim is instruction, propaganda, etc. But at the same time, they acquire a new need—the need for society—and what appears as a means has become an end."[18] It is "in the gatherings of French socialist workers," he notes, that "smoking, eating and drinking, etc. are no longer means of creating links between people. Company, association, conversation, which in its turn has society as its goal, is enough for them. The brotherhood of man is not a hollow phrase, it is a reality."[19]

In some sense, these forms and practices of workers' association became the model for Marx's vision of a disalienated society. Rejecting any understanding of "society" as an abstract entity that exists "over against the individual," he argues that "the individual *is* the *social being*. His vital expression . . . is therefore an expression and confirmation of *social life*."[20] This formulation is then echoed in his sixth thesis on Feuerbach (to which Balibar pays particular attention): "The human essence is no abstraction inherent in each single individual. In its reality it is the ensemble of the social relations."[21] Accordingly, Marx praises "activity and consumption that express and confirm themselves directly in *real association* with other men."[22] He characterizes communism as "activity in direct association with others,"[23] and contends that "in a real community . . . individuals obtain their freedom in and through their association."[24] For Marx, association thus indexed a form of sociality that points beyond alienated oppositions between self and society, or individuality and humanity.

This emphasis on the emancipatory character of collective association was not restricted to Marx's early writings. The *Communist Manifesto* (1848) envisions a postcapitalist order in which "class distinctions have disappeared, and all production [is] concentrated in the hands of a vast association of the whole nation."[25] As Marx and Engels famously declare, "we shall have an association, in which the free development of each is the condition for the free development of all."[26] The *Grundrisse* (1858) contrasts capitalism, in which individuals produce "for society" to a system in which they produce in a "*directly* social" manner as the "offspring of association" in order to "manage" their "common wealth."[27] In *Capital* (1867), Marx repeatedly employs the image of "freely associated producers" as his standpoint of critique and emancipatory possibility.[28]

In 1871, worldly events intersected with Marx's proleptic social analysis when the Paris Commune attempted to transform land and capital into "mere instruments of free and associated labour."[29] By these means, Marx believed, "united cooperative societies" could "regulate national production upon a common plan" and thereby institute a form of "'possible' communism."[30] Through "the reabsorption of state power by society as its own living forces," he explained, the "popular masses themselves" made the Paris Commune into "the political form of their social emancipation."[31] In this sense, the Commune seemed to have realized, however fleetingly, Marx's earlier hope and call for human emancipation: "Only when man has recognized and organized his *forces propres* as *social forces* so that social force is no longer separated from him in the form of *political* force, only then will human emancipation be completed."[32] For Marx, association pointed beyond the alienating distinction within modern bourgeois society between public and private, state and society, citizen and man.

Marx also regarded the Paris Commune as the herald of a revolutionary internationalism that would be the cause and consequence of new solidarity practices. Beyond being the "true representative of . . . French society" as well as "the truly national government," Marx explains, "as a working men's government, as the bold champion of the emancipation of labor, emphatically international . . . the Commune annexed to France the working people of the world."[33] Marx praises the Commune for rejecting the nationalist "chauvinism of the bourgeoisie" and argues that "the international cooperation of the working classes" is "the first condition of their emancipation."[34] He contends that the revolutionary aim was not only to create an international alliance of struggling workers against bourgeois class rule but to institute a new epoch of human history in which all "mankind" could be freely associated "through the Communal form of political organization."[35] By linking communal self-management and human emancipation on a planetary scale, "association" would be a *concrete universal*; it would transcend the opposition between concrete particularity and abstract universality.

Marx, of course, had long been committed to internationalist solidarity. *The Communist Manifesto* famously ended with a call: "Working Men of All Countries Unite!" It pledged that "Communists everywhere [will] support every revolutionary movement against the existing social and political order of things.... They labour everywhere for the union and agreement of the democratic parties of all countries."[36] Recall that Marx and Engels were originally commissioned to write the *Manifesto* at the November 1847 convention of the Communist League, which Marx had described as "an international association of workers."[37] Almost twenty years later, in September 1864, they helped form the International Working Men's Association in the wake of the Europe-wide counterrevolution.

In his inaugural address to the first International, Marx attributes the failures of 1848 to the absence of "solidarity of action between the British and continental working classes."[38] He warns that "disregard of that bond of brotherhood, which ought to exist between workmen of different countries, and incite them to stand firmly by each other in all their struggles for emancipation, will be chastised by... their incoherent efforts."[39] For Marx, international labor solidarity was not merely a matter of abstract morality or disinterested empathy. He insisted that the failure of one fraction of the working class would ensure the failure of the movement as a whole; their conditions of domination were interrelated, and their common future depended on one another. Accordingly, the "working classes" had a "duty to master... the mysteries of international politics" in order to "counteract" the "diplomatic acts of their respective governments."[40] Marx thus praises English workers for opposing Atlantic slavery and called on European labor movements to defend Poland against Russian imperial conquest. The provisional rules of the International held that "the emancipation of labour is neither a local nor a national, but a social problem embracing all the countries in which modern society exists, and depending for its solution on the concurrence, practical, and theoretical, of the most advanced countries."[41] To this end, the organization affirms that "when immediate practical steps should be needed, as, for instance, in case of international quarrels, the action of the associated societies [will] be simultaneous and uniform."[42] More prosaically, but no less importantly, each national association pledges to provide "the fraternal support of the associated working men" to any individual member who moves residence from one country to another.⁴³ In matters of solidarity, overarching principles could not be separated from everyday practices.

Marx's understanding of international solidarity is nicely condensed in an 1870 letter on Irish nationalism to Siegfried Meyer and August Vogt, German comrades in the United States. He explains that because England is the world "metropolis of capital," a social revolution there is indispensable to the emancipation of labor everywhere.⁴⁴ Additionally, he observes that English wealth and power depended largely on the colonization of Ireland, that is, on the expropriation of land and dispossession of peasants, cheap raw materials and a surplus population to fuel industrialization at home, and religio-nationalist prejudices to keep the metropolitan working class divided. Finally, he notes that revolution would be more easily accomplished in Ireland than in England. Marx therefore concludes that "the decisive blow against the English ruling classes (and it will be decisive for the workers' movement all over the world) cannot be delivered *in England* but *only in Ireland*."⁴⁵ These are the grounds on which he calls on the International to support Irish national liberation. Its "special task" was "to make the English workers realise that *for them* the *national emancipation of Ireland* is not a question of abstract justice or humanitarian sentiment but the *first condition of their own social emancipation*."⁴⁶

Marx's revolutionary internationalism was a form of radical universalism, not bourgeois humanism. He insisted that international solidarity was both a tactical necessity and a good in itself, declaring that "all societies and individuals adhering to [the International] will acknowledge truth, justice, and morality, as the basis of their conduct towards each other, and towards all men, without regard to color, creed, or nationality; they hold it the duty of a man to claim the rights of a man and a citizen, not only for himself, but for every man who does his duty."⁴⁷ In contrast to the kind of abstract universalism that would homogenize peoples and standardize differences, Marx does not propose the eventual dissolution of specific worker associations or their amalgamation into a central governing body. On the contrary, by "joining the International Association," workers "will preserve their existent organizations intact."⁴⁸ Marx envisions a global federation of self-managing "working men's societies" that would be "united in a perpetual bond of fraternal cooperation."⁴⁹ For Marx, both local self-management and planetary internationalism were grounded in a concept and practice of solidarity. He hoped to conjugate both within a new form of *differential unity*. This was a vision of concrete universalism rooted in translocal networks of socialist association.

The forces of *belle-époque* European order feared precisely the kinds of revolutionary solidarity promoted by Marxism and embodied by the Paris Commune.

Solidarity also animated the "general strike" of enslaved African Americans during the US Civil War, the 1865 Morant Bay peasant rebellion in Jamaica, the rent strikes and boycotts against landlords and evictions during the Irish Land War, and the coordinated actions of anarchist networks linking Europe, Asia, and the Caribbean.[50] National states, colonial administrations, ruling classes, industrial oligarchs, and ancien régime autocrats were equally opposed to the prospect of a global federation of self-managing and freely associated producers. Their counterrevolutionary fear—along with the new requirements of mass production, mass politics, and colonial administration—set in motion the historic compromise among labor, capital, and the state that led first to social democracy and the Second International and, eventually, to Fordist capitalism and Keynesian welfarism (Balibar's "national-social state").[51] Perversely, this attempt to reform liberal capitalism in order to neutralize Marxism and preempt class war was also articulated in the language of "solidarity."

Solidarisme, as elaborated by Léon Bourgeois, famously became a state ideology in Third Republic France. At the same time, the new field of academic sociology, dominated by Durkheim and his circle, elevated social solidarity to an object of analysis, a normative ideal, and a reformist desire. Republican politicians and scholars began to question liberal assumptions about society by conceptualizing individuals as intrinsically social beings, born into webs of interdependence, and society as founded upon reciprocity, mutuality, and shared risk. In this story, individuals assumed responsibility for their neighbors, employers for their workers, and the state for the welfare of its citizens. This new discourse of solidarity appropriated, in order to domesticate, workerist, socialist, and Marxist critiques of liberal capitalism. Its aim was to ensure social integration and public order, not to realize social justice and public freedom. Accordingly, it naturalized solidarity as a (depoliticized) social fact rather than recognize it as an emancipatory political practice. The new politics of solidarity may have blurred the categorical distinction between state and society that Marx regarded as a source of alienation. But it did so in order to consolidate a more powerful form of capitalism, to expand further the scale and scope of national state power, and to ground new strategies of imperial rule.[52]

Of course, social democrats, liberal sociologists, welfare states, and colonial administrators were never able to recuperate fully the radical struggles and imaginaries associated with the concept of solidarity. Marcel Mauss's reflections on the contemporary importance of "archaic" forms of exchange associated with "the gift," for example, indicate how the transformative implications of solidarity practices could point beyond even scholars' own reformist intentions.[53] More broadly, the legacy and spirit of solidarity politics was equally present in various popular cooperative movements from the 1880s through the mid-twentieth century among workers and peasants in Europe, the United States, Latin America, the Caribbean, West Africa, and South Asia.[54] The solidarity ethos also informed mutual-aid societies, multiracial labor unions, and mass movements for colonial emancipation among colonized workers and students living in European metropoles between the world wars.

Solidarity politics were central to the thinking of Antonio Gramsci, who participated in the Turin factory occupation and council movement that culminated in the 1920 General Strike. The latter depended on effective solidarity relations between urban and rural actors in order to link factories, cities, and the region in a broad movement for workers' democracy.[55] Gramsci then confronted the challenge and necessity of revolutionary solidarity in his analysis of "the Southern Question." Contending that capitalism, rather than cultural backwardness, was the reason for uneven development in twentieth-century Italy, Gramsci argued for a new alliance between northern workers and southern peasants.[56] The point was not to recruit peasants to orthodox Marxism but to have workers assume peasant struggles as their own. Gramsci's subsequent prison reflections on relations of force, political blocs, and socialist hegemony further engaged the problem of solidarity.

Gramsci may be usefully related to W. E. B. Du Bois, his American contemporary, who also inherited a legacy of solidarity practices (in this case from the black radical tradition) that he, too, related to his specific historical situation. During the 1930s Great Depression, Du Bois elaborated a program for black self-management through consumer cooperatives that would serve as both model and catalyst for transforming liberal democracy in the United States into a new "cooperative commonwealth."[57] For Du Bois, solidarity worked in multiple registers. It was a tactic for community survival under conditions of severe deprivation and persecution. It was also part of a long-term strategy of cross-group alliance (including with traditionally racist white working classes) within a broad movement to transform American society into a multiracial socialist democracy composed of federated cooperatives. Solidarity also indexed the mutualist principle of sociality that would be practiced within black cooperative associations and, eventually, the larger society.[58]

Both Gramsci and Du Bois were heterodox Marxists who confronted the challenge of human emancipation in relation to historically specific political situations within unevenly developed and culturally divided societies. Their respective commitments to solidarity struggles and associative politics were inspired, even enabled, by the Russian Revolution. Yet they embraced and extended solidarity traditions in ways that diverged sharply from the authoritarian centralism favored by Soviet state socialism and the Moscow-led Third International. The latter purported to extend the tradition of Marxist internationalism by creating a worldwide network of revolutionary anticapitalist and anti-imperial organizations (whose skeleton was formed by various national or protonational Communist Parties). But given its preoccupation with ideological orthodoxy, its universal normative assumptions about history, revolution, and Communism, its embrace of bureaucratic statism, and its opposition to democratic self-management, the Third International may be seen as another instance through which the radical legacy of solidarity practices and politics was instrumentalized and domesticated.

Yet the Third International also facilitated and extended networks of anti-imperial internationalists across Europe, Asia, Africa, the Middle East, Latin America, North America, and the Caribbean.[59] Such transversal connections proved invaluable to struggles for decolonization. They often promoted forms of political association and associative politics that transgressed bureaucratic statism and Cold War geopolitics. Anticolonial internationalists linked struggles within and across regions and empires. The worldwide mobilization against the Italian invasion of Ethiopia, Frantz Fanon joining the anticolonial revolution in Algeria, C. L. R. James organizing black revolutionaries in the United States, and Cuban fighters and aid workers joining their comrades in Congo and Angola are only a few of many such examples. The African American civil-rights struggle identified and allied explicitly with anticolonial national liberation movements (and vice versa). The legendary 1955 Bandung Conference of newly decolonized nations seeking to form a nonaligned bloc in the global order for a new era of world history was organized under the rubric of Afro-Asian solidarity. More radical yet was the Tricontinental Congress, created in Havana in 1966, which gave birth to the Organization of Solidarity with the People of Asia, Africa, and Latin America.

May 1968 may be regarded as having inherited the solidarity legacies of the Paris Commune and colonial liberation. The insurrection in France was largely enabled by mutualist *groupuscules* that promoted unprecedented solidarity practices among students, factory workers, intellectuals, and technocrats, among the capital, provincial cities, and the countryside, and among white metropolitan and colonized subaltern communities.[60] Moreover, it was part of a global wave of antisystemic rebellion that linked Paris to places such as Prague, Mexico City, and Dakar. Since the 1980s, solidarity practices have been central to the internal organization and international networks mobilized by Sandinistas and Zapatistas, the antiapartheid struggle in South Africa and the Central American sanctuary movement, the World Social Forum and *alterglobalization* movement, and, more recently, mass assembly and occupation movements in the Middle East, Turkey, Europe, and the United States.

Concurrent with many of these developments, the concept of solidarity has been instrumentalized in deplorable ways. From one side, it has been deployed by statist and populist nationalist, nativist, and racist movements; they are identitarian and internalist. From another side, it has been deployed by liberal internationalists who support Western states, international agencies, and the forces of "global governance," and who justify imperial military interventions through doctrines of human rights, humanitarianism, just war, and the Responsibility to Protect. Moreover, the global internet has allowed solidarity to be depoliticized through individuals' immediate capacity to express digital support for distant catastrophes. Social media displaces, by perversely mimicking, socialist internationalism.

SOLIDARITY AS A CRITICAL POLITICAL CONCEPT

In Reinhart Koselleck's terms, we might say that solidarity has been an ambiguous or plastic concept that has "registered" historical shifts and experiences of struggle.[61] We may also usefully recall Mikhail Bakhtin's insights about how a language, discourse, or text can be a "heteroglot unity" that condenses diverse, competing, and interrelated social and ideological forces within a given social field and across multiple historical periods.[62] I have tried to suggest that the plastic character of "solidarity" may be linked directly to its potency as a concept that both registers a series of historical shifts and crystallizes a set of political practices and possibilities that may speak to our historical present. I propose treating the concept as an untimely and heteroglot unity that indexes modes of thinking, sets of practices, and a political tradition that point beyond many of the limiting frameworks and false oppositions that continue to overdetermine both radical and liberal political thinking today. Solidarity refers to both a method of struggle (in concert) and a principle of sociality (in common) for which the struggle is waged. It conveys forms of political unity *within* and *across* social groups (or formations). Solidarity helps us to think about nonliberal forms of concrete universality, founded on interconnected singularities, or federated associations.

Balibar writes about the need to engage the tensions of Marx's thought in order "to find the keys" to its "intrinsic incompletion" and "thus to its potentiality for reactivation at other conjunctures."[63] Similarly, I hope that historicizing "solidarity" may help revitalize this seemingly mundane category by allowing it to disclose, across generations, the kind of analytic and political work it has done. To this end, I distill from my historical sketch a set of provisional propositions about this concept for our times.

1. *We might usefully distinguish three types of solidarity.*

    First are those forms associated with *solidarity as a principle of struggle* whereby actors recognize shared or related conditions of domination and coordinate collective responses. Second are those forms associated with *solidarity as a principle of sociality* whereby actors pursue self-organization according to principles of interdependent reciprocity, mutual responsibility, shared risks, and common futures. Third, and related, is *solidarity as a principle of cosmopolitan or international linkage across collectivities.*

2. *Solidarity is never given.*

    In contrast to the Durkheimian tradition, solidarity is a political act, not a social fact. It does not flow naturally from primordial social groupings. Nor should it be conflated with the fiction of self-interested individuals entering social compacts to guarantee security and maximize material welfare. *Solidarity presupposes and produces social subjects.* The concept points beyond the conventional opposition between natural communities (which are supposed to precede politics) and transhistorical individuals (who are supposed to precede society).

3. *Solidarity is a practice, not a sentiment.*

    The different motives of solidarity practices are less important than the political, social, and ethical work that they pursue are. Many forms; as many, and different, motives. These matter less than the actual work that these practices pursue.

4. *Solidarity requires risk.*

    In contrast to feelings of compassion or acts of charity from a safe distance, solidarity is a *standing-with where something is at stake*. It means renouncing safety and sharing risk, putting oneself on the line by propelling oneself over the line that is supposed to mark an outside.

5. *Solidarity starts from entanglement.*

    The nonindifferent commitment to *stand with* flows from the fact of mutual implication, from actors' recognition that they are already involved in each other's situations, that they share a common world, and that their future prospects are somehow bound together. They may share conditions of oppression, recognize a common enemy, or be linked through a broader system of intersecting domination. Alternatively, members of socially dominant groups may recognize their own implication in and responsibility for others' domination, whether near or far. In both cases, solidarity starts from the fact that in an unevenly shared world, forms of domination create relations of mutual responsibility whereby the fate of each depends on all and all on each.

Radical solidarity politics thus contrast with the kind of liberal logic that underlies something like the "Right to Protect," whereby atomized individuals delegate their social power to alien agencies (such as states) that act, often violently, to "protect" suffering individuals, always absolute others, in the name of humanity. But it also contrasts with Levinas's and Derrida's infinite responsibility for the absolute other, which situates self and other on different ontological and ethical planes. *Solidarity is the response to a call*, not the obligation to a face. Solidarity does not claim that privileged majorities and dominated minorities are equally responsible to one another. It figures *horizontal* relationships among *social* individuals, within and across struggling collectives, who are already concretely implicated in each other's history and fate.

6. *Solidarity is a practice of identification that cuts across conventional oppositions between identity and difference.*

It calls into question categorical divisions between insiders and outsiders, the threatened and the protected, the implicated and the indifferent, those who must take sides and the spectators or commentators who can afford to stay off the field. But this does not mean that solidarity presupposes sameness, levels differences, or assimilates heterogeneity into a singular identity or undifferentiated totality. Nor does it expect consensus. It is an uneven, messy, and risky enterprise, ever incomplete, that reveals systemic contradictions, acknowledges power differentials, and generates real conflicts (think here of Balibar's "conflictual citizenship").

7. *Solidarity emerges from and creates differential unities.*

It is not based on the concrete particular identity of primordial communities that naturally stick together or act in unison. Nor is it based on the abstract universal identity of generic humans who supposedly share a common essence (e.g., reason, will, compassion, pain). Solidarity recognizes the existence of differences that need to be provisionally coordinated. Yet, at every scale, it also calls into question categorical separations by recognizing or creating networks of interdependent singularities. It establishes forms of *heterogeneous commonality* and *concrete universality* that challenge false oppositions between plurality and totality, the singular and the shared. Solidarity refers to mutuality and reciprocity *within and across* heterogeneous formations. It displaces commonsense divisions between inside and outside, here and there, us and them, now and then.

8. *Solidarity practices work to create new subjects for a different kind of social order and to create new social arrangements for a different kind of social subjectivity.*

    Solidarity is both a means and an end in itself, an instrument of politics and a political good, an ethical practice and a practical ethics, a strategy that enacts the relations it hopes to institute. It refers both to a historical legacy and a future aspiration. If solidarity indicates a kind of political practice and envisions a set of social arrangements, it also signals a political challenge to which there can be no definitive solution. In contrast to pragmatic realism and regulative idealism, *solidarity is a real practice* that has no intrinsic limits.

9. *Solidarity is as much a temporal as a spatial concept.*

    Just as it seeks to connect diverse groups, solidarity may also link groups across seemingly separate historical epochs. We can think of traditions and legacies as forms of *temporal* solidarity that invite actors to assume responsibility for past and future generations. Recall Kant's claim that humans "cannot be indifferent even to the most remote epoch which may eventually affect our species," and of Benjamin's "secret agreement between past generations and the present one" that endows predecessors with moral claims on existing actors.[64]

    Solidarity reworks conventional assumptions about the grounds of political association. It contends that emancipation struggles should create solid blocs and dense networks in order to overcome multiple and intersecting forms of domination. It also suggests that the aim of such struggles is to create a social world and form of life based on precisely the principles of reciprocity, mutuality, and collectivity prefigured by the struggle. In other words, solidarity *anticipates* futures; *it calls for in order to call forth*. It thereby displaces conventional oppositions between doing and waiting, the actual and the possible, realism and utopianism. Solidarity practices *take place* and *stretch time*. Propelled by the dialectics of gap and link, distinction and connection, multiplication and unification, its work can never reach a boundary or come to a stop.

10. *Solidarity indexes aspirations for democratic sociality in an interdependent world.*

The concept helps us engage the political antinomy—frontally taken on by Kant, Arendt, and Balibar—that continues to haunt current politics: popular sovereignty in determinate polities is both indispensable for and antithetical to a human freedom that must somehow be based on local self-management *and* encompass all of humanity.[65] The concept indexes (the imperative for) association within and across social groups. It simultaneously affirms and calls into question determinate social communities and the boundaries of polities.

In short, "solidarity" expresses what Balibar identifies as the "essential element of uncertainty" and the intrinsically conflictual character of concepts.[66] Rather than grasping the world as it really is or settling questions, he suggests, concepts "exhibit dilemmas" by pointing to a "conflictual horizon" where it is impossible to come to a "universal agreement."[67] As in nineteenth-century Europe, solidarity today remains an ambiguous concept that may be claimed by radicals, reformers, and reactionaries. The radical legacy I have traced may be discerned in the practices of Boycott, Divest, Sanctions activists fighting for justice in Palestine, Palestinians texting encouragement and advice to black militants protesting police violence in Ferguson, Missouri, the emergence of the broad-based and planetary-minded Movement for Black Lives, the extraordinary mobilization of solidarity politics to halt construction of the Dakota Access Pipeline, and the experiment in confederal democracy in Rojava. The political questions both raised and addressed by the concept of solidarity also run through Balibar's writings about our shared political present.

BEING(S)-IN-COMMON

Although Balibar has not written extensively about solidarity per se, the concept embodies the many political dilemmas and possibilities that his work explores regarding entanglement and interdependence, mutual responsibility and shared risk, cooperation and coordination, insurgent blocs and nonidentitarian forms of association.

In response to Jean-Luc Nancy's 1986 question "Who comes after the subject?," Balibar responds: "the citizen."[68] He has since elaborated on this answer by developing historical, political, and theoretical arguments about the *becoming citizen of the subject* and the *becoming subject of the citizen*. But I also read his response as a comment on the state and future of critical theory. In the wake of the deconstructive critique of the subject, he seems to imply, we need to re-engage democratic politics accordingly. In this moment of world-historical transformation, it is not enough to reiterate the familiar antihumanist critique. His analyses begin by elaborating the dilemmas, antinomies, and aporias that haunt modern political concepts, projects, and imaginaries. But these are only a starting point for his attempt to envision new forms of substantive democracy adequate to our global present. They would be grounded neither in primordial communities nor in abstract humanity. They would not allow constitutive social power to be alienated in sovereign states, transnational bureaucracies, or a world government. This is the perspective from which I read Balibar's rich reflections on being(s)-in-common, equaliberty, citizenship without community, conflictual and co-citizenship, and the need to democratize democracy.[69]

Balibar's political thinking proceeds from the observation that "every political community (local or global) is a community of fate . . . whose members are at once radically foreign to each other . . . and unable to survive without each other."[70] For when "heterogeneous people and groups have been 'thrown together' by history and economy, in situations where their interests or cultural ideals cannot spontaneously converge," they "also cannot completely diverge without risking mutual destruction (or common elimination by external forces)."[71]

In response, he attempts to conceptualize citizenship "without an a priori principle of unity"; he hopes to "dissolve borders without . . . instituting humanity as a political subject" or opening a pathway for the institution of supranational security states, authoritarian world government, and an even more complete surveillance society.[72] Such politics, Balibar suggests, would both require and create "new forms of transindividuality" that would embrace rather than erase what he calls "anthropological differences."[73] Such differences would have to ground rather than to obstruct the kind of democratic political universalism toward which equaliberty points. Accordingly, he figures "liberation as a right to equality in difference, that is, not as the restoration of an original identity or the neutralization of differences in the equality of rights, but as the production of an equality without precedents or models that would be difference itself, the complementarity and reciprocity of singularities."[74] Likewise, he calls for "the incorporation of differences and singularities into the very conception of the universal—as the invention and institution of a system of 'equivalences without a general equivalent,' the translation and retranslation of the human to infinity in the ensemble of its variants."[75] With characteristic modesty, Balibar confesses that he does not know how to conceptualize this kind of universalism. Yet he also suggests that "this process is already underway" and "the very malaise of our political civilization must be read as evidence of the rise of new forms of transindividuality."[76] Here, we can see how political practice may require theory, or an understanding of how existing arrangements may already be creating new imperatives and possibilities. Balibar reminds us that "*action in the present*" requires "*theoretical* knowledge of the material conditions which constitute 'the present.'"[77]

The global drift toward authoritarian statism and populism compels all those actors who can *stand with* the many precarious communities targeted by forms of violent nationalism, nativism, and White supremacy. In the United States, for example, any successful resistance movement will have to create solidary blocs composed of diverse collectives *and* need to be part of an internationalist effort to challenge capitalism, imperialism, and authoritarianism. Americans will need to learn from and coordinate with comrades in places such as Britain, Germany, Russia, Turkey, India, Egypt, Brazil, and Palestine, to name only a few. Any number of currently unfolding political situations demand a politics (and an understanding) of solidarity: the war in Syria, the Mediterranean refugee crisis, and the policies of Fortress Europe, the occupation of Palestine, violent imperial interventions perpetrated under US–UN auspices, the predicament faced by small sovereign nations that are utterly dependent on the international financial system (from Greece to Africa), climate change and imminent environmental catastrophe.

The life prospects of most of the world's peoples and populations are determined by systemic forces and distant deciders that are beyond the reach of any state's sovereign power. Demographic, economic, geopolitical, and environmental entanglement and interdependence have never been denser. Processes of structural violence are creating impossible situations for greater numbers of people, a growing number of whom are permanently displaced. The need to coordinate struggles, assume responsibility, and share risks across spurious divisions has never been greater. Equally urgent is the imperative to envision and enact democratic social orders based on principles of reciprocity, mutuality, and collective self-management. Only then could we hope to overcome the rule of capital, the sovereignty of reified states, and social hierarchies based on invidious "anthropological distinctions." Under current conditions, any movement for human emancipation will require plural and postnational frameworks through which to articulate political autonomy and planetary politics, popular sovereignty and cosmopolitan association. The concept of solidarity contains the risks of voluntarism, instrumentalism, paternalism, and patriarchy. But as both means and aim of struggle, it also suggests a way of addressing these central political dilemmas of our time. It may be an indispensable resource and modality of meeting Balibar's call, rooted in Marxian critique and fueled by democratic commitments, to expand "the capacity for individuals collectively to control their own conditions of existence."

NOTES

1. Louis Althusser and Étienne Balibar, *Reading Capital* (New York: Verso, 1997), 223–345.

2. Étienne Balibar, *The Philosophy of Marx*, trans. Chris Turner (New York: Verso, 2014).

3. Balibar, *Philosophy of Marx*, 120, 122.

4. Balibar, *Philosophy of Marx*, 92.

5. Peter Linebaugh and Marcus Rediker, *The Many-Headed Hydra: Sailors, Slaves, Commoners, and the Hidden History of the Revolutionary Atlantic* (Boston: Beacon Press, 2000).

6. See, for example, Jean Casimir, *La culture opprimée* (Mexico City: Nueva Imagen, 1981); Thomas C. Holt, *The Problem of Freedom: Race, Labor and Politics in Jamaica and Britain, 1832–1938* (Baltimore: Johns Hopkins University Press, 1992); and Laurent Dubois, *Haiti: The Aftershocks of History* (New York: Metropolitan Books, 2012).

7. E. P. Thompson, *The Making of the English Working Class* (New York: Vintage, 1966); William H. Sewell Jr., *Work and Revolution in France: The Language of Labor from the Old Regime to 1848* (Cambridge, UK: Cambridge University Press, 1980).

8. Pierre-Joseph Proudhon, *Proudhon's Solution of the Social Problem* (New York: Vanguard Press, 1927).

9. Proudhon, *Solution*, 510.

10. Proudhon, *Solution*, 643.

11. Proudhon, *Solution*, 646.

12. Proudhon, *Solution*, 650.

13. Proudhon, *Solution*, 776.

14. Proudhon, *Solution*, 452.

15. Karl Marx and Friedrich Engels, *The Communist Manifesto* (New York: International Publishers, 1948), 21.

16. Marx and Engels, *Communist Manifesto*, 18.

17. Marx and Engels, *Communist Manifesto*, 18.

18. Karl Marx, *Early Writings* (London: Penguin, 1992), 365.

19. Marx, *Early Writings*, 365.

20. Marx, *Early Writings*, 350.

21. Karl Marx, "Theses on Feuerbach," in *The Marx-Engels Reader*, ed. Robert C. Tucker, 2nd ed. (New York: Norton, 1978), 145.

22. Marx, *Early Writings*, 350.

23. Marx, *Early Writings*, 352.

24. Karl Marx, "The German Ideology," in *The Marx-Engels Reader*, ed. Robert C. Tucker, 2nd ed. (New York: Norton, 1978), 197.

25. Marx and Engels, *Communist Manifesto*, 31.

26. Marx and Engels, *Communist Manifesto*, 31.

27. Karl Marx, *Grundrisse: Foundations of the Critique of Political Economy* (London: Penguin, 1993), 158.

28. Karl Marx, *Capital*, vol. 1, *A Critique of Political Economy* (London: Penguin, 1992).

29. Karl Marx, *The First International and After*, vol. 3, *Marx's Political Writings* (London: Penguin, 1992), 213.

30. Marx, *First International*, 250.

31. Marx, *First International*, 250.

32. Karl Marx, *Early Writings*, trans. Gregor Benton (Harmondsworth, UK: Penguin, 1975), 234.

33. Marx, Marx, *First International*, 216. "Captive Paris" gave "body to the aspirations of the working class of all countries" (Marx, *First International*, 252).

34. Marx, *First International*, 263.

35. Marx, *First International*, 254.

36. Marx and Engels, *Communist Manifesto*.

37. Marx and Engels, *Communist Manifesto*.

38. Marx, *First International*, 78.

39. Marx, *First International*, 81.

40. Marx, *First International*, 81.

41. Marx, *First International*, 82.

42. Marx, *First International*, 83–84.

43. Marx, *First International*, 84.

44. Marx, *First International*, 220.

45. Marx, *First International*, 222.

46. Marx, *First International*, 223.

47. Marx, *First International*, 82–83.

48. Marx, *First International*, 82–83.

49. Marx, *First International*, 82–83.

50. W. E. B. Du Bois, *Black Reconstruction in America, 1860–1880* (New York: Free Press, 1997); Holt, *Problem of Freedom*; Samuel Clark, *Social Origins of the Irish*

Land War (Princeton: Princeton University Press, 1979); Benedict Anderson, *Under Three Flags: Anarchism and the Anti-Colonial Imagination* (New York: Verso, 2007).

51. Étienne Balibar, "The Nation-Form: History and Ideology," in Étienne Balibar and Immanuel Wallerstein, *Race, Nation, Class: Ambiguous Identities*, trans. Chris Turner (London: Verso, 1991), 92.

52. The political logic of productivism, cooperation, and welfarism also allowed colonial states to instrumentalize "association" in order to preempt radical movements for either national liberation or democratic citizenship in Africa, Asia, and the Caribbean. See Gary Wilder, *The French Imperial Nation-State: Negritude and Colonial Humanism between the World Wars* (Chicago: University of Chicago Press, 2005).

53. Marcel Mauss, *The Gift: The Form and Reason for Exchange in Archaic Societies* (New York: Norton, 1990).

54. Marx refers to "the cooperative movement" as a "victory of the political economy of labor over the political economy of property" and a "great social experiment" that "cannot be overrated," even as he warns that "however excellent in principle, and however useful in practice, cooperative labour, if kept within the narrow circle of the casual efforts of private workmen, will never be able to . . . free the masses" (*First International*, 79–80).

55. Antonio Gramsci, "Unions and Councils," *L'ordine nuovo* 11 (October 1919): 98–102.

56. Antonio Gramsci, *Modern Prince and Other Writings* (New York: International Publishers, 1957), 28–51.

57. W. E. B. Du Bois, *Writings* (New York: Library of America, 1987), 712.

58. See Gary Wilder, "Reading Du Bois's Revelation," in *The Postcolonial Contemporary: Political Imaginaries for the Global Present*, ed. Jini Kim Watson and Gary Wilder (New York: Fordham University Press, 2018), 95–125.

59. Manu Goswami, "Imaginary Futures and Colonial Internationalisms," *American Historical Review* 117, no. 5 (December 2012): 1461–85.

60. Kristin Ross, *May 68 and Its Afterlives* (Chicago: University of Chicago Press, 2002).

61. Reinhart Koselleck, "Introduction and Prefaces to the *Geschichtliche Grundbegriffe*," *Contributions to the History of Concepts* 6, no. 1 (Summer 2011): 1–37.

62. M. M. Bakhtin, *The Dialogic Imagination: Four Essays* (Austin: University of Texas Press, 1981), 284.

63. Étienne Balibar, *Citizen Subject: Foundations for Philosophical Anthropology* (New York: Fordham University Press, 2017), 149.

64. Immanuel Kant, *Political Writings* (Cambridge, UK: Cambridge University Press, 1970), 50; Walter Benjamin, *Selected Writings*, vol. 4, *1938–1940* (Cambridge, UK: Belknap, 2006), 389–401.

65. Kant, *Political Writings*, especially "Universal History with a Cosmopolitan Purpose" (41–53) and "Perpetual Peace: A Philosophical Sketch" (93–130); Hannah

Arendt, *The Origins of Totalitarianism* (New York: Harcourt, 1979); Hannah Arendt, *The Human Condition*, 2nd ed. (Chicago: University of Chicago Press, 1998); Hannah Arendt, *Eichmann in Jerusalem: A Report on the Banality of Evil* (New York: Penguin, 1977); Hannah Arendt, *The Jewish Writings* (New York: Schocken Books, 2007).

66. Étienne Balibar, "Concept" (this volume). Certain concepts, Balibar explains, "are not used *despite* their conflictual nature but precisely *because* of the *dissensus* they provoke and crystallize."

67. Balibar, "Concept" (this volume).

68. Balibar, *Citizen Subject*, especially "Citizen Subject: Response to Jean-Luc Nancy's Question 'Who Comes after the Subject?'"

69. Étienne Balibar, *We, the People of Europe?: Reflections on Transnational Citizenship*, trans. James Swenson (Princeton: Princeton University Press, 2003); Étienne Balibar, *Equaliberty: Political Essays*, trans. James Ingram (Durham, N.C.: Duke University Press, 2014); Étienne Balibar, *Citizenship*, trans. Thomas Scott-Railton (New York: Polity Press, 2015); Étienne Balibar, *Violence and Civility: On the Limits of Political Philosophy* (New York: Columbia University Press, 2015); Balibar, *Citizen Subject*.

70. Balibar *Equaliberty*, 144.

71. Balibar, *We, the People of Europe?*, 132.

72. Balibar, *Equaliberty*, 144.

73. Balibar, *Equaliberty*, 130. Recall his emphasis on Marx's definition of the human essence as an ensemble of social relations.

74. Balibar, *Equaliberty*, 59.

75. Balibar, *Equaliberty*, 131.

76. Balibar, *Equaliberty*, 130.

77. Balibar, *Philosophy of Marx*, 120.

BIBLIOGRAPHY OF THE WORKS OF ÉTIENNE BALIBAR

Compiled by Alexis Dianda and Jacques Lezra

2019

(With Emanuela Fornari and Iain Halliday.) *Boundary Lines: Philosophy and Postcolonialism*. Albany: State University of New York Press, 2019.

(With Jean-Claude Monod, and Myriam Revault d'Allonnes.) "Le concept de totalitarisme est-il encore pertinent?" *Esprit*, no. 1 (2019): 83–98.

Cukier, Alexis, and Isabelle Garo, eds. *Avec Marx, philosophie et politique: Entretiens*. Paris: La Dispute, 2019.

de Rudder, Véronique, and Marguerite Cognet. *Sociologie du racisme*. Paris: Éditions Syllepse, 2019.

(With William Callison, Zachary Manfredi, Sören Brandes, Wendy Brown, Melinda Cooper, Julia Elyachar, Michel Feher, Megan C. Moodie, and Christopher Newfield.) *Mutant Neoliberalism: Market Rule and Political Rupture*. New York: Fordham University Press, 2019.

"Politics and Translation: Reflections on Lyotard, Derrida, and Said." *Positions: East Asia Cultures Critique* 27, no. 1 (2019): 99–114.

"Revisiting the 'Expropriation of Expropriators' in Marx's 'Capital.'" In *Marx's Capital after 150 Years: Critique and Alternative to Capitalism*, Vol. 1, edited by Marcello Musto, 39–54. 1st ed. Milton, Eng.: Routledge, 2019.

2018

(With Emilio de Ipola and Gavin Arnall.) *Althusser, the Infinite Farewell*. Durham, N.C.: Duke University Press, 2018.

"Exploitation." In *Political Concepts: A Critical Lexicon*, edited by J. M. Bernstein, 131–44. New York: Fordham University Press, 2018.

"The Expropriation of Expropriators." *Revue de métaphysique et de morale* 100, no. 4 (2018): 479–90.

(Interview with Fabienne Brugère and Guillaume le Blanc.) "Le fantasme du corps étranger." *Esprit*, nos. 7–8 (2018): 173–82.

(Interview with Vadim Kamenka.) "Die Geschichte wird über uns urteilen." Translated by Frieder Otto Wolf. *Der Freitag* (July 4, 2018). https://www.freitag.de/autoren

/der-freitag/die-geschichte-wird-ueber-uns-urteilen. First published in *L'humanité* (June 21, 2018).

(With Jean-Claude Monod, Myriam Revault D'allonnes, Michaël Fœssel, and Justine Lacroix.) "Is the Concept of Totalitarianism Still Relevant?" *Esprit*, no. 1 (2018): 83–98.

Libre parole. Paris: Éditions Galilée, 2018.

"Mehrwert." *Actuel Marx* 63, no. 1 (2018): 114–33.

"Philosophies of the Transindividual: Spinoza, Marx, Freud." *Australasian Philosophical Review* 2, no. 1 (2018): 5–25.

(With Immanuel Wallerstein.) *Rasse, klasse, nation: Ambivalente identitäten*. Hamburg, Ger.: Argument Verlag, 2018.

Secularism and Cosmopolitanism: Critical Hypotheses on Religion and Politics. New York: Columbia University Press, 2018.

Spinoza politique: Le transindividuel. Paris: Presses Universitaires de France, 2018.

"Transindividuality in Dispute: A Response to My Readers." *Australasian Philosophical Review* 2, no.1 (2018): 113–17.

(With Gérard Bras.) *Les voies du peuple: Éléments d'une histoire conceptuelle*. Paris: Éditions Amsterdam, 2018.

2017

"È ancora possible una critica Marxista dei diritti umani?" *Parolechiave* 57, no. 1 (2017): 35–50.

"After Utopia, Imagination?" In *Political Uses of Utopia: New Marxist, Anarchist, and Radical Democratic Perspectives*, edited by S. D. Chrostowska and James D. Ingram, 161–64. New York: Columbia University Press, 2017.

(With Sandra Laugier.) "Agency." Entry in *Dictionary of Untranslatables: A Philosophical Lexicon*, edited by Barbara Cassin. Princeton: Princeton University Press, 2017.

(With Michel Wieviorka.) *Antiracistes: Connaitre le racisme et l'antisémitisme pour mieux les combattre*. Paris: Robert Laffont, 2017.

"Consciousness," "I," "Praxis (Greek)," "Soul," and "Subject." Entries in *Dictionary of Untranslatables: A Philosophical Lexicon*, edited by Barbara Cassin. Princeton: Princeton University Press, 2017.

Citizen Subject: Foundations for Philosophical Anthropology. Translated by Steven Miller. New York: Fordham University Press, 2017.

"Die drei Endspiele des Kapitalismus." In *RE: Das Kapital: Politische Ökonomie im 21 Jahrhundert*, edited by Mathias Greffrath, 213–35. Munich: Verlag Antje Kunstmann, 2017.

"Europe Provincial, Common, Universal." *Annali de scienze religiose* 10 (2017): 37–49.

"Fremde, nicht Feinde: In Richtung eines neuen Kosmopolitismus?" *Allgemeine Zeitschrift für Philosophie* 42, no. 2 (2017): 127–43.

(Interview with Olivier de France and Marc Verzeroli.) "From the Triumph of Capitalism to the Defeat of Democracy?" *Revue internationale et stratégique* 106, no. 2 (2017): 51–63.

(With Immanuel Maurice Wallerstein, James K. Galbraith, Johan Galtung, Nilüfer Göle, Pablo González Casanova, Michel Wieviorka.) *La gauche globale: Hier, aujourd'hui, demain.* Paris: Éditions de la Maison des Sciences de l'Homme, 2017.

La igualibertad. Translated by Victor Goldstein. Barcelona: Herder, 2017.

(With Christine Delory-Momberger, François Durpaire, and Béatrice Mabilon-Bonfils.) *Lettre ouverte contre l'instrumentalisation politique de la laïcité.* Paris: Éditions de l'Aube, 2017.

"A New Querelle of Universals." *Philosophy Today* 61, no. 4 (2017): 929–45.

"Our European Incapacity." In *Shifting Baselines of Europe: New Perspectives beyond Neoliberal Nationalism*, edited by Daphne Büllesbach, Marta Cillero, and Lukas Stoltz, 18–25. Bielefeld: Transcript, 2017.

The Philosophy of Marx. London: Verso, 2017.

"Reinventing the Stranger: Walls All over the World, and How to Tear Them Down." *Symploke* 25, no. 1–2 (2017): 25–41.

(With Olivier de France and Marc Verzeroli.) "De la victoire du capitalisme à la défaite de la démocratie?" *Revue international et stratégique* 106, no. 2 (2017): 51–63.

2016

"Après la fin de l'Europe." *Vacarme* 74, no. 1 (2016,): 153–58.

"La crise de la construction européenne: Une fin de cycles?" *Revue française d'histoire des idées politiques* 43, no. 1 (2016): 25–43.

"Critique in the 21st Century: Political Economy Still, and Religion Again." *Radical Philosophy*, no. 200 (2016): 11.

"Démocratisations." *Vacarme* 76, no. 3 (2016): 136–41.

Eşitliközgürlük. Istanbul: Metis, 2016.

Europa: Krise und Ende? Translated by Frieder Otto Wolf. Münster: Westfälisches Dampfboot, 2016.

"Europe at the Limits." *Interventions* 18, no. 2 (2016): 165–71.

Europe crise et fin? Lormont, Fr.: Éditions le Bord de l'Eau, 2016.

Foreword to *Radikaldemokratische Volkssouveränität für ein postnationales Europa: Eine Aktualisierung Rousseaus*, by Dagmar Comtesse. Baden-Baden, Ger.: Nomos, 2016.

"Group Psychology and the Analysis of the Ego." *Research in Psychoanalysis* 21, no. 1 (2016): 43–53.

(With Gonzalo Ricci Cernadas.) "El Hobbes de Schmitt, el Schmitt de Hobbes." *Las torres de Lucca: Revista internacional de filosofía política*, no. 9 (2016): 201–59.

"L'instance de la lettre et la dernière instance." *Actuel Marx* 59, no. 1 (2016): 42–52.

(With Gayatri Chakravorty Spivak.) "Interview on subalternity." *Cultural Studies* 30, no. 5 (2016): 856–71.

(With Clara Lecadet.) *Le manifeste des expulsés: Errance, survie et politique au Mali*. Tours, Fr.: Presses Universitaires François-Rabelais, 2016.

"Note sur la théorie du discoure." *Décalages* 2, no. 1 (2016): 1–37.

"Un point d'hérésie du marxisme occidental: Althusser et Tronti lecteurs du *Capital*." *Période* (July 4, 2016). http://revueperiode.net/un-point-dheresie-du-marxisme-occidental-althusser-et-tronti-lecteurs-du-capital/.

"La política de la deuda." Translated by Giulia Colaizzi and Elisa Hernández Pérez. *Pasajes: Revista de pensamiento contemporáneo*, no. 50 (2016): 50–82.

"Psychologie des masses et analyse du moi." *Research in Psychoanalysis* 21, no. 1 (2016): 43a–53a.

Preface to Bérard Cénatus, Stéphane Douailler, Michèle Duvivier Pierre-Louis, and Étienne Tassin, *Haïti: De la dictature à la démocratie?* Quebec: Mémoire d'Encrier, 2016.

(Interview with Thomas Casadei.) "Il ritorno della razza: Tra società e istituzioni." In Thomas Casadei, *Il rovescio dei diritti umani: Razza, discriminazione, schiavitù*, 93–125. Rome: Derive Approdi, 2016.

Des universels: Essais et conférences. Paris: Éditions Galilée, 2016.

Yurttaşlık. Istanbul: Monokl, 2016.

2015

"Althusser's Dramaturgy and the Critique of Ideology." *Differences* 26, no. 3 (2015): 1–22.

(With Yves Duroux.) "Althusser: Une nouvelle pratique de la philosophie entre politique et idéologie; conversation avec Étienne Balibar et Yves Duroux (partie I)." Interview with Fabio Bruschi and Eva Mancuso. In "Althusser: Politique et subjectivité I," edited by Fabio Bruschi and Eva Mancuso. Special issue, *Cahiers du GRM* 7 (2015). http://journals.openedition.org/grm/641.

(With Yves Duroux.) "Althusser: Une nouvelle pratique de la philosophie entre politique et idéologie; conversation avec Étienne Balibar et Yves Duroux (partie II)." Interview with Fabio Bruschi and Eva Mancuso. In "Althusser: Politique et subjectivité II," edited by Fabio Bruschi and Eva Mancuso. Special issue, *Cahiers du GRM* 8 (2015). http://journals.openedition.org/grm/722.

"L'anti-Marx de Michel Foucault." In *Marx & Foucault: Lectures, usages, confrontations*, edited by Christian Laval, Luca Paltrinieri, and Ferhat Taylan, 84–102. Paris: La Découverte, 2015.

Citizenship. Translated by Thomas Scott-Railton. Cambridge, Eng.: Polity Press, 2015.

"Dall'antropologia filosofica all'ontologia sociale e ritorno: Che fare con la sesta tesi di Marx su Feuerbach?" *Nóema* 6, no. 1 (2015): 35–59.

"Essere Principe, Essere Populare: The Principle of Antagonism in Machiavelli's Epistemology." In *The Radical Machiavelli: Politics, Philosophy, and Language*, edited by Filippo Del Lucchese, Fabio Frosini, and Vittorio Morfino, 349–67. Leiden, Neth.: Brill, 2015.

"Europe and Refugees: Enlargement." *Multitudes* 61, no. 4 (2015): 153–61.

(With Frédéric Boccara, Thomas Coutrot, Alexis Cukier, Cedric Durand, Michel Husson, Pierre Khalfa, Sandro Mezzadra, Catherine Samary, and Frieder Otto Wolf.) *Europe, l'expérience Grecque: Le débat stratégique*. Bellecombe-en-Bauges, Fr.: Éditions du Croquant, 2015.

"L'Europe-frontière et le 'défi migratoire.'" *Vacarme* 73, no. 4 (2015): 136–42.

"Evropa in begunci: Demografska širitev 1." *Casopis za kritiko znanosti* no. 262 (2015): 207–15.

"Foucault's Point of Heresy: 'Quasi-Transcendentals' and the Transdisciplinary Function of the Episteme." *Culture & Society* 32, no. 5–6 (2015): 45–77.

"L'hypothèse formulée dans violence et civilite." *Rue Descartes* 85–86, nos. 2–3 (2015): 11–12.

(With Vittorio Morfino.) "Introduzione al transindividuale." *Nóema* 6, no. 1 (2015): 1–34.

(With Louis Althusser, Roger Establet, Pierre Macherey, and Jacques Rancière.) *Das Kapital lessen*. Münster, Ger.: Westfälisches Dampfboot, 2015.

"Marx, Freud, Spinoza: Tre concezioni del transindividuale." *Nóema* 6, no. 1 (2015). https://riviste.unimi.it/index.php/noema/issue/view/627.

"Marxism and the Idea of Revolution: The Messianic Moment in Marx." In *Historical Teleologies in the Modern World*, edited by Henning Truper, Dipesh Chakrabarty, and Sanjay Subrahmanyam, 235–50. London: Bloomsbury, 2015.

(With Ahmet Insel, Marie-Claire Caloz-Tschopp, and Ilaria Possenti.) "Philosophie et politique: La turquie, l'Europe en devenir." *Rue Descartes* 85–86, nos. 2–3 (2015): 231–66.

"Plus que jamais, pour l'autre Europe! Thèses du 29 août 2015." In *Écrits sur la Grèce: Points de vue européens*, edited by Elisabeth Gauthier and Dominique Crozat, 21–50. Vulaines-sur-Seine, Fr.: Éditions du Croquant, 2015.

"La política y sus sujetos en el interregno." Prologue to Wendy Brown, *Estados amurallados, soberanía en declive*. Barcelona: Herder Editorial, 2015.

(With Louis Althusser, Roger Establet, Pierre Macherey, and Jacques Rancière.) *Reading Capital: The Complete Edition*. Brooklyn: Verso, 2015.

Sobre la dictadura del proletariado. 2nd ed. Madrid: Siglo XXI, 2015.

"Stunde der Wahrheit." *Zeit Online*, no. 41, October 8, 2015. https://www.zeit.de /2015/41/asypolitik-europa-fluechtlinge-angela-merkel.

"Sujeción y subjetivación." *Política común* 6, no. 2018. http://dx.doi.org/10.3998/pc .12322227.0006.004.

Violence and Civility: On the Limits of Political Philosophy. Translated by G. M. Goshgarian. New York: Columbia University Press, 2015.

(With Marie-Claire and Caloz-Tschopp.) *Violence, civilité, révolution: Autour d'Étienne Balibar*. La Dispute, 2015.

"Violencia, política, civilidad." *Ciencia política* 10, no. 19 (2015): 45–67.

2014

Ciudadano sujeto. Vol. 2, *Ensayos de antropología filosófica*. Buenos Aires: Editorial Prometeo, 2014.

"Los dilemas históricos de la democracia y su relevancia contemporánea para la ciudadanía." *Enrahonar: Quaderns de filosofia*, no. 48 (2012): 9–29.

Equaliberty: Political Essays. Translated by James Ingram. Durham, N.C.: Duke University Press, 2014.

"Europa, aber richtig: Plädoyer für ein einzigartiges Projekt." Emanzipatorische Linke (April 2014). https://emanzipatorische-linke.org/2014/04/11/etienne-balibar-europa-aber-richtig-pladoyer-fur-ein-einzigartiges-projekt/.

"Europe at the Limits." *Interventions* 18, no. 2 (2016): 165–71.

"Europe-Nations: The Missing People and the Crisis of Legitimacy." In *United Europe, Divided Europe: Transform!*, edited by Walter Baier, Eric Canepa, and Eva Himmelstoss. London: Merlin Press, 2015. https://www.transform-network.net/en/publications/yearbook/overview/article/yearbook-2015/europe-nations-the-missing-people-and-the-crisis-of-legitimacy.

(With Yannis Stavrakakis, Bruno Théret, Dēmētrēs Christopoulos, Wojciech Kalinowski, Dimitris Kousouris, Antonio Negri, Elsa Papageōrgiou, et al.). *To Hellēniko symptōma: Hē krisē, to chreos, ta kinēmata kai hē aristera*. Athens: Nisos, 2014.

(With Louis Althusser, Roger Establet, Pierre Macherey, and Jacques Rancière.) *Lire* Le capital. Paris: Presses Universitaires de France, 2014.

"Nancy's Inoperative Community." In *Nancy Now*, edited by Verena Andermatt Conley and Irving Goh, 20–36. Cambridge, Eng.: Polity Press, 2014.

"A New Impulse—But for Which Europe?" *Belgrade Journal of Media and Communications* 3, no. 6 (2014): 111–22.

"Un nouvel élan, mais pour quelle Europe?" *Le Monde Diplomatique* 70, no. 3 (March 2014): 16–17. https://www.monde-diplomatique.fr/2014/03/BALIBAR/50208.

(With Louis Althusser.) *On the Reproduction of Capitalism: Ideology and Ideological State Apparatuses*. London: Verso, 2014.

La philosophie de Marx. Paris: La Découverte, 2014.

Philosophy of Marx. New York: Verso, 2014.

(With Daho Djerbal.) "Pour une nouvelle épistémê." In *Guerre d'Algérie: Les mots pour la dire*, edited by Catherine Brun, 255–86. Paris: CNRS Éditions, 2014.

Preface to Silyane Larcher, *L'autre citoyen: L'idéal républicain et les Antilles après l'esclavage*. Paris: Armand Colin, 2014.

Preface to Thomas Boccon-Gibod, *Autorité et démocratie: L'exercice du pouvoir dans les sociétés modernes*. PhD diss., Institut Universitaire Varenne, 2014.

"Rasa, Nacija, Klasa." *Forum Bosnae*, no. 66 (2014): 22–31.

"The Rise and Fall of the European Union: Temporalities and Teleologies." *Constellations* 21, no. 2 (2014): 202–12.

Şiddet ve medenilik: Wellek Library konferansları ve diğer siyaset felsefesi denemeleri. Translated by Sevgi Tamgüç. Istanbul: İletişim Yayınları, 2014.

(With Vittorio Morfino.) *Il transindividuale: Soggetti, relazioni, mutazioni*. Milan, It.: Mimesis, 2014.

Des universels: Trois conférences. Paris: Éditions Galilée, 2014.

(With Marie-Clarie Caloz-Tschopp, Pinar Selek, and Ahmet Insel.) *Violence, politique et civilité aujourd'hui: La Turquie aux prises avec ses tourments*. Paris: L'Harmattan, 2014.

(With James Swenson.) *We, the People of Europe?: Reflections on Transnational Citizenship*. Princeton: Princeton University Press, 2014.

2013

"Avant-propos." *Tumultes* 40, no. 1 (2013): 7–11.

"Ce qu'il reste de la politique." *Lignes* 41, no. 2 (2013): 11–14.

Ciudadanía. Translated by Rodrigo Molina-Zavalía. Buenos Aires: Adriana Hidalgo, 2013.

Ciudadano sujeto. Translated by César Marchesino. Buenos Aires: Prometeo, 2013.

"Du commun et de l'universel dans la phénoménologie de Hegel." In *Jean Hyppolite, entre structure et existence*, edited by Giuseppe Bianco, 265–94. Paris: Rue d'Ulm, 2013.

"Europe: Final Crisis?: Some Thesis Again." *Belgrade Journal of Media and Communications* 2, no. 4 (2013): 69–74.

"Europe: L'impuissance des nations et la question 'populiste.'" *Actuel Marx* 54, no. 2 (2013): 13–23.

"His Name Is Legion." *Tumultes* 40 (2013): 7–11.

Identity and Difference: John Locke and the Invention of Consciousness. Translated by Warren Montag. London: Verso, 2013.

"La justice ou l'égalité: Pascal, Hegel, Marx." In *L'injustice sociale: Quelles voies pour la critique?*, edited by Julia Christ and Florian Nicodème, 17–38. Paris: Presses Universitaires de France, 2013.

"'Klassenkampf' als Begriff des Politischen." In *Nach Marx: Philosophie, Kritik, Praxis*, edited by Rahel Jaeggi and Daniel Loick. Berlin: Suhrkamp, 2013.

Marx' Philosophie. Berlin: B-Book, 2013.

Masses, Classes, Ideas: Studies on Politics and Philosophy before and after Marx. Hoboken, N.J.: Taylor & Francis, 2013.

"Il momento messianico di Marx." *Consecutio rerum: Rivista critica della postmodernità*, no. 5 (2013). http://www.consecutio.org/2013/10/il-momento-messianico-di-marx/.

"On the Politics of Human Rights." *Constellations* 20, no. 1 (2013): 18–26.

The Philosophy of Marx. Translated by Chris Turner. London: Verso, 2013.

"Politics of the Debt." *Postmodern Culture* 23, no. 3 (2013). https://doi.org/10.1353/pmc.2013.0049.

"Propositions on Citizenship." In *Citizenship Rights*, edited by Jo Shaw and Igor Štiks. Farnham, Eng.: Ashgate, 2013.

"Réflexions sur la crise européenne." *Temps modernes* 673 (April–June 2013): 128–51.

"Secularism and/or Cosmopolitanism." *Islam and Public Controversy in Europe*, edited by Nilüfer Göle, 37–44. London: Taylor & Francis, 2013.

"Uspon i pad Europske unije: Temporalnosti i teleologije." *Europski glasnik: Le messager européen*, no. 18 (2013): 357–75.

2012

(With Gunter Gebauer, Roberto Nigro, and Diogo Sardinha.) "L'anthropologie philosophique et l'anthropologie historique en débat." *Rue Descartes* 75, no. 3 (2012): 81–101.

(Edited with Sandra Mezzadra and Raṇṇabīra Samāddāra.) *The Borders of Justice*. Philadelphia: Temple University Press, 2011.

Cittadinanza. Translated by Fabrizio Grillenzoni. Turin, It.: Bollati Boringhieri, 2012.

"Civic Universalism and Its Internal Exclusions: The Issue of Anthropological Difference." *boundary 2* 39, no. 1 (2012): 207–29.

"De la crise grecque à la refondation de l'Europe." *Lignes* 39, no. 3 (2012): 48–59.

"Los dilemas históricos de la democracia y su relevancia contemporánea para la ciudadanía."*Enrahonar* 48 (2012): 9–29.

"Els dilemes històrics de la democràcia i la seva rellevància contemporània per a la ciutadania." *Enrahonar: Quaderns de filosofia* 48 (2012): 9–29.

(Interview with Christine Delory-Momberger and Valérie Melin.) "'Droit de cité' et citoyenneté dans le contexte de l'Europe et de la mondialisation." *Le sujet dans la cité* 2, no. 3 (2012): 69–79.

"From Philosophical Anthropology to Social Ontology and Back: What to Do with Marx's Sixth Thesis on Feuerbach?" *Postmodern Culture* 22, no. 3 (2012). http://www.pomoculture.org/2015/06/10/from-philosophical-anthropology-to-social-ontology-and-back-what-to-do-with-marxs-sixth-thesis-on-feuerbach-2/.

Gleichfreiheit: Politische Essays. Translated by Christine Pries. Berlin: Suhrkamp, 2012.

"The 'Impossible' Community of the Citizens: Past and Present Problems." *Environment and Planning D: Society and Space* 30, no. 3 (2012): 437–49.
"L'introuvable humanité du sujet moderne: L'universalité 'civique-bourgeoise' et la question des différences anthropologiques." In "Anthropologie début de siècle." Special issue, *L'homme* 203–4 (2012): 19–50.
"Justice and Equality: A Political Dilemma?: Pascal, Plato, Marx." In *The Borders of Justice*, edited by Étienne Balibar, Sandro Messadra, and Ranabir Samaddar, 9–32. Philadelphia: Temple University Press, 2012.
"Kant, critique du 'paralogisme' de Descartes. Le 'je pense' (*Ich denke*) comme sujet et comme substance." *Intellectica* 57, no. 1 (2012): 21–33.
"Lenin and Gandhi: A Missed Encounter?" *Radical Philosophy* 172 (2012): 9–17.
"Lovence in Rousseau's *Julie, ou la Nouvelle Héloïse*." In *The Political Archive of Paul De Man: Property, Sovereignty and the Theotropic*, edited by Martin McQuillan, 13–24. Edinburgh: Edinburgh University Press, 2012.
"La metamorfosis de la pulsión de muerte." Prologue to Jacques Lezra, *Materialismo salvaje: La ética del terror y la república moderna*, 11–24. Madrid: Biblioteca Nueva, 2012.
(With Yves Duroux.) "A Philosophical Conjuncture." In *Concept and Form*. Volume 2, *Interviews and Essays on the* Cahiers pour l'Analyse, edited by Peter Hallward and Knox Peden, 169–86. Brooklyn: Verso, 2012.
(Edited with Graham L. Hammill and Julia Reinhard Lupton.) *Political Theology and Early Modernity*. Chicago: University of Chicago Press, 2012.
"Postscript: The Idea of 'New Enlightenment' [Nouvelles Lumières] and the Contradictions of Universalism." *Political Theology and Early Modernity*, edited by Graham L. Hammill and Julia Reinhard Lupton, 299–305. Chicago: University of Chicago Press, 2012.
Saeculum: Culture, religion, idéologie. Paris: Éditions Galilée, 2012.
"Spinoza's Three Gods and the Modes of Communication." *European Journal of Philosophy* 20, no. 1 (2012): 26–49.

2011

"Althusser et les 'appareils idéologiques d'état.'" In Louis Althusser, *Sur la reproduction*, 7–18. Paris: Presses Universitaires de France, 2011.
Citoyen sujet, et autres essais d'anthropologie philosophique. Paris: Presses Universitaires de France, 2011.
"Comme si une philosophie état née." In Diogo Sardinha, *Ordre et temps dans la philosophie de Foucault*, 11–21. Paris: L'Harmattan, 2011.
"Cosmopolitanism and Secularism: Controversial Legacies and Prospective Interrogations." *Grey Room* 44 (2011): 7–25.
(Interview with Catherine Portevin and Mathilde Blottière.) "La condition d'étranger se définit moins par le passeport que par le statut précaire." *Télérama*, April 24,

2011. https://www.telerama.fr/idees/etienne-balibar-la-condition-d-etranger-se-definit-moins-par-le-passeport-que-par-le-statut-precaire,67997.php.

"Les 'deux Découvertes' de Marx." *Actuel Marx* 50, no. 2 (2011): 44–60.

(Edited with John Rajchman and Anne Boyman.) *French Philosophy since 1945: Problems, Concepts, Inventions*. Translated by Aurthur Goldhammer. New York: New Press, 2011.

"La philosophie et l'actualité: Au-delà de l'évènement?" *Le moment philosophique des années 1960 en France*, edited by Patrice Maniglier, 211–34. Paris: Presses Universitaires de France.

(Interview with Thierry Labica and Razmig Keucheyan.) "Pour Marx et au-delà." In *Penser à gauche: Figures de la pensée critique aujourd'hui*, edited by Christian Laval, 253–66. Paris: Éditions Amsterdam, 2011.

(With Michel Prigent.) *Pourquoi Marx?: Philosophie, politique, sciences sociales*. Paris: Presses Universitaires de France, 2011.

Preface to Emanuela Fornari and Étienne Balibar, *Linee Di Confine: Filosofia e Postcolonialismo*, 9–18. Turin, It.: Bollati Boringhieri, 2011.

"Racisme et politique communautaire: Les Roms." *Lignes* 34, no. 1 (2011): 135–44.

"Lo schema genealogico: Razza o cultura?" *La società degli individui* 41, no. 2 (2011): 11–21.

Spinoza et la politique. 4th ed. Philosophies. Paris: Presses Universitaires de France, 2011.

Spinoza y la política. Translated by Diego Tatián. Buenos Aires: Prometeo, 2011.

"Structure: Method or Subversion of the Social Sciences?" *Radical Philosophy* 165 (2011): 17–22.

"Toward a Diasporic Citizen?: From Internationalism to Cosmopolitics." In *The Creolization of Theory*, edited by Françoise Lionnet and Shu-Mei Shih, 207–25. Durham, N.C.: Duke University Press, 2011.

"Крај Политике Или Политика Без Краја?: Маркс и Апорија 'Комунистичке Политике.'" *Nova srpska politička misao* 19, nos. 3–4 (2011): 9–28.

"Философија и Границе Политичког." *Nova Srpska politička misao* 19, nos. 3–4 (2011): 231–67.

2010

"Antinomies of Citizenship." *Journal of Romance Studies* 10, no. 2 (2010): 1–20.

"Arendt, le droit aux droits et la désobéissance civique." In *La proposition de l'égaliberté*, 201–27. Actuel Marx Confrontations. Paris: Presses Universitaires de France, 2010.

"At the Borders of Citizenship: A Democracy in Translation?" *European Journal of Social Theory* 13, no. 3 (2010): 315–22.

"Avant-propos." In *La proposition de l'égaliberté*, 7–9. Actuel Marx Confrontations. Paris: Presses Universitaires de France, 2010.

"Communism as commitment, imagination, and politics." In *The Idea of Communism*. Volume 2, *The New York Conference*, edited by Slavoj Žižek, 13–35. New York: Verso, 2010.

"Communisme et citoyenneté sur Nicos Poulantzas." In *La proposition de l'égaliberté*, 179–200. Actuel Marx Confrontations. Paris: Presses Universitaires de France, 2010.

"Dissonances dans la laïcité: La nouvelle 'affaire des Foulards.'" In *La proposition de l'égaliberté*, 253–70. Actuel Marx Confrontations. Paris: Presses Universitaires de France, 2010.

(Interview with Gabrieal Basterra, Ghislaine Glasson Deschaumes, Rada Ivekovic, Boyan Manchev, and Francisco Naishtat.) "Entretien avec et entre Étienne Balibar et Ernesto Laclau." *Rue Descartes* 67, no. 1 (2010): 78–99.

"Europe: Final Crisis?: Some Theses." *Theory and Event* 13, no. 2 (2010). https://muse.jhu.edu/article/384016.

"Fermeture: Résistance insurrection insoumission." In *La proposition de l'égaliberté*, 339–58. Actuel Marx Confrontations. Paris: Presses Universitaires de France, 2010.

(Edited with John Rajchman and Anne Boyman.) *French Philosophy since 1945: Problems, Concepts, Inventions*. Translated by Aurthur Goldhammer. New York: New Press, 2010.

"The Greek Crisis." *Journal of Modern Greek Studies* 28, no. 2 (2010): 306–09.

"Laïcité et universalité le paradoxe libéral." In *La proposition de l'égaliberté*, 271–79. Actuel Marx Confrontations. Paris: Presses Universitaires de France, 2010.

"Marxism and War." *Radical Philosophy* 160 (2010): 9–18.

"La mort, cette faucheuse. . . ." *Lignes* 32, no. 2 (2010): 27–30.

"Nouvelles réflexions sur l'égaliberté." In *La proposition de l'égaliberté*, 127–64. Actuel Marx Confrontations. Paris: Presses Universitaires de France, 2010.

"Ouverture: L'antinomie de la citoyenneté." In *La proposition de l'égaliberté*, 11–52. Actuel Marx Confrontations. Paris: Presses Universitaires de France, 2010.

(With Louis Althusser.) *Para leer El Capital*. Mexico City: Siglo XXI, 2010.

(With Alain Badiou.) "Philosophical View: Middlesex, Think Again." *Times Higher Education Supplement*, May 6, 2010, 34.

"Philosophy and the Frontiers of the Political: A Biographical-Theoretical Interview with Emanuela Fornari." *Iris: European Journal of Philosophy and Public Debate* 2, no. 3 (2010): 23–64.

"Populisme et politique: le retour du contrat." In *La proposition de l'égaliberté*, 229–38. Actuel Marx Confrontations. Paris: Presses Universitaires de France, 2010.

(Interview with Pierre Sauvêtre and Cécile Lavergne.) "Pour une phénoménologie de la cruauté." *Tracés: Revue de sciences humaines* 19 (2010). https://journals.openedition.org/traces/4926.

"La proposition de l'égaliberté." In *La proposition de l'égaliberté*, 53–89. Actuel Marx Confrontations. Paris: Presses Universitaires de France, 2010.

La proposition de l'égaliberté: Essais politiques 1989–2009. Paris: Presses Universitaires de France, 2010.

"Qu'est-ce que la philosophie politique?: Notes pour une topique." In *La proposition de l'égaliberté*, 165–78. Actuel Marx Confrontations. Paris: Presses Universitaires de France, 2010.

"De quoi les exclus sont-ils exclus?" In *La proposition de l'égaliberté*, 239–51. Actuel Marx Confrontations. Paris: Presses Universitaires de France, 2010.

"Remarques de circonstance sur le communisme." *Actuel Marx* 48, no. 2 (2010): 33–45.

"Le renversement de l'individualisme possessif." In *La proposition de l'égaliberté*, 91–126. Actuel Marx Confrontations. Paris: Presses Universitaires de France, 2010.

"Séjourner dans la contradiction: L'idée de 'nouvelles lumières' et les contradictions de l'universalisme." In *Formen des Nichtwissens der Aufklärung*, edited by Hans Adler and Rainer Godel. Volume 4. Munich: Wilhelm Fink, 2010.

"Sur *Guerre et paix* de Tolstoï: Un essai de 'philosophie littéraire.'" In *War and Peace: The Role of Science and Art*, edited by Soraya Nour and Olivier Remaud, 266–80. Berlin: Duncker & Humbolt, 2010.

"Uprisings in the Banlieues." In *La proposition de l'égaliberté*, 281–315. Actuel Marx Confrontations. Paris: Presses Universitaires de France, 2010.

"Vers la co-citoyenneté." In *La proposition de l'égaliberté*, 317–37. Actuel Marx Confrontations. Paris: Presses Universitaires de France, 2010.

Violence et civilité: Wellek Library lectures et autres essais de philosophie politique. Paris: Éditions Galilée, 2010.

에티엔 발리바르 "정치의 종언인가, 종언 없는 정치인가?" 레프트대구, no. 1 (2010): 137–65.

2009

"Althusser and the Rue d'Ulm." *New Left Review* 28 (2009): 91–107.

"Derrida and the 'Aporia of the Community.'" *Philosophy Today* 53, supplement (2009): 5–18.

"Eschatology versus Teleology: The Suspended Dialogue between Derrida and Althusser." In *Derrida and the Time of the Political*, edited by Pheng Cheah and Suzanne Guerlac, 57–73. Durham, N.C.: Duke University Press, 2009.

(Interview with Emanuela Fornari.) "Étienne Balibar: La filosofia e le frontiere del politico." *Iride* 56, no. 1 (2009): 31–70.

"Europe as Borderland." *Environment and Planning D: Society and Space* 27, no. 2 (2009): 190–215.

"Un feu d'artifice du structuralisme en politique." In Ernesto Laclau and Chantal

Mouffe, *Hégémonie et stratégie socialiste: Vers une politique démocratique radicale*, 5–15. Besançon, Fr.: Les Solitaires Intempestifs, 2009.

Gleichfreiheit. Translated by Christine Preis. Frankfurt: Suhrkamp, 2012.

"'God Will Not Remain Silent': Zionism, Messianism and Nationalism." *Human Architecture: Journal of the Sociology of Self-Knowledge* 7, no. 2 (2009): 123–34.

"Ideas of Europe: Civilization and Constitution." *Iris: European Journal of Philosophy and Public Debate* 1, no. 1 (2009): 3–17.

(With Yves Sintomer, Guillaume Garrets, and Hugues Jallon.) "Insurrection et constitution: La citoyenneté ambiguë." In *Pensées critiques: Dix itinéraires de la revue mouvements 1998–2008*, 9–28. Paris: La Découverte, 2009.

"Louis Althusser." *New Left Review* 58 (2009): 91–108.

(With Cory Browning.) "On the Aporias of Marxian Politics: From Civil War to Class Struggle." *Diacritics* 39, no. 2 (2009): 59–73.

"Die Proposition *Égaliberté* ('Gleichfreiheit')." *Trivium* 3 (2009). https://journals.openedition.org/trivium/3337.

"Reflections on *Gewalt*." *Historical Materialism* 17, no. 1 (2009): 99–125.

"Une rencontre en Romagne." In Louis Althusser, *Machiavel et nous*, 9–30. Paris: Tallandier, 2009.

"Violence and Civility: On the Limits of Political Anthropology." Translated by Stephanie Bundy. *Differences* 20, nos. 2–3 (2009): 9–35.

Violence et civilité: "Welleck library lectures" et autres essais de philosophie politique. Paris: Éditions Galilée, 2009.

We, the People of Europe?: Reflections on Transnational Citizenship. Translated by James Swenson. Princeton: Princeton University Press, 2009.

"What Is Political Philosophy?: Contextual Notes." In *Jacques Rancière: History, Politics, Aesthetics*, edited by Gabriel Rockhill and Philip Watts, 95–104. Durham, N.C.: Duke University Press, 2009.

2008

Biz, Avrupa Halkı?: Ulusaşırı Yurttaşlık Üzerine Düşünümler. Istanbul: Ara-Lik, 2008.

"Cosmopolitisme et internationalisme aujourd'hui." In *Marx contemporain: Acte 2*, 347–56. Paris: Éditions Syllepse, 2008.

"From Cosmopolitanism to Cosmopolitics." *Revista internacional de filosofía política*, no. 31 (2008): 85–100.

"Del cosmopolitismo a la cosmopolítica." *Revista internacional de filosofía política* 31 (2008): 85–100.

"Historical Dilemmas of Democracy and Their Contemporary Relevance for Citizenship." *Rethinking Marxism* 20, no. 4 (2008): 522–38.

(Interview with Razmig Keucheyan and Michaël Löwy.) "Identités conflictuelles et violences identitaires." In *Politiquement incorrects: Entretiens du XXI e siècle*, edited by Daniel Bensaïd, 181–186. Paris: Éditions Textuel, 2008.

"Le moment messianique de Marx." In "Politische Theologie des Vormärz." Special issue, *Revue germanique internationale* 8 (2008): 143–60.

"Obéir? Désobéir?: L'enfant, l'école et le nouveau métier de citoyen." *Après-demain* 5, no. 1 (2008): 41–46.

"Racism Revisited: Sources, Relevance, and Aporias of a Modern Concept." *PMLA* 123, no. 5 (2008): 1630–39.

"Toward a Politics of the Universal." *Graduate Faculty Philosophy Journal* 29, no. 1 (2008): 5–25.

"Violencia: Idealidad y crueldad." *Polis: Revista latinoamericana* 19 (2008): 1–16.

"What's in a War? (Politics as War, War as Politics)." *Ratio Juris* 21, no. 3 (2008): 365–86.

2007

(With Arnaud Lechevalier, Monique Chemillier-Gendreau, Alain Caillé, Paul Magnette, Julien Lusson, and Lionel Larqué.) "Citoyenneté et institutions européennes" [Citizenship and European institutions]. *Mouvements* 49, no. 1 (2007): 154–64.

"Constructing and Deconstructing the Universal: Jacques Derrida's *Sinnliche Gewissheit*." In *Adieu Derrida*, edited by Costas Douzinas, 61–83. Basingstoke, Eng.: Palgrave Macmillan, 2007.

"Constructions and Deconstructions of the Universal." In *Recognition, Work, Politics: New Directions in French Critical Theory*. Vol 5, edited by Jean-Philippe Deranty, 47–69. Leiden, Neth.: Brill, 2007.

"De la critique des droits de l'homme à la critique des droits sociaux." In *Bentham contre les droits de l'homme*, edited by Bertrand Binoche and Jean-Pierre Cléro, 249–69. Paris, Presses Universitaires de France, 2007.

"(De)Constructing the Human as Human Institution: A Reflection on the Coherence of Hannah Arendt's Practical Philosophy." *Social Research: An International Quarterly* 74, no. 3 (2007): 727–38.

"Eschatologie/téléologie: Un dialogue philosophique interrompu et son enjeu actuel." *Lignes* 23–24, no. 2 (2007): 183–208.

"El estructuralismo: ¿Una destitución del sujeto?" *Instantes y azares: Escrituras Nietzscheanas* 4 (2007): 155–72.

Irk ulus sinif. Istanbul: Metis, 2007.

Kapitali okumak. Istanbul: İthaki, 2007.

"The Philosophical Moment in Politics Determined by War: Lenin 1914–16." In *Lenin Reloaded: Toward a Politics of Truth*, edited by Sebasian Budgen, Stathis Kouvelakis, and Slavoj Žižek, 207–21. Durham, N.C.: Duke University Press, 2007.

The Philosophy of Marx. New student ed. London: Verso, 2007.

Preface to Yoshiyuki Sato, *Pouvoir et résistance: Foucault, Deleuze, Derrida, Althusser*. Paris: L'Harmattan, 2007.

(With Immanuel Wallerstein.) *Race, nation, classe: Les identités ambiguës*. Paris: La Découverte, 2007.

"The Return of Race." *Movements* 50, no. 2 (2007): 162–71.

Il ritorno della razza: Identità etniche e paradigmi politici. Modena, It.: Fondazione Collegio San Carlo per festivalfilosofia, 2007.

Très loin et tous près. Paris: Bayard, 2007.

"Uprisings in the Banlieues." *Constellations* 14, no. 1 (2007): 47–71.

"Vers la co-citoyenneté." *Après-demain* 4, no. 4 (2007): 44–46.

"Zur 'Sache Selbst': Comune e universale nella 'fenomenologia' di Hegel." *Iride: Filosofia e discussione pubblica* 20, no. 3 (2007): 553–58.

2006

"Capovolgimenti performativi del nome 'razza' e dilemma delle vittime." *Iride: Filosofia e discussione pubblica* 19, no. 3 (2006): 561–76.

"Communisme et citoyenneté: Réflexions sur la politique d'émancipation à partir de Nicos Poulantzas" [Communism and citizenship: Reflections on Nicos Poulantzas's politics of emancipation]. *Actuel Marx* 40, no. 2 (2006): 136–55.

"Constructions and Deconstructions of the Universal." *Critical Horizons: A Journal of Philosophy and Social Theory* 7, no. 1 (2006): 21–43.

(With Nicolau Leitão.) "A Europa, a América, a guerra, reflexões sobre a mediação Europeia." *Análise social* 41, no. 181 (2006): 1241–43.

Europa cittadinanza confini: Dialogando con Étienne Balibar. Lecce, It.: Pensa Multimedia, 2006.

"Exclusion of Whom? Exclusion from What?" Paper presented at the 16th International Sociological Association World Congress of Sociology, Durban, South Africa, July 2006.

(With Jean-Marc Lévy-Leblond.) "A Mediterranean Way for Peace in Israel-Palestine?" *Radical Philosophy* 140 (2006): 2–8.

"'Monotheismus': Anmerkung zu Ursprung und Gebrauch des Begriffs." *Mittelweg 36* 15, no. 5 (2006): 65–86.

"My Self and My Own: One and the Same?" In *Accelerating Possession: Global Futures of Property and Personhood*, edited by Bill Maurer and Gabriele Schwab, 21–44. New York: Columbia University Press, 2006.

"Note sur l'origine et les usages du terme 'monothéisme.'" *Critique* 704–5, no. 1 (2006): 19–45.

Preface to Thomas Hippler, *Soldats et citoyens: Naissance du service militaire en France et en Prusse*, 1–8. Paris: Presses Universitaires de France, 2006.

Der Schauplatz des Anderen. Formen der Gewalt und Grenzen der Zivilität. Translated by Thomas Laugstien. Hamburg, Ger.: Hamburger Edition, 2006.

"Sub specie universitatis." *Topoi* 25, no. 1–2 (2006): 3–16.

"Le sujet de la nation dans l'encyclopédie: 'Caractère' et 'université.'" *Corpus: Revue de philosophie* 51 (2006): 201–13.

"Uprisings in the Banlieues." *Lignes* 21, no. 3 (2006): 50–101.

(With Barbara Cassin and Alain de Libera.) "Vocabulary of European Philosophies, Part 1 (Subject)." *Radical Philosophy* 138, no. 1 (July/August 2006): 15–41.

2005

"À demain, Jacques Derrida." *Rue Descartes* 48, no. 2 (2005): 45–47.

"La construction du racisme" [The construction of racism]. *Actuel Marx* 2, no. 38 (2005): 11–28.

(Interview with Diane Enns.) "A Conversation with Étienne Balibar." *Symposium* 9, no. 2 (2005): 375–99.

Derecho de ciudad: Cultura y política en democracia. Translated by Maria de los Angeles Serrano. Buenos Aires: Nueva Visión, 2004.

"Difference, Otherness, Exclusion." *Parallax* 11, no. 1 (2005): 19–34.

Escritos por Althusser. Buenos Aires: Nueva Visión Argentina, 2005.

L'Europe, l'Amérique, la guerre: Réflexions sur la médiation européenne. Paris: La Découverte, 2005.

Europe, constitution, frontière. Paris: Éditions du Passant, 2005.

"Human Rights and Democratic Radicalism." In *Human Rights in Crisis: The Sacred and the Secular in Contemporary French Thought*, edited by Geneviève Souillac, 157–206. Lanham, Md.: Lexington Books, 2005.

"Kombet dhe nacionalizmi." *Revistë mikste debatike për çështje shoqërore, politikë, kulturë dhe letërsi* 8–9 (2005): 19–21.

"Lenin i Gandhi." Translated by Andrzej Staroń. *Nowa krytyka* 18 (2005): 7–18.

"Lenin und Gandhi—eine verfehlte Begegnung?" *Das argument* 47, no. 5 (2005): 29–38.

(With Richard Rorty and Diane Enns.) "In Memoriam Jacques Derrida." *Symposium* 9, no. 1 (2005): 5–10.

"Une philosophie des droits du citoyen est-elle possible?: Nouvelles réflexion sur l'églaliberté." *Revue universelle des droits de l'homme* 16, no. 1–4 (2005): 2–6.

"Potentia multitudinis, quae una veluti mente ducitur: Spinoza on the Body Politic." In *Current Continental Theory and Modern Philosophy*, edited by Stephen H. Daniel, 70–99. Evanston, Il.: Northwestern University Press, 2005.

"Racism after the Races." *Actuel Marx* 38 (2005): 11–133.

"Structuralism: A Negation of the Subject?" In "Rethinking Structures" edited by Guy Félix Duportail. Special issue, *Revue de métaphysique et de morale* 1 (2005): 5–22.

"Le structuralisme: Une destitution du sujet?" *Revue de métaphysique et de morale* 1, no. 1 (2005): 5–22.

Violencias, identidades y civilidad. Barcelona: Gedisa Editorial, 2005.

"Was fur enine Europaische verfassung?" *PROKLA: Zeitschrift fuer kritische Sozialwissenschaft* 35, no. 2 (2005): 287–300.

"World Borders, Political Boundaries." *Alteridades* 15, no. 30 (2005): 87–96.

2004

"Agency," "Âme," "Conscience," "Je, Moi, Soi," "Praxis," and "Sujet." Entries in *Vocabulaire Européen des philosophies*, edited by Barbara Cassin. Paris: Seuil, 2004.

"Le contrat social des marchandises et la constitution marxienne de la monnaie (contribution à la question de l'universalité de l'argent)." In *L'argent: Croyance, mesure, spéculation*, edited by Marcel Drach, 95–112. Paris: La Découverte, 2004.

Derecho de ciudad: Cultura y política en la democracia. Buenos Aires: Nueva Visión Argentina, 2004.

"Dissonances dans la laïcité." In *Le foulard islamique en questions*, edited by Charlotte Nordmann, 15–27. Paris: Éditions Amsterdam, 2004.

"Dissonances dans la laïcité." *Mouvements* 33–34, no. 3 (2004): 148–61.

"Dissonances within Laïcité." *Constellations* 11, no. 3 (2004): 353–67.

(Edited with Ghislaine Glasson Deschaumes.) "L'Europe en partage." Special issue, *Lignes* 13 (2004): 11–94.

"Europe: Vanishing Mediator?" In *Who If Not We Should at Least Try to Imagine the Future of All This?*, edited by Maria Hlavajova, 211–30. Amsterdam: Artimo, 2004.

"Is a Philosophy of Human Civic Rights Possible?: New Reflections on Equaliberty. *South Atlantic Quarterly* 103, no. 2/3 (2004): 311–22.

"Une philosophie des droits du citoyen est-elle possible?: Nouvelles réflexions sur l'égaliberté." *Revue universelle des droits de l'homme* 16, no. 1–4 (2004): 2–6.

(Edited with Dominique Lecourt.) Pratiques Théoriques [series]. Paris: Presses Universitaires de France, 1981–2004.

"Quelle 'constitution' de l'Europe?" Introduction to "L'Europe en partage." Special issue, *Lignes* 13 (2004): 13–32.

"Rasismen nygranskad—ett modernt begrepps ursprung, relevans och paradoxer." In *Rasismer i Europa, kontinuitet och förändring*, edited by Katarina Matsson and Ingemar Lindberg. Stockholm: Agora, 2004.

"Le renversement de l'individualisme possessif." In *La propriété, le propre, l'appropriation*, edited by Hervé Guineret and Arnaud Milanese, 9–32. Paris, Édition Ellipses, 2004.

"Scène tragique et structure psychanalytique." In *La pulsion de mort entre psychanalyse et philosophie*, edited by Michel Plon and Henri Rey-Flaud, 109–17. Ramonville Saint-Agne, Fr.: Erès, 2004.

Spinoza ve siyaset. Istanbul: Otonom, 2004.

"Sur la constitution de l'Europe: Crise et virtualités." *Le passant ordinaire* 49 (2004): 10–13.

"Universalité d'une cause." *Manière de voir* 78, no. 12 (2004): 80.

"Universalité de la cause palestinienne." *Le Monde Diplomatique* 602, no. 5 (2004): 26A.

"Violence et civilité: Sur les limites de l'anthropologie politique." In *La question de l'humain entre l'éthique et l'anthropologie*, edited by Alfredo Gómez-Muller, 157–93. Ouverture Philosophique. Paris: L'Harmattan, 2004.

We, the People of Europe?: Reflections on Transnational Citizenship. Translated by James Swenson. Princeton: Princeton University Press, 2004.

2003

(Edited with Rony Brauman, Judith Butler, Sylvain Cypel, Éric Hazan, Daniel Lindenberg, Marc Saint-Upéry, Denis Sieffert, and Michel Warschawski.) *Antisémitisme: L'intolérable chantage; Israël-Palestine, une affaire française?* Paris: La Découverte, 2003.

L'Europa, l'America, la guerra. Rome: Manifestolibri, 2003.

L'Europe, l'Amérique, la guerre: Réflexions sur la médiation européenne. Paris: La Découverte, 2003.

"Europe, an 'Unimagined' Frontier of Democracy." Translated by Frank Collins. *Diacritics* 33, no. 3–4 (2003): 36–44.

"Europe: Vanishing Mediator." *Constellations* 10, no. 3 (2003): 312–38.

Mi, građani Evrope? Translated by Aljoša Mimica. Belgrade, Serb.: Beogradski krug, 2003.

"The New Frontiers of the European Democracy." *Critique internationale*, no. 1 (2003): 169–78.

Nosotros, ¿ciudadanos de Europa?: Las fronteras, el estado, el pueblo. Madrid: Tecnos, 2003.

"Un nouvel antisémitisme?" In *Antisémitisme: L'intolérable chantage; Israël-Palestine, une affaire française?*, edited by Étienne Balibar, Rony Brauman, Judith Butler, Sylvain Cypel, Éric Hazan, Daniel Lindenberg, Marc Saint-Upéry, Denis Sieffert, and Michel Warschawski, 89–96. Paris: La Découverte, 2003.

(Interview with Jean-François Bayart, Béatrice Hibou, and Évelyne Ritaine.) "Les nouvelles frontières de la démocratie européenne." *Critique internationale* 18 (2003): 169–78.

"Présentation par Étienne Balibar et Dominique Lecourt." In Georges Canguilhem, Georges Lapassade, Jacques Piqumal, and Jacques Ulmann, *Du développement à l'évolution au XIXe siècle* [1962], 5–8. Paris: Presses Universitaires de France, 2003.

"Prolegomena za pitanje suvereniteta." *Beogradski krug*, nos. 1–4 (2003): 83–104.

(Interview with Verónica Gago.) "Los racismos del mañana." Radar libros, *Página 12* (November 9, 2003). https://www.pagina12.com.ar/diario/suplementos/libros/10-808-2003-11-09.html.

"Schmitt: Une lecture conservatrice de Hobbes?" *Droits* 38 (2003): 149–57.

Sind wir Bürger Europas?: Politische Integration, soziale Ausgrenzung und die Zukunft des Nationalen. Hamburg, Ger.: Hamburger Edition, 2003.

"Structuralism: A Destitution of the Subject?" Translated by James Swenson. "On Humanism," edited by Elizabeth Weed and Ellen Rooney. Special issue, *differences: A Journal of Feminist Cultural Studies* 14, no. 1 (2003): 1–21.

"The Subject." In "Ignorance of the Law," edited by Joan Copjec. Special issue, *UMBR(a)* (2003): 9–24.

(With Friedrich A. Kittler and Martin Van Creveld.) *Vom Krieg zum Terrorismus?: Mosse-Lectures Winter 2002/2003.* Berlin: Humbolt-Universität, 2003.

We, the People of Europe?: Reflections on Transnational Citizenship. Translated by James Swenson. Princeton: Princeton University Press, 2003.

"Which Power? Whose Weakness?: On Robert Kagan's Critique of European Ideology." *Theory and Event* 6, no. 4 (2003). https://muse.jhu.edu/article/44779/summary.

2002

"Apories Rousseauistes: Subjectivité, communauté, propriété." In "L'anthropologie et le politique selon Jean-Jacques Rousseau," edited by Michèle Cohen-Halimi. Special issue, *Cahiers philosophiques de Strasbourg* 13 (2002): 13–36.

"Avant-propos." In Olivier Le Cour Grandmaison, *Haine(s): Philosophie et politique*, 1–7. Paris: Presses Universitaires de France, 2002.

"La démocratisation des frontières." *Rue Descartes* 37, no. 3 (2002): 122–28.

"'The History of Truth': Alain Badiou in French Philosophy." *Radical Philosophy* 115 (2002): 16–28.

"Le Hobbes de Schmitt, le Schmitt de Hobbes," preface to Carl Schmitt, *Le léviathan dans la doctrine de l'État de Hobbes: Sens et échec d'un symbole politique*, 7–65. Paris: Éditions du Seuil, 2002.

"The Nation Form: History and Ideology." In Philomena Essed and David Theo Goldberg, *Race Critical Theories: Text and Context*, chap. 12. Malden, Ma.: Blackwell, 2002.

(Interview with Bruno Karsenti.) "Une philosophie politique de la différence anthropologique." *Multitudes* 9 (2002): 66–68.

Politics and the Other Scene. Translated by Christine Jones, James Swenson, and Chris Turner. London: Verso, 2002.

"'Possessive Individualism' Reversed: From Locke to Derrida." *Constellations* 9, no. 3 (2002): 299–317.

"Quelques enjeux du travail de Jan Assmann." *Transeuropéennes* 22 (2002). http://www.transeuropeennes.org/fr/articles/118/Numero_22_Traduire_entre_les_cultures.html.

Spinoza: Il transindividuale. Milan, It.: Edizioni Ghibi, 2002.

"World Borders, Political Borders." Translated by Erin M. Williams. *PMLA* 117, no. 1 (2002): 68–78.

2001

"La crainte des masses: Politique et philosophie avant et après Marx." *Revue philosophique de la France et de l'étranger* 191, no. 1 (2001): 75–76.

"Europe from the Outside." *Critica Marxista* 5 (2001): 33–38.

"Granice Evrope." *Dijalog—Časopis za filozofiju i društvenu teoriju* 3, no. 4 (2001): 29–41.

"Jus-Pactum Lex: On the Constitution of the Subject in the Theologico-Political Treatise." In *Spinoza: Critical Assessments*, edited by Genevieve Lloyd, 171–205. London: Routledge, 2001.

(Edited with Gérard Raulet) *Marx démocrate: Le manuscrit de 1843*. Paris: Presses Universitaires de France, 2001.

Nous, citoyens d'Europe?: Les frontières, l'état, le peuple. Paris: La Découverte, 2001.

"Outlines of a Topography of Cruelty: Citizenship and Civility in the Era of Global Violence." *Constellations* 8, no. 1 (2001): 15–29.

La philosophie de Marx. 2nd rev. ed. Paris: Éditions Découverte, 2001.

"Postface." In *Marx démocrate: Le manuscrit de 1843*, edited by Étienne Balibar and Gérard Raulet, 119–28. Paris: Presses Universitaires de France, 2001.

"Le structuralisme: Une destitution du sujet?" *Revue de métaphysique et de morale* 45, no. 1 (2001): 5–22.

2000

La filosofía de Marx. Buenos Aires: Nueva Visión Argentina, 2000.

Marx'ın felsefesi. Istanbul: Birikim, 2000.

"Prolégomènes à la Souveraineté: La Frontière, L'État, Le Peuple." *Temps modernes* 610 (2000): 47–75.

"Quel communisme après le communisme?" In *Marx 2000*, edited by Eustache Kouvélakis, 77–88. Paris: Presses Universitaires de France, 2000.

"Qu'est-ce que la philosophie politique?: Notes pour une topique." *Actuel Marx* 28, no. 2 (2000): 11–22.

"What Makes a People a People?: Rousseau and Kant." Translated by Erin Post. In *Masses, Classes, and the Public Sphere*, edited by Mike Hill and Warren Montag, 105–31. London: Verso, 2000.

1999

"Le droit de cité ou l'apartheid?" In *Sans-papiers: L'archaïsme fatal*, edited by Étienne Balibar, Monique Chemillier-Gendreau, Jacqueline Costa-Lascoux, and Emmanuel Terray, 68–92. Paris: La Découverte, 1999.

(Interview with Peter Osborne.) "Étienne Balibar: Conjectures and Conjunctures." *Radical Philosophy* 97 (1999): 30–41.

"Is Citizenship Possible?" In *Cities and Citizenship*, edited by James Holston, 195–215. Durham, N.C.: Duke University Press, 1999.
(With Monique Chemillier-Gendreau, Jacqueline Costa-Lascoux, and Emmanuel Terray.) *Sans-papiers: L'archaïsme fatal*. Paris: La Découverte, 1999.

1998

"The Borders of Europe." In *Cosmopolitics: Thinking and Feeling beyond the Nation*, edited by Pheng Cheah and Bruce Robbins, 216–29. Minneapolis: University of Minnesota Press, 1998.
"Citizenship, Nationality, Sovereignty." *Crítica Marxista* 2–3 (1998): 59–63.
Dersimiz yurttaşlik. Istanbul: Kesit, 1998.
Droit de cite: Culture et politique en démocratie. Paris: Éditions de l'Aube, 1998.
Identité et différence: L'invention de la conscience (John Locke's An Essay Concerning Human Understanding). Translated by Étienne Balibar. Paris: Seuil, 1998.
Spinoza and Politics. Translated by Peter Snowdon. London: Verso, 1998.
"Violence, Ideality, and Cruelty." *New Formations*, no. 35 (1998): 7.

1997

"Algérie, France: Une ou deux nations?" *Lignes* 30, no. 1 (1997): 7–22.
La crainte des masses: Politique et philosophie avant et après Marx. Paris: Éditions Galilée, 1997.
"Critical Reflections." Translated by Jeanine Herman. *Artforum* 36, no. 3 (November 1997): 100–2.
"Une culture mondiale?" *Lignes* 32, no. 3 (1997): 171–202.
"L'enseignement de la philosophie du droit: Enquête dans les facultés de philosophie." In "L'enseignement de la philosophie du droit," edited by Michel Troper. Special issue, *Droit et société* 40 (1998).
"Frontières et violence." *Dialogue International Edition*, nos. 5–6 (1997): 107–16.
"Für ein politisches Konzept des Auschlusses." In *Inklusion: Exklusion, Versuch einer neuen Kartographie der Kunst im Zeitalter von postkolonialismus und globaler Migration*, edited by Peter Weibal. Cologne, Ger.: Dumont, 1996.
"Globalization/Civilization: Parts 1 & 2." In *Documenta X: Politics, Poetics*. Edited by Catherine David and Jean-François Chevrier. Ostfildern, Ger.: Cantz, 1997.
"Granice i nasilje." *Dijalog—Časopis za filozofiju i društvenu teoriju*, no. 3 (1997): 9–17.
"*Jus-Pactum-Lex*: On the Constitution of the Subject in the *Theologico-Political Treatise*." Translated by Ted Stolze. In *The New Spinoza*, edited by Warren Montag and Ted Stolze, 171–206. Minneapolis: Minnesota University Press, 1997.
(Translated with François Matheron and Antonio Negri.). *Le pouvoir constituant: Essai sur les alternatives de la modernité*. Pratiques théoriques, edited by Étienne Balibar and Dominique Lecourt. Paris: Preses Universitaires de France, 1997.
"Il problema della civiltà." *Theoria* 17, no. 1 (1997): 21–36.

(With Thomas Ferenczi.) *De quoi sommes-nous responsables?: Huitième forum* Le Monde *Le Mans*. Paris: Le Monde Éditions, 1997.

"Racisme et universalisme." *Raison présente* 122, no. 1 (1997): 63–77.

(With Louis Althusser.) *Reading Capital*. London: Verso, 1997.

"Le structuralisme: Méthode ou subversion des sciences sociales." In *Structure, système, champ et théorie du sujet*, edited by Tony Andréani and Menahem Rosen, 223–36. Paris: L'Harmattan, 1997.

1996

"Emancipation, Transformation, Civility." *Temps modernes* 587 (1996): 409–49.

"Fictive ethnicity and ideal nation." In *Ethnicity*, edited by John Hutchinson and Anthony D. Smith, 164–67. Oxford, Eng.: Oxford University Press, 1996.

"Individualité et transindividualité chez Spinoza." In *Architectures de la raison: Mélanges offerts à Alexandre Matheron*, edited by P. F. Moreau, 65–46. Fontenay-aux-Roses, Fr.: ENS Editions, 1996.

"Is European Citizenship Possible?" *Public Culture: Society for Transnational Cultural Studies* 8, no. 2 (1996): 355–76.

"Murs contre murs: Impressions de Saint-Maur." *Lignes* 27, no. 1 (1996): 63–77.

"The Nation Form: History and Ideology." In *Becoming National: A Reader*, edited by Geoff Eley and Ronald Grigor Suny, 132–49. New York: Oxford University Press, 1996.

"Racism and Anti-Racism." *UNESCO Courier* 3 (March 1996): 14–16.

Razza, nazione, classe: Le identità ambigue. Rome: Edizioni Associate Editrice Internazionale, 1996.

"Structural Causality, Overdetermination, and Antagonism." *Postmodern Materialism and the Future of Marxist Theory: Essays in the Althusserian Tradition*, edited by Antonio Callari and David F. Ruccio, 109–19. Hanover, N.H.: Wesleyan University Press, 1996.

Spinoza e la política. Rome: Manifestolibri, 1996.

Spinoza: From Individuality to Transindividuality. Medendelingen vanwege het Spinozahuis 71. Delft, Neth.: Eburon, 1997.

"Violence." In Françoise Héritier, *De la violence*. Vol. 2, *Séminaire de Françoise Héritier*. Paris: Odile. Jacob, 1996.

"What Is 'Man' in Seventeenth-Century Philosophy?" In *The Individual in Political Theory and Practice*, edited by Janet Coleman, 215–42. Oxford, Eng.: Clarendon Press, 1996.

1995

"Ambiguous Universality." *Differences: A Journal of Feminist Cultural Studies* 7, no. 1 (1995): 48–74.

"Une citoyenneté européenne est-elle possible?" In *L'état, la finance et le social*, edited by Bruno Théret, 533–53. Paris: La Découverte, 1995.

"Culture and Identity (Working Notes)." In *The Identity in Question*, edited by John Rajchman, 173–96. New York: Routledge, 1995.

"Has 'the World' Changed?" In *Marxism in the Postmodern Age: Confronting the New World Order*, edited by Antonio Callari, Stephen Cullenberg, and Carole Biewener, 405–14. New York: Guilford, 1995.

"Identité et conscience de soi dans l'essai de Locke." *Revue de métaphysique et de morale* 100, no.4 (1995): 455–77.

"The Infinite Contradiction." Translated by Jean-Marc Poisson and Jacques Lezra. In "Depositions: Althusser, Balibar, Macherey, and the Labor of Reading." Special issue, *Yale French Studies* 88 (1995): 142–64.

Nombres y lugares de la verdad. Buenos Aires: Nueva Visión Argentina, 1995.

The Philosophy of Marx. Translated by Chris Turner. London: Verso, 1995.

(With Bertrand Ogilvie.) "Présentation." *Lignes* 25, no. 2 (1995): 5–8.

(Edited with Helmut Seidel and Manfred Walther.) *Spinoza and Modernity: Ethics and Politics*. Würzburg, Ger.: Königshausen and Neumann, 1995.

(With Hélène Cixous, Jacques Derrida, Philippe Lacoue-Labarthe, and Jean-Luc Nancy.) "La vérité?" *Le Monde* (August 13–14, 1995).

"La violence des intellectuels." *Lignes* 25, no. 2 (1995): 9–22.

에티엔 발리바르 "바슐라르에서 알튀세르로." 이론 (1995): 157–200.

1994

"Althusser's Object." *Social Praxis* 39 (Summer 1994): 157–88.

"¿Es posible una ciudadanía Europea?" *Revista internacional de filosofía política* 4 (1994): 22–40.

La filosofia di Marx. Translated by Andrea Catone. Rome: Manifestolibri, 1994.

(Edited with Helmut Seidel and Manfred Walther.) *Freiheit und Notwendigkeit: Ethische und politische Aspekte bei Spinoza und in der Geschichte des (Anti-)Spinozismus*. Würzburg, Ger.: Königshausen und Neumann, 1994.

Für Althusser. Translated by Renate Nentwig and Peter Schöttler. Mainz, Ger.: Decaton, 1994.

"Identité culturelle, identité nationale." *Quaderni* 22, no. 1 (1994): 53–65.

Introduction to *Denk-Prozesse nach Althusser*, edited by Henning Böke. Hamburg, Ger.: Argument-Verlag, 1994.

"Kann es ein europäisches Staatsbürgertum geben?" *Das argument* 36, no. 206 (1994): 621–38.

Lieux et noms de la vérité. La Tour-d'Aigues, Fr.: Éditions de l'Aube, 1994.

"Man and Citizen: Who's Who?" *Journal of Political Philosophy* 2, no. 2 (1994): 99–114.

Masses, Classes, Idea: Studies on Politics and Philosophy before and after Marx. Translated by James Swenson. New York: Routledge, 1994.

"'Le monde' a-t-il changé?" In *Le nouveau système du monde*, edited by Jacques Texier and Jacques Bidet, 125–34. Paris: Presses Universitaires de France, 1994.

"La philosophie de Marx." *Revue philosophique de la France et de l'étranger* 184, no. 4 (1994): 458–58.

Preface to *Spinoza contra Leibniz: Documenti di uno scontro intelettuale (1676–1678)*, edited by Vittorio Morfino. Milan, It.: Unicopli, 1994.

"Subjection and Subjectivation." In *Supposing the Subject*, edited by Joan Copjec, 1–15. London: Verso, 1994.

"Violence et politique: Quelques questions." In *Le passage des frontière: Autour du travail de Jacques Derrida*, edited by Marie-Louise Mallet, 203–10. Paris: Éditions Galilée, 1994.

1993

"Althusser (1939)." In *Association amicale de secours des anciens élèves de l'École normale supérieure*, edited by École Normale Supérieure, 425–36. Paris, École Normale Supérieure Éditions, 1993.

(With Dominique Lecourt.) "Avant-propos." *Politique et philosophie dans l'œuvre de Louis Althusser*, edited by Sylvain Lazarus, 7–8. Pratiques théoriques, edited by Étienne Balibar and Dominique Lecourt. Paris: Presses Universitaires de France, 1993.

(Edited in collaboration with the Bibliothèque du Collège International de Philosophie.) *Georges Canguilhem: Philosophe, historien des sciences; Actes du Colloque du Collège International de Philosophie, 6–8 décembre 1990*. Paris: Éditions Albin Michel, 1993.

"Europa efter kommunismen." *Ord och Bild* 102, nos. 4–5 (1993): 26–39.

Le frontiere della democrazia. Translated by Andrea Catone. Rome: Manifestolibri, 1993.

"Gibt es einen 'Europäischen Rassismus'?: Elemente einer Analyse und einer Handlungsorientierung." In *Schwierige Fremdheit: Über Integration Und Ausgrenzung in Einwanderungsländern*, edited by Friedrich Balke, Rebekka Habermas, Patrizia Nanz, and Peter Sillem, 119–34. Frankfurt: Fischer Taschenbuch Verlag, 1993.

Die Grenzen der Demokratie. Translated by Thomas Laugstien, Frieder O. Wolf, Nora Räthzel, and Jan Rehmann. Hamburg, Ger.: Argument-Verlag, 1993.

"Il mondo è cambiato?: Strutturalismo e marxismo." *Prometeo* 44 (1993): 30–37.

"Louis Althusser: Bibliographie choisie." In *Politique et philosophie dans l'œuvre de Louis Althusser*, edited by Sylvain Lazarus, 177–79. Pratiques théoriques, edited by Étienne Balibar and Dominique Lecourt. Paris: Presses Universitaires de France, 1993.

Masses, Classes, Ideas: Studies on Politics and Philosophy before and after Marx. New York: Routledge, 1993.
"The Non-Contemporaneity of Althusser." In *The Althusserian Legacy*, edited by E. Ann Kaplan and Michael Sprinker, 1–16. London: Verso, 1993.
"L'objet d'Althusser." In *Politique et philosophie dans l'œuvre de Louis Althusser*, edited by Sylvain Lazarus, 81–116. Paris: Presses Universitaires de France, 1993.
La philosophie de Marx. Paris: La Découverte, 1993.
"Le politique, la politique: De Rousseau à Marx, de Marx à Spinoza." *Studia Spinozana: An International and Interdisciplinary Series* 9 (1993): 203–16.
"Racism, Nation, and Class." *Critica Marxista* 1–2 (1993): 73.
"Science et vérité dans la philosophie de Georges Canguilhem." In *Georges Canguilhem: Philosophe, historien des sciences; Actes du Colloque du Collège International de Philosophie, 6–8 décembre 1990*, edited by Bibliothèque du Collège International de Philosophie, 58–76. Paris: Éditions Albin Michel, 1993.
"Some Questions on Politics and Violence." *Assemblage: A Critical Journal of Architecture and Design Culture* 20 (April 1993): 12.

1992

The Boundaries of Democracy. 1992.
(Ed.) *Conservatisme, libéralisme, socialisme. Genèses*, 9, 1992.
"Conservatisme, libéralisme, socialisme." *Genèses: Sciences sociales et histoire* 9, no. 1 (1992): 2–6.
"Culture and Identity." *NAQD* 2, no. 1 (1992): 9–21.
(With Michaël Lowy and Sami Nair.) "Le droit de vote des immigrés: Le moment est venu." *Le Monde* (May 6, 1992).
"'Ego sum, ego existo': Descartes au point d'hérésie." *Bulletin de la société française de philosophie* 86, no. 3 (1992): 77–123.
"Europa nach dem kommunismus." *Das argument* 34, no. 191 (1992): 7–26.
"Europe after Communism." *Rethinking Marxism: A Journal of Economics, Culture, and Society* 5, no. 3 (1992): 29–49.
"L'Europe après le communisme." *Temps modernes* 547 (February 1992): 56–89.
"Foucault and Marx: The Question of Nominalism." In *Michel Foucault Philosopher: Essays Translated from the French and German*, edited by Timothy J. Armstrong, 38–56. New York: Routledge, 1992.
Les frontières de la démocratie. Paris: La Découverte, 1992.
"Gramsci, Marx, et le rapport social." In *Modernité de Gramsci?: Actes du colloque franco-italien de Besançon, 23–25 novembre 1989*, edited by André Tosel, 259–70. Paris: Belles Lettres, 1992.

"L'institution de la vérité: Hobbes et Spinoza." In *Hobbes e Spinoza, scienza e politica; Atti del convegno internationale*, edited by Daniela Bostrenghi, 3–22. Naples, It.: Bibliopolis, 1992.

"Internationalisme ou barbarie." *Lignes* 17 (October 1992): 21–42.

"Le mot race n'est pas "de trop" dans la Constitution Française." *Mots: Les langages du politique* 33, no. 1 (1992): 241–56.

"A Note on 'Consciousness/Conscience' in the 'Ethics.'" *Studia Spinozana: An International and Interdisciplinary Series* 8 (1992): 37–54.

(With Immanuel Wallerstein.) "Race, Nation, Class: Ambiguous Identities." *Science and Society* 56, no. 4 (1992): 482–84.

"Le socialisme et les catégories politiques de la modernité." In *L'idée du socialisme a-t-elle un avenir?*, edited by Jacques Bidet and Jacques Texier, 31–42. Paris: Presses Universitaires de France, 1992.

"Spinoza's Psychology and Social Psychology." *Studia Spinozana: An International and Interdisciplinary Series* 8 (1992): 23–25.

(Edited with Helmut Seidel and Manfred Walther). *Spinoza's Psychology and Social Psychology*. Special issue, *Studia Spinozana: An International and Interdisciplinary Series* 8 (1992).

1991

Althusser için yazılar. Istanbul: İletişim, 1991.

"Citizen Subject." Translated by James B. Swenson Jr. In *Who Comes after the Subject?*, edited by Eduardo Cadava, Peter Connor, and Jean-Luc Nancy, 33–57. New York: Routledge, 1991.

"Crime privé, folie publique." In *Le citoyen fou*, edited by Nathalie Rabatel. Paris: Presses Universitaires de France, 1991.

Écrits pour Althusser. Paris: La Découverte, 1991.

(With Jacqueline Lalouette.) "Entretien avec le professeur André Mandouze." *Mots: Les langages du politique* 27, no. 1 (1991): 92–98.

"'Es Gibt keinen Staat in Europa': Racism and Politics in Europe Today." *New Left Review* 186 (1991): 5–19.

"Faut-il qu'une laïcité soit ouverte ou fermée?" *Mots: Les langages du politique* 27 (June 1991): 73–80.

"For Louis Althusser." *Rethinking Marxism: A Journal of Economics, Culture, and Society* 4, no. 1 (1991): 9–16.

"From Class Struggle to Struggle without Classes?" *Graduate Faculty Philosophy Journal* 14, no. 1 (1991): 7–21.

(Edited with Simone Bonnafous and Pierre Fiala). "Laïc, laïque, laïcité." *Mots: Les langages du politique* 27 (June 1991).

"Oração fúnebre para Louis Althusser." *Vértice* (1991): 93.

Per Althusser. Translated by Andrea Catone. Roma: Manifestolibri, 1991.
(With Simone Bonnafous and Pierre Fiala.) "Présentation." *Mots: Les Langages Du Politique* 27, no. 1 (1991): 3–4.
(Interview with Maxim Silverman.) "Race, Nation, and Class." In *Race, Discourse, and Power in France*, edited by Maxim Silverman, translated by Clare Hughes, 71–83. Avebury, Eng.: Aldershot, 1991.
(With Immanuel Wallerstein.) *Race, Nation, Class: Ambiguous Identities*. Translated by Chris Turner. London: Verso, 1991.
(With Immanuel Wallerstein.) *Raza, nación y clase*. Madrid: Iepala, 1991.
Razzismi. Milan, It.: F. Angeli, 1991.
"Réponse à Natalia Avtonomova: Lacan avec Kant: L'idée du symbolisme." In *Lacan avec les philosophes*, edited by Natalia Avtonomova, 87–97. Paris: Éditions Albin Michel. 1991.

1990

"Actualités d'Althusser à l'étranger." *Actuel Marx* 7, no. 1 (1990): 164–67.
"Les apories de la 'transition' et les contradictions de Marx." *Sociologie et sociétés* 22, no. 1 (1990): 83–91.
"'Droits de l'homme' et 'droits du citoyen': La dialectique moderne de l'égalité et de la liberté." *Actuel Marx* 8 (1990): 13–32.
"Fichte et la frontière intérieure: A propos des *Discours à la nation allemande*." *Cahiers de Fontenay* 58/59 (June 1990): 57–81.
Lock, Grahame. "Le marxisme analytique entre la philosophie et la science." Translated by Étienne Balibar. *Actuel Marx* 7 (1990): 131–38.
"The Nation Form: History and Ideology." *Review: A Journal of the Fernand Braudel Center* 13, no. 3 (1990): 329–61.
"Paradoxes of Universality." In *Anatomy of Racism*. Edited by David Theo Goldberg, 283–94. Minneapolis: University of Minnesota Press, 1990.
(With Immanuel Wallerstein.) *Rasse, klasse, nation: Ambivalente identitäten*. Translated by Michael Haupt and Ilse Utz. Hamburg, Ger.: Argument, 1990.
"Ultimi barbarorum—Espinoza: O temor das massas." *Discurso* 18 (1990): 7–36.

1989

"Analysis of Contemporary Racism." *Critica sociologica* 89 (1989): 5–38.
"Ce qui fait qu'un peuple est un peuple: Rousseau et Kant." *Revue de synthèse* 110, nos. 3–4 (1989): 391–417.
"Citoyen sujet: Réponse à la question de Jean-Luc Nancy; Qui vient après le sujet?" *Cahiers confrontation* 20 (Winter 1989): 23–47.
"Cultura e identità." In *Problemi del socialismo* 3 (1989): 13–34.
"Foucault et Marx: L'enjeu du nominalisme." In *Michel Foucault philosophe: Rencontre*

internationale Paris 9, 10, 11 janvier 1988, edited by Georges Canguilhem, 54–75. Paris: Seuil, 1989.

"Gibt es einen 'neuen rassismus'?" *Das argument* 31, no. 173 (1989): 175.

"Jus-pactum-lex." *Studia Spinozana: An International and Interdisciplinary Series* 1 (1989): 105.

Permanences de la révolution: Pour un autre bicentenaire. Montreuil, Fr.: La Brèche-PEC, 1989.

"La proposition de l'égaliberté." *Les conférences du perroquet* 22 (1989).

"Racism as Universalism." *New Political Science* 16 (Fall–Winter 1989): 9–22.

"Racisme: Encore un universalisme." *Mots: Les langages du politique* 18 (March 1989): 7–20.

"¡Sigue callado, Althusser!" *Cuadernos políticos* 57 (1989): 70.

"Spinoza, the Anti-Orwell: The Fear of the Masses." Translated by Ted Stolze. *Rethinking Marxism* 2, no.3 (Fall 1989): 104–39.

"Spinoza, politique et communication." *Cahiers philosophiques: Centre national de documentation pédagogique* 39 (June 1989): 17–42.

(With Grahame Lock and Herman van Gunsteren.) *Sterke posities in de politieke filosofie*. Leiden, Neth.: Stenfert Kroese, 1989.

"Lo stesso o l'altro? Per un'analisi del razzismo contemporaneo." Translated by Maria Teresa Maiullari and Clara Gallini. *La critica sociologica* 89 (April–June 1989): 5–38.

"Thèses." *Raison présente* 89, no. 1 (1989): 15–17.

1988

"A propos du Différend: Entretien avec Jean-François Lyotard." *Cahiers de philosophie* 5 (1988): 50–51.

"L'avenir du racisme." *Lignes* 1, no. 2 (1988): 7–12.

Droit de cite: Culture et politique en démocratie. Paris: Éditions de l'Aube, 1988.

"Un jacobin nommé Marx?: Liberté, égalité, fraternité: A chacun de ces trois mots de la devise républicaine se rattache un moment de la pensée de Marx." *Magazine littéraire* 258 (October 1988): 66–69.

"Mao: Critica interna dello Stalinismo." In *Mao Zedong dalla politica alla storia*, edited by Enrica Collotti Pischel, Emilia Giancotti, and Aldo Natoli, 252–63. Rome: Editori Riuniti, 1988.

"Mao: Critique interne du stalinisme?" *Actuel Marx* 3 (1988): 145–54.

"Le moment philosophique déterminé par la guerre dans la politique: Lénine 1914–1916." In *Les philosophes et la guerre de 14*, edited by Philippe Soulez, 105–20. Saint-Denis, Fr.: Presses Universitaires de Vincennes, 1988.

"The Notion of Class Politics in Marx." Translated by Dominique Parent-Ruccio and Frank R. Annunziato. *Rethinking Marxism: A Journal of Political Economy and Social Analysis* 1, no. 2 (Summer 1988): 18–51.

"Propositions on Citizenship." Translated by Simon Critchley. *Ethics*, 98, no. 4 (1988): 723–30.
(With Immanuel Wallerstein.) *Race, nation, classe: Les identités ambiguës*. Paris: La Découverte, 1988.
"Tais-toi, encore, Althusser." *Temps modernes* 509 (December 1988):1–29.
"The Vacillation of Ideology." Translated by Andrew Ross and Constance Penley. In *Marxism and the Interpretation of Culture*, edited by Cary Nelson and Lawrence Grossberg, 159–210. Chicago: University of Illinois Press, 1988.

1987

"Causalità strutturale e antagonismo." In *Il marxismo di Louis Althusser*, edited by Étienne Balibar, M. Giacometti, G. Lock, F. Pogliani, C. Preve, and M. Turchetto, 19–31. Verbania, It.: Vallerini, 1987.
"La contradiction infinie: Eléments d'une philosophie de l'histoire." Soutenance de thèse, Katholieke Universiteit Nihmegen, 1987.
"Nouvelle-Calédonie et racisme." *Le Monde* (December 15, 1987).
Review of *Substanz und Begriff: Zur Spinoza-Rezeption Marxens*, by Fred E. Schrader. *Studia Spinozana: An International and Interdisciplinary Series* 3 (1987): 521–23.

1986

(Interview with Frédéric Darmau and Pierre-Yves Mate.) "Entretien avec Étienne Balibar." *Raison présente* 79, no. 1 (1986): 5–12.
"Solidarité." *Le Monde* (April 3, 1986).
"Zu *Apparat, Absterben des Staates* und *Bakunismus*." *Das argument* 157 (1986): 409.

1985

"Entretien sur la finalité de l'éducation." *Monde de l'éducation* (July 1985): 17–18.
"L'idée d'une politique de classe chez Marx." In *Marx en perspective*, edited by Bernard Chavance, 497–526. Paris: L'Ecole des Hautes Etudes en Sciences Sociales, 1985.
"Intellectuels, idéologues, idéologie: Quelques réflexions." *Raison présente* 73 (1985): 23–38.
"Jus, pactum, lex: Sur la constitution du sujet dans le traite theologico-politique." *Studia Spinozana: An International and Interdisciplinary Series* 1 (1985): 105–42.
"Marx, the Joker in the Pack (or the Included Middle)." Translated by David Watson. *Economy and Society* 14, no. 1 (February, 1985): 1–27.
"Spinoza, l'anti-Orwell: La crainte des masses." *Temps modernes* 41 (September 1985): 353–98.
Spinoza et la politique. Paris: Presses Universitaires de France, 1985.

1984

"L'idée d'une politique de classe chez Marx." *Temps modernes* 40 (February 1984): 1357–406.

"'Ideologia' e 'concezione del mondo' in Engels." *Paradigmi: Rivista di storia filosofica* 2, no. 5 (1984): 235–70.

"Les masques de la politique." *Raison présente* 69, no. 1 (1984): 147–52.

"La société métissée." *Le Monde* (December 1, 1984).

"Sujets ou citoyens? (Pour l'égalité)." *Temps modernes* 40 (February 1984): 1726–53.

1983

"Après l'autre mai." In *La gauche, le pouvoir, le socialisme: Hommage à Nicos Poulantzas*. Edited by Christine Buci-Glucksmann, 99–119. Paris: Presses Universitaires de France, 1983.

"Longue marche pour la paix." In *L'exterminisme: Armement nucléaire et pacifisme*, edited by Edward Thompson, 199–228. Translated by Jean-Jacques Lecercle, Yvette le Guillou, and Robert Fischer. Paris: Presses Universitaires de France, 1983.

(With Yves Benot.) "Suffrage universel!" *Le Monde* (May 4, 1983).

"Sur le concept marxiste de la 'division du travail manuel et du travail intellectuel' et la lutte des classes." In *L'intellectuel: L'intelligentsia et les manuels*, edited by Jean Belkhir, 97–117. Paris: Éditions Anthropos, 1983.

"La vacillation de l'idéologie dans le marxisme." *Raison présente* 66, no. 2 (1983): 97–116.

1982

L'altro maggio francese: Contraddizioni e prospettive delle sinistre al governo della v repubblica. Milan, It.: F. Angeli, 1982.

"Le concept de 'coupure épistémologique' de Gaston Bachelard à Louis Althusser." *Cahiers philosophiques: Centre National Documentation Pédagogique* 12 (September 1982).

"Interview: Étienne Balibar and Pierre Macherey." *Diacritics* 12, no. 1 (Spring 1982): 46–51.

Kavanagh, James H. "Marxism's Althusser: Toward a Politics of Literary Theory." Review of *For Marx*, by Louis Althusser; *Lenin and Philosophy*, by Louis Althusser; *Essays in Self-Criticism*, by Louis Althusser; *Reading Capital*, by Louis Althusser and Étienne Balibar; *Formalism and Marxism*, by Tony Bennett; *Criticism and Ideology*, by Terry Eagleton; *A Theory of Literary Production*, by Pierre Macherey; and "Literature as an Ideological Form: Some Marxist Hypotheses," by Pierre Macherey and Étienne Balibar. *Diacritics* 12, no. 1 (1982): 25–45.

"Die Krise der Parteiform in der Arbeiterbewegung." Translated by Herbert Bosch and Jan Rehmann. *Das argument* 24, no. 3 (1982): 347–62.

"The Long March for Peace." In *Exterminism and Cold War*, edited by New Left Review, 135–52. London: Verso, 1982.

"Il marxismo è all'origine di una nuova pratica della politica?" *Fenomenologia e società* 5 (1982):178–202.

Preface to Niccolò Machiavelli, *Le Prince*, edited by Patrick Dupouey, 3–5. Paris: Nathan, 1982.

1981

"Acerca de los problemas de 'método' en *El capital*." *Investigación económica* 40 (1981): 43–71.

"Estado, partido, transición." *Revista mexicana de sociología* 43, no. 3 (July–September 1981): 967–79.

"Estado, superestructura, reproducción de las relaciones capitalistas." *Investigación económica* 40, no. 155 (1981): 147–60.

"Literature as an Ideological Form: Some Marxist Hypotheses." *Praxis: A Journal of Cultural Criticism* 5 (1981): 43–58.

(With Pierre Macherey.) "On Literature as an Ideological Form: Some Marxist Propositions." In *Untying the Text: A Post-Structuralist Reader*, edited by Robert Young, 79–99. London: Routledge and Kegan Paul, 1981.

"Marx le joker—ou le tiers inclus." In *Rejouer le politique*, edited by Philippe Lacoue-Labarthe and Jean-Luc Nancy, 135–69. Paris: Éditions Galilée, 1981.

"PCF: De Charonne à Vitry." *Le nouvel observateur* 852 (March 9–15, 1981): 56–60.

(With Luc Ferry, Philippe Lacoue-Labarthe, Jean-François Lyotard, and Jean-Luc Nancy.) *Rejouer le politique*. Paris: Éditions Galilée, 1981.

"State, Party, Transition." *Revista mexicana de sociología* 43, no. 3 (1981): 967–79.

"Der Widerspruch hat die Grenzen des Erträglichen überschritten." *PROKLA: Zeitschrift für kritische Sozialwissenschaft* 11, no. 43 (1981): 147–60.

1980

(With Guy Bois, Georges Labica and Jean-Pierre Lefebvre.) "Is the Crisis 'Above All National'?: A View of the Policy of the French Communist Party." *Contemporary Marxism: Journal of the Institute for the Study of Labor and Economic Crisis* 2 (Winter 1980): 40–55.

(With Louis Althusser.) *Lire* Le capital. Montreuil, Fr.: Maspero, 1980.

1979

"État, parti, transition." *Dialectiques* 27 (Spring 1979): 81–92.

(With André Tosel and Cesare Luporini.) *Marx et sa critique de la politique*. Paris: Maspero, 1979.

(With Guy Bois, Georges Labica, and Jean-Pierre Lefebvre.) *Ouvrons la fenêtre, camarades!* Paris: F. Maspero, 1979.

(With Louis Althusser) *Reading Capital*. London: Verso, 1979.

"Sur la lutte idéologique et le travail théorique." In *Ouverture d'une discussion?: Dix interventions à la rencontre des 400 intellectuels communistes à Vitry*, edited by Christine Buci-Glucksmann, 97–111. Paris: Maspero, 1979.

1978

"From Bachelard to Althusser: The Concept of 'Epistemological Break.'" Translated by Elizabeth Kingdom. *Economy and Society* 7, no. 3 (August 1978): 207–37.

(With Louis Althusser, Guy Bois, Georges Labica, Jean-Pierre Lefebvre, and Maurice Moissonnier.) "Des intellectuels communistes signent 'une véritable discussion politique.'" *Le Monde* (April 6, 1978).

"Introduction to Cerroni." *Economy and Society* 7, no. 3 (1978): 238–40.

"Irrationalism and Marxism." Translated by Patrick Camiller. *New Left Review* 107 (January–February 1978): 3–18.

(With Pierre Macherey.) "Literature as an Ideological Form: Some Marxist Propositions." Translated by Ian McLeod, John Whitehead, and Ann Wordswoth. *Oxford Literary Review* 3, no. 1 (1978): 1–12.

"Marx, Engels and the Revolutionary Party." *Marxist Perspectives* 1, no. 4 (1978): 124–43.

"Marx, Engels et le parti révolutionnaire." *La pensée* 201 (September–October 1978): 120–35.

"Marx, Engels y El Partido Revolucionario." *Cuadernos políticos* 18 (1978): 35–46.

(With Jean-Pierre Lefebvre.) "Plus-value ou survaleur?" *La pensée* 197 (January–February 1978): 32–42.

"La responsabilité des communistes." *Dialectiques* 23 (Spring 1978): 15–61.

(With Guy Besse, Jean-Pierre Cotten, Pierre Jaeglé, Georges Labica, and Jacques Texier.) "Sur la dialectique." *Revue philosophique de la France et de l'étranger* 168, no. 3 (1978): 372–73.

"Sur la dictature du prolétariat: Postface pour l'édition anglaise." *Politique aujourd'hui* 1 (1978): 97–110.

1977

The Dictatorship of the Proletariat. Translated by Grahame Lock. London: Verso, 1977.

"The Dictatorship of the Proletariat." *Marxism Today: Theoretical and Discussion Journal of the Communist Party* 21, no. 5 (May 1977): 144–53.

"Les *Entretiens sur le matérialisme dialectique* de Bob Claessens." In *Bob Claessens: Le temps d'une vie*, edited by Colette Fontaine. Brussels: Éditions du Cercle d'Éducation Populaire, 1977.

"Klassen, Staat und 'Diktatur des Proletariats.'" *Das argument* 19 (1977): 795–808.

"A nouveau sur la contradiction: Dialectiques des luttes de classes et lutte de classes dans la dialectique." In *Sur la dialectique*, edited by Guy Besse, 17–63. Paris: CERM-Éditions Sociales, 1977.

(With Louis Althusser.) *Reading* Capital. 2nd ed. London: NLB, 1977.

"Socialisme: 1948–1917." In *Politieke Theorieën*, edited by Herman van Gunsteren and Grahame Lock. Alphen aan den Rijn, Neth.: Samson, 1977.

Sobre la dictadura del proletariado. Translated by Josefa Cordero and Gabriel Albaic. Madrid: Siglo XXI, 1977.

(With Christine Buci-Glucksmann, Marc Abeles, David Kaisergruber, Jacques Guilhaumou, and Georges Labica.) "Table-ronde: Sur et autour de la dictature du prolétariat." *Dialectiques* 17 (Winter 1977): 3–34.

1976

"Au nom de la raison?: Marxisme, rationalisme, irrationalisme." *La nouvelle critique* 99 (December 1976): 69–76.

Cinco ensayos de materialismo histórico. Translated by Gabriel Albiac. Barcelona: Editorial Laia, 1976.

Cinque studi di materialismo storico. Translated by Claudia Mancina. Bari, It.: De Donato, 1976.

"Réponses aux camarades." *La nouvelle critique* 90 (January 1976): 73–78.

Sur la dictature du prolétariat. Paris: Maspero, 1976.

Über die Diktatur des Proletariats: Mit Dokumenten des 22; Parteitages der KPF. Translated by Rolf Löper, Klaus Riepe, and Peter Schöttler. Hamburg, Ger.: VSA, 1976.

1975

"Dialectique, contradiction, lutte des classes: quelques thèses philosophiques." *Poznan Studies in the Philosophy of the Sciences and the Humanities* 1, no. 2 (1975): 11–31.

1974

"Acerca de la dialéctica histórica: Algunas observaciones críticas con respecto a leer *El capital*." *Revista mexicana de ciencia política* 20, no. 78 (1974): 29.

Cinque études du matérialisme historique. Paris: Maspero, 1974.

(With Pierre Macherey.) "Lingua nazionale e lotte di classe nella rivoluzione francese." *Critica Marxista* 2 (1974): 97–115.

(With Pierre Macherey.) "Présentation." In *Les français fictifs: Le rapport des styles littéraires au français national*, edited by Renée Balibar, Geneviève Merlin, and Gilles Tret, 7–49. Paris: Hachette, 1974.

(With Pierre Macherey). "Sur la littérature comme forme idéologique: Quelques hypothèses marxistes." *Littérature* 4, no. 13 (1974): 29–48.

(With Pierre Macherey.) "Thesen zum materialistischen Verfahren." *Alternative* 17 (October 1974): 193–221.

1973

"Les formations sociales capitalistes." *L'économie*. Paris: Hachette, 1973.

"Self-Criticism—an Answer to Questions from *Theoretical Practice*." *Theoretical Practice* 7–8 (January 1973): 56–72.

"Sur la dialectique historique: Quelques remarques critiques à propos de *Lire* Le capital." *La pensée* 170 (July–August 1973): 27–47.

1972

Das Kapital lessen. Rev. ed. Translated by Klaus-Dieter Thieme. Reinbek, Ger.: Rowohlt, 1972.

"Le passé composé fictif dans *L'étranger* d'Albert Camus." *Littérature* 7, no. 3 (1972): 102–19.

"La rectification du *Manifeste communiste*." *La pensée* 1, no. 164 (1972): 38–64.

1970

(With Louis Althusser). *Reading Capital*. Translated by Ben Brewster. London: New Left Books, 1970.

1969

(With Michel Pécheux). "Définitions." In *Sur l'histoire des sciences*, edited by Michel Fichant and Michel Pécheux, 8–12. Paris: Maspero, 1969.

"Pour une politique de l'enseignement." *Revue de l'enseignement philosophique* (June–July 1969).

1968

"Marxismus und Linguistik." In *Marxismus und Fragen der Sprachwissenschaft*, edited by H. P. Gente, 9–19. (Munich: Rogner & Bernhard, 1968).

1967

(With Lucien Goldman and Pierre Macherey). *Le centenaire du capital*. Paris: Éditions Mouton, 1967.

"La science du capital." In *Le centenaire du capital*, edited by Étienne Balibar, Lucien Goldman, and Pierre Machery, 68–85. Paris: Éditions Mouton, 1967.

1966

"Les idéologies pseudo-marxistes de l'aliénation." *Clarté* 59 (1966): 28–35.

"Marxisme et linguistique." *Les cahiers marxistes-leninistes* 12–13 (July–October 1966): 19–25.

1965

(With Louis Althusser, Roger Establet, Pierre Macherey, and Jacques Rancière.) *Lire* Le capital. Paris: F. Maspero, 1965.

"Sur les concepts fondamentaux du matérialisme historique." In Louis Althusser, Pierre Macherey, Jacques Rancière, Roger Etablet, and Étienne Balibar, 419–568. *Lire* Le capital, 419–568. Paris: F. Maspero, 1965.

CONTRIBUTORS

Emily Apter is Silver Professor of Comparative Literature and French at New York University. She has published extensively in translation theory and is the author of *Against World Literature: On the Politics of Untranslatability* (Verso, 2013) and coeditor with Jacques Lezra and Michael Wood of the *Dictionary of Untranslatables: A Philosophical Lexicon* (Princeton University Press, 2014). Her most recent book is *Unexceptional Politics: On Obstruction, Impasse and the Impolitic* (Verso, 2018).

Étienne Balibar, Emeritus Professor at Paris Nanterre University, currently Professor at Columbia University and Kingston University London, is a French philosopher. Among his books are *Reading Capital* (with Louis Althusser); *Race, Nation, Class: Ambiguous Identities* (with Immanuel Wallerstein); *Citizen Subject: Foundations for Philosophical Anthropology*; and *Violence and Civility*.

J. M. Bernstein is University Distinguished Professor of Philosophy at the New School for Social Research. His writings include *The Fate of Art: Aesthetic Alienation from Kant to Derrida and Adorno* (1992), *Recovering Ethical Life: Jürgen Habermas and the Future of Critical Theory* (1995), *Adorno: Disenchantment and Ethics* (2002), and *Against Voluptuous Bodies: Late Modernism and the Meaning of Painting* (2006). His most recent book is *Torture and Dignity: An Essay on Moral Injury* (2015). He is working on a manuscript with the tentative title *Human Rights: On the Foundations of Ecological Socialism*, from which the essay in this volume is drawn.

Judith Butler is Maxine Elliot Professor of Comparative Literature and Critical Theory at the University of California at Berkeley. She is the author of several books, including *The Force of Non-Violence*, forthcoming with Verso in 2020. She is currently a Codirector of the International Association of Critical Theory Programs.

Monique David-Ménard is a psychoanalyst and philosopher. She has taught at the Université de Paris VII–Diderot and at universities throughout North and South America and Europe, and she maintains a private psychoanalysis practice. Her publications include *L'hystérique entre Freud et Lacan: Corps et langage en psychanalyse* (*Hysteria from Freud to Lacan: Body and Language in Psychoanalysis*) and *Deleuze et la psychanalyse: L'altercation*.

Hanan Elsayed is Associate Professor of French and Arabic at Occidental College in Los Angeles. Her research interests include Islam and history in Francophone literature from the Arab world, twentieth-century French literature and thought, and the French colonial legacy. She is the author of *L'histoire sacrée de l'Islam dans la fiction maghrébine*.

Didier Fassin is Professor of Social Science at the Institute for Advanced Study in Princeton and the École des Hautes Études en Sciences Sociales in Paris. He holds an Annual Chair at the Collège de France. He is recently the author of *Life: A Critical User's Manual* (Polity) and *The Will to Punish* (Oxford University Press).

Stathis Gourgouris is Professor of Comparative Literature and Society at Columbia University. He is author of *Dream Nation: Enlightenment, Colonization, and the Institution of Modern Greece*; *Does Literature Think?: Literature as Theory for an Antimythical Era*; *Lessons in Secular Criticism*; and Ενδεχομένως αταξίες (*Contingent Disorders*). His most recent book is *The Perils of the One*.

Bernard E. Harcourt is the Isidor and Seville Sulzbacher Professor of Law and Professor of Political Science at Columbia University, and Director d'Études at the École des Hautes Études en Sciences Sociales in Paris. He is the author most recently of *The Counterrevolution: How Our Government Went to War against Its Own Citizens* (Basic Books, 2018) and an editor of the work of Michel Foucault.

Jacques Lezra is Professor in the Department of Hispanic Studies at the University of California, Riverside. His most recent publications are *República salvaje* (2019), *On the Nature of Marx's Things* (2018), *Untranslating Machines: A Genealogy for the Ends of Global Thought* (2017), and *Contra todos los fueros de la muerte* (2016).

Patrice Maniglier is Maître de Conférences in the Philosophy Department of Paris Nanterre University. He has written on Saussure, Lévi-Strauss, Sartre, Merleau-Ponty, Foucault, Deleuze, Derrida, Badiou, and Latour. He is the author of *La vie énigmatique des signes: Saussure et la naissance du structuralisme*, *Foucault va au cinéma*, and *La philosophie qui se fait*.

Warren Montag is the Brown Family Professor of Literature at Occidental College in Los Angeles. His most recent books include *Althusser and His Contemporaries* (Duke University Press, 2013) and *The Other Adam Smith* (Stanford University Press, 2014).

Adi Ophir is a Visiting Professor at the Cogut Institute for the Humanities at Brown University and Professor Emeritus at Tel Aviv University. Among his recent works are *Goy: Israel's Multiple Others and the Birth of the Gentile*, coauthored with Ishay Rosen-Zvi (Oxford University Press, 2018); *Divine Violence: Two Essays on God and Disaster* (Van Leer Institute, 2013); and *The One-State Condition* (coauthored with Ariella Azoulay; Stanford University Press 2012).

Bruce Robbins is Old Dominion Foundation Professor of the Humanities at Columbia University. His latest books are *The Beneficiary* (2017) and *Cosmopolitanisms*

(2017), which was coedited with Paulo Lemos Horta. He is also the director of a short documentary titled "Some of My Best Friends Are Zionists."

Ann Laura Stoler is Willy Brandt Distinguished University Professor of Anthropology and Historical Studies at The New School for Social Research, Founding Director of its Institute for Critical Social Inquiry since 2014, and one of the founding editors of *Political Concepts: A Critical Lexicon*. Her books include *Race and the Education of Desire* (1995), *Carnal Knowledge and Imperial Power* (2002), *Along the Archival Grain* (2009), and *Duress* (2016).

Gary Wilder is Professor in Anthropology and French in the Graduate Center at City University of New York. His publications include *The French Imperial Nation-State: Negritude and Colonial Humanism between the Two World Wars* (2005).

INDEX

Page numbers in **bold** refer to the specific essays written by the named contributors to the book.

Adorno, Theodor W., 69
Agamben, Giorgio, 104, 110
Agee, James, 66, 133
Ahmed, Sarah, 99
Althusser, Louis, 3, 5–7, 11–13, 17, 26, 56, 58, 62, 64–66, 68, 70, 91, 93, 143, 146, 149–57, 197–98, 228, 270
Anderson, Benedict, 95
Anderson, Perry, 22
Appadurai, Arjun, 95
Apter, Emily, **94–116**
Arendt, Hannah, 170, 171, 175–76, 181, 231–35, 240–42, 244, 246, 250, 267
Aristotle, 3–4, 20, 33–34, 54, 59, 106, 171, 211, 213, 220–21, 224, 225–26, 227, 229
Asad, Talal, 18, 21, 50
Auerbach, Erich, 101–2

Bachelard, Gaston, 7
Bakhtin, Mikhail, 263
Balakrishnan, Gopal, 22
Balibar, Étienne, **54–70**
Barrada, Yto, 104–5
Benjamin, Walter, 30, 38, 65, 166, 266
Bennington, Geoffrey, 105–7
Benveniste, Émile, 188, 226
Bernstein, J. M., **230–52**
Bilgrami, Akeel, 139
Bloch, Ernst, 69
Boethius, 225
Bradley, F. H., 228–29
Buber, Martin, 49
Butler, Judith, 33, **45–53**, 132, 139

Canguilhem, Georges, 2, 6–9, 12–13, 62, 68, 69, 197

Capdevila, Nestor, 59, 69
Cassin, Barbara, 97, 111
Cassirer, Ernst, 142
Cavaillès, Jean, 2–4, 6–7, 12–13
Celan, Paul, 81–82
Chakrabarty, Dipesh, 21
Cheah, Pheng, 95–96
Clastres, Pierre, 39
Condorcet, Marquis de, 97, 114
Conrad, Joseph, 71–73, 76, 79, 81
Culler, Jonathan, 229

David-Ménard, Monique, **85–93**
Davidson, Arnold, 76, 78–79
de Castro, Eduardo Viveiros, 96
Deleuze, Gilles, 38, 47, 55, 59, 65, 156–57
Demos, T. J., 104
Derrida, Jacques, 30, 63, 95, 105, 107, 110, 226, 265
Descartes, René, 5–6, 55, 142, 144, 215, 216
Deuchar, Hannah Scott, 108
Diawara, Manthia, 115
Dolcerocca, Ozen Nergis, 107
Dosemeci, Mehmet, 43
Du Bois, W. E. B., 124, 261
Dumont, Gérard-François, 206, 210
Durkheim, Émile, 185, 189, 260, 264
Dworkin, Ronald, 68

Eco, Umberto, 100
Eliot, George, 25
Elliott, Gregory, 17
Elsayed, Hanan, **193–210**
Empson, William, 106
Engels, Friedrich, 11, 142, 144, 146, 257, 258

Epicurus, 91
Evans, Walker, 66

Fanon, Frantz, 131, 198–200, 262
Fassin, Didier, 26, **183–92**
Feher, Michel, 26, 75
Feuerbach, Ludwig, 146, 211, 218, 222, 256
Feyerabend, Paul, 79
Fichte, Johann Gottlieb, 28, 117–36
Foucault, Michel, 2, 8–12, 18–19, 23–24, 26, 33, 37, 56, 63–66, 68, 73–79, 82, 83, 86, 128–30, 190
Forster, E. M., 224
Frege, Gottlob, 105
Freud, Sigmund, 49, 64, 89, 91–93
Furetière, Antoine, 214–16, 220, 227

Gallie, W. B., 7–8, 59, 68–69
Gourgouris, Stathis, **28–44**, 115
Gramsci, Antonio, 143, 154, 261
Green, André, 126–32
Greenblatt, Stephen, 217
Gündoğdu, Ayten, 237

Habermas, Jürgen, 252
Hamacher, Werner, 105
Harcourt, Bernard, **71–84**
Hart, H. L. A., 68, 184–85
Hegel, G. W. F., 11, 12, 18, 20, 52, 64, 67, 68, 69, 71, 77, 85–89, 91, 93, 105, 134, 152
Herodotus, 31
Hertz, Neil, 106–7
Hobbes, Thomas, 20, 86, 173
Holt, Thomas C., **255**
Horta, Paulo Lemos, 96
Huertas, Hubert, 207, 210
Hume, David, 4
Husserl, Edmund, 2–3, 142, 146

James, C. L. R., 262
Jameson, Fredric, 59, 68, 111, 112
Jones, Kristin M., 104

Kafka, Franz, 30
Kant, Immanuel, 18–19, 55, 59, 60, 63–68, 69, 70, 71, 77, 87, 89, 94, 95, 102–3, 105, 112, 140, 142, 230, 266–67
Kojève, Alexandre, 18
Koselleck, Reinhart, 50, 60–62, 263

Lacan, Jacques, 62, 70, 87, 89, 126
Laclau, Ernesto, 40
Lacroix, Jean, 143
Lane, Edward, 108
Laruelle, François, 140
Latour, Bruno, 21, 155, 157
Le Bras, Hervé, 205–7, 209
Lenin, Vladimir Ilyich, 11, 37, 75, 91, 144–49, 154, **155**
Levinas, Emmanuel, 10, 265
Lévi-Strauss, Claude, 17, 18, 65, 88, 154, 189
Lezra, Jacques, 22, **211–29**
Lilla, Mark, 15–16, 25–26
Locke, John, 3, 51, 97, 157, 214–16, 227
Lowell, Robert, 106
Lukács, Georg, 69
Lukes, Steven, 68
Luxemburg, Rosa, 36
Lyotard, François, 56, 252

Macherey, Pierre, 198–99
Machiavelli, Niccolò, 86
Mahmood, Saba, 50
Maniglier, Patrice, **140–57**
Margalit, Avishai, 252
Marx, Karl, 11, 19–20, 22, 28, 29, 37–39, 47, 50, 56, 64, 67, 69, 70, 75, 77, 83, 87, 91, 112, 129, 141–42, 146, 149–50, 152, 211, 218, 221–22, 230, 237–38, 253–54, 256–62, 270, 273
Mauss, Marcel, 18, 260
Mbembe, Achille, 132
Meillassoux, Quentin, 140, 157
Merleau-Ponty, Maurice, 49, 63, 66
Mezzadra, Sandro, 31
Mirowski, Philip, 17
Montag, Warren, **1–13**, 70
Montesquieu, Charles Louis de Secondat, 171
Mosse, Richard, 115
Mouffe, Chantal, 40–42
Mufti, Aamir, 31, 50, 101
Muntadas, Antoni, 104

Nancy, Jean-Luc, 95, 98, 267
Nietzsche, Friedrich, 50, 74, 76, 123, 189, 244
Nixon, Rob, 96
Nozick, Robert, 186

Ophir, Adi, vii, 22, 32, 109–10, 116, 134, **158–82**, 276, 312
Orwell, George, 24
Osborne, Peter, 35

Pascal, Blaise, 64, 70
Plato, 56, 57, 142, 171, 240, 243
Poulantzas, Nicos, 129
Proudhon, Pierre-Joseph, 255–56

Quine, W. V. O., 57, 68

Rajchman, John, 18
Rancière, Jacques, 65–66, 70, 132, 169–71, 181, 252
Raspail, Jean, 206–7, 210
Rawls, John, 68
Revel, Judith, 63
Rigouste, Mathieu, 133
Robbins, Bruce, **15–27**, 30, 95, 96, 111
Rooney, Ellen, 17
Rousseau, Jean-Jacques, 86, 238

Said, Edward W., 50, 101, 129
Sangiovanni, Andrea, 252
Sartre, Jean-Paul, 17–18, 149, 150

Saunders, George, 16, 26
Saunders, Simon, 226
Schelling, F. W., 69
Schmitt, Carl, 50, 60, 174
Searle, John R., 229
Simmel, Georg, 189
Simondon, Gilbert, 215, 218–19, 223, 227–28
Socrates, 9, 76–77, 213, 221
Spinoza, Baruch, viii, 3–6, 13, 28, 34, 43, 45–53, 67, 156, 228, 276
Spitzer, Leo, 102
Spivak, Gayatri Chakravorty, 96
Stoler, Ann Laura, 111, **117–39**
Strathern, Marilyn, 212, 215, 220

Thompson, E. P., 22, 255

Vico, Giambattista, 89

Wacquant, Loïc, 130
Waldron, Jeremy, 69
Wallerstein, Immanuel, 29, 162, 196
Wehr, Hans, 108
Wilder, Gary, **253–73**
Williams, Raymond, 124
Wolin, Sheldon, 33

IDIOM: INVENTING WRITING THEORY
Jacques Lezra and Paul North, series editors

Werner Hamacher, *Minima Philologica*. Translated by Catharine Diehl and Jason Groves

Michal Ben-Naftali, *Chronicle of Separation: On Deconstruction's Disillusioned Love*. Translated by Mirjam Hadar. Foreword by Avital Ronell

Daniel Hoffman-Schwartz, Barbara Natalie Nagel, and Lauren Shizuko Stone, eds., *Flirtations: Rhetoric and Aesthetics This Side of Seduction*

Jean-Luc Nancy, *Intoxication*. Translated by Philip Armstrong

Márton Dornbach, *Receptive Spirit: German Idealism and the Dynamics of Cultural Transmission*

Sean Alexander Gurd, *Dissonance: Auditory Aesthetics in Ancient Greece*

Anthony Curtis Adler, *Celebricities: Media Culture and the Phenomenology of Gadget Commodity Life*

Nathan Brown, *The Limits of Fabrication: Materials Science, Materialist Poetics*

Jay Bernstein, Adi Ophir, and Ann Laura Stoler, eds., *Political Concepts: A Critical Lexicon*

Willy Thayer, *Technologies of Critique*. Translated by John Kraniauskas

Julie Beth Napolin, *The Fact of Resonance: Modernist Acoustics and Narrative Form*

Ann Laura Stoler, Stathis Gourgouris, and Jacques Lezra, eds., *Thinking with Balibar: A Lexicon of Conceptual Practice*

www.ingramcontent.com/pod-product-compliance
Lightning Source LLC
Chambersburg PA
CBHW030434300426
44112CB00009B/995